HARLEY QUINN

HARLEY VS. APOKOLIPS

VOL. 1

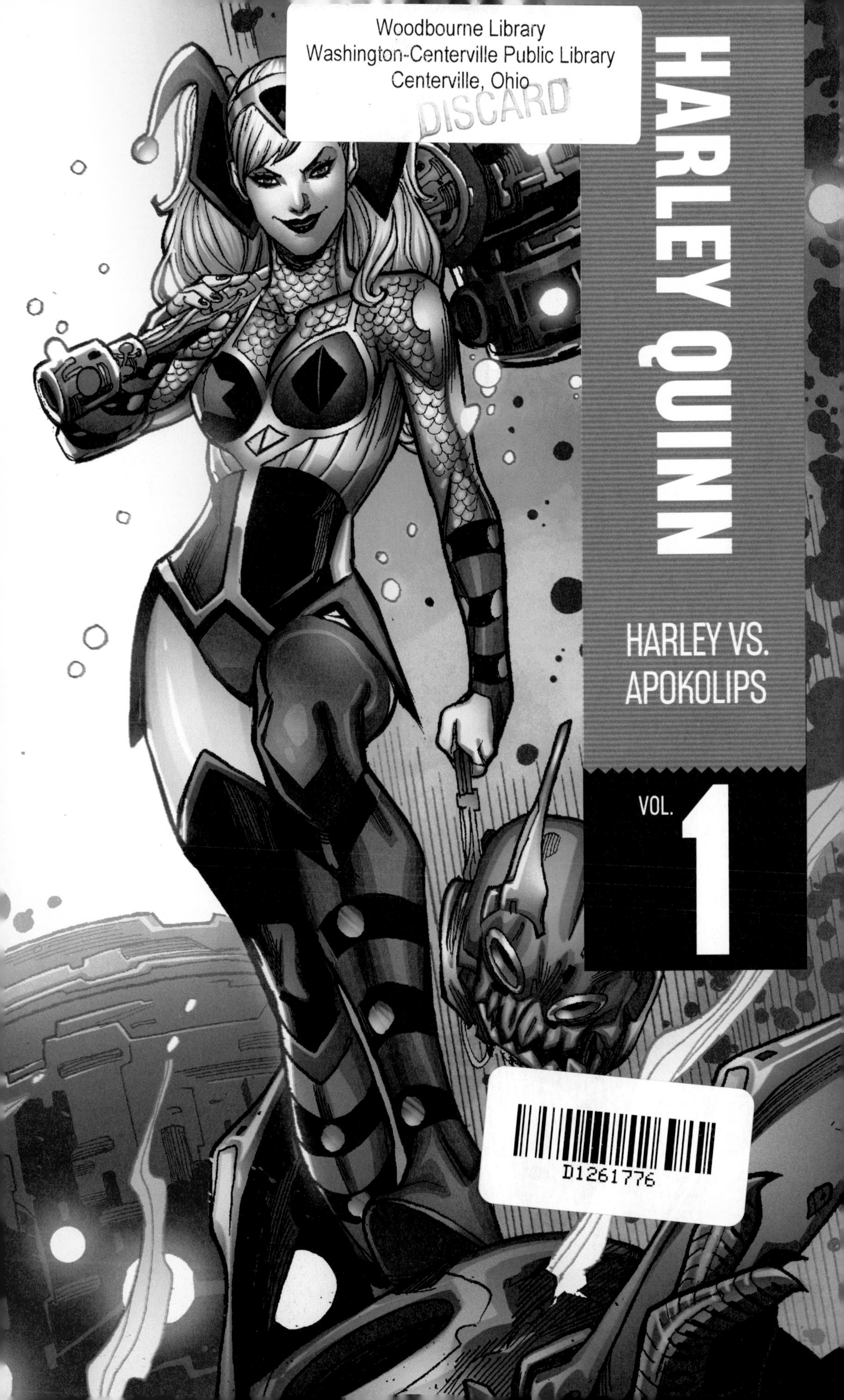

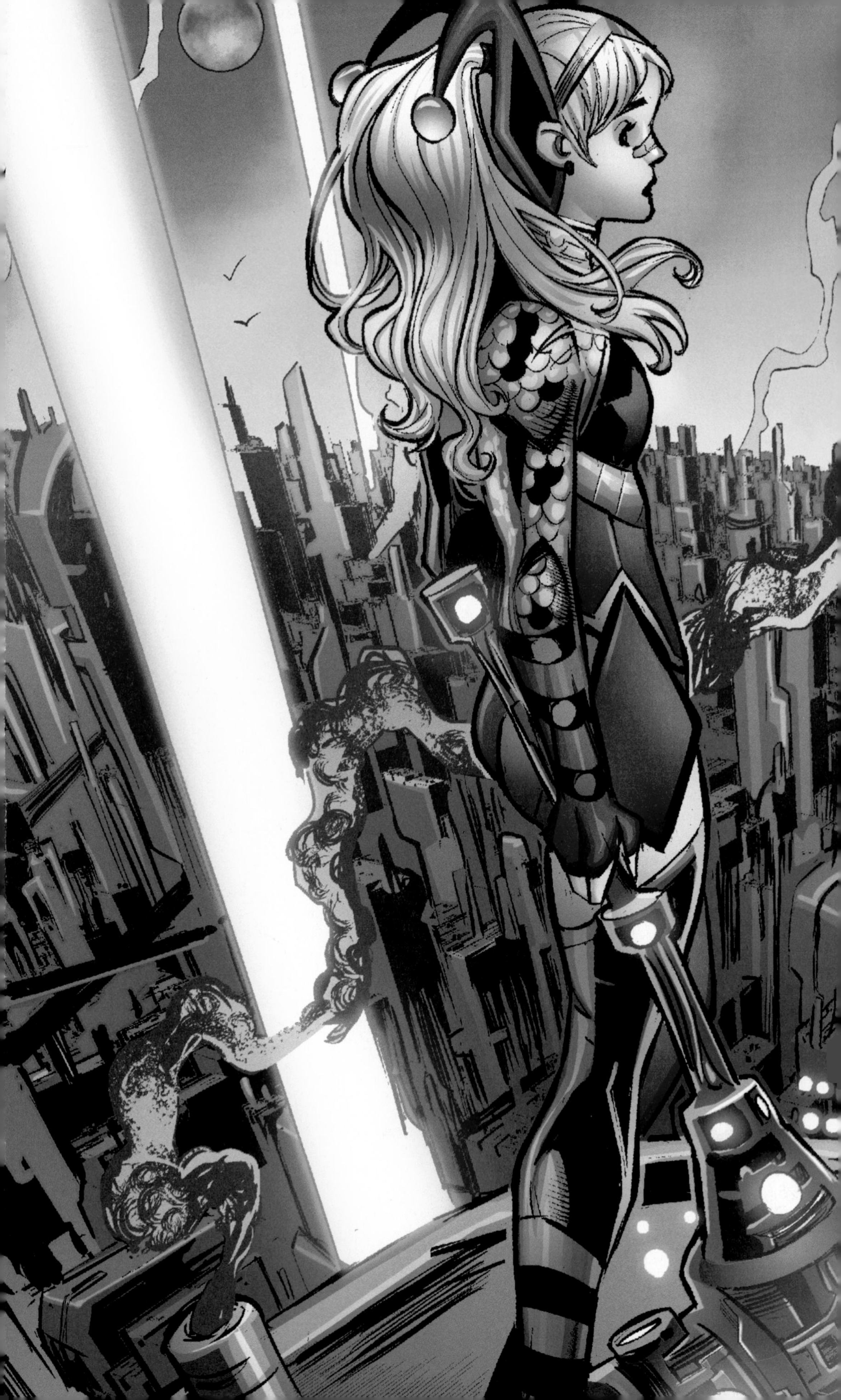

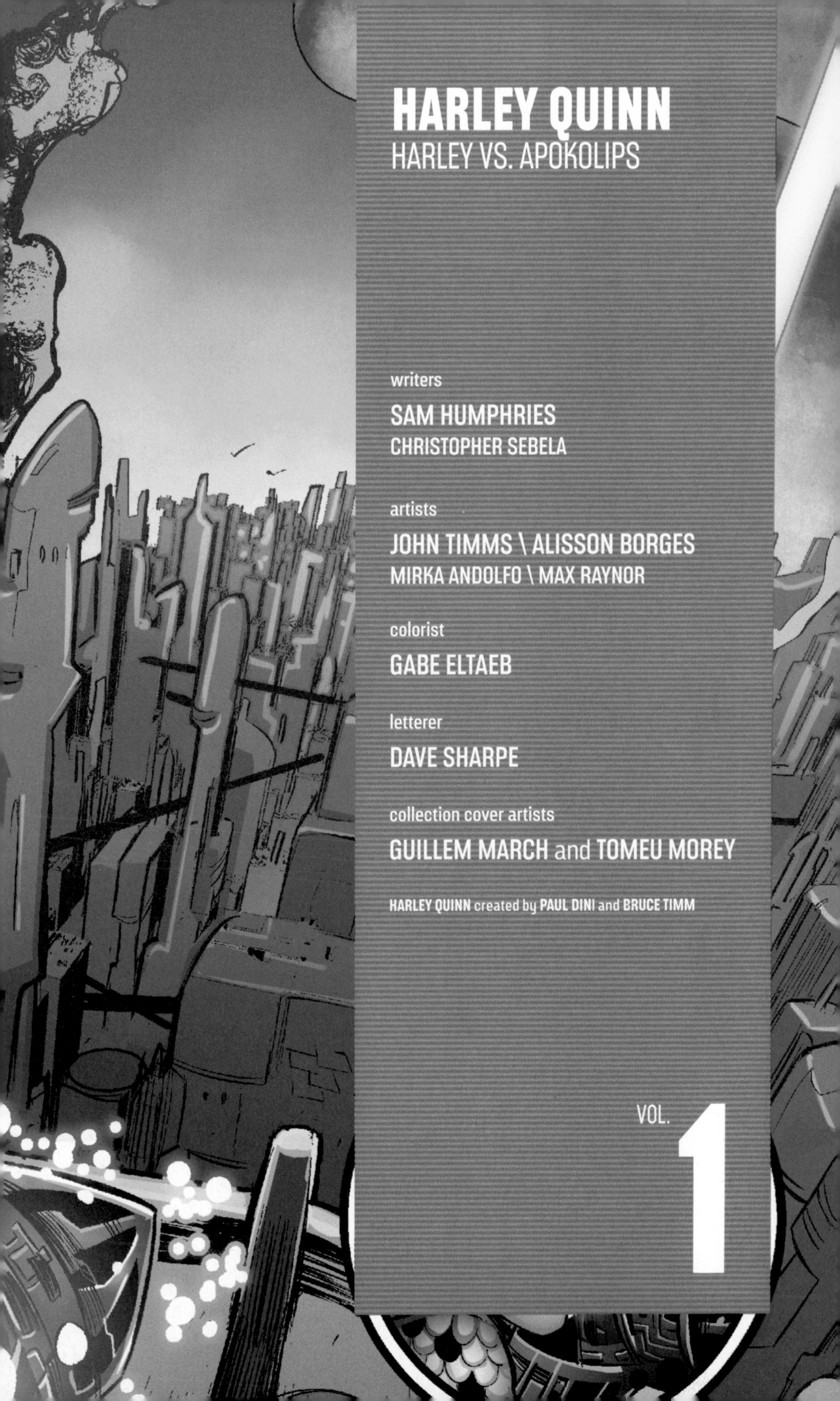

HARLEY QUINN
HARLEY VS. APOKOLIPS

writers

SAM HUMPHRIES
CHRISTOPHER SEBELA

artists

JOHN TIMMS \ ALISSON BORGES
MIRKA ANDOLFO \ MAX RAYNOR

colorist

GABE ELTAEB

letterer

DAVE SHARPE

collection cover artists

GUILLEM MARCH and **TOMEU MOREY**

HARLEY QUINN created by **PAUL DINI** and **BRUCE TIMM**

VOL. **1**

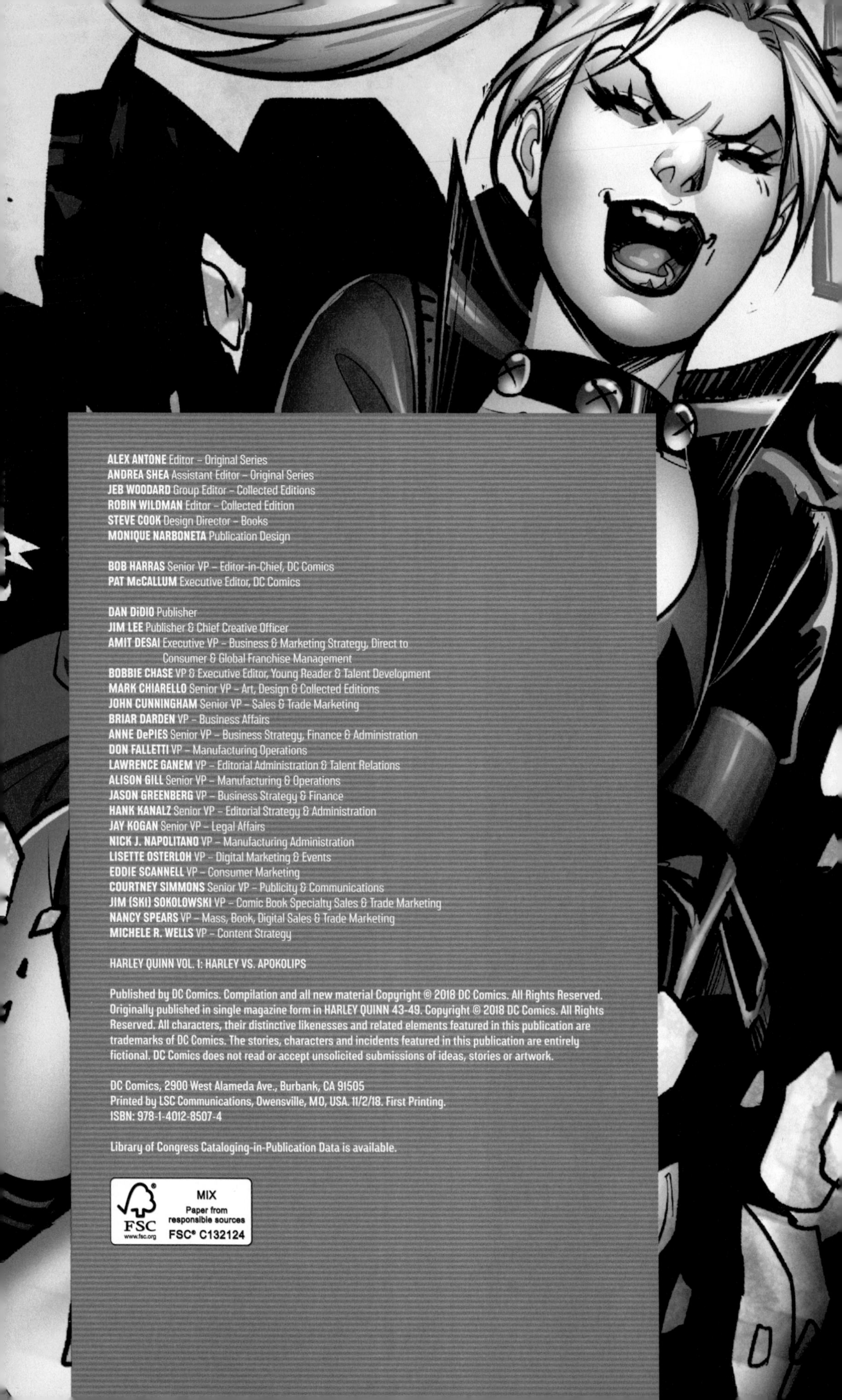

ALEX ANTONE Editor – Original Series
ANDREA SHEA Assistant Editor – Original Series
JEB WOODARD Group Editor – Collected Editions
ROBIN WILDMAN Editor – Collected Edition
STEVE COOK Design Director – Books
MONIQUE NARBONETA Publication Design

BOB HARRAS Senior VP – Editor-in-Chief, DC Comics
PAT McCALLUM Executive Editor, DC Comics

DAN DiDIO Publisher
JIM LEE Publisher & Chief Creative Officer
AMIT DESAI Executive VP – Business & Marketing Strategy, Direct to Consumer & Global Franchise Management
BOBBIE CHASE VP & Executive Editor, Young Reader & Talent Development
MARK CHIARELLO Senior VP – Art, Design & Collected Editions
JOHN CUNNINGHAM Senior VP – Sales & Trade Marketing
BRIAR DARDEN VP – Business Affairs
ANNE DePIES Senior VP – Business Strategy, Finance & Administration
DON FALLETTI VP – Manufacturing Operations
LAWRENCE GANEM VP – Editorial Administration & Talent Relations
ALISON GILL Senior VP – Manufacturing & Operations
JASON GREENBERG VP – Business Strategy & Finance
HANK KANALZ Senior VP – Editorial Strategy & Administration
JAY KOGAN Senior VP – Legal Affairs
NICK J. NAPOLITANO VP – Manufacturing Administration
LISETTE OSTERLOH VP – Digital Marketing & Events
EDDIE SCANNELL VP – Consumer Marketing
COURTNEY SIMMONS Senior VP – Publicity & Communications
JIM (SKI) SOKOLOWSKI VP – Comic Book Specialty Sales & Trade Marketing
NANCY SPEARS VP – Mass, Book, Digital Sales & Trade Marketing
MICHELE R. WELLS VP – Content Strategy

HARLEY QUINN VOL. 1: HARLEY VS. APOKOLIPS

DC Comics, 2900 West Alameda Ave., Burbank, CA 91505
Printed by LSC Communications, Owensville, MO, USA. 11/2/18. First Printing.
ISBN: 978-1-4012-8507-4

Library of Congress Cataloging-in-Publication Data is available.

FSC www.fsc.org
MIX
Paper from responsible sources
FSC® C132124

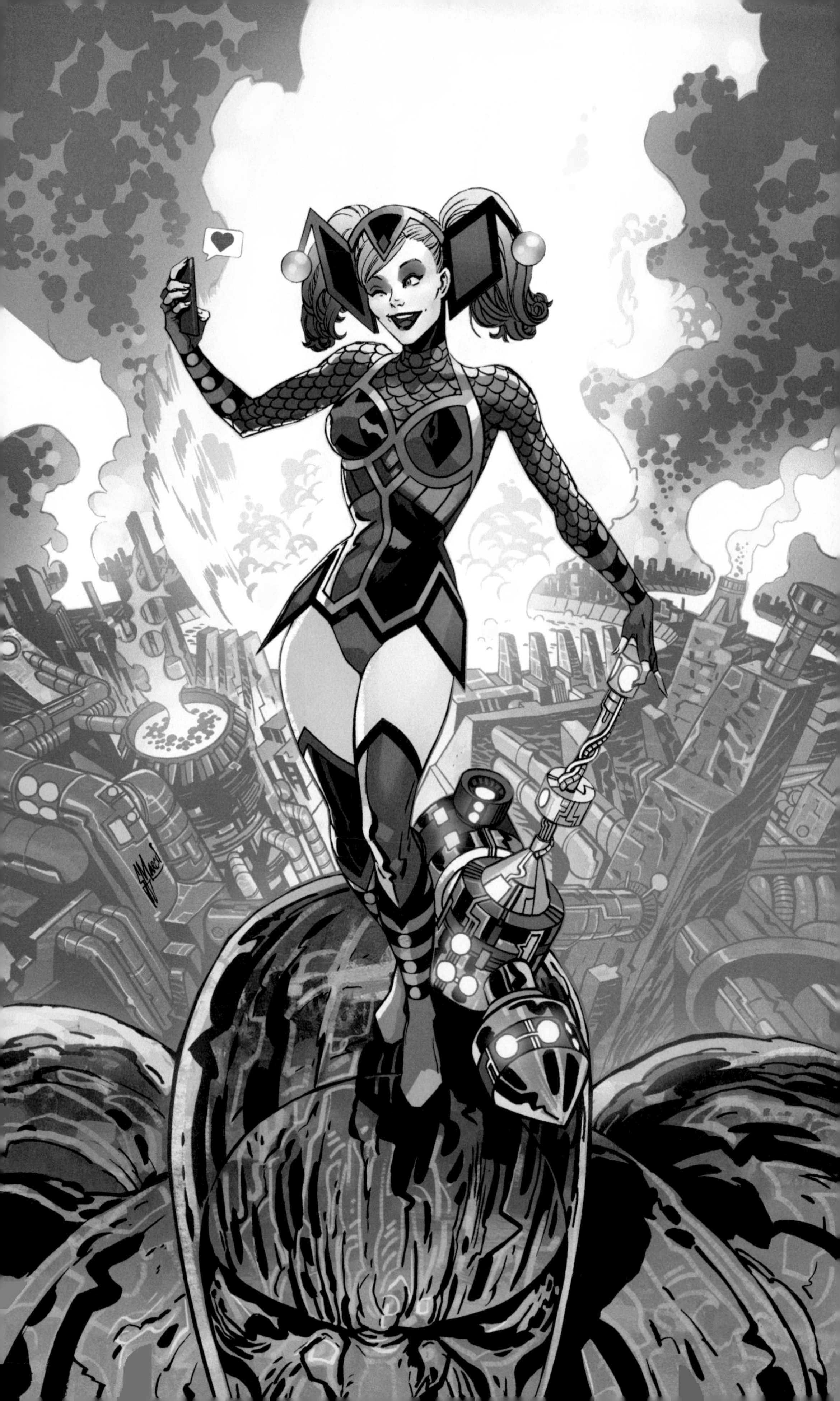

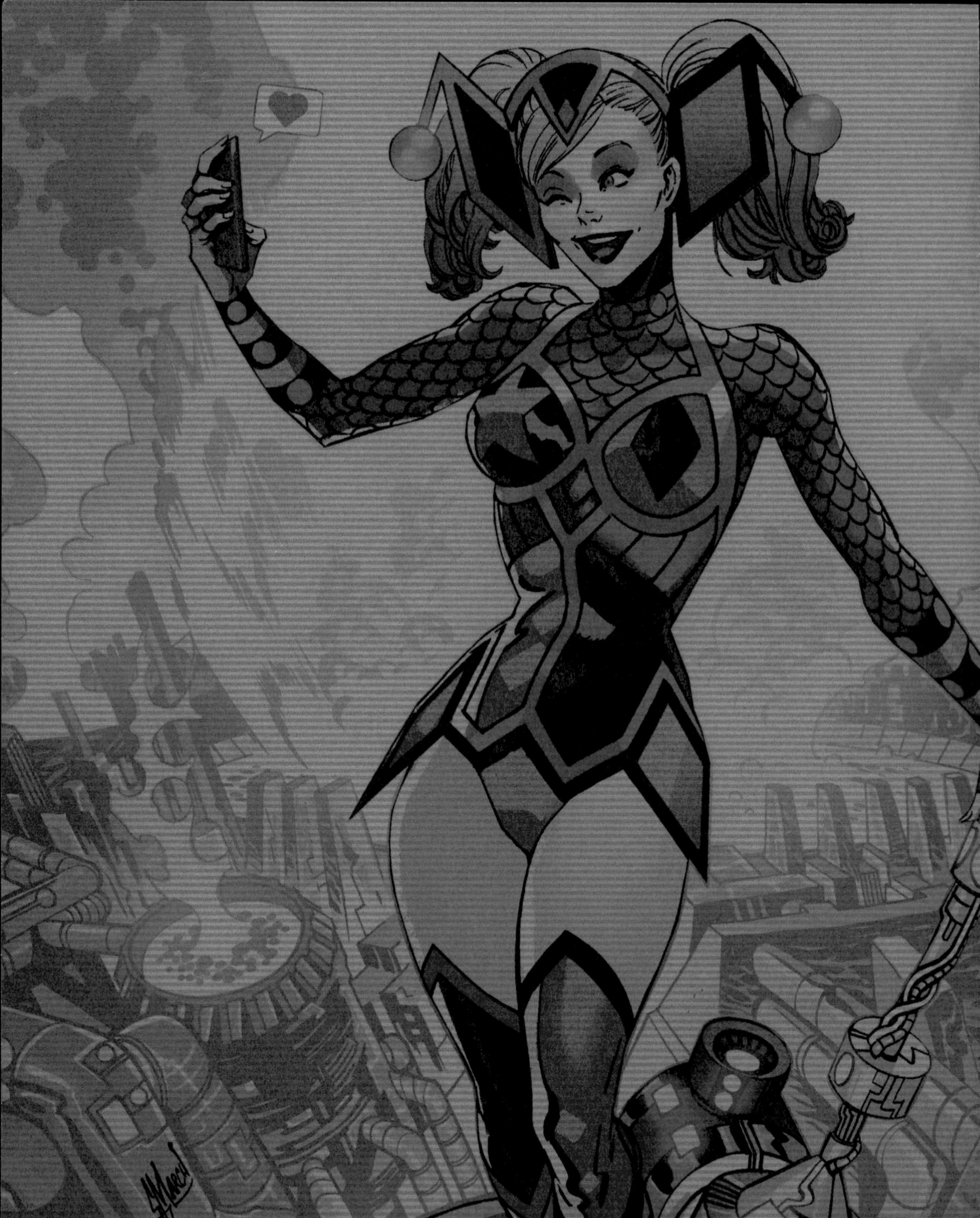

HARLEY QUINN
#45

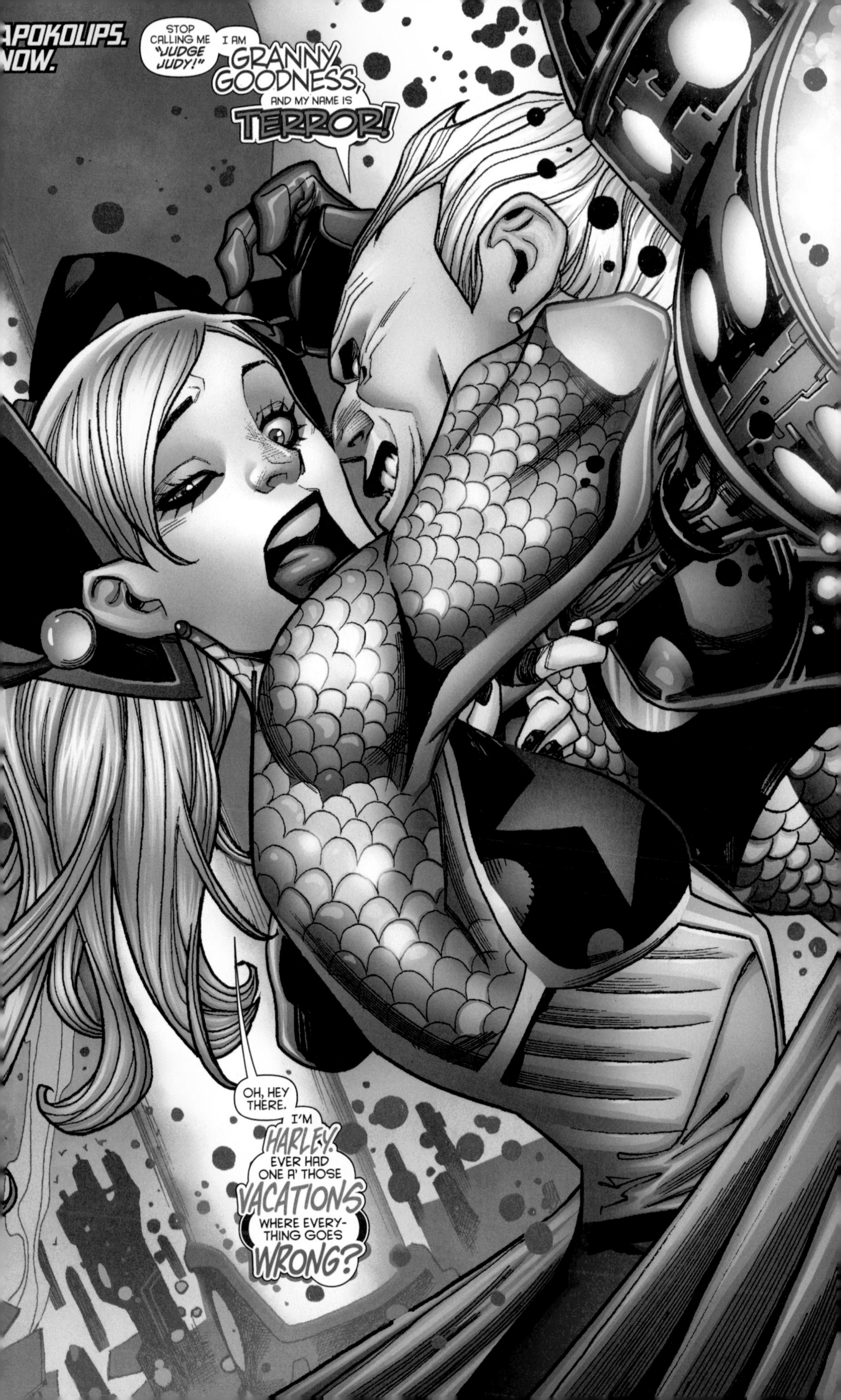
APOKOLIPS. NOW.
STOP CALLING ME "JUDGE JUDY!"
I AM GRANNY GOODNESS, AND MY NAME IS TERROR!
OH, HEY THERE.
I'M HARLEY. EVER HAD ONE A' THOSE VACATIONS WHERE EVERY-THING GOES WRONG?

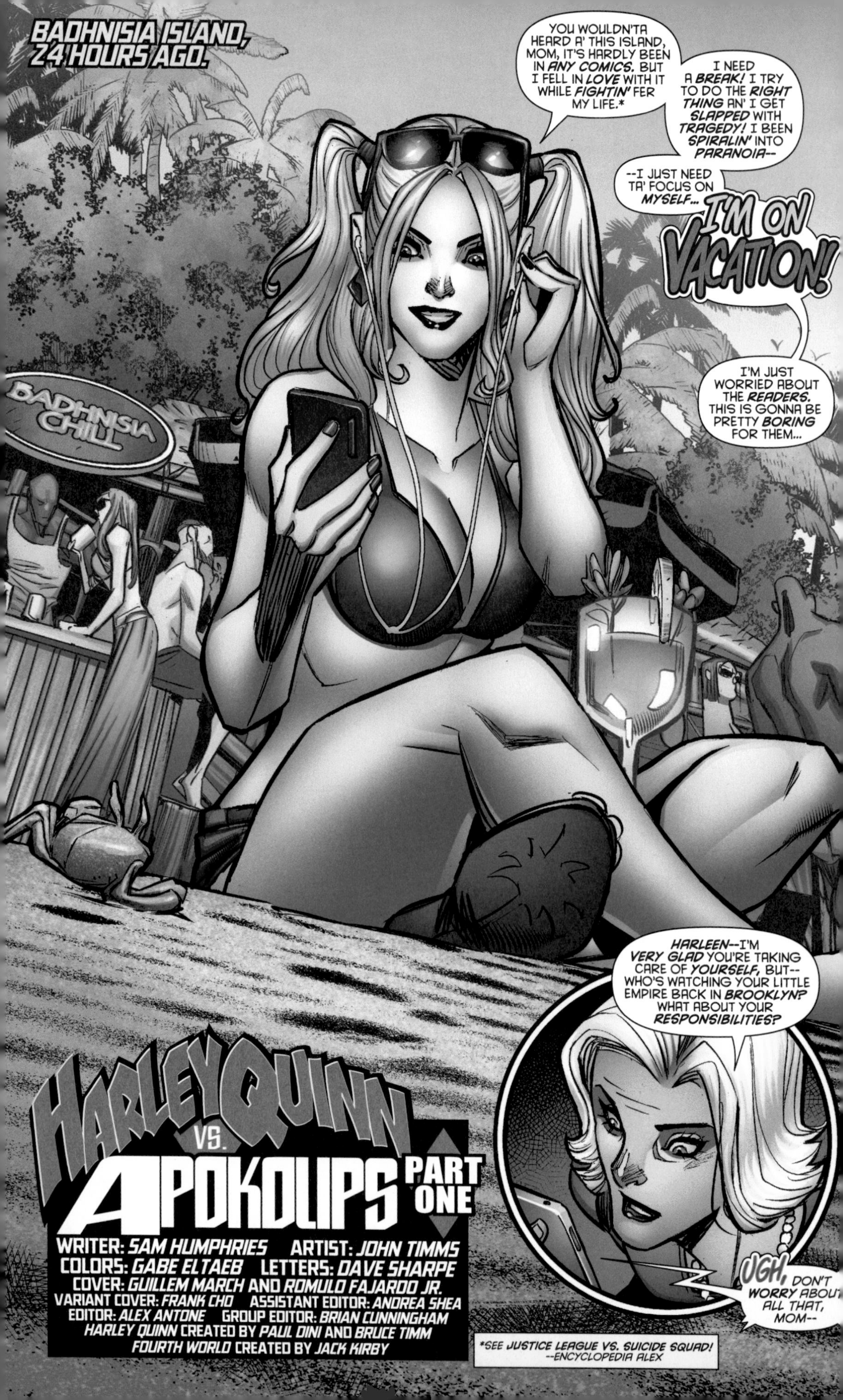
BADHNISIA ISLAND, 24 HOURS AGO.
YOU WOULDN'TA HEARD A' THIS ISLAND, MOM, IT'S HARDLY BEEN IN ANY COMICS. BUT I FELL IN LOVE WITH IT WHILE FIGHTIN' FER MY LIFE.*
I NEED A BREAK! I TRY TO DO THE RIGHT THING AN' I GET SLAPPED WITH TRAGEDY! I BEEN SPIRALIN' INTO PARANOIA--
--I JUST NEED TA' FOCUS ON MYSELF... I'M ON VACATION!
I'M JUST WORRIED ABOUT THE READERS. THIS IS GONNA BE PRETTY BORING FOR THEM...
BADHNISIA CHILL
HARLEEN--I'M VERY GLAD YOU'RE TAKING CARE OF YOURSELF, BUT--WHO'S WATCHING YOUR LITTLE EMPIRE BACK IN BROOKLYN? WHAT ABOUT YOUR RESPONSIBILITIES?
UGH, DON'T WORRY ABOUT ALL THAT, MOM--
HARLEY QUINN VS. APOKOLIPS PART ONE
WRITER: SAM HUMPHRIES ARTIST: JOHN TIMMS
COLORS: GABE ELTAEB LETTERS: DAVE SHARPE
COVER: GUILLEM MARCH AND ROMULO FAJARDO JR.
VARIANT COVER: FRANK CHO ASSISTANT EDITOR: ANDREA SHEA
EDITOR: ALEX ANTONE GROUP EDITOR: BRIAN CUNNINGHAM
HARLEY QUINN CREATED BY PAUL DINI AND BRUCE TIMM
FOURTH WORLD CREATED BY JACK KIRBY
*SEE JUSTICE LEAGUE VS. SUICIDE SQUAD! --ENCYCLOPEDIA ALEX

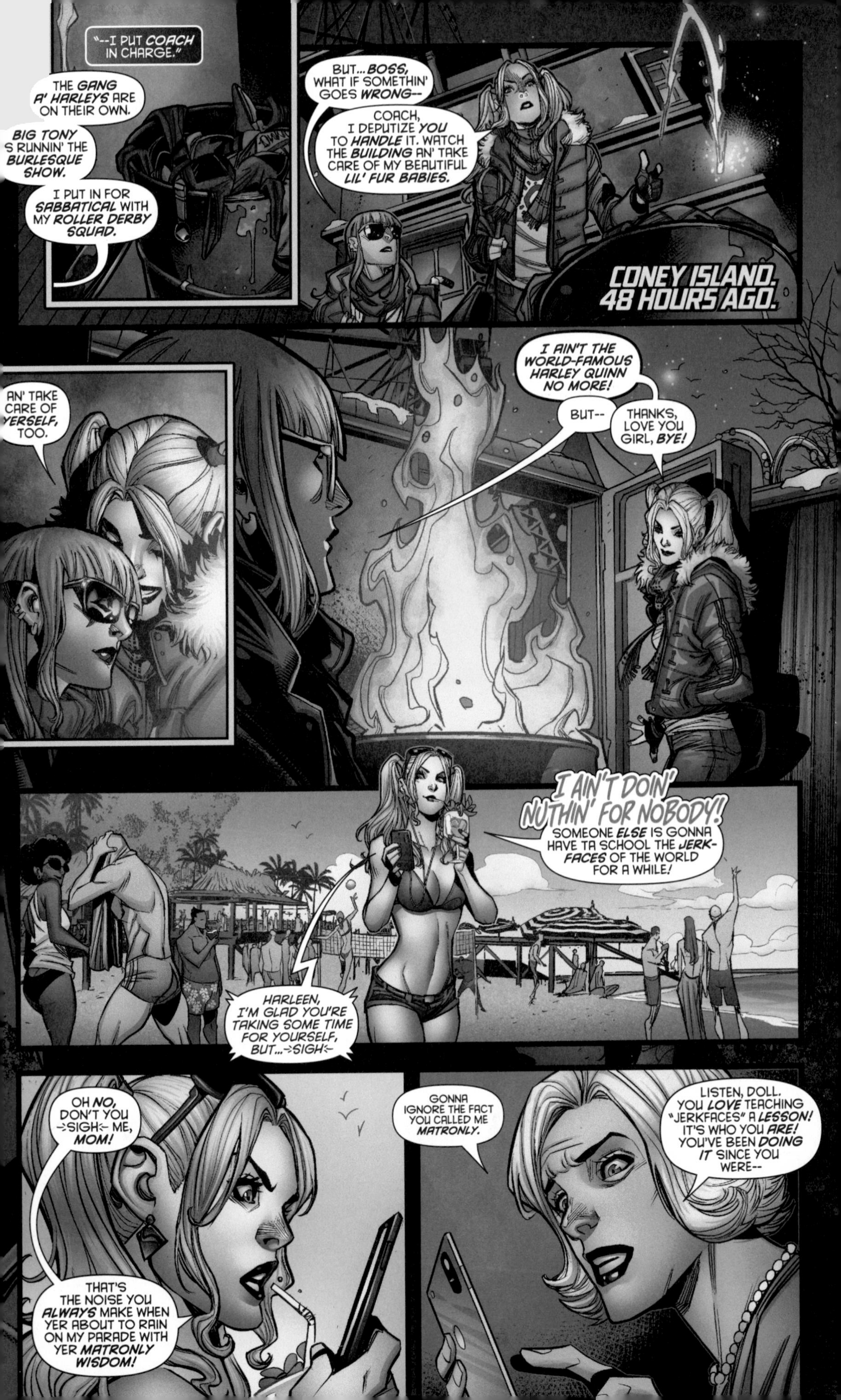

"--I PUT COACH IN CHARGE."
THE GANG A' HARLEYS ARE ON THEIR OWN.
BIG TONY 'S RUNNIN' THE BURLESQUE SHOW.
I PUT IN FOR SABBATICAL WITH MY ROLLER DERBY SQUAD.
BUT... BOSS, WHAT IF SOMETHIN' GOES WRONG--
COACH, I DEPUTIZE YOU TO HANDLE IT. WATCH THE BUILDING AN' TAKE CARE OF MY BEAUTIFUL LIL' FUR BABIES.
CONEY ISLAND. 48 HOURS AGO.
AN' TAKE CARE OF YERSELF, TOO.
BUT--
I AIN'T THE WORLD-FAMOUS HARLEY QUINN NO MORE!
THANKS, LOVE YOU GIRL, BYE!
I AIN'T DOIN' NUTHIN' FOR NOBODY!
SOMEONE ELSE IS GONNA HAVE TA SCHOOL THE JERK-FACES OF THE WORLD FOR A WHILE!
HARLEEN, I'M GLAD YOU'RE TAKING SOME TIME FOR YOURSELF, BUT... >SIGH<
OH NO, DON'T YOU >SIGH< ME, MOM!
THAT'S THE NOISE YOU ALWAYS MAKE WHEN YER ABOUT TO RAIN ON MY PARADE WITH YER MATRONLY WISDOM!
GONNA IGNORE THE FACT YOU CALLED ME MATRONLY.
LISTEN, DOLL. YOU LOVE TEACHING "JERKFACES" A LESSON! IT'S WHO YOU ARE! YOU'VE BEEN DOING IT SINCE YOU WERE--

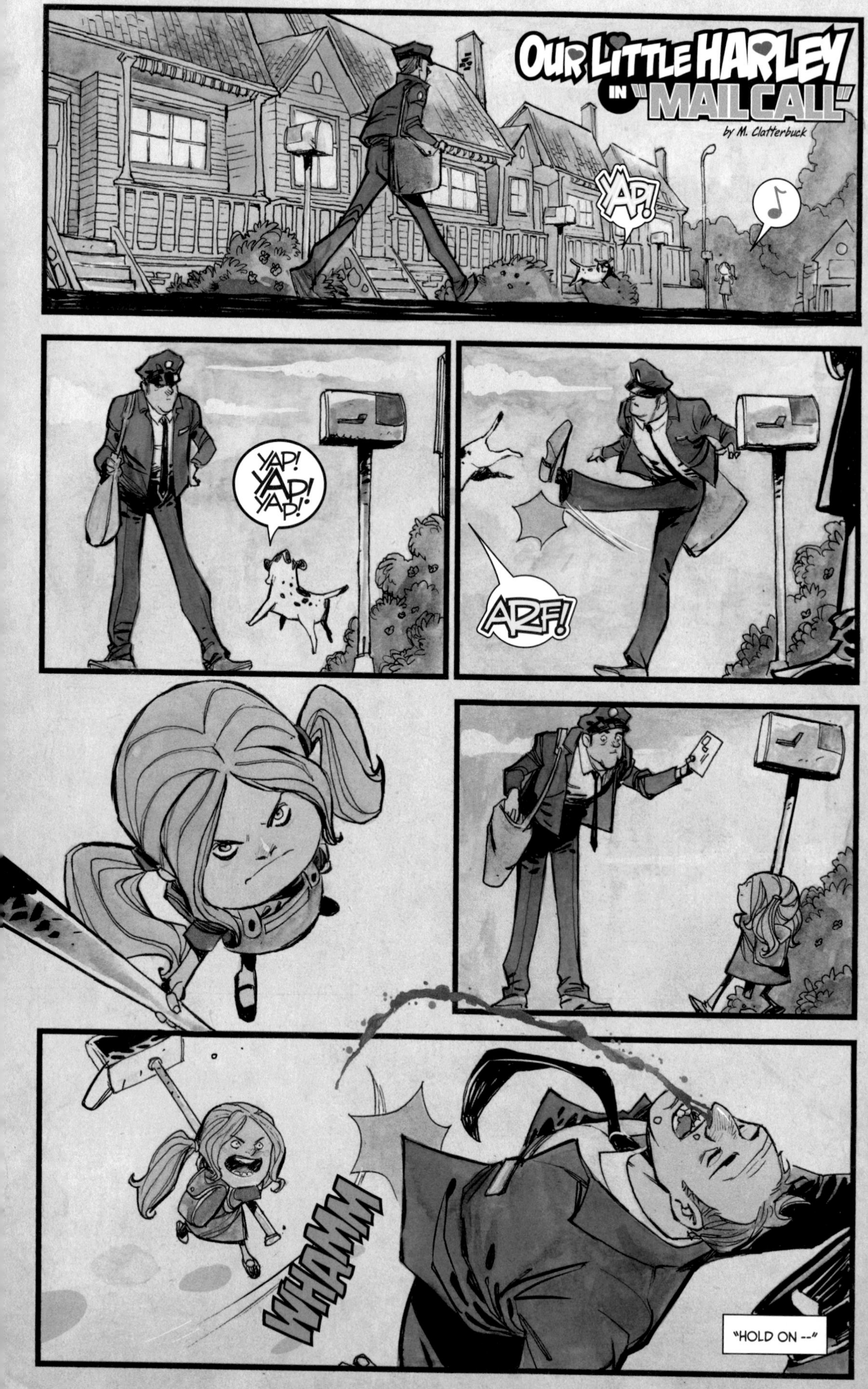
OUR LITTLE HARLEY IN "MAIL CALL"
by M. Clatterbuck
YAP!
♪
YAP! YAP! YAP!
ARF!
WHAMM
"HOLD ON --"

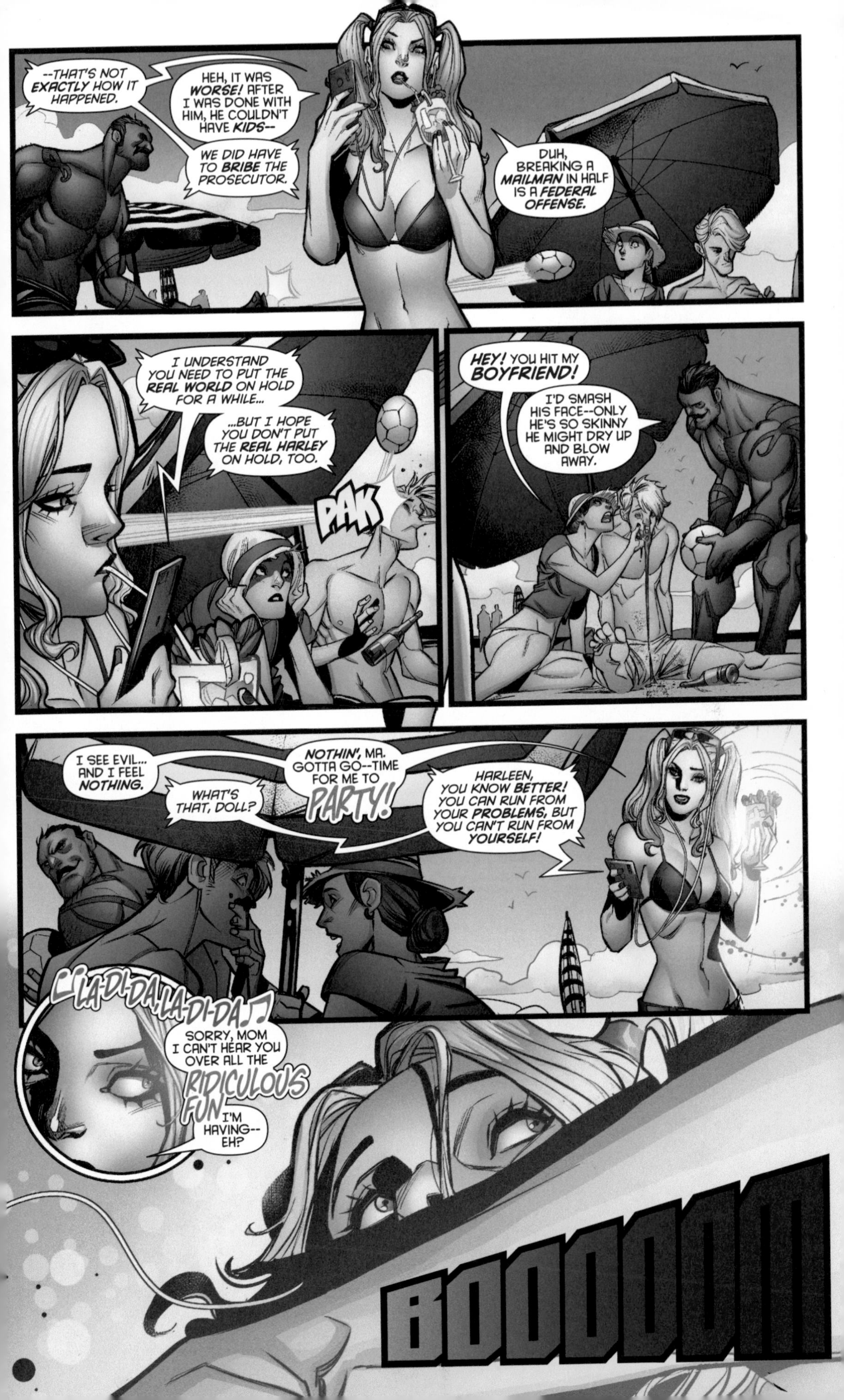

--THAT'S NOT EXACTLY HOW IT HAPPENED.
HEH, IT WAS WORSE! AFTER I WAS DONE WITH HIM, HE COULDN'T HAVE KIDS--
WE DID HAVE TO BRIBE THE PROSECUTOR.
DUH, BREAKING A MAILMAN IN HALF IS A FEDERAL OFFENSE.
I UNDERSTAND YOU NEED TO PUT THE REAL WORLD ON HOLD FOR A WHILE...
...BUT I HOPE YOU DON'T PUT THE REAL HARLEY ON HOLD, TOO.
PAK
HEY! YOU HIT MY BOYFRIEND!
I'D SMASH HIS FACE--ONLY HE'S SO SKINNY HE MIGHT DRY UP AND BLOW AWAY.
I SEE EVIL... AND I FEEL NOTHING.
WHAT'S THAT, DOLL?
NOTHIN', MA. GOTTA GO--TIME FOR ME TO PARTY!
HARLEEN, YOU KNOW BETTER! YOU CAN RUN FROM YOUR PROBLEMS, BUT YOU CAN'T RUN FROM YOURSELF!
♫LA-DI-DA, LA-DI-DA♫
SORRY, MOM I CAN'T HEAR YOU OVER ALL THE RIDICULOUS FUN I'M HAVING--EH?
BOOOOOM

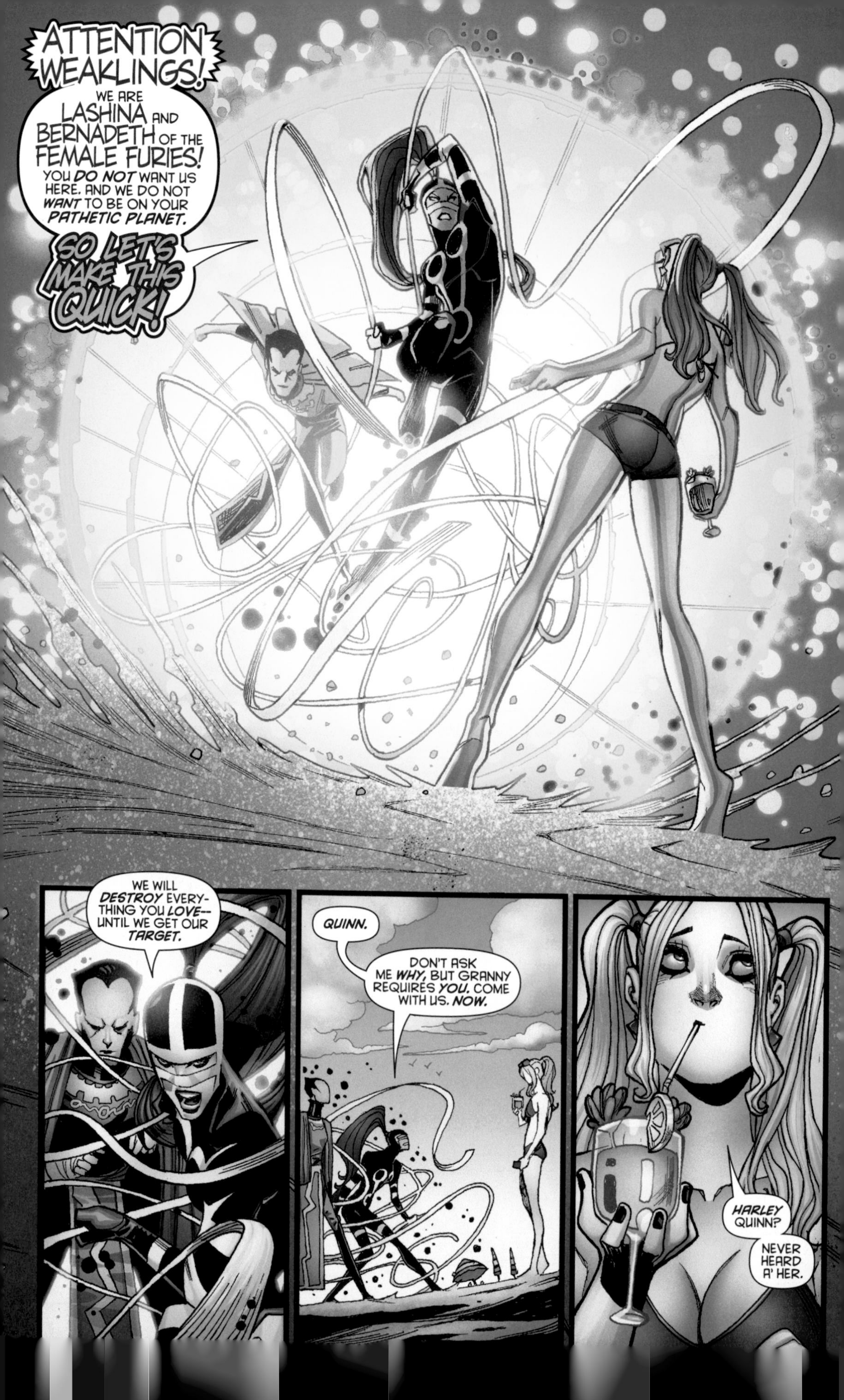
ATTENTION WEAKLINGS!
WE ARE LASHINA AND BERNADETH OF THE FEMALE FURIES! YOU DO NOT WANT US HERE. AND WE DO NOT WANT TO BE ON YOUR PATHETIC PLANET.
SO LET'S MAKE THIS QUICK!
WE WILL DESTROY EVERYTHING YOU LOVE-- UNTIL WE GET OUR TARGET.
QUINN.
DON'T ASK ME WHY, BUT GRANNY REQUIRES YOU. COME WITH US. NOW.
HARLEY QUINN?
NEVER HEARD A' HER.

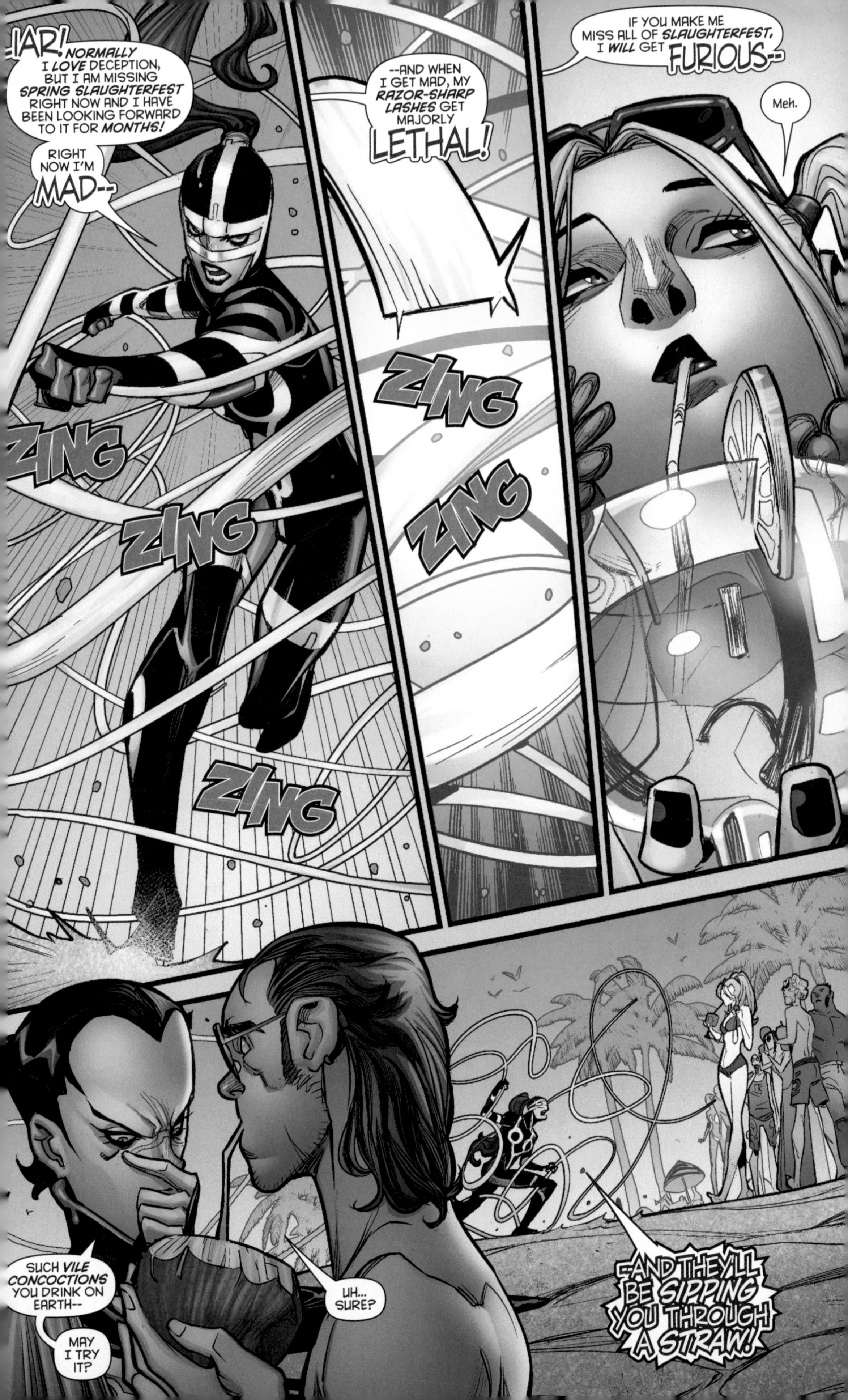
LIAR! NORMALLY I LOVE DECEPTION, BUT I AM MISSING SPRING SLAUGHTERFEST RIGHT NOW AND I HAVE BEEN LOOKING FORWARD TO IT FOR MONTHS!
RIGHT NOW I'M MAD--
ZING
ZING
ZING
--AND WHEN I GET MAD, MY RAZOR-SHARP LASHES GET MAJORLY LETHAL!
ZING
ZING
IF YOU MAKE ME MISS ALL OF SLAUGHTERFEST, I WILL GET FURIOUS--
Meh.
SUCH VILE CONCOCTIONS YOU DRINK ON EARTH--
MAY I TRY IT?
UH... SURE?
--AND THEY'LL BE SIPPING YOU THROUGH A STRAW!

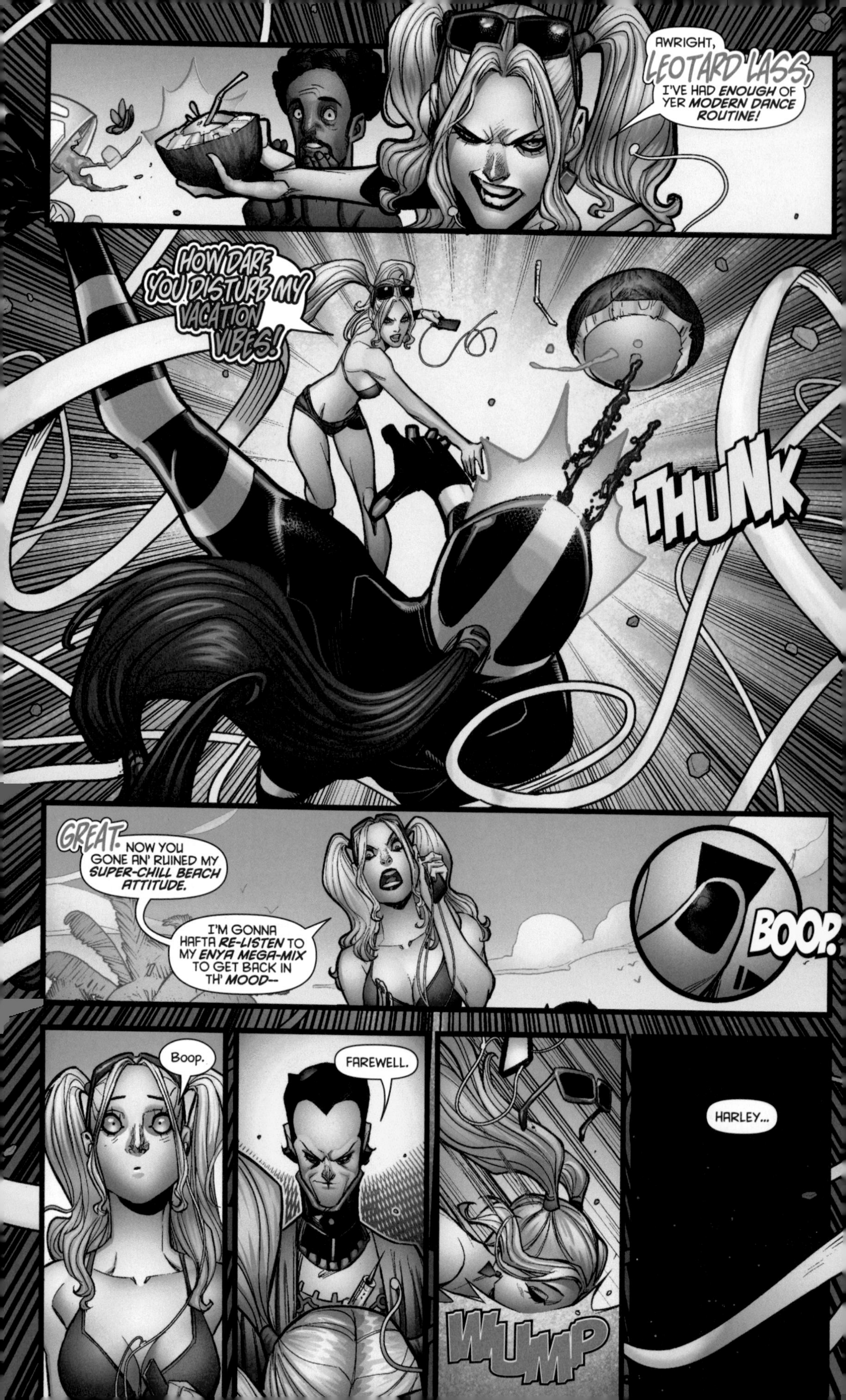
AWRIGHT, LEOTARD LASS, I'VE HAD ENOUGH OF YER MODERN DANCE ROUTINE!
HOW DARE YOU DISTURB MY VACATION VIBES!
THUNK
GREAT. NOW YOU GONE AN' RUINED MY SUPER-CHILL BEACH ATTITUDE.
I'M GONNA HAFTA RE-LISTEN TO MY ENYA MEGA-MIX TO GET BACK IN TH' MOOD--
BOOP.
Boop.
FAREWELL.
WUMP
HARLEY...

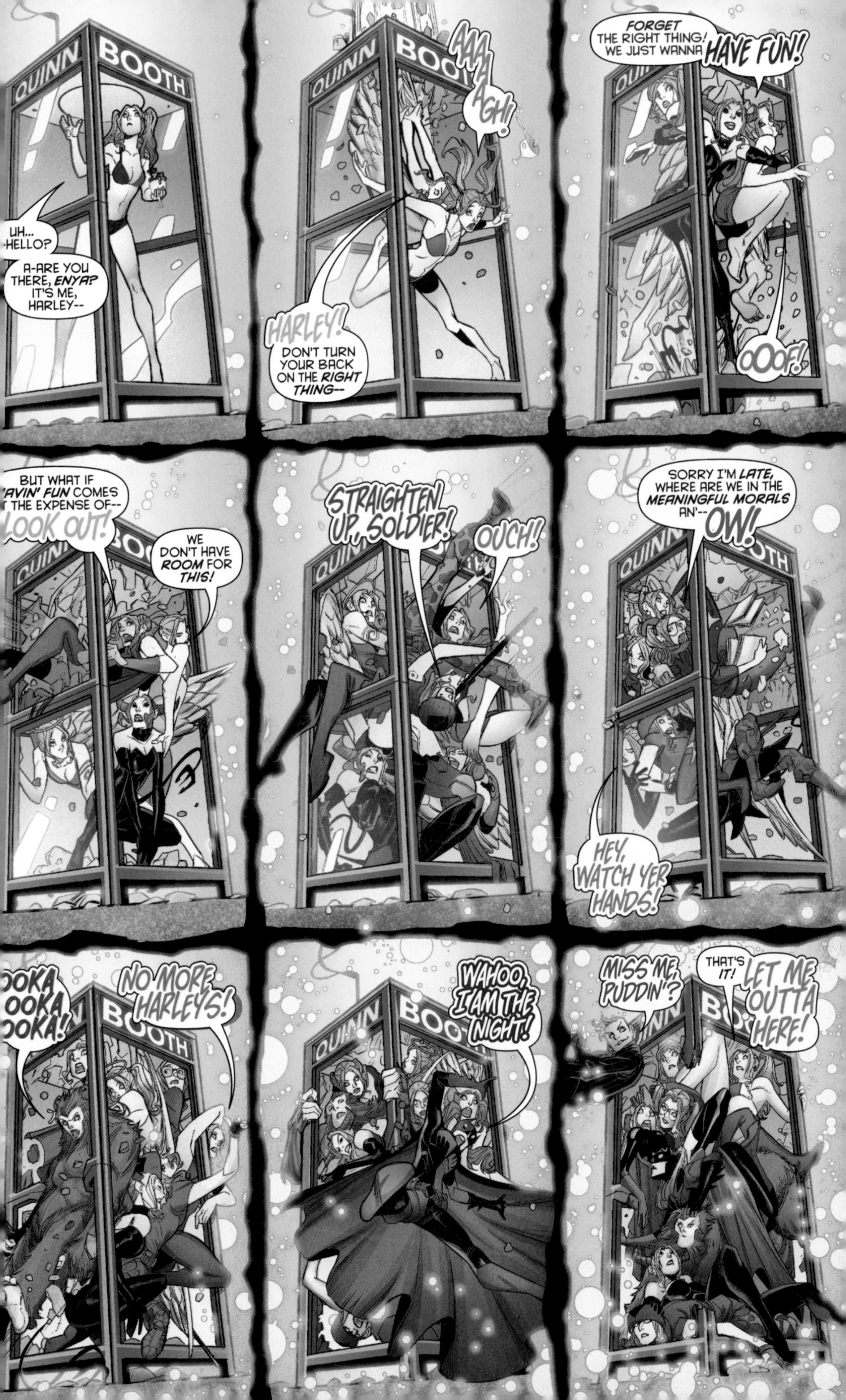
QUINN BOOTH
UH... HELLO?
A-ARE YOU THERE, ENYA? IT'S ME, HARLEY--
AAAAAAGH!
HARLEY! DON'T TURN YOUR BACK ON THE RIGHT THING--
FORGET THE RIGHT THING! WE JUST WANNA HAVE FUN!
OOOF!
BUT WHAT IF HAVIN' FUN COMES AT THE EXPENSE OF-- LOOK OUT!
WE DON'T HAVE ROOM FOR THIS!
STRAIGHTEN UP, SOLDIER!
OUCH!
SORRY I'M LATE, WHERE ARE WE IN THE MEANINGFUL MORALS AN'-- OW!
HEY, WATCH YER HANDS!
OOKA OOKA OOKA!
NO MORE HARLEYS!
WAHOO, I AM THE NIGHT!
MISS ME, PUDDIN'?
THAT'S IT! LET ME OUTTA HERE!

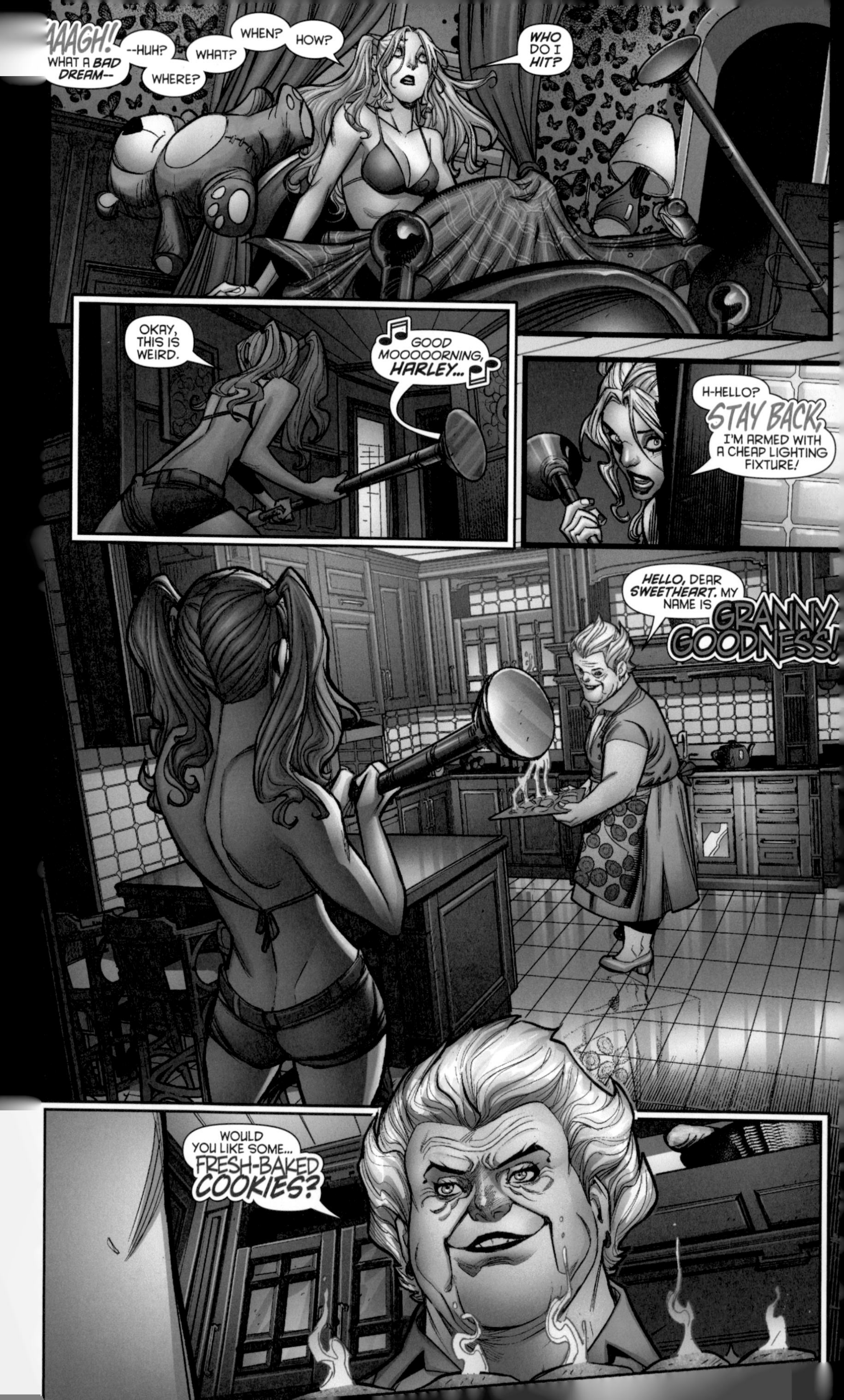
AAAGH! WHAT A BAD DREAM--
--HUH?
WHERE?
WHAT?
WHEN?
HOW?
WHO DO I HIT?
OKAY, THIS IS WEIRD.
GOOD MOOOOORNING, HARLEY...
H-HELLO? STAY BACK, I'M ARMED WITH A CHEAP LIGHTING FIXTURE!
HELLO, DEAR SWEETHEART. MY NAME IS GRANNY GOODNESS!
WOULD YOU LIKE SOME... FRESH-BAKED COOKIES?

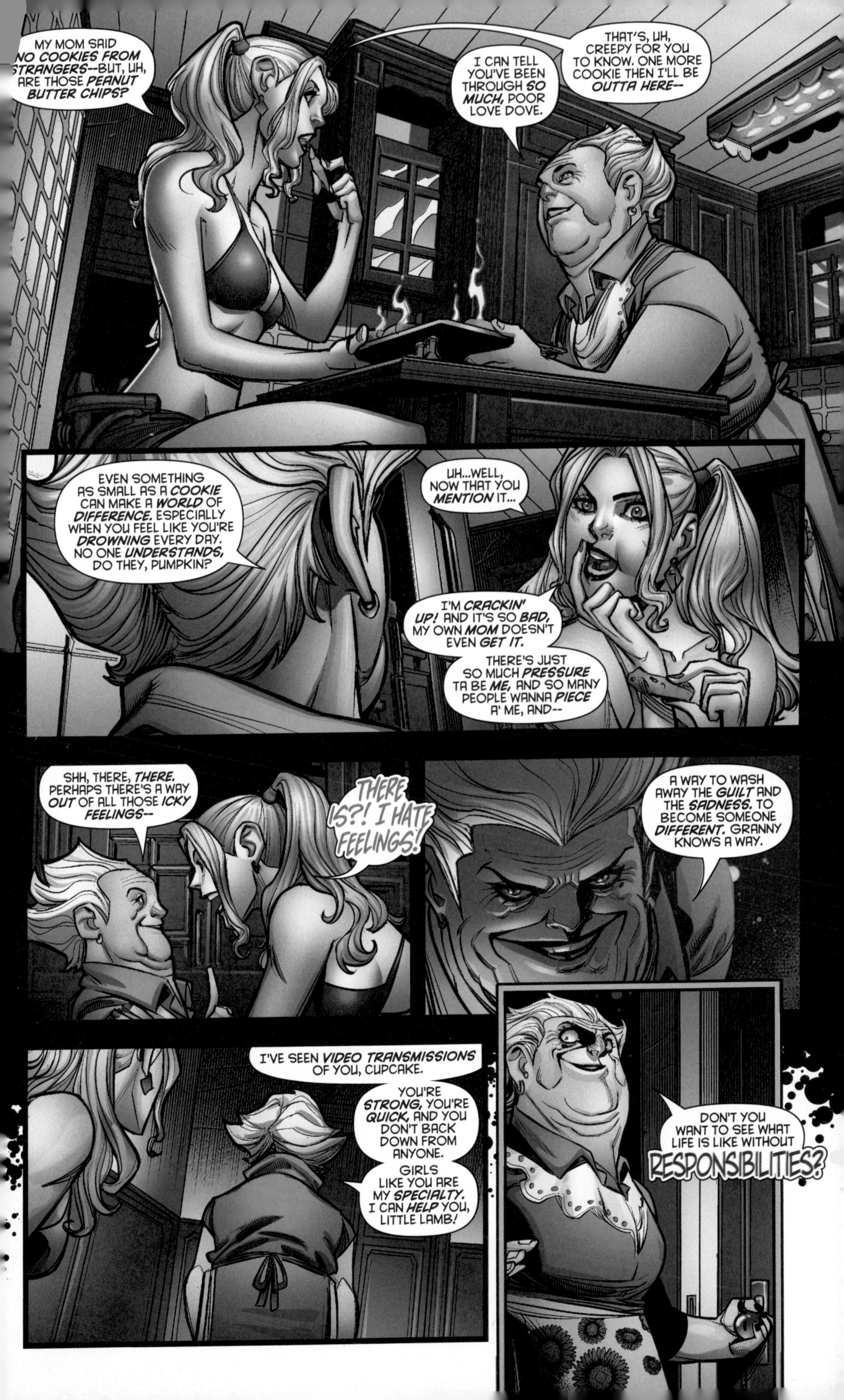
MY MOM SAID NO COOKIES FROM STRANGERS--BUT, UH, ARE THOSE PEANUT BUTTER CHIPS?
I CAN TELL YOU'VE BEEN THROUGH SO MUCH, POOR LOVE DOVE.
THAT'S, UH, CREEPY FOR YOU TO KNOW. ONE MORE COOKIE THEN I'LL BE OUTTA HERE--
EVEN SOMETHING AS SMALL AS A COOKIE CAN MAKE A WORLD OF DIFFERENCE. ESPECIALLY WHEN YOU FEEL LIKE YOU'RE DROWNING EVERY DAY. NO ONE UNDERSTANDS, DO THEY, PUMPKIN?
UH...WELL, NOW THAT YOU MENTION IT...
I'M CRACKIN' UP! AND IT'S SO BAD, MY OWN MOM DOESN'T EVEN GET IT.
THERE'S JUST SO MUCH PRESSURE TA BE ME, AND SO MANY PEOPLE WANNA PIECE A' ME, AND--
SHH, THERE, THERE. PERHAPS THERE'S A WAY OUT OF ALL THOSE ICKY FEELINGS--
THERE IS?! I HATE FEELINGS!
A WAY TO WASH AWAY THE GUILT AND THE SADNESS. TO BECOME SOMEONE DIFFERENT. GRANNY KNOWS A WAY.
I'VE SEEN VIDEO TRANSMISSIONS OF YOU, CUPCAKE.
YOU'RE STRONG, YOU'RE QUICK, AND YOU DON'T BACK DOWN FROM ANYONE.
GIRLS LIKE YOU ARE MY SPECIALTY. I CAN HELP YOU, LITTLE LAMB!
DON'T YOU WANT TO SEE WHAT LIFE IS LIKE WITHOUT RESPONSIBILITIES?

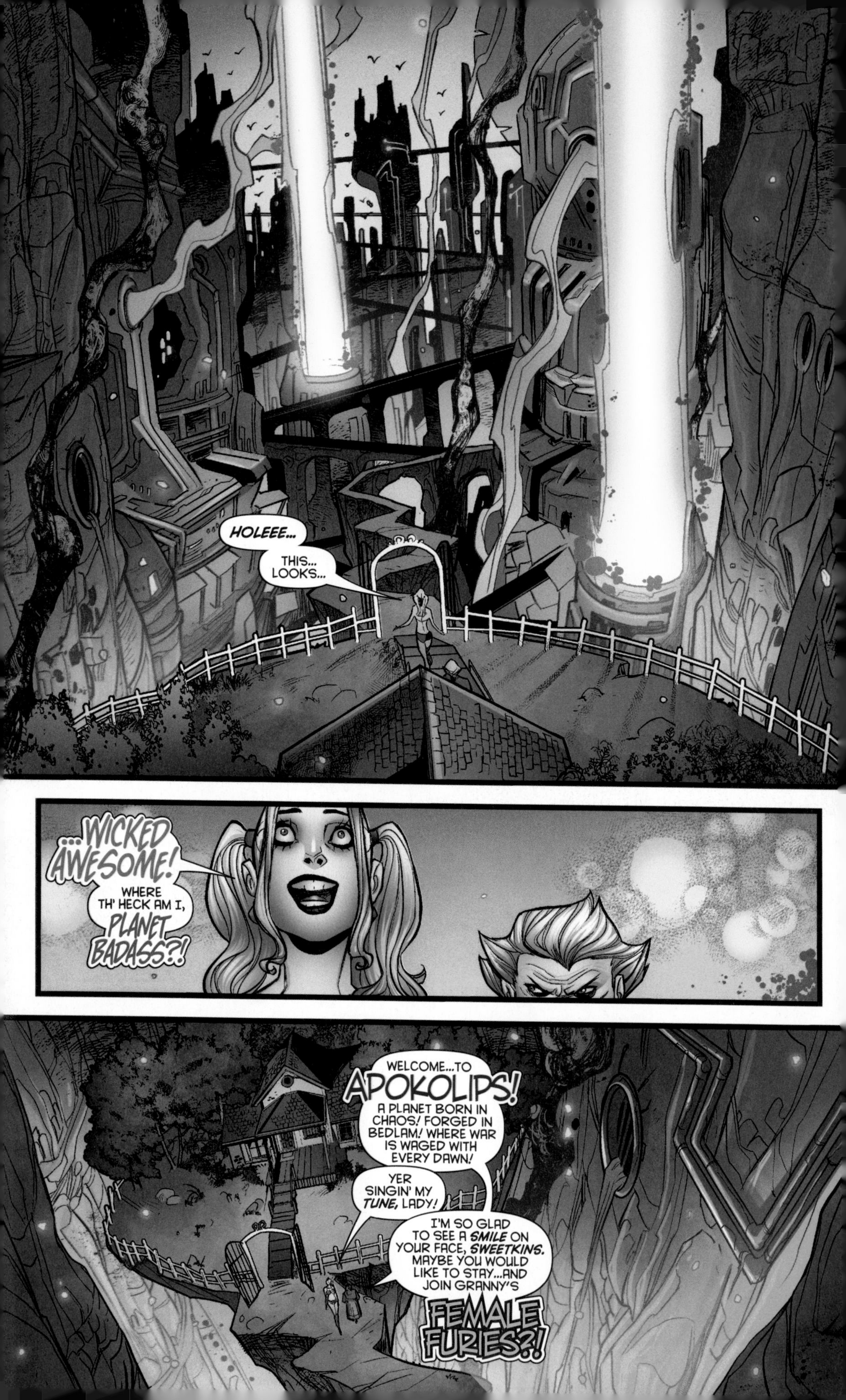
HOLEEE...
THIS... LOOKS...
...WICKED AWESOME!
WHERE TH' HECK AM I, PLANET BADASS?!
WELCOME...TO APOKOLIPS!
A PLANET BORN IN CHAOS! FORGED IN BEDLAM! WHERE WAR IS WAGED WITH EVERY DAWN!
YER SINGIN' MY TUNE, LADY!
I'M SO GLAD TO SEE A SMILE ON YOUR FACE, SWEETKINS. MAYBE YOU WOULD LIKE TO STAY...AND JOIN GRANNY'S FEMALE FURIES?!

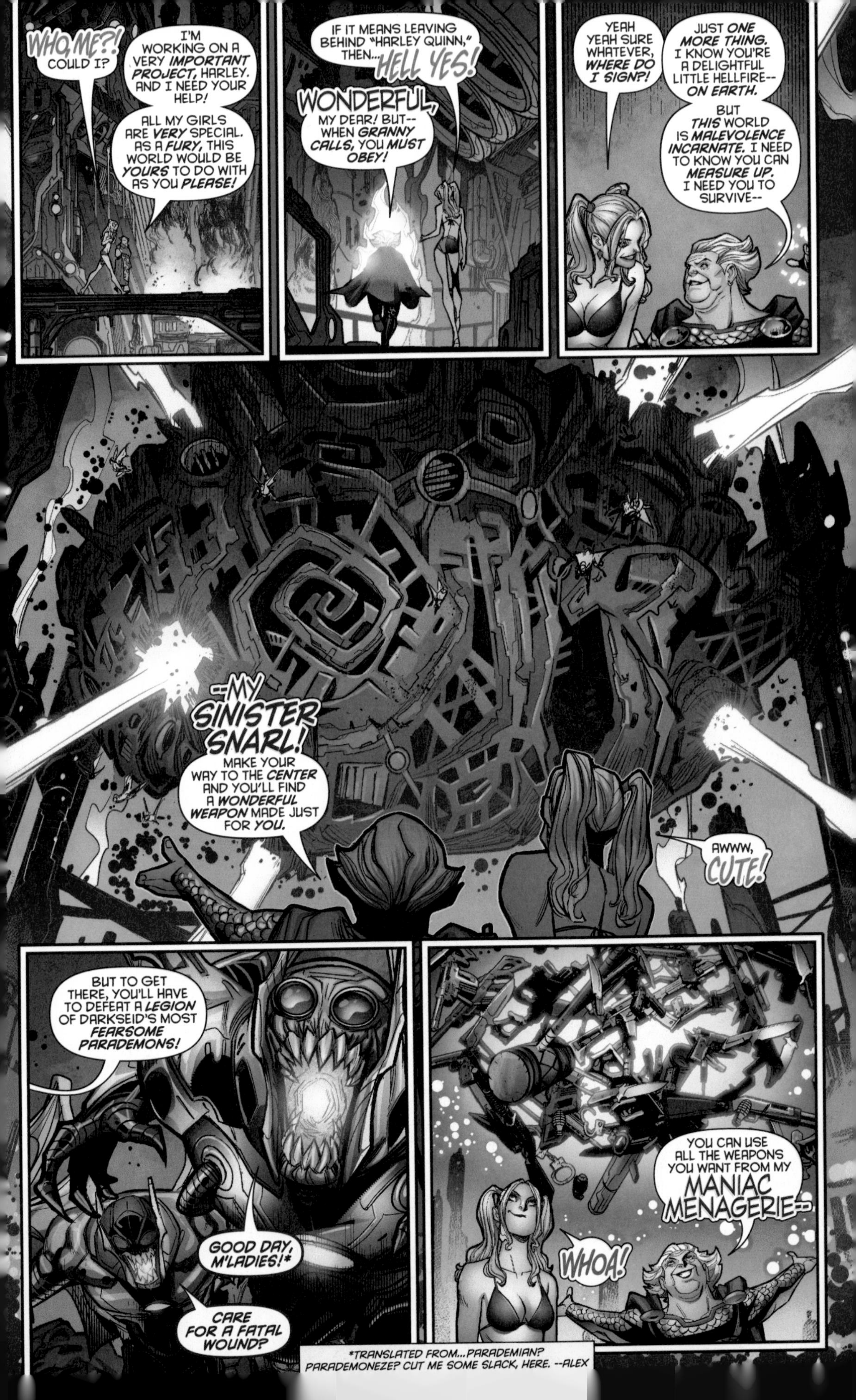
WHO, ME?! COULD I?
I'M WORKING ON A VERY IMPORTANT PROJECT, HARLEY. AND I NEED YOUR HELP!
ALL MY GIRLS ARE VERY SPECIAL. AS A FURY, THIS WORLD WOULD BE YOURS TO DO WITH AS YOU PLEASE!
IF IT MEANS LEAVING BEHIND "HARLEY QUINN," THEN...HELL YES!
WONDERFUL, MY DEAR! BUT-- WHEN GRANNY CALLS, YOU MUST OBEY!
YEAH YEAH SURE WHATEVER, WHERE DO I SIGN?!
JUST ONE MORE THING. I KNOW YOU'RE A DELIGHTFUL LITTLE HELLFIRE-- ON EARTH.
BUT THIS WORLD IS MALEVOLENCE INCARNATE. I NEED TO KNOW YOU CAN MEASURE UP. I NEED YOU TO SURVIVE--
--MY SINISTER SNARL! MAKE YOUR WAY TO THE CENTER AND YOU'LL FIND A WONDERFUL WEAPON MADE JUST FOR YOU.
AWWW, CUTE!
BUT TO GET THERE, YOU'LL HAVE TO DEFEAT A LEGION OF DARKSEID'S MOST FEARSOME PARADEMONS!
GOOD DAY, M'LADIES!*
CARE FOR A FATAL WOUND?
YOU CAN USE ALL THE WEAPONS YOU WANT FROM MY MANIAC MENAGERIE--
WHOA!
*TRANSLATED FROM...PARADEMIAN? PARADEMONEZE? CUT ME SOME SLACK, HERE. --ALEX

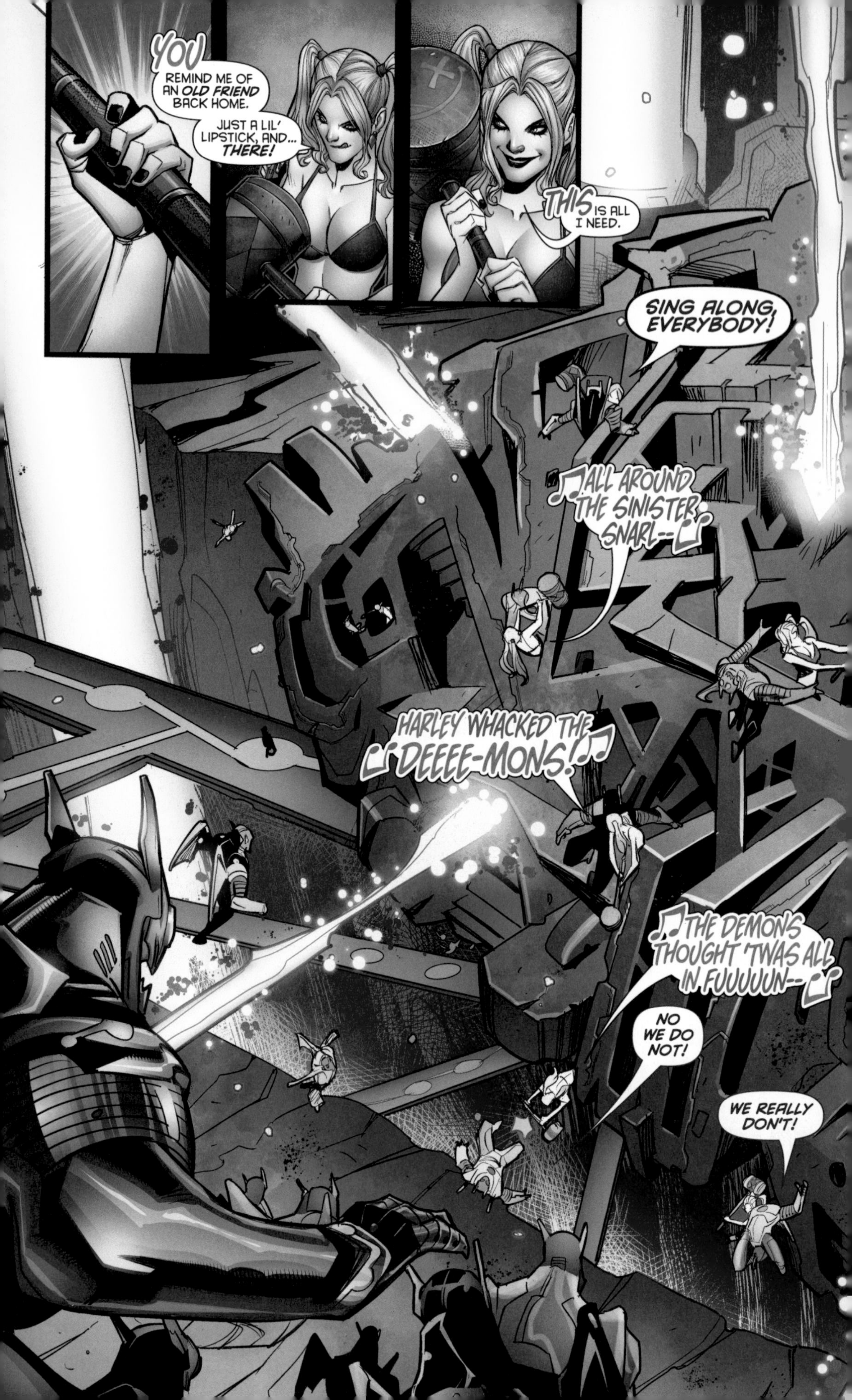
YOU REMIND ME OF AN OLD FRIEND BACK HOME.
JUST A LIL' LIPSTICK, AND... THERE!
THIS IS ALL I NEED.
SING ALONG, EVERYBODY!
♫ ALL AROUND THE SINISTER SNARL-- ♫
HARLEY WHACKED THE ♫ DEEEE-MONS! ♫
♫ THE DEMONS THOUGHT 'TWAS ALL IN FUUUUUN-- ♫
NO WE DO NOT!
WE REALLY DON'T!

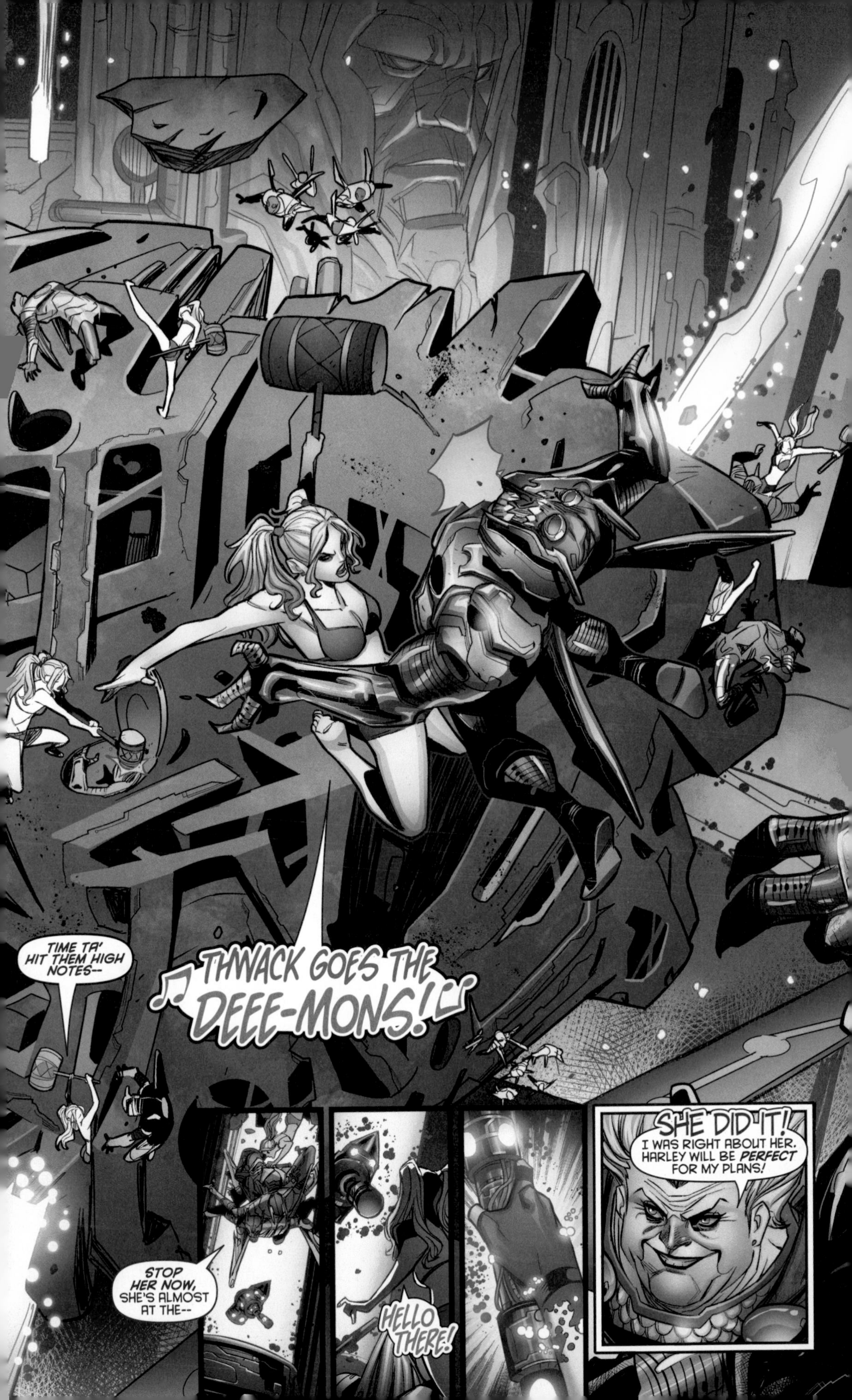

TIME TA' HIT THEM HIGH NOTES--
THWACK GOES THE DEEE-MONS!
STOP HER NOW, SHE'S ALMOST AT THE--
HELLO THERE!
SHE DID IT! I WAS RIGHT ABOUT HER. HARLEY WILL BE *PERFECT* FOR MY PLANS!

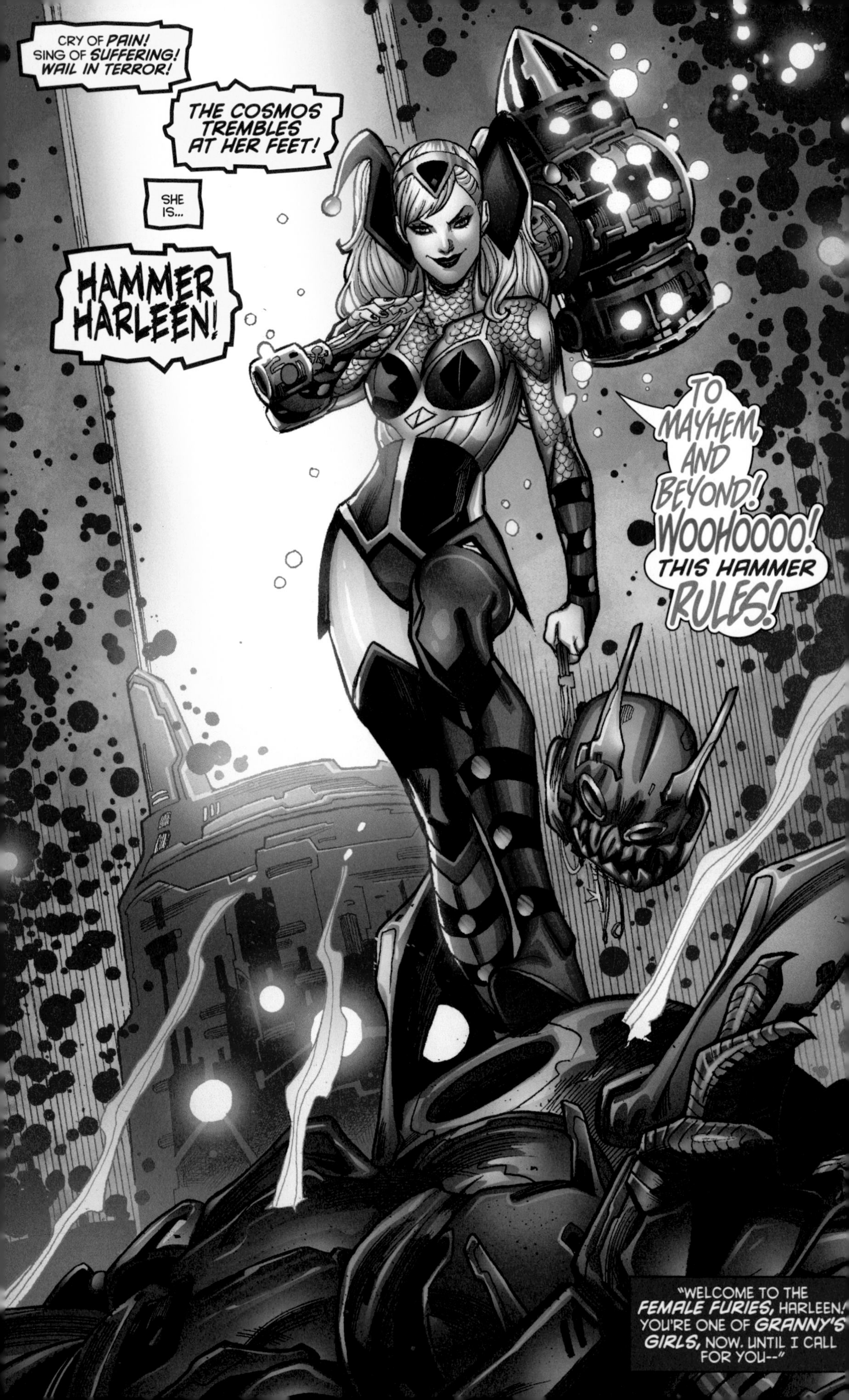

CRY OF PAIN! SING OF SUFFERING! WAIL IN TERROR!
THE COSMOS TREMBLES AT HER FEET!
SHE IS...
HAMMER HARLEEN!
TO MAYHEM, AND BEYOND! WOOHOOOO! THIS HAMMER RULES!
"WELCOME TO THE FEMALE FURIES, HARLEEN! YOU'RE ONE OF GRANNY'S GIRLS, NOW. UNTIL I CALL FOR YOU--"

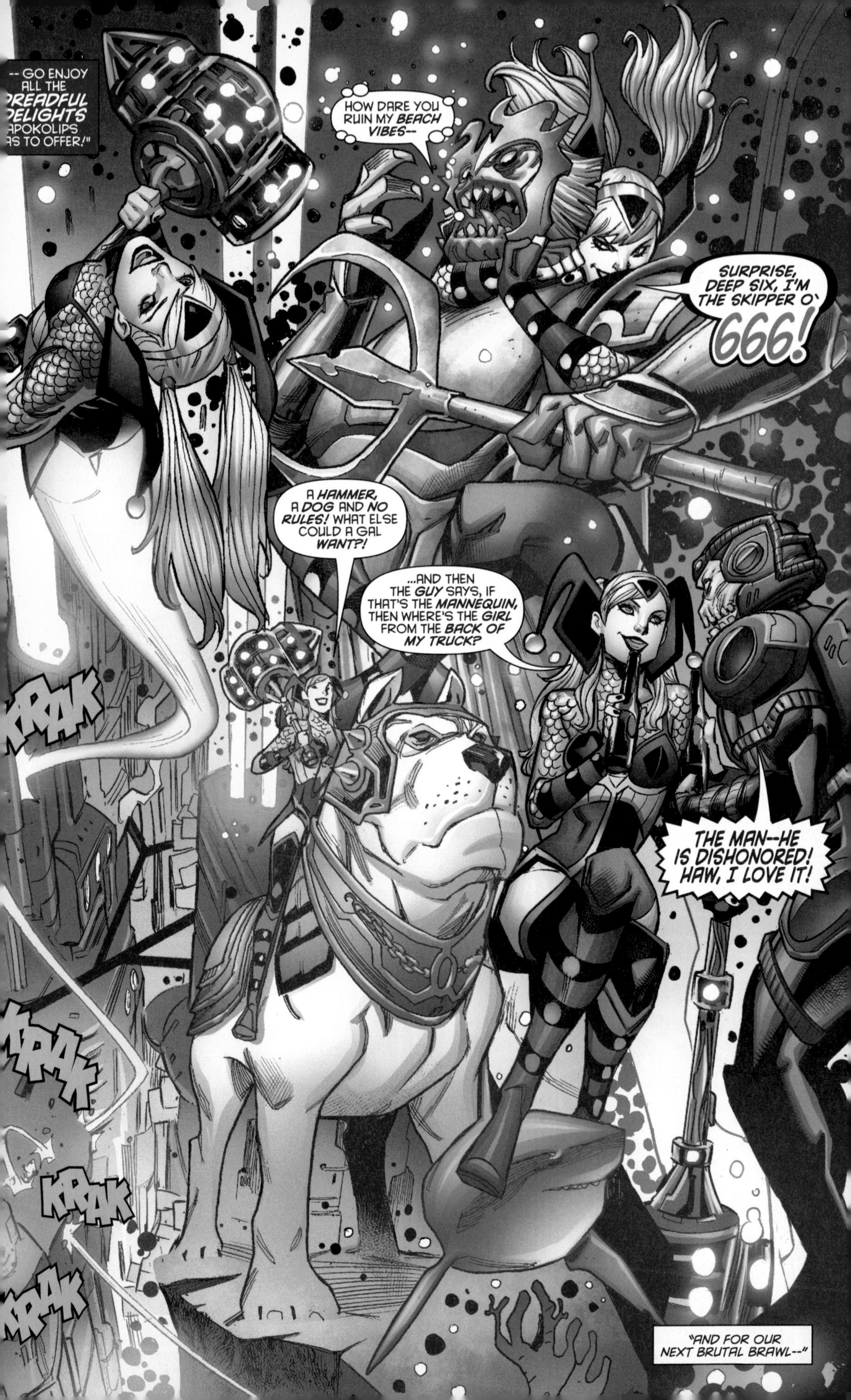
-- GO ENJOY ALL THE DREADFUL DELIGHTS APOKOLIPS HAS TO OFFER!"
HOW DARE YOU RUIN MY BEACH VIBES--
SURPRISE, DEEP SIX, I'M THE SKIPPER O' 666!
A HAMMER, A DOG AND NO RULES! WHAT ELSE COULD A GAL WANT?!
...AND THEN THE GUY SAYS, IF THAT'S THE MANNEQUIN, THEN WHERE'S THE GIRL FROM THE BACK OF MY TRUCK?
THE MAN--HE IS DISHONORED! HAW, I LOVE IT!
KRAK
KRAK
KRAK
KRAK
"AND FOR OUR NEXT BRUTAL BRAWL--"

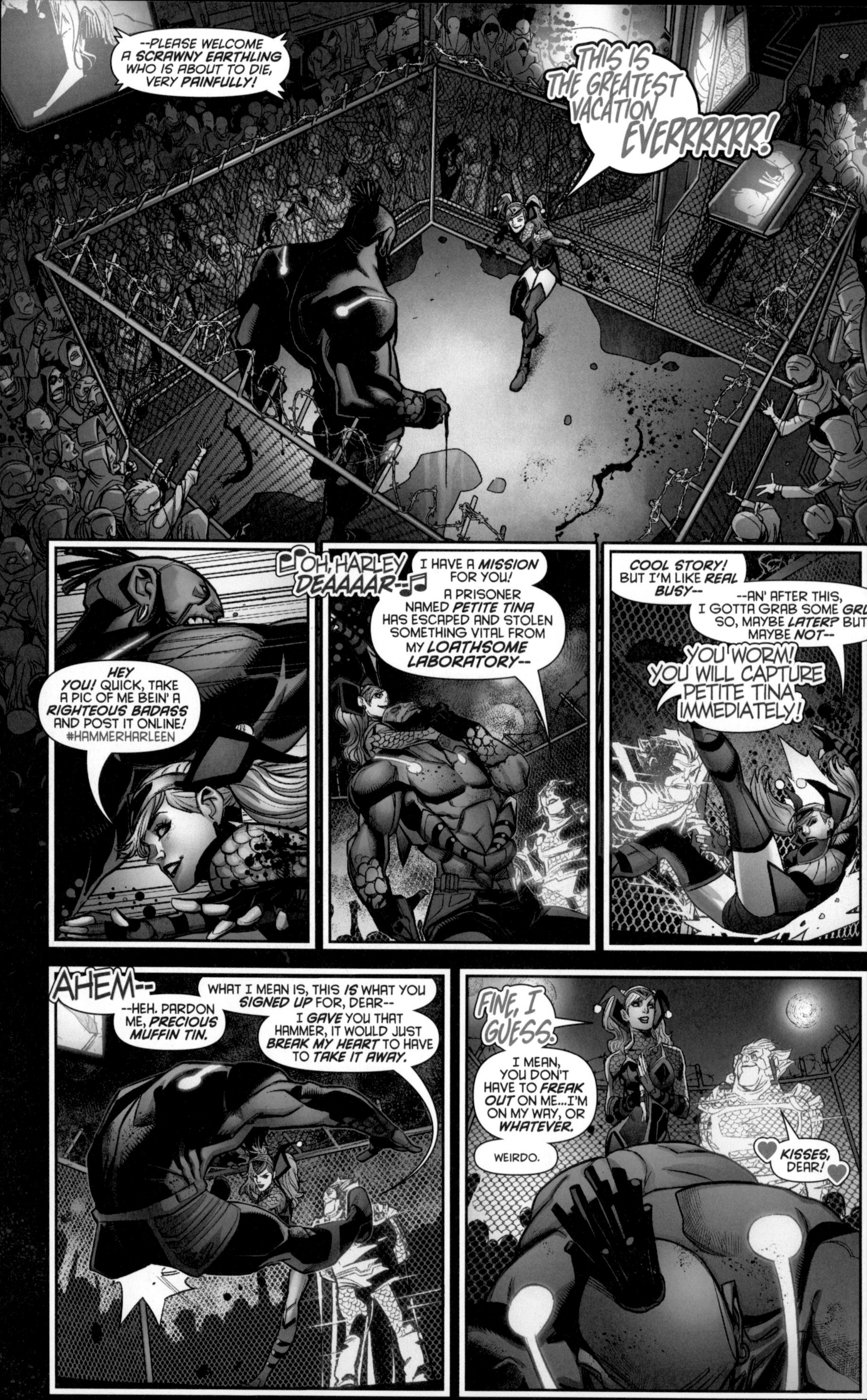

--PLEASE WELCOME A SCRAWNY EARTHLING WHO IS ABOUT TO DIE, VERY PAINFULLY!
THIS IS THE GREATEST VACATION EVERRRRRR!
HEY YOU! QUICK, TAKE A PIC OF ME BEIN' A RIGHTEOUS BADASS AND POST IT ONLINE! #HAMMERHARLEEN
OH, HARLEY DEAAAAR--
I HAVE A MISSION FOR YOU!
A PRISONER NAMED PETITE TINA HAS ESCAPED AND STOLEN SOMETHING VITAL FROM MY LOATHSOME LABORATORY--
COOL STORY! BUT I'M LIKE REAL BUSY--
--AN' AFTER THIS, I GOTTA GRAB SOME GRU SO, MAYBE LATER? BUT MAYBE NOT--
YOU WORM! YOU WILL CAPTURE PETITE TINA IMMEDIATELY!
AHEM--
--HEH. PARDON ME, PRECIOUS MUFFIN TIN.
WHAT I MEAN IS, THIS IS WHAT YOU SIGNED UP FOR, DEAR--
I GAVE YOU THAT HAMMER, IT WOULD JUST BREAK MY HEART TO HAVE TO TAKE IT AWAY.
FINE, I GUESS.
I MEAN, YOU DON'T HAVE TO FREAK OUT ON ME...I'M ON MY WAY, OR WHATEVER.
WEIRDO.
KISSES, DEAR!

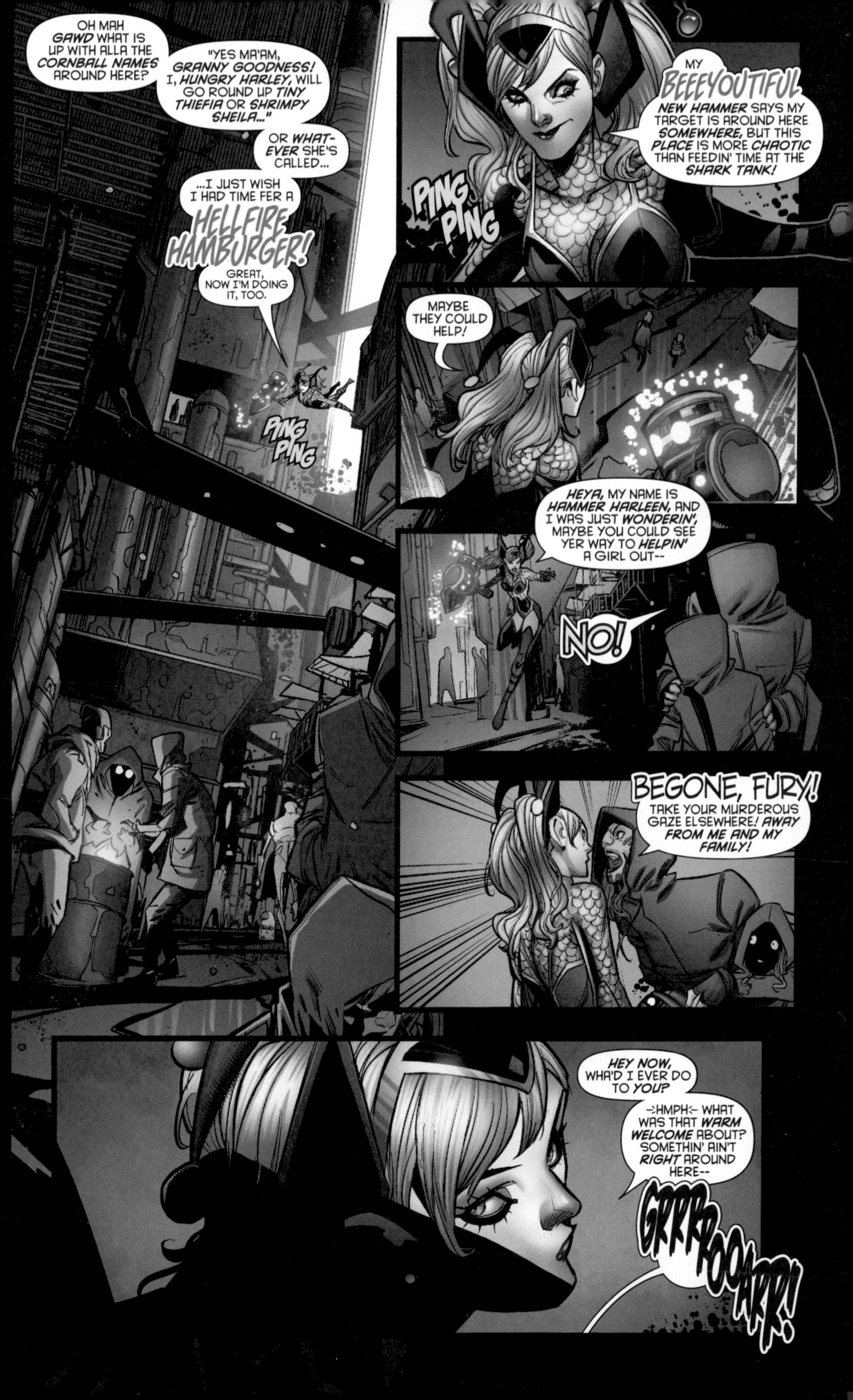

OH MAH GAWD WHAT IS UP WITH ALLA THE CORNBALL NAMES AROUND HERE?
"YES MA'AM, GRANNY GOODNESS! I, HUNGRY HARLEY, WILL GO ROUND UP TINY THIEFIA OR SHRIMPY SHEILA..."
OR WHAT-EVER SHE'S CALLED...
...I JUST WISH I HAD TIME FER A HELLFIRE HAMBURGER!
GREAT, NOW I'M DOING IT, TOO.
PING PING
PING PING
MY BEEEYOUTIFUL NEW HAMMER SAYS MY TARGET IS AROUND HERE SOMEWHERE, BUT THIS PLACE IS MORE CHAOTIC THAN FEEDIN' TIME AT THE SHARK TANK!
MAYBE THEY COULD HELP!
HEYA, MY NAME IS HAMMER HARLEEN, AND I WAS JUST WONDERIN', MAYBE YOU COULD SEE YER WAY TO HELPIN' A GIRL OUT--
NO!
BEGONE, FURY! TAKE YOUR MURDEROUS GAZE ELSEWHERE! AWAY FROM ME AND MY FAMILY!
HEY NOW, WHA'D I EVER DO TO YOU?
-HMPH- WHAT WAS THAT WARM WELCOME ABOUT? SOMETHIN' AIN'T RIGHT AROUND HERE--
GRRRROOARR!

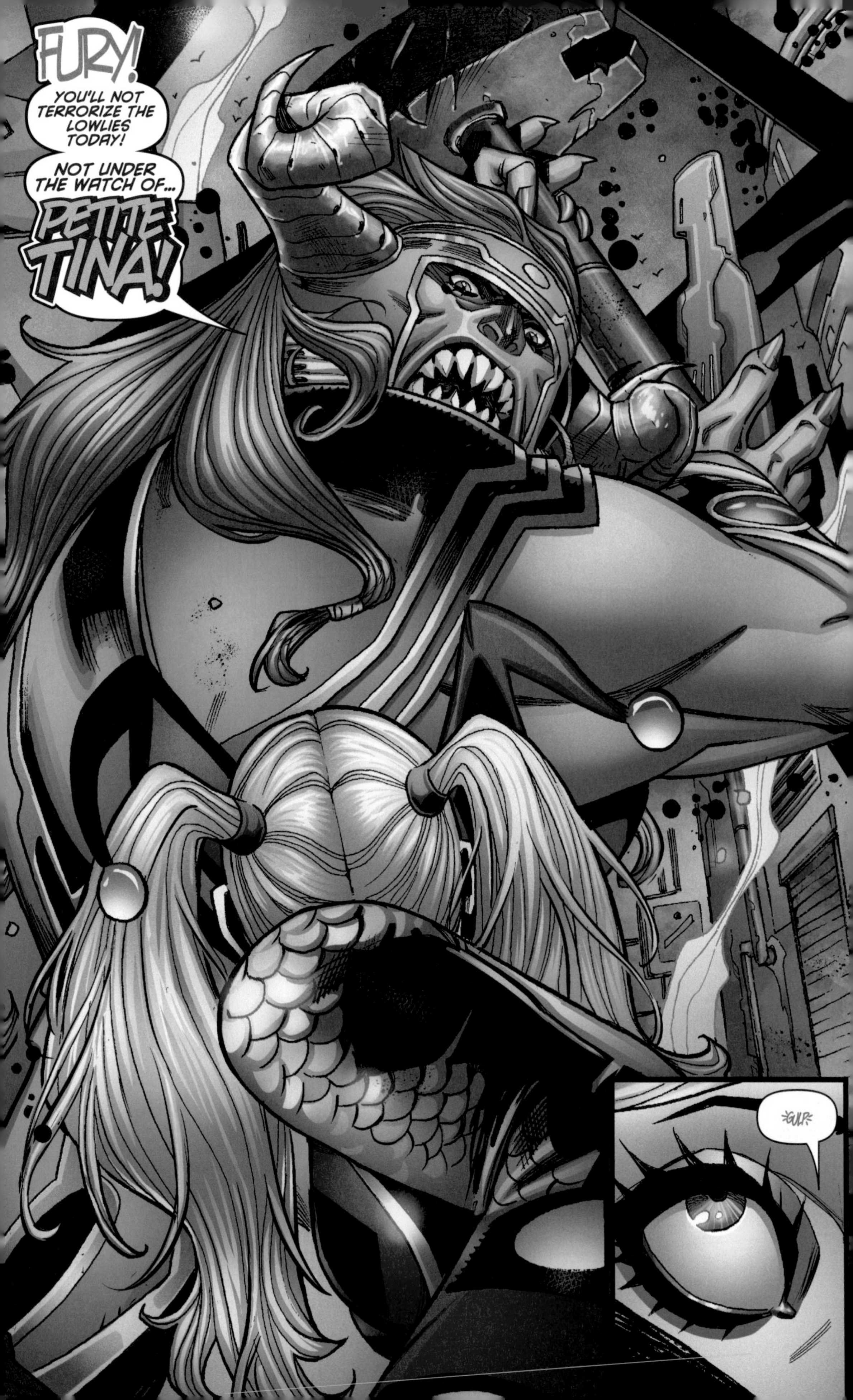
FURY!
YOU'LL NOT TERRORIZE THE LOWLIES TODAY!
NOT UNDER THE WATCH OF... PETITE TINA!
GULP

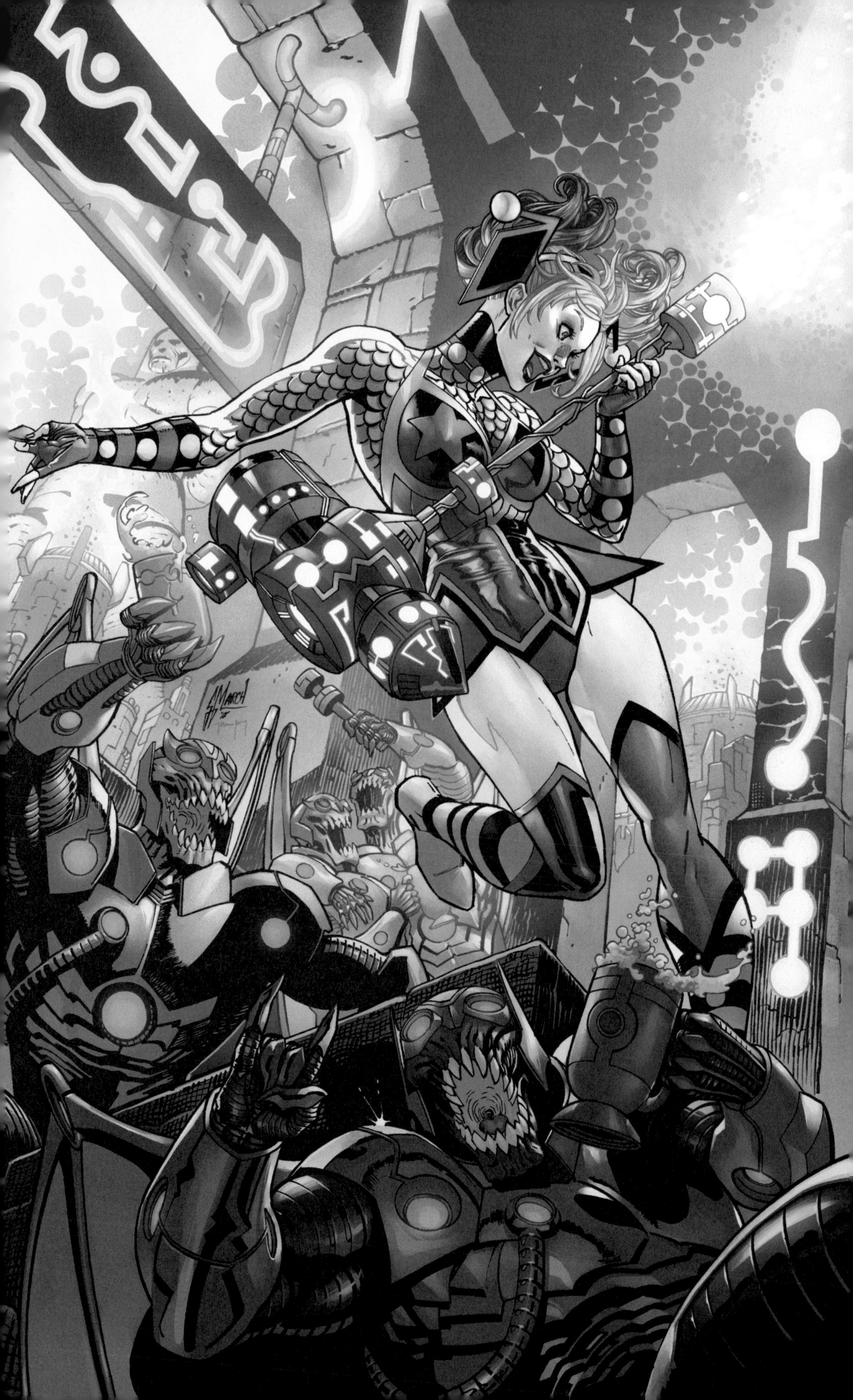

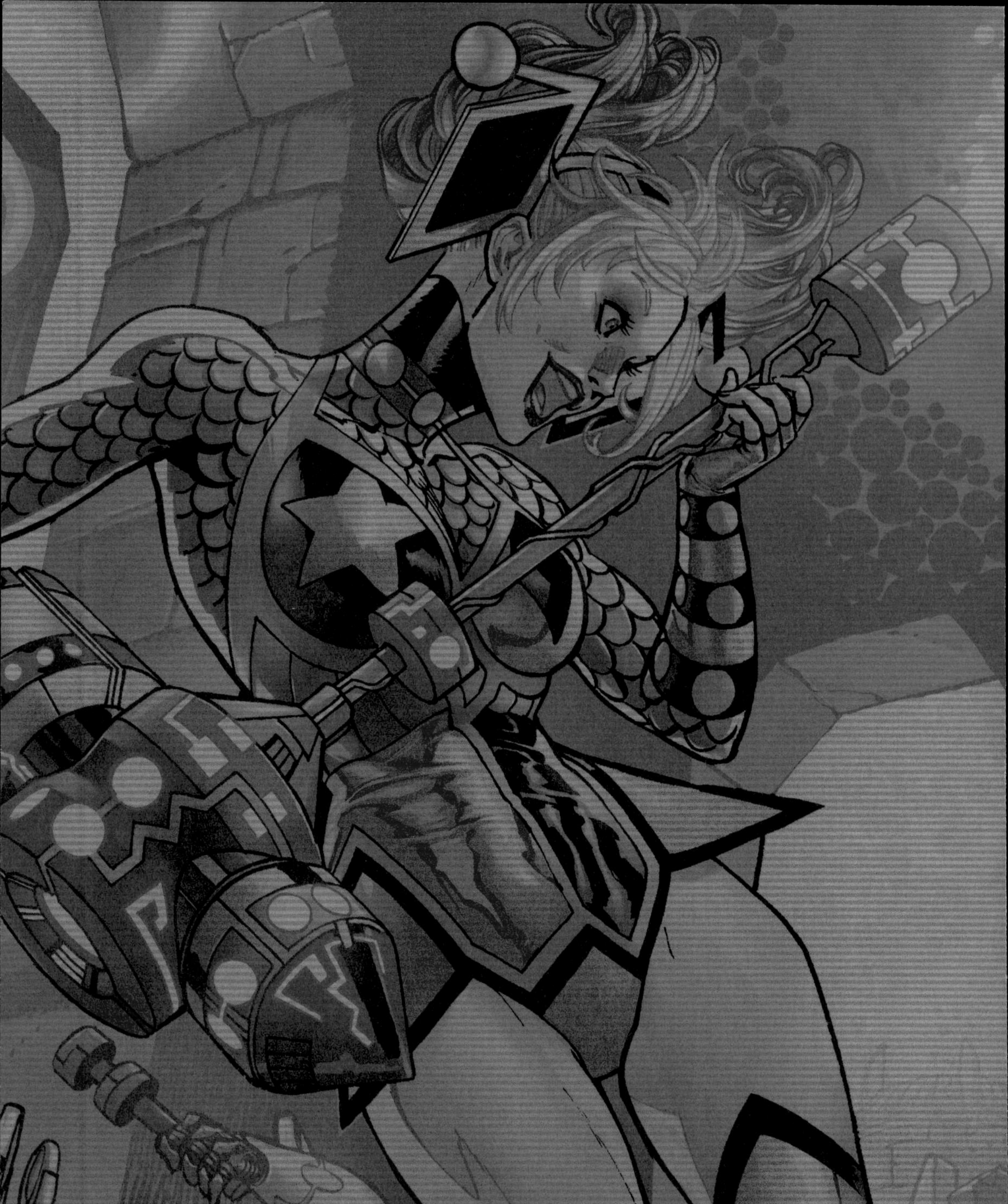

HARLEY QUINN
#46

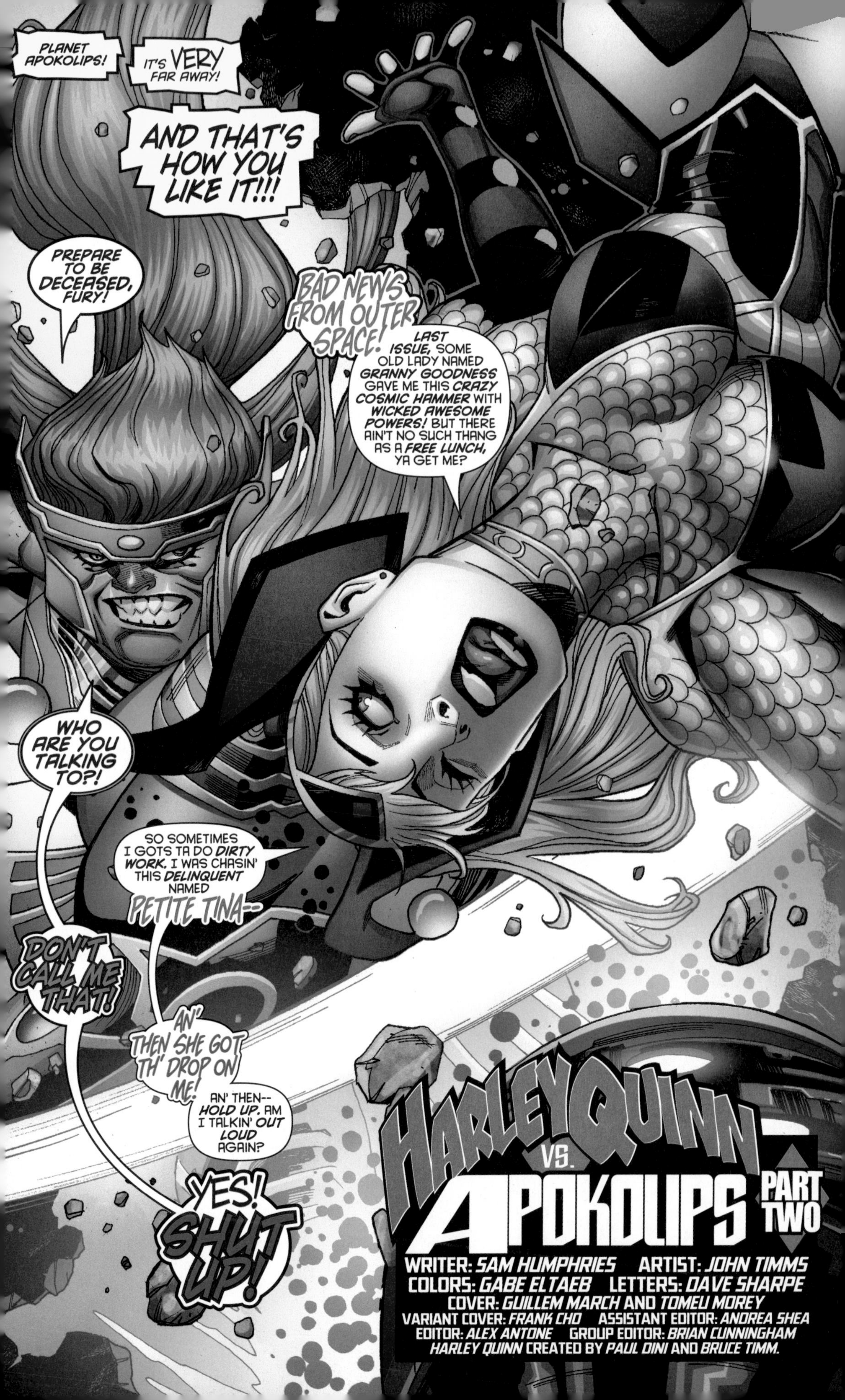
PLANET APOKOLIPS!
IT'S VERY FAR AWAY!
AND THAT'S HOW YOU LIKE IT!!!
PREPARE TO BE DECEASED, FURY!
BAD NEWS FROM OUTER SPACE!
LAST ISSUE, SOME OLD LADY NAMED GRANNY GOODNESS GAVE ME THIS CRAZY COSMIC HAMMER WITH WICKED AWESOME POWERS! BUT THERE AIN'T NO SUCH THANG AS A FREE LUNCH, YA GET ME?
WHO ARE YOU TALKING TO?!
SO SOMETIMES I GOTS TA DO DIRTY WORK. I WAS CHASIN' THIS DELINQUENT NAMED
PETITE TINA--
DON'T CALL ME THAT!
AN' THEN SHE GOT TH' DROP ON ME!
AN' THEN-- HOLD UP. AM I TALKIN' OUT LOUD AGAIN?
YES! SHUT UP!
HARLEY QUINN VS. APOKOLIPS PART TWO
WRITER: SAM HUMPHRIES ARTIST: JOHN TIMMS
COLORS: GABE ELTAEB LETTERS: DAVE SHARPE
COVER: GUILLEM MARCH AND TOMEU MOREY
VARIANT COVER: FRANK CHO ASSISTANT EDITOR: ANDREA SHEA
EDITOR: ALEX ANTONE GROUP EDITOR: BRIAN CUNNINGHAM
HARLEY QUINN CREATED BY PAUL DINI AND BRUCE TIMM.

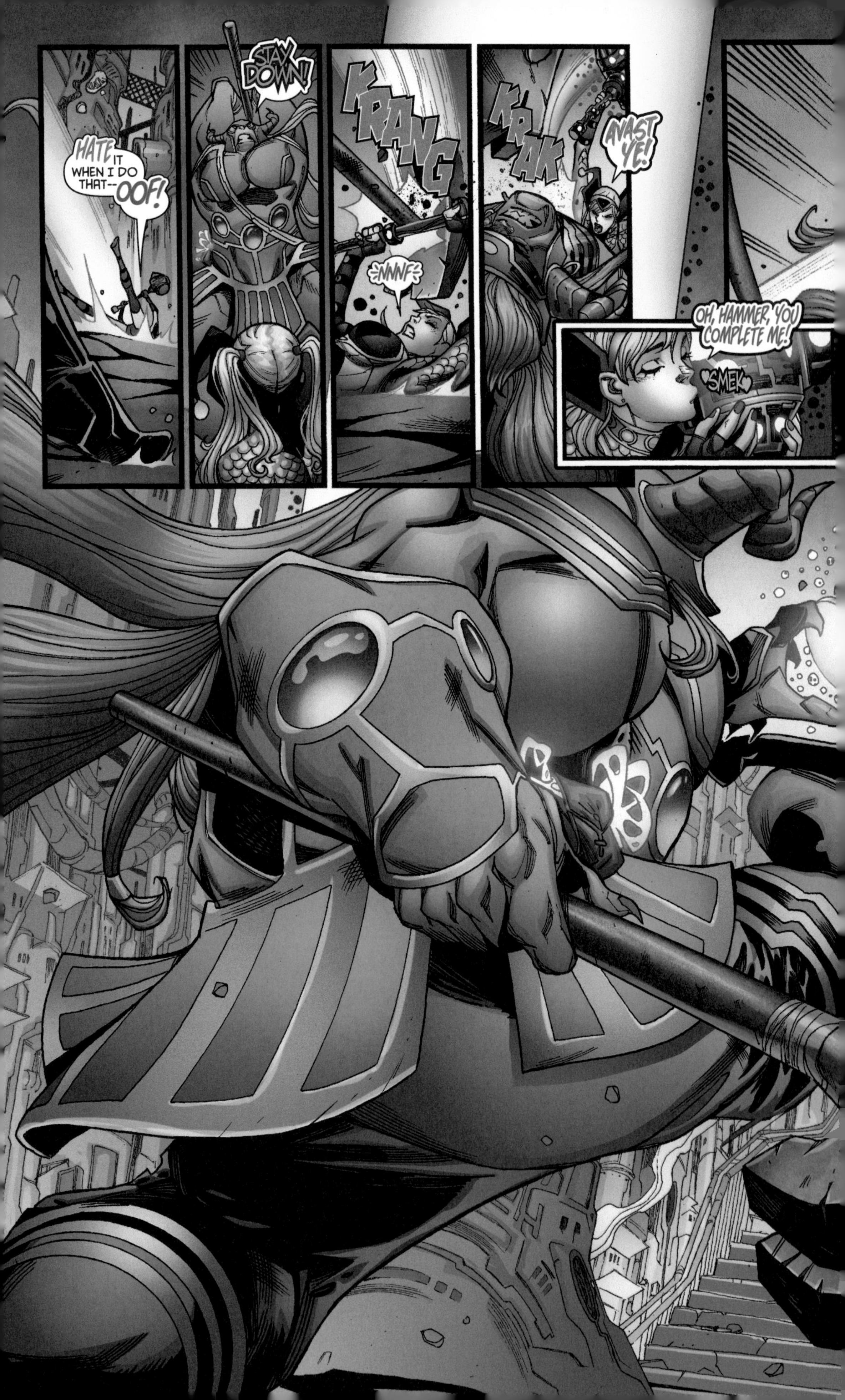
HATE IT WHEN I DO THAT--OOF!
STAY DOWN!
KRANG
NNNF
KRAK
AVAST YE!
OH, HAMMER, YOU COMPLETE ME!
SMEK

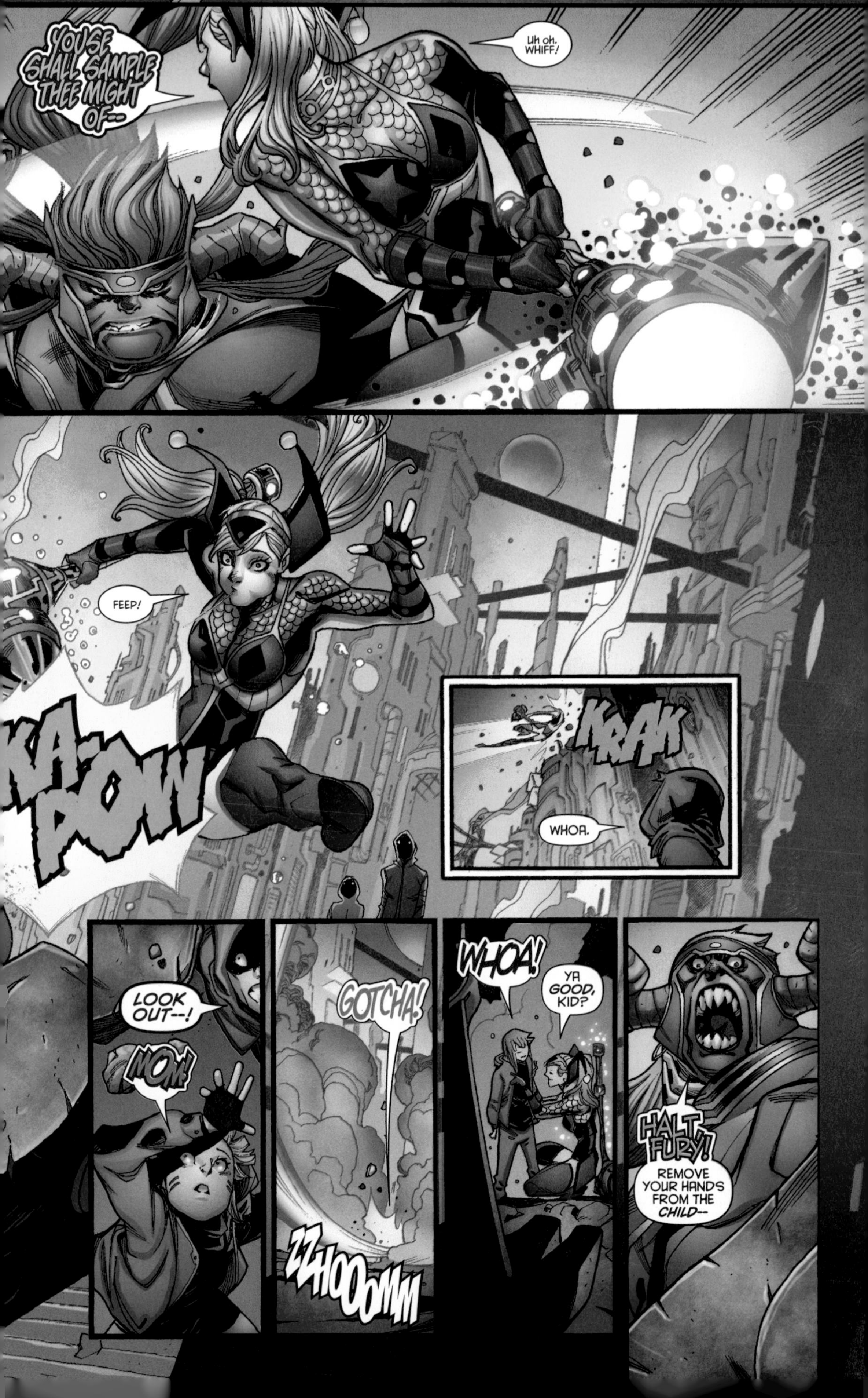
YOUSE SHALL SAMPLE THEE MIGHT OF--
Uh oh. WHIFF!
FEEP!
KA-DOW
KRAK
WHOA.
LOOK OUT--!
MOM!
GOTCHA!
ZZHOOOMMM
WHOA!
YA GOOD, KID?
HALT, FURY!
REMOVE YOUR HANDS FROM THE CHILD--

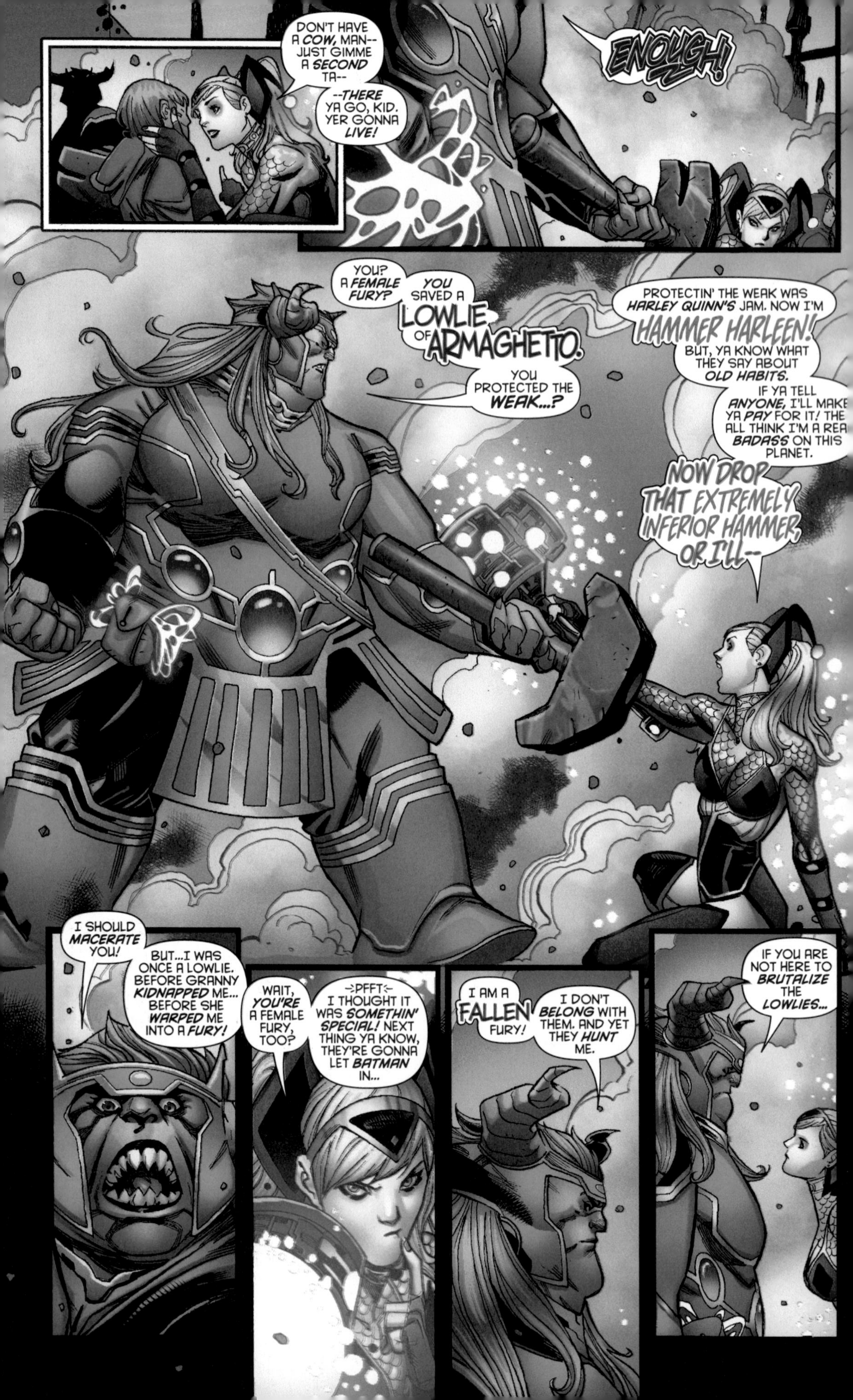
DON'T HAVE A COW, MAN-- JUST GIMME A SECOND TA--
--THERE YA GO, KID. YER GONNA LIVE!
ENOUGH!
YOU? A FEMALE FURY?
YOU SAVED A LOWLIE OF ARMAGHETTO.
YOU PROTECTED THE WEAK...?
PROTECTIN' THE WEAK WAS HARLEY QUINN'S JAM. NOW I'M HAMMER HARLEEN!
BUT, YA KNOW WHAT THEY SAY ABOUT OLD HABITS.
IF YA TELL ANYONE, I'LL MAKE YA PAY FOR IT! THE ALL THINK I'M A REA BADASS ON THIS PLANET.
NOW DROP THAT EXTREMELY INFERIOR HAMMER, OR I'LL--
I SHOULD MACERATE YOU!
BUT...I WAS ONCE A LOWLIE. BEFORE GRANNY KIDNAPPED ME... BEFORE SHE WARPED ME INTO A FURY!
WAIT, YOU'RE A FEMALE FURY, TOO?
PFFT I THOUGHT IT WAS SOMETHIN' SPECIAL! NEXT THING YA KNOW, THEY'RE GONNA LET BATMAN IN...
I AM A FALLEN FURY!
I DON'T BELONG WITH THEM. AND YET THEY HUNT ME.
IF YOU ARE NOT HERE TO BRUTALIZE THE LOWLIES...

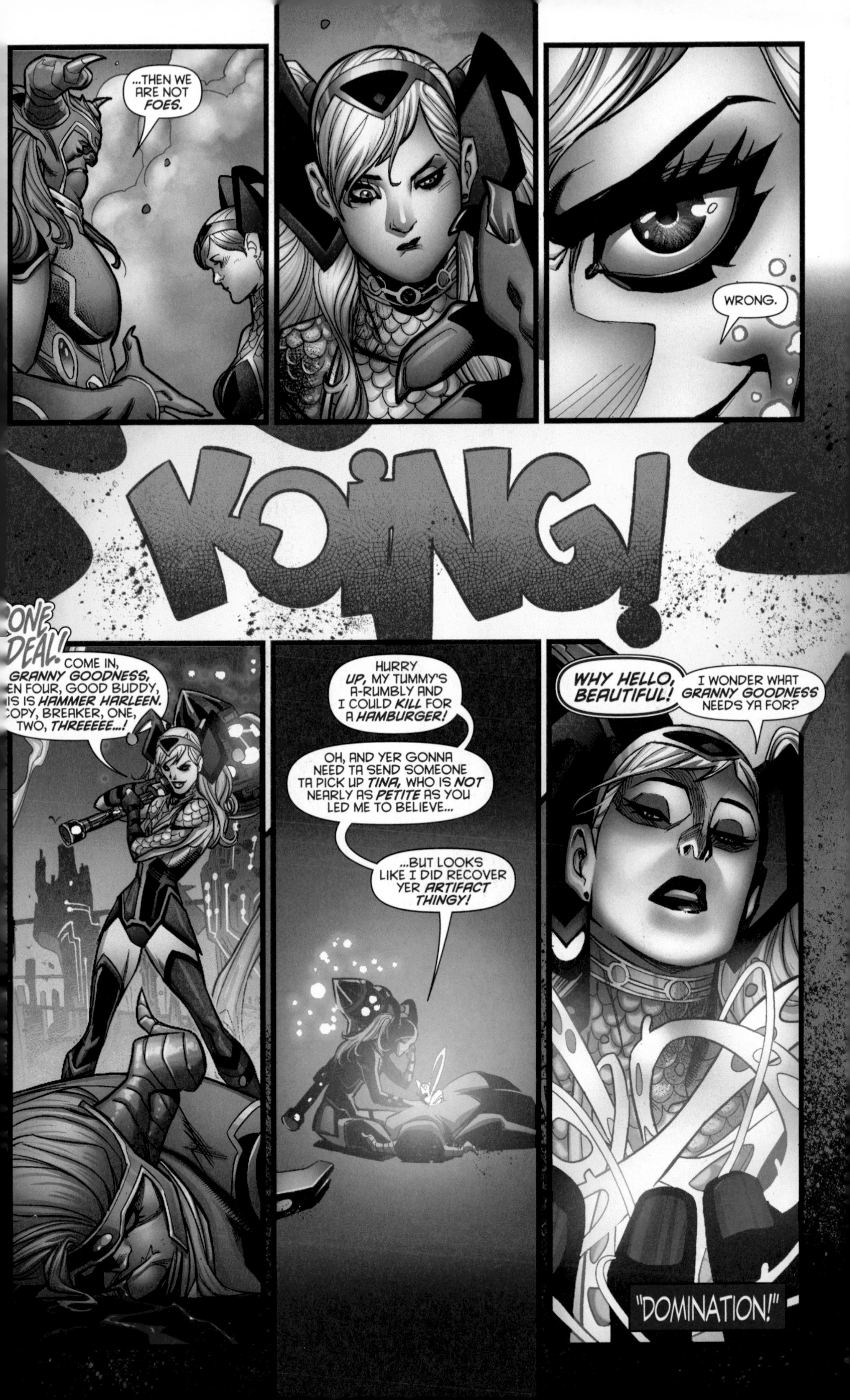
...THEN WE ARE NOT FOES.
WRONG.
KOING!
ONE DEAL!
COME IN, GRANNY GOODNESS, EN FOUR, GOOD BUDDY, IS IS HAMMER HARLEEN. COPY, BREAKER, ONE, TWO, THREEEEE...!
HURRY UP, MY TUMMY'S A-RUMBLY AND I COULD KILL FOR A HAMBURGER!
OH, AND YER GONNA NEED TA SEND SOMEONE TA PICK UP TINA, WHO IS NOT NEARLY AS PETITE AS YOU LED ME TO BELIEVE...
...BUT LOOKS LIKE I DID RECOVER YER ARTIFACT THINGY!
WHY HELLO, BEAUTIFUL!
I WONDER WHAT GRANNY GOODNESS NEEDS YA FOR?
"DOMINATION!"

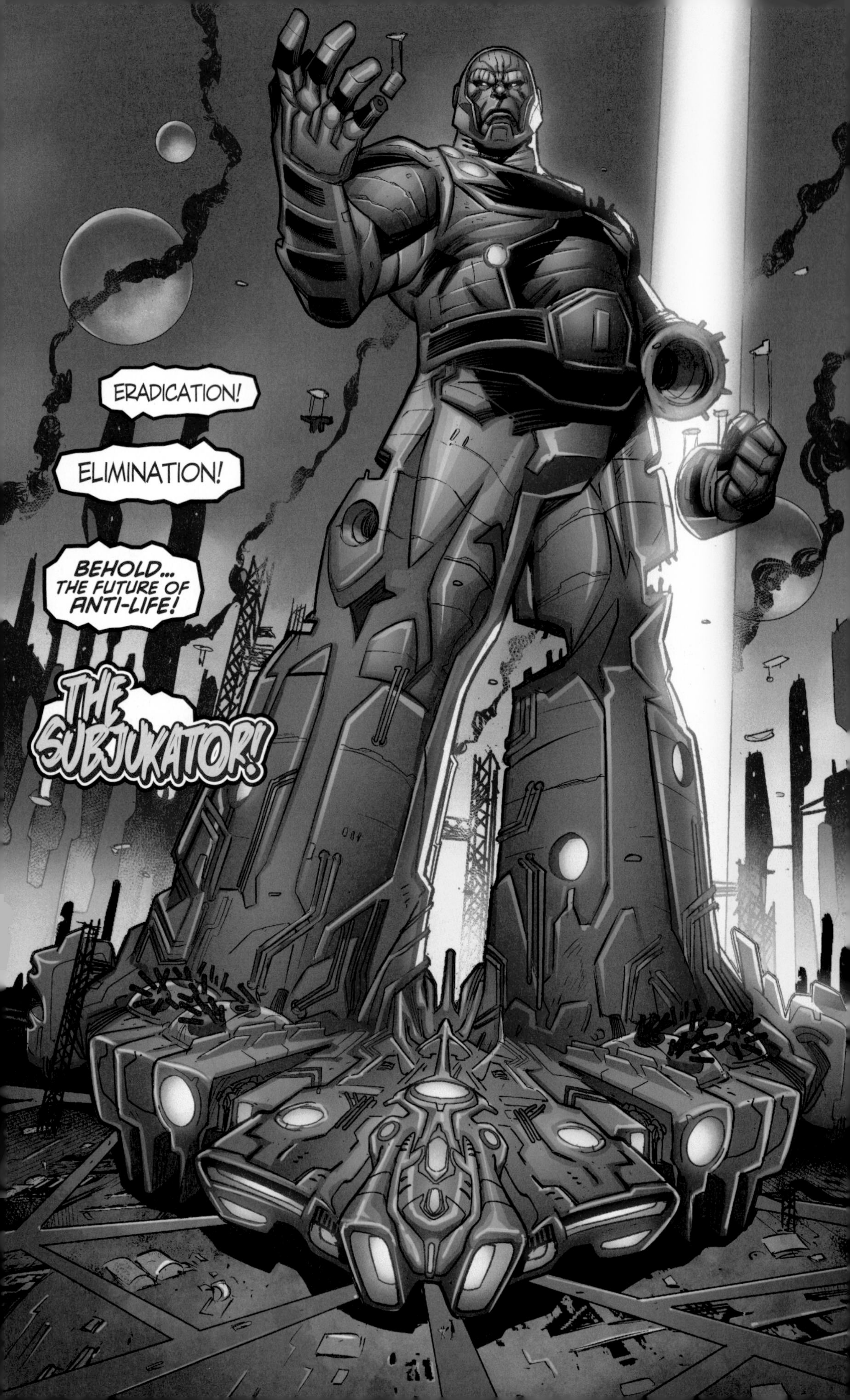
ERADICATION!
ELIMINATION!
BEHOLD... THE FUTURE OF ANTI-LIFE!
THE SUBJUKATOR!

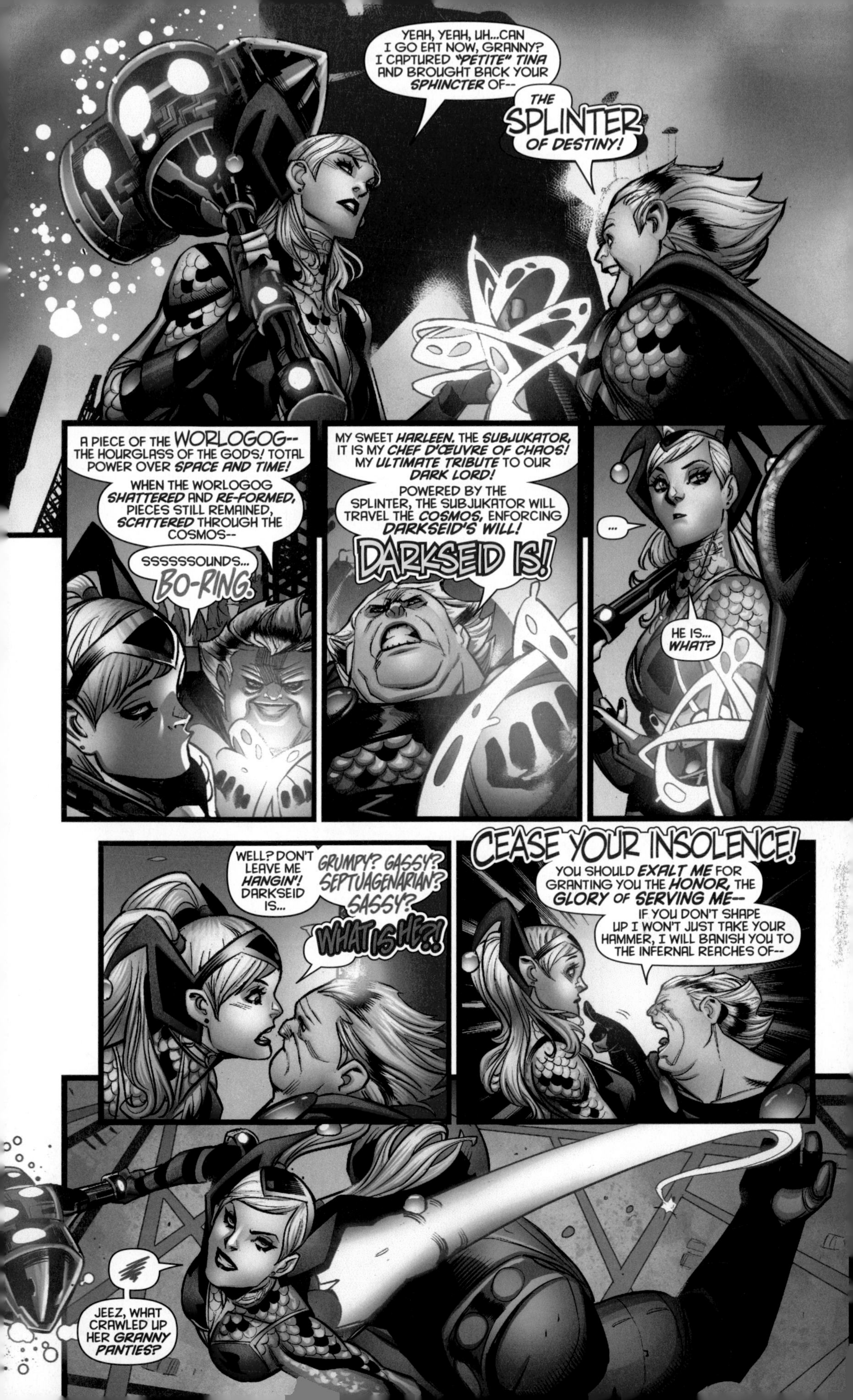

YEAH, YEAH, UH...CAN I GO EAT NOW, GRANNY? I CAPTURED "PETITE" TINA AND BROUGHT BACK YOUR SPHINCTER OF--
THE SPLINTER OF DESTINY!
A PIECE OF THE WORLOGOG-- THE HOURGLASS OF THE GODS! TOTAL POWER OVER SPACE AND TIME!
WHEN THE WORLOGOG SHATTERED AND RE-FORMED, PIECES STILL REMAINED, SCATTERED THROUGH THE COSMOS--
SSSSSSOUNDS... BO-RING.
MY SWEET HARLEEN. THE SUBJUKATOR, IT IS MY CHEF D'ŒUVRE OF CHAOS! MY ULTIMATE TRIBUTE TO OUR DARK LORD!
POWERED BY THE SPLINTER, THE SUBJUKATOR WILL TRAVEL THE COSMOS, ENFORCING DARKSEID'S WILL!
DARKSEID IS!
...
HE IS... WHAT?
WELL? DON'T LEAVE ME HANGIN'! DARKSEID IS...
GRUMPY? GASSY? SEPTUAGENARIAN? SASSY?
WHAT IS HE?!
CEASE YOUR INSOLENCE!
YOU SHOULD EXALT ME FOR GRANTING YOU THE HONOR, THE GLORY OF SERVING ME--
IF YOU DON'T SHAPE UP I WON'T JUST TAKE YOUR HAMMER, I WILL BANISH YOU TO THE INFERNAL REACHES OF--
JEEZ, WHAT CRAWLED UP HER GRANNY PANTIES?

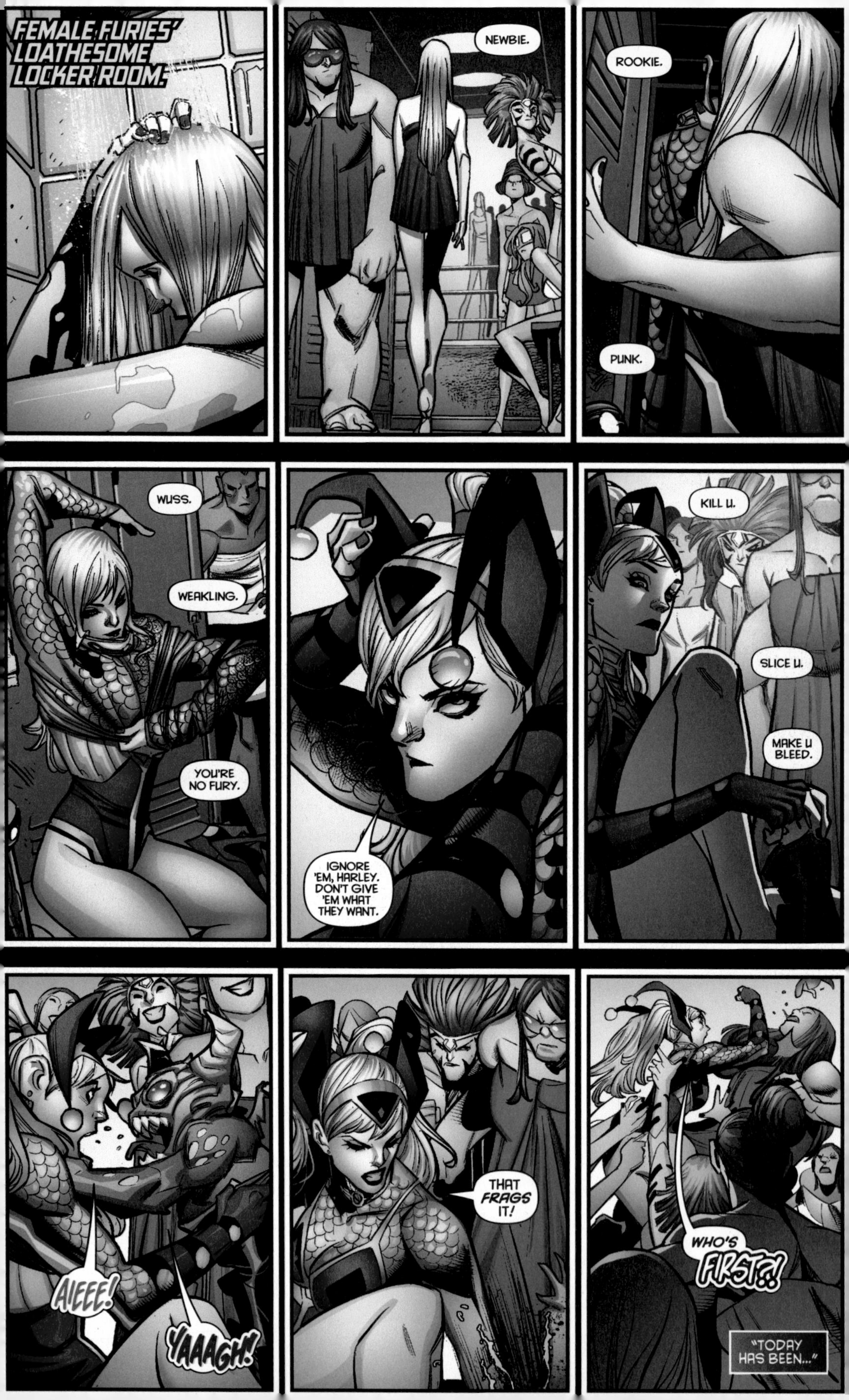
FEMALE FURIES' LOATHESOME LOCKER ROOM.
NEWBIE.
ROOKIE.
PUNK.
WUSS.
WEAKLING.
YOU'RE NO FURY.
IGNORE 'EM, HARLEY. DON'T GIVE 'EM WHAT THEY WANT.
KILL U.
SLICE U.
MAKE U BLEED.
AIEEE!
YAAAGH!
THAT FRAGS IT!
WHO'S FIRST?!
"TODAY HAS BEEN..."

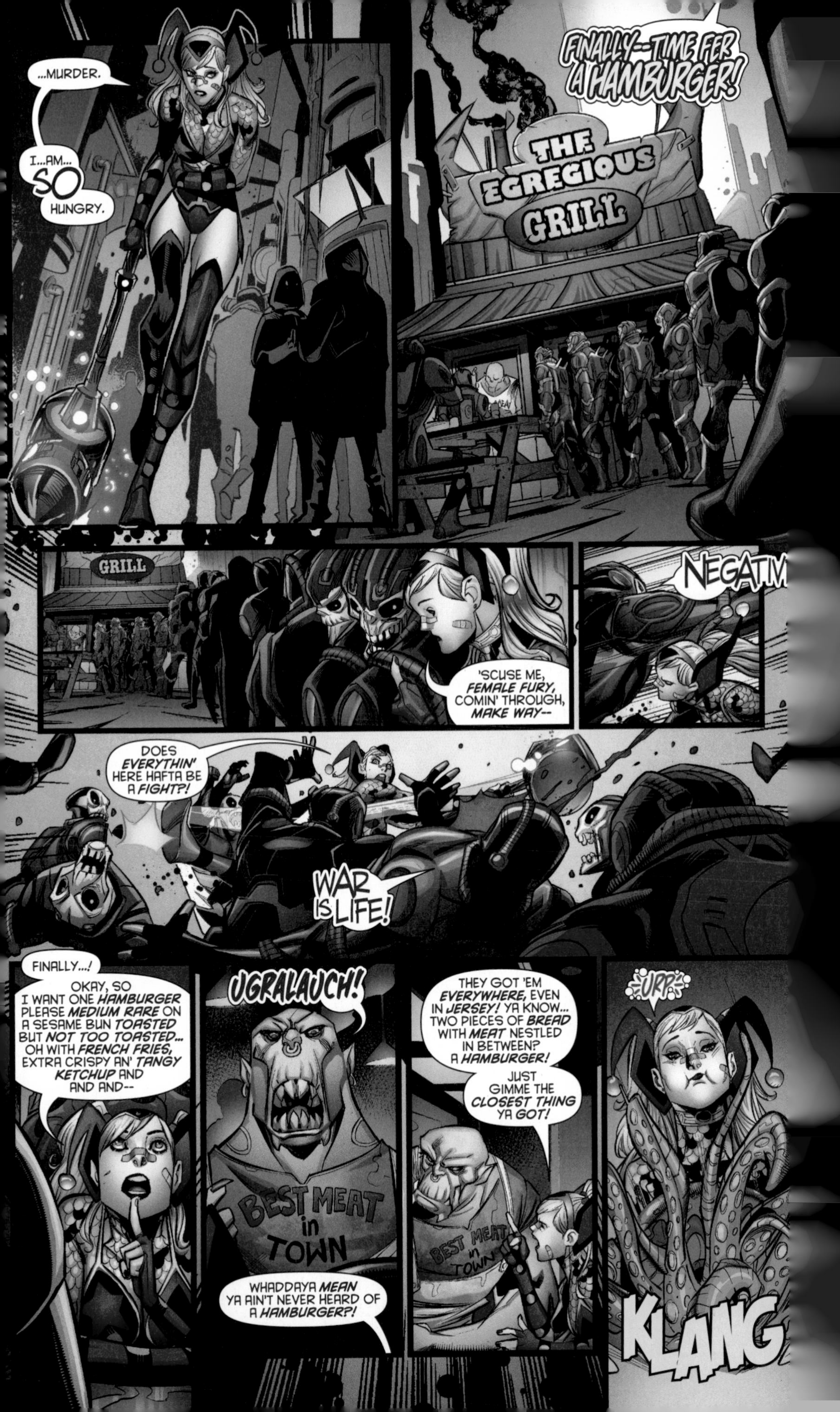
...MURDER.
I...AM... SO HUNGRY.
FINALLY--TIME FER A HAMBURGER!
THE EGREGIOUS GRILL
GRILL
'SCUSE ME, FEMALE FURY, COMIN' THROUGH, MAKE WAY--
NEGATIV
DOES EVERYTHIN' HERE HAFTA BE A FIGHT?!
WAR IS LIFE!
FINALLY...!
OKAY, SO I WANT ONE HAMBURGER PLEASE MEDIUM RARE ON A SESAME BUN TOASTED BUT NOT TOO TOASTED... OH WITH FRENCH FRIES, EXTRA CRISPY AN' TANGY KETCHUP AND AND AND--
UGRALAUCH!
BEST MEAT in TOWN
WHADDAYA MEAN YA AIN'T NEVER HEARD OF A HAMBURGER?!
THEY GOT 'EM EVERYWHERE, EVEN IN JERSEY! YA KNOW... TWO PIECES OF BREAD WITH MEAT NESTLED IN BETWEEN? A HAMBURGER!
JUST GIMME THE CLOSEST THING YA GOT!
BEST MEAT in TOWN
URP
KLANG

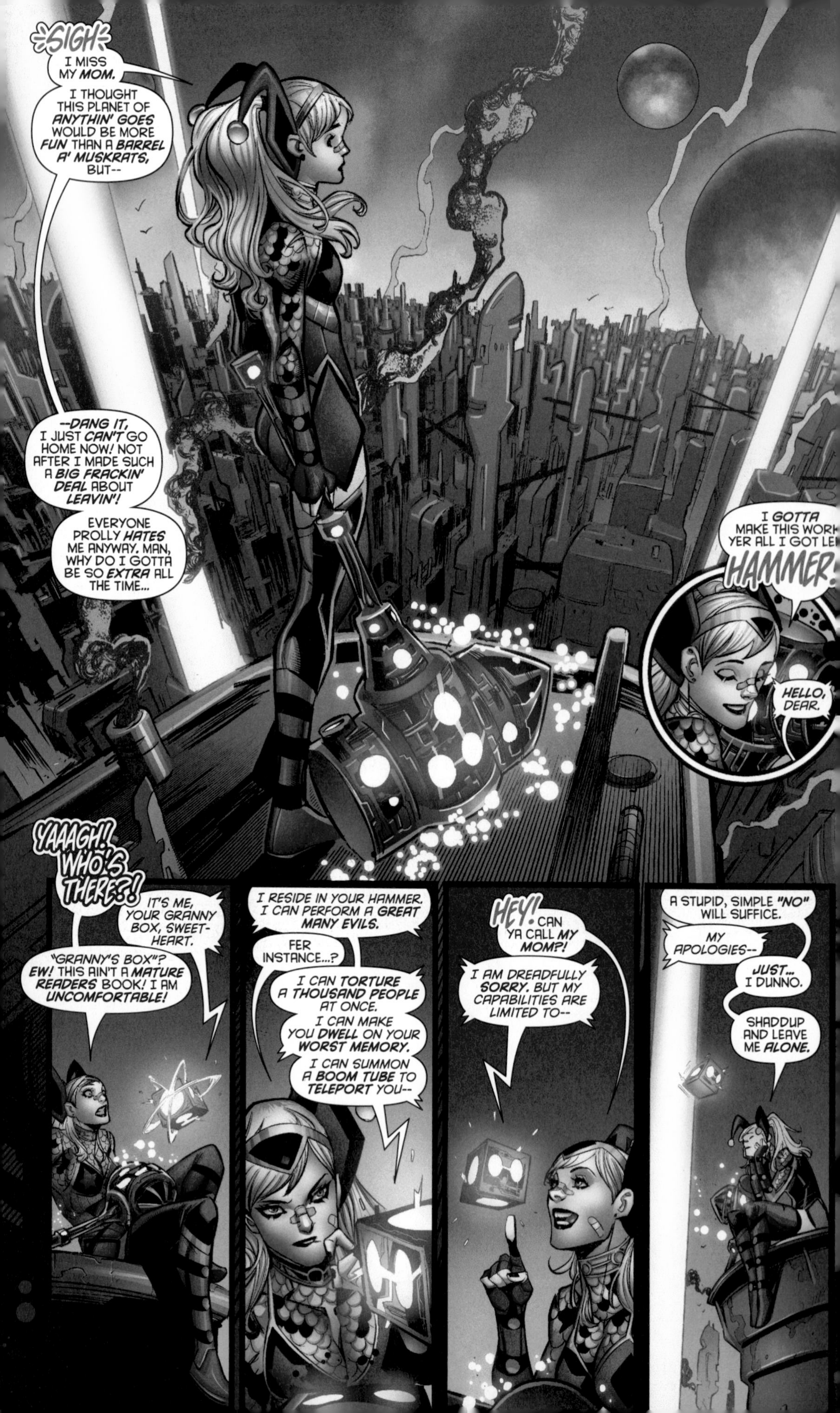
SIGH
I MISS MY MOM.
I THOUGHT THIS PLANET OF ANYTHIN' GOES WOULD BE MORE FUN THAN A BARREL A' MUSKRATS, BUT--
--DANG IT, I JUST CAN'T GO HOME NOW! NOT AFTER I MADE SUCH A BIG FRACKIN' DEAL ABOUT LEAVIN'!
EVERYONE PROLLY HATES ME ANYWAY. MAN, WHY DO I GOTTA BE SO EXTRA ALL THE TIME...
I GOTTA MAKE THIS WORK
HAMMER!
HELLO, DEAR.
YAAAGH! WHO'S THERE?!
IT'S ME, YOUR GRANNY BOX, SWEET-HEART.
"GRANNY'S BOX"? EW! THIS AIN'T A MATURE READERS BOOK! I AM UNCOMFORTABLE!
I RESIDE IN YOUR HAMMER. I CAN PERFORM A GREAT MANY EVILS.
FER INSTANCE...?
I CAN TORTURE A THOUSAND PEOPLE AT ONCE.
I CAN MAKE YOU DWELL ON YOUR WORST MEMORY.
I CAN SUMMON A BOOM TUBE TO TELEPORT YOU--
HEY! CAN YA CALL MY MOM?!
I AM DREADFULLY SORRY, BUT MY CAPABILITIES ARE LIMITED TO--
A STUPID, SIMPLE "NO" WILL SUFFICE.
MY APOLOGIES--
JUST... I DUNNO.
SHADDUP AND LEAVE ME ALONE.

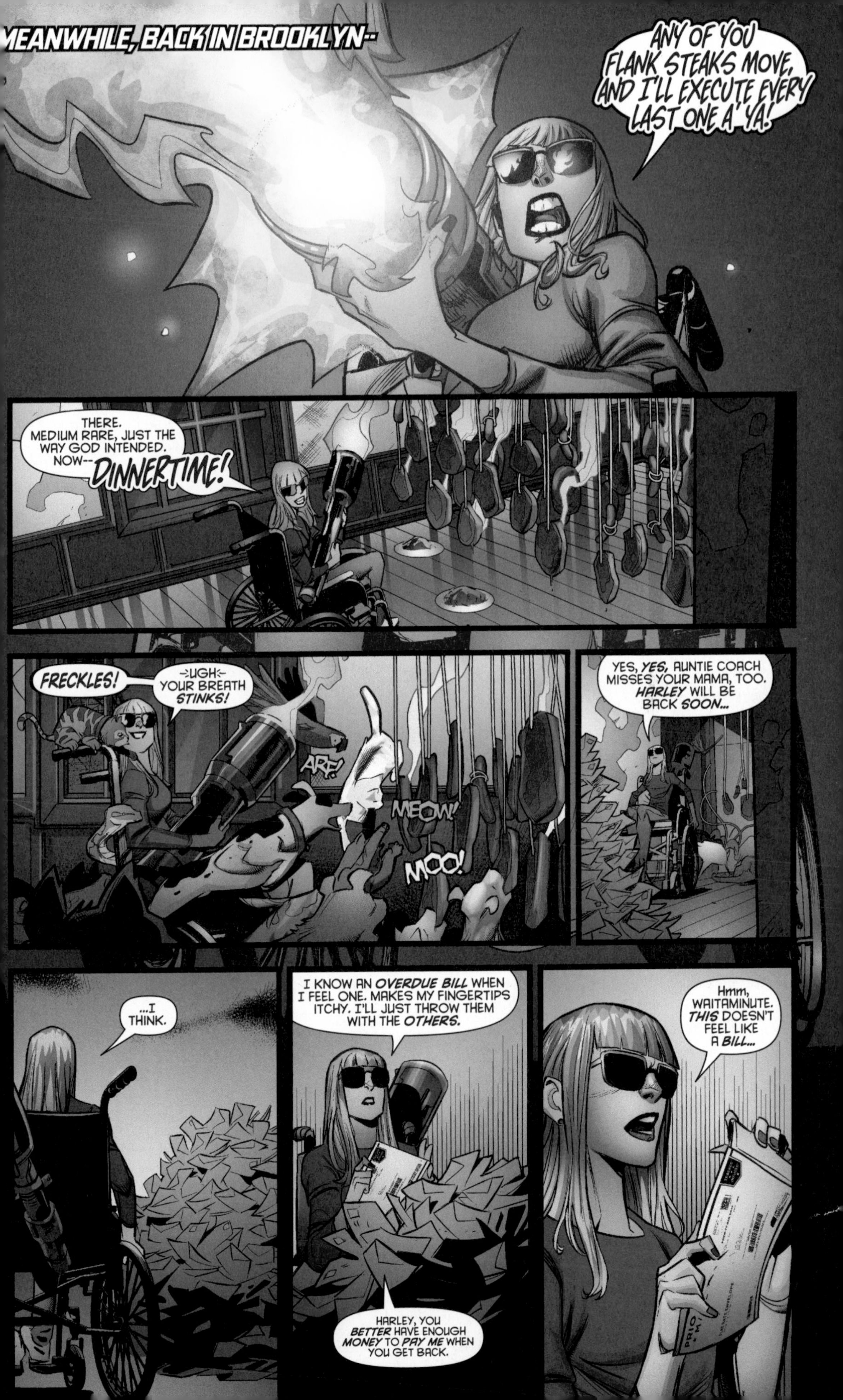
MEANWHILE, BACK IN BROOKLYN--
ANY OF YOU FLANK STEAKS MOVE, AND I'LL EXECUTE EVERY LAST ONE A' YA!
THERE. MEDIUM RARE, JUST THE WAY GOD INTENDED. NOW-- DINNERTIME!
FRECKLES!
UGH YOUR BREATH STINKS!
ARF!
MEOW!
MOO!
YES, YES, AUNTIE COACH MISSES YOUR MAMA, TOO. HARLEY WILL BE BACK SOON...
...I THINK.
I KNOW AN OVERDUE BILL WHEN I FEEL ONE. MAKES MY FINGERTIPS ITCHY. I'LL JUST THROW THEM WITH THE OTHERS.
HARLEY, YOU BETTER HAVE ENOUGH MONEY TO PAY ME WHEN YOU GET BACK.
Hmm, WAITAMINUTE. THIS DOESN'T FEEL LIKE A BILL...

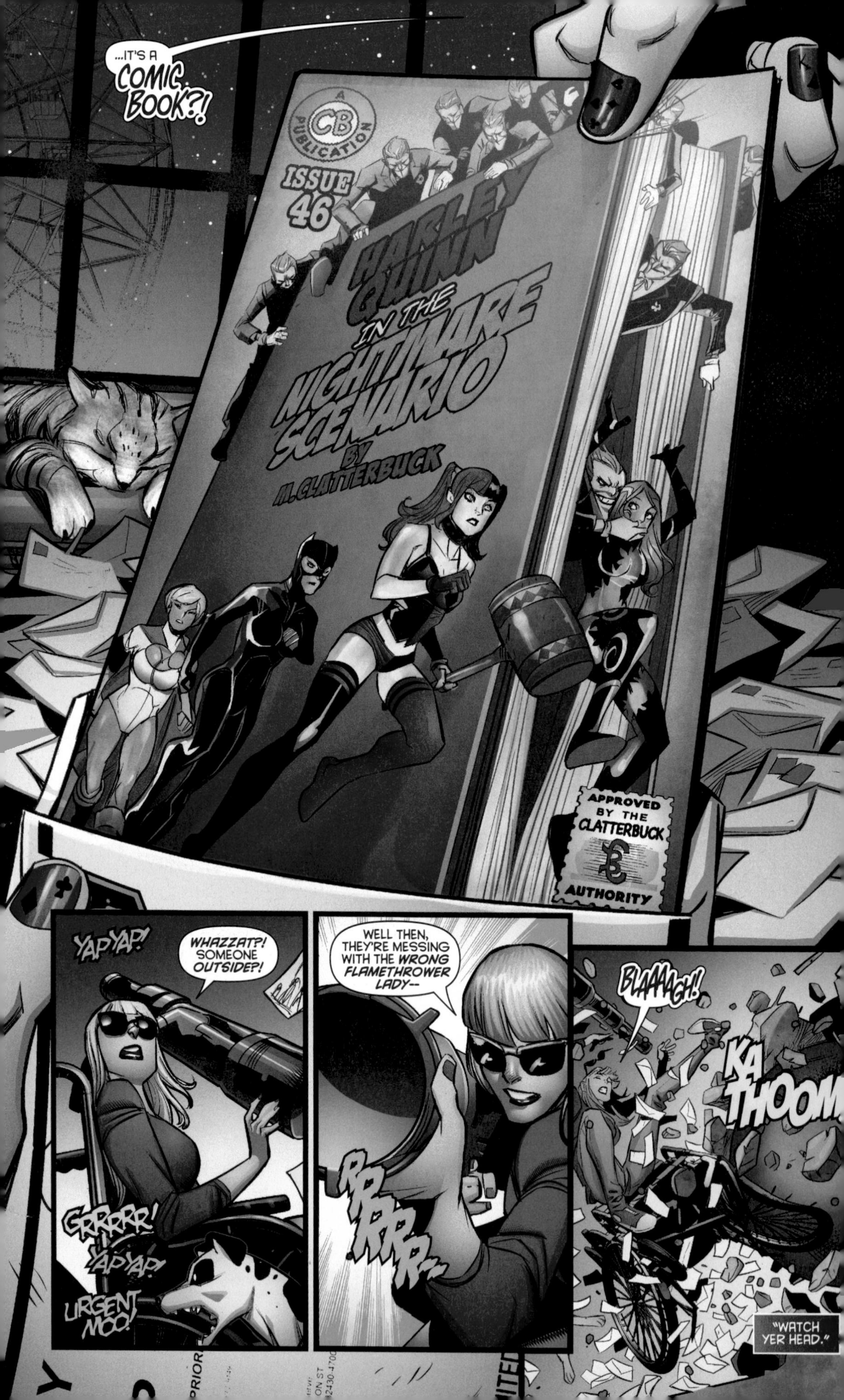

...IT'S A COMIC BOOK?!
A CB PUBLICATION
ISSUE 46
HARLEY QUINN IN THE NIGHTMARE SCENARIO BY M. CLATTERBUCK
APPROVED BY THE CLATTERBUCK AUTHORITY
YAP YAP!
WHAZZAT?! SOMEONE OUTSIDE?!
GRRRRR!
YAP YAP!
URGENT MOO!
WELL THEN, THEY'RE MESSING WITH THE WRONG FLAMETHROWER LADY--
RRRRRR...
BLAAAAGH!
KA THOOM
"WATCH YER HEAD."

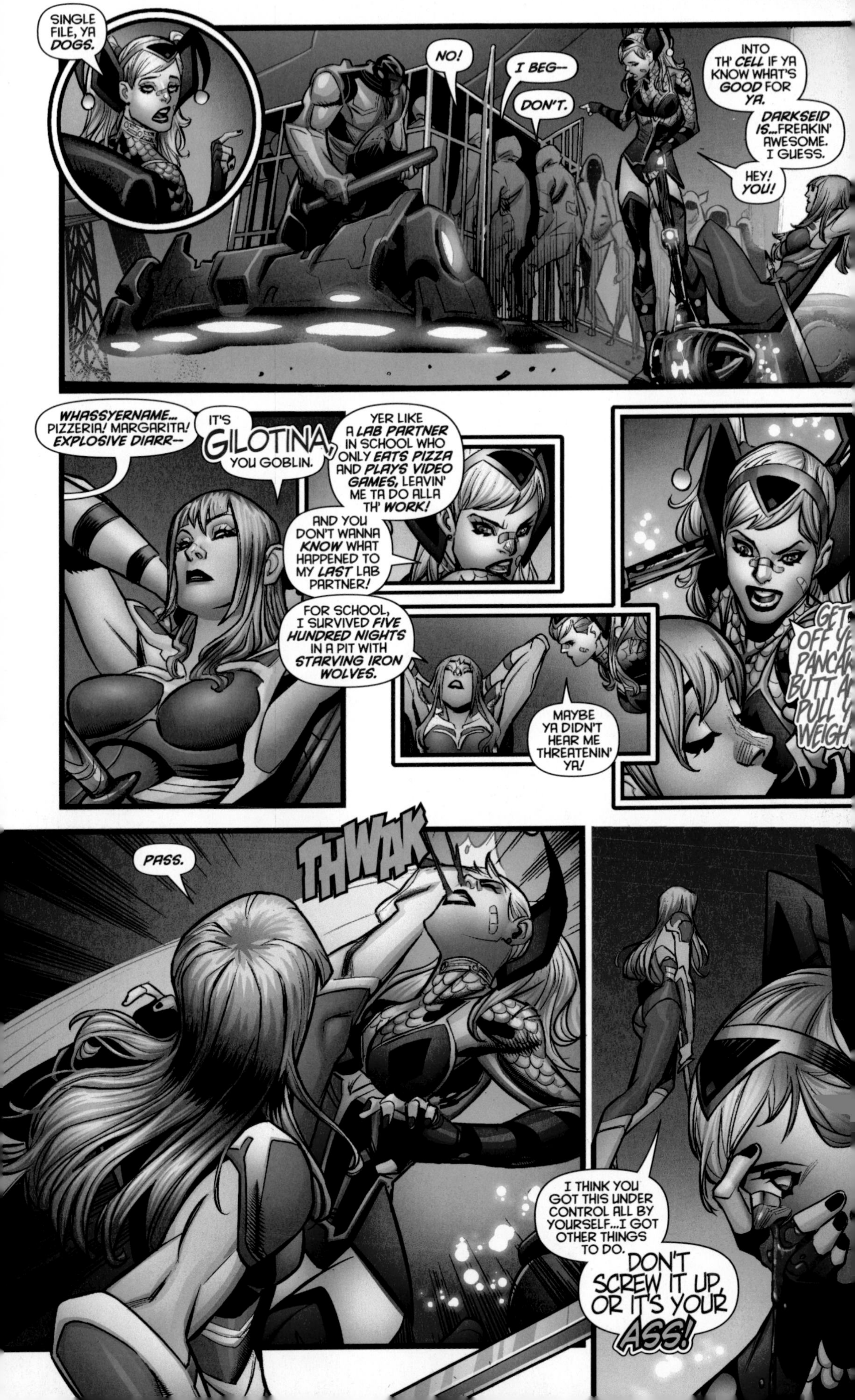

SINGLE FILE, YA DOGS.
NO!
I BEG--
DON'T.
INTO TH' CELL IF YA KNOW WHAT'S GOOD FOR YA.
DARKSEID IS...FREAKIN' AWESOME. I GUESS.
HEY! YOU!
WHASSYERNAME... PIZZERIA! MARGARITA! EXPLOSIVE DIARR--
IT'S GILOTINA, YOU GOBLIN.
YER LIKE A LAB PARTNER IN SCHOOL WHO ONLY EATS PIZZA AND PLAYS VIDEO GAMES, LEAVIN' ME TA DO ALLA TH' WORK!
AND YOU DON'T WANNA KNOW WHAT HAPPENED TO MY LAST LAB PARTNER!
FOR SCHOOL, I SURVIVED FIVE HUNDRED NIGHTS IN A PIT WITH STARVING IRON WOLVES.
MAYBE YA DIDN'T HEAR ME THREATENIN' YA!
PASS.
THWAK
I THINK YOU GOT THIS UNDER CONTROL ALL BY YOURSELF...I GOT OTHER THINGS TO DO.
DON'T SCREW IT UP, OR IT'S YOUR ASS!

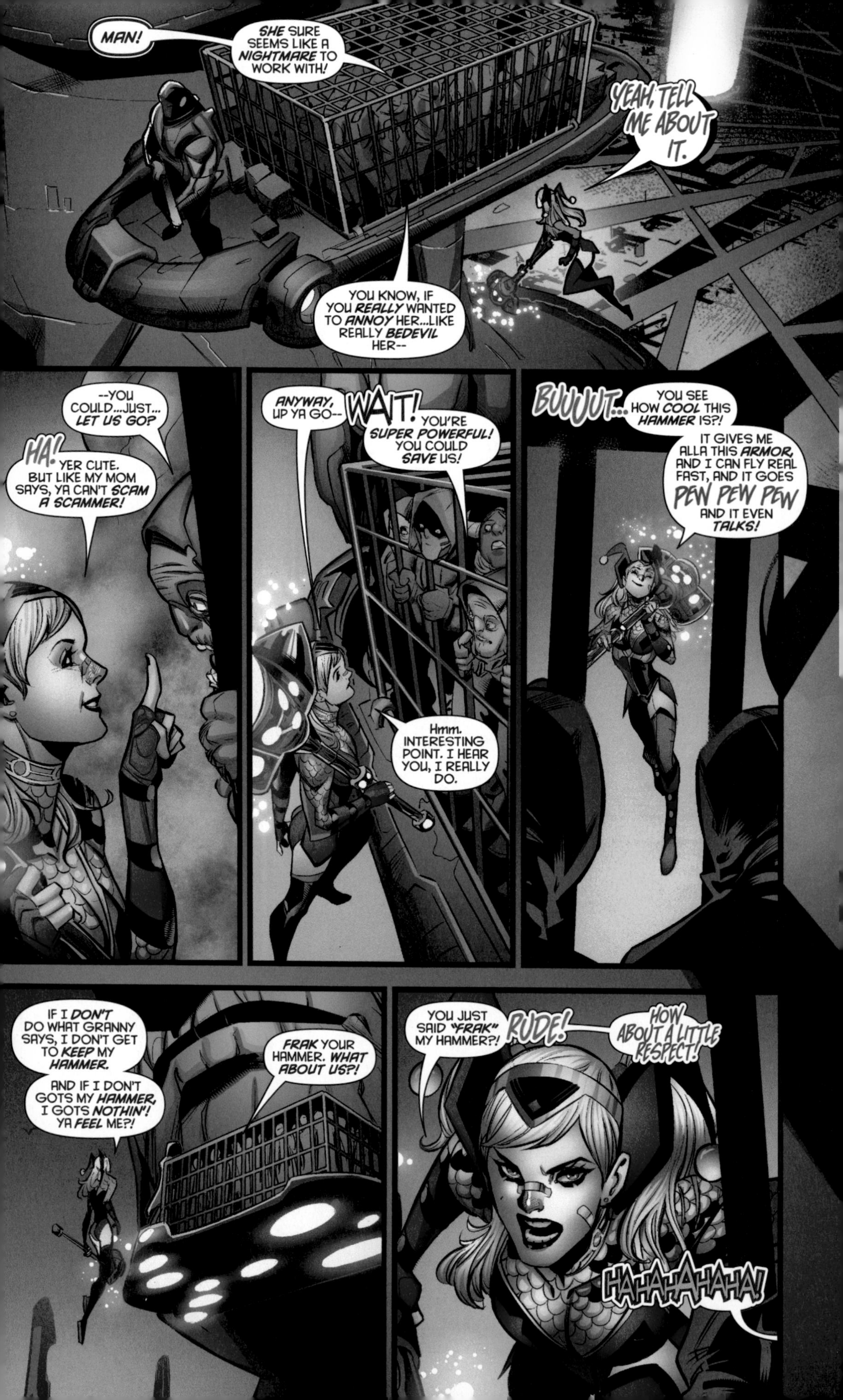

MAN!
SHE SURE SEEMS LIKE A NIGHTMARE TO WORK WITH!
YEAH, TELL ME ABOUT IT.
YOU KNOW, IF YOU REALLY WANTED TO ANNOY HER...LIKE REALLY BEDEVIL HER--
--YOU COULD...JUST... LET US GO?
HA! YER CUTE. BUT LIKE MY MOM SAYS, YA CAN'T SCAM A SCAMMER!
ANYWAY, UP YA GO--
WAIT!
YOU'RE SUPER POWERFUL! YOU COULD SAVE US!
Hmm. INTERESTING POINT. I HEAR YOU, I REALLY DO.
BUUUUT...
YOU SEE HOW COOL THIS HAMMER IS?!
IT GIVES ME ALLA THIS ARMOR, AND I CAN FLY REAL FAST, AND IT GOES PEW PEW PEW AND IT EVEN TALKS!
IF I DON'T DO WHAT GRANNY SAYS, I DON'T GET TO KEEP MY HAMMER.
AND IF I DON'T GOTS MY HAMMER, I GOTS NOTHIN'! YA FEEL ME?!
FRAK YOUR HAMMER. WHAT ABOUT US?!
YOU JUST SAID "FRAK" MY HAMMER?!
RUDE!
HOW ABOUT A LITTLE RESPECT!
HAHAHAHAHA!

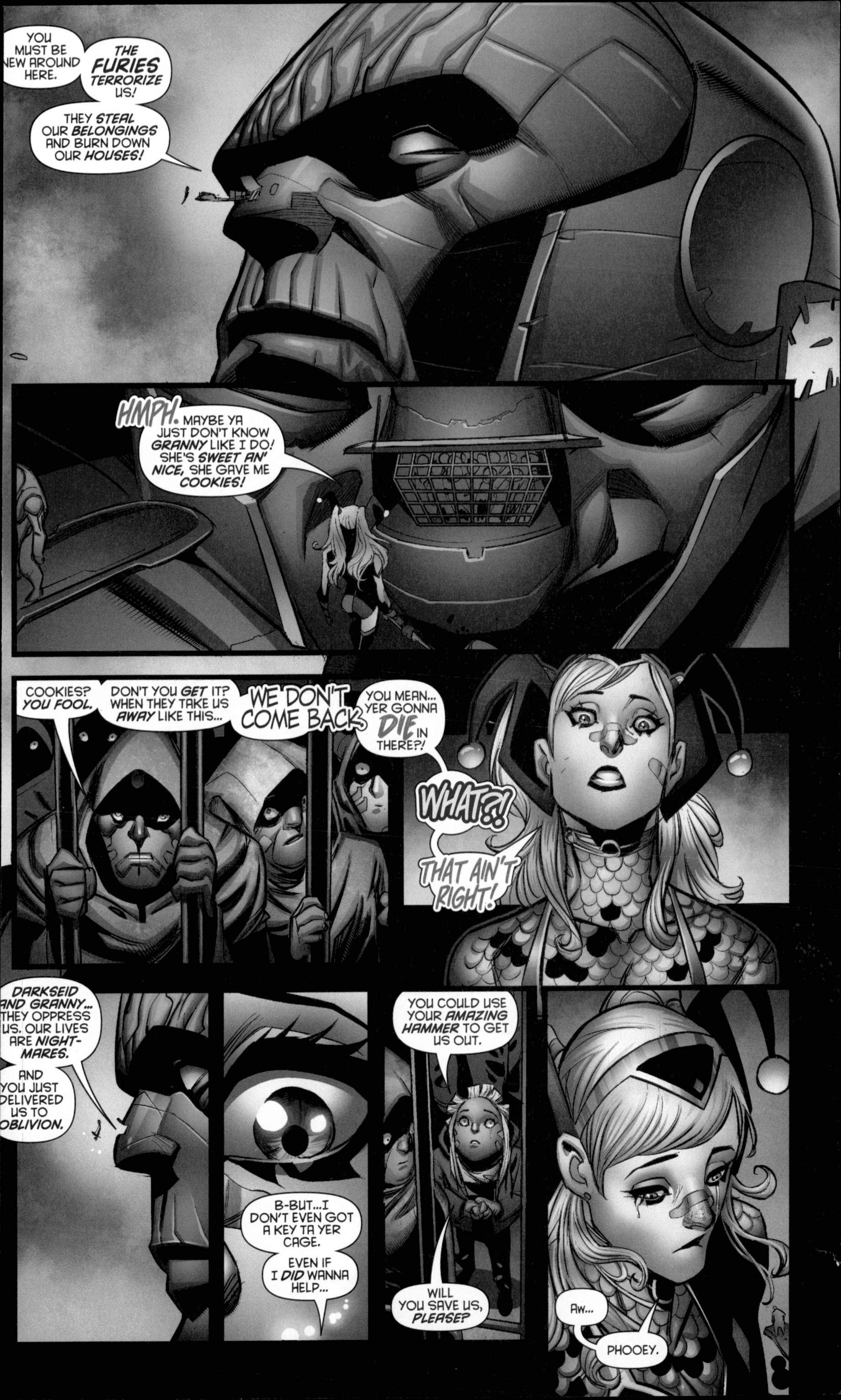
YOU MUST BE NEW AROUND HERE.
THE FURIES TERRORIZE US!
THEY STEAL OUR BELONGINGS AND BURN DOWN OUR HOUSES!
HMPH. MAYBE YA JUST DON'T KNOW GRANNY LIKE I DO! SHE'S SWEET AN' NICE, SHE GAVE ME COOKIES!
COOKIES? YOU FOOL.
DON'T YOU GET IT? WHEN THEY TAKE US AWAY LIKE THIS...
WE DON'T COME BACK.
YOU MEAN... YER GONNA DIE IN THERE?!
WHAT?!
THAT AIN'T RIGHT!
DARKSEID AND GRANNY... THEY OPPRESS US. OUR LIVES ARE NIGHT-MARES.
AND YOU JUST DELIVERED US TO OBLIVION.
B-BUT...I DON'T EVEN GOT A KEY TA YER CAGE.
EVEN IF I DID WANNA HELP...
YOU COULD USE YOUR AMAZING HAMMER TO GET US OUT.
WILL YOU SAVE US, PLEASE?
AW...
PHOOEY.

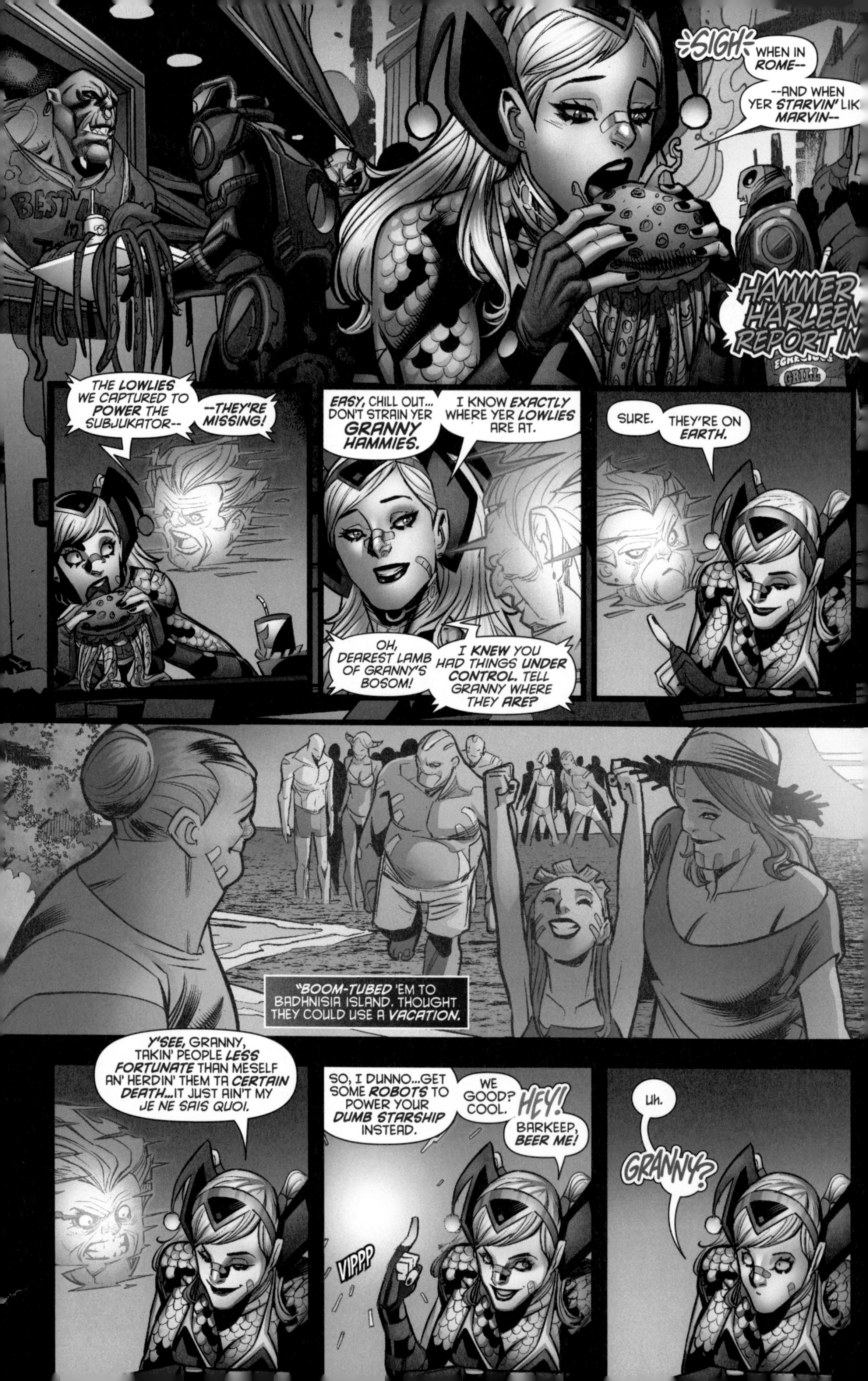
SIGH WHEN IN ROME--
--AND WHEN YER STARVIN' LIK MARVIN--
HAMMER HARLEEN REPORT IN
GRILL
THE LOWLIES WE CAPTURED TO POWER THE SUBJUKATOR--
--THEY'RE MISSING!
EASY, CHILL OUT... DON'T STRAIN YER GRANNY HAMMIES.
I KNOW EXACTLY WHERE YER LOWLIES ARE AT.
OH, DEAREST LAMB OF GRANNY'S BOSOM!
I KNEW YOU HAD THINGS UNDER CONTROL. TELL GRANNY WHERE THEY ARE?
SURE.
THEY'RE ON EARTH.
"BOOM-TUBED 'EM TO BADHNISIA ISLAND. THOUGHT THEY COULD USE A VACATION.
Y'SEE, GRANNY, TAKIN' PEOPLE LESS FORTUNATE THAN MESELF AN' HERDIN' THEM TA CERTAIN DEATH...IT JUST AIN'T MY JE NE SAIS QUOI.
SO, I DUNNO...GET SOME ROBOTS TO POWER YOUR DUMB STARSHIP INSTEAD.
WE GOOD? COOL.
HEY!
BARKEEP, BEER ME!
VIPPP
uh.
GRANNY?

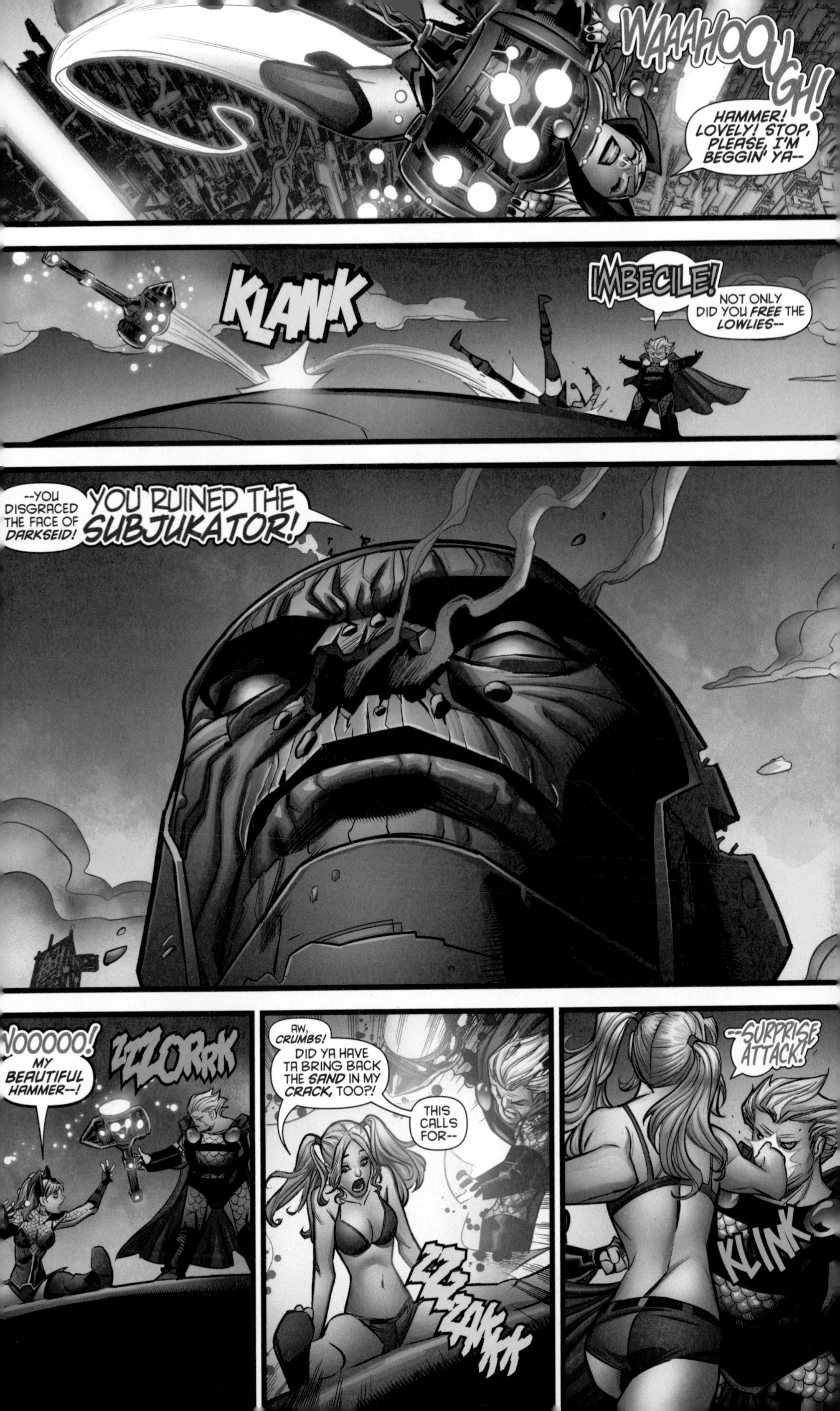
WAAAHOOOUGH!
HAMMER! LOVELY! STOP, PLEASE, I'M BEGGIN' YA--
KLANK
IMBECILE!
NOT ONLY DID YOU FREE THE LOWLIES--
--YOU DISGRACED THE FACE OF DARKSEID!
YOU RUINED THE SUBJUKATOR!
NOOOOO! MY BEAUTIFUL HAMMER--!
ZZZORRRK
AW, CRUMBS! DID YA HAVE TA BRING BACK THE SAND IN MY CRACK, TOO?!
THIS CALLS FOR--
ZZZAKKK
--SURPRISE ATTACK!
KLINK

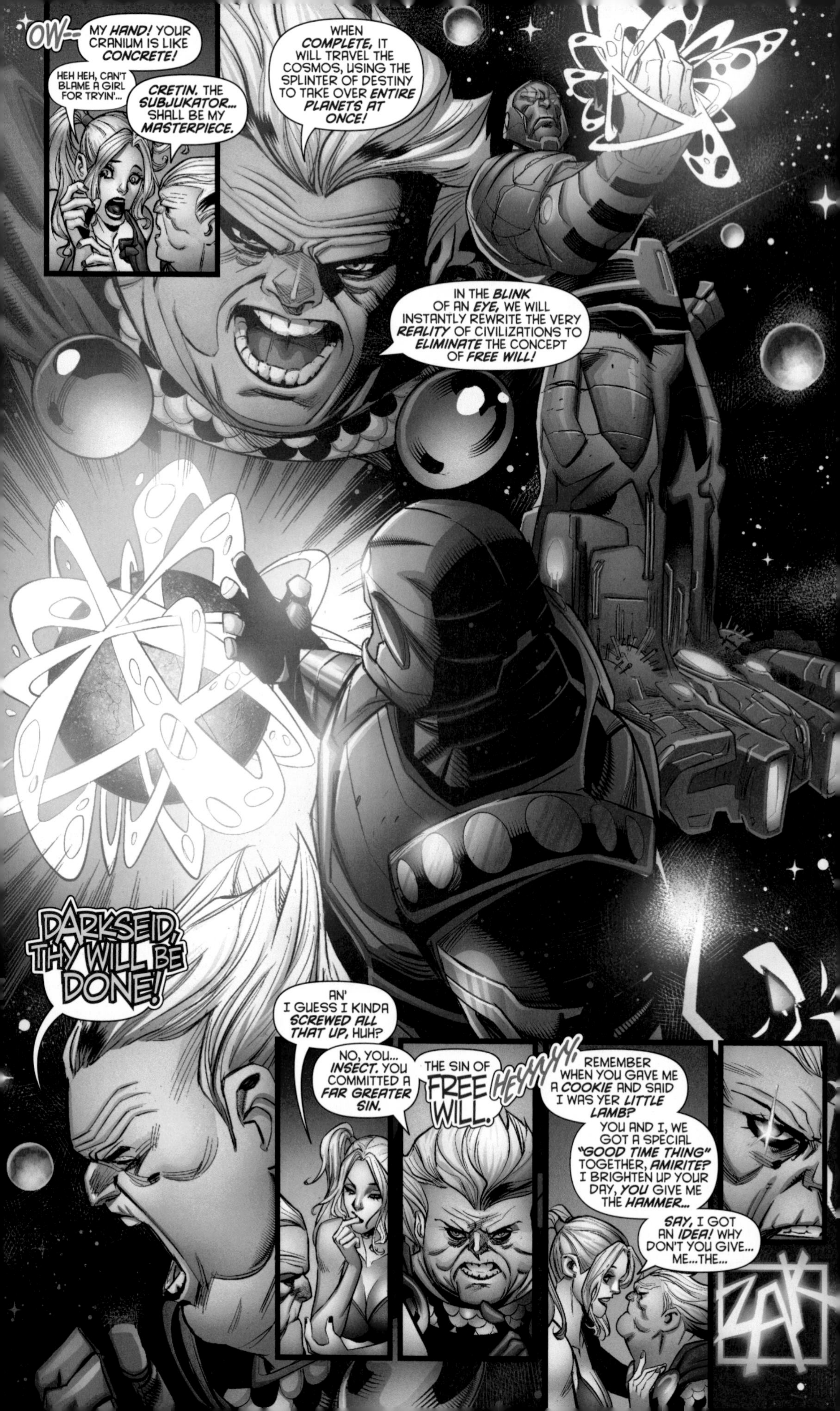
OW--
MY HAND! YOUR CRANIUM IS LIKE CONCRETE!
HEH HEH, CAN'T BLAME A GIRL FOR TRYIN'...
CRETIN. THE SUBJUKATOR... SHALL BE MY MASTERPIECE.
WHEN COMPLETE, IT WILL TRAVEL THE COSMOS, USING THE SPLINTER OF DESTINY TO TAKE OVER ENTIRE PLANETS AT ONCE!
IN THE BLINK OF AN EYE, WE WILL INSTANTLY REWRITE THE VERY REALITY OF CIVILIZATIONS TO ELIMINATE THE CONCEPT OF FREE WILL!
DARKSEID, THY WILL BE DONE!
AN' I GUESS I KINDA SCREWED ALL THAT UP, HUH?
NO, YOU... INSECT. YOU COMMITTED A FAR GREATER SIN.
THE SIN OF FREE WILL.
HEYYYYY.
REMEMBER WHEN YOU GAVE ME A COOKIE AND SAID I WAS YER LITTLE LAMB?
YOU AND I, WE GOT A SPECIAL "GOOD TIME THING" TOGETHER, AMIRITE? I BRIGHTEN UP YOUR DAY, YOU GIVE ME THE HAMMER...
SAY, I GOT AN IDEA! WHY DON'T YOU GIVE... ME...THE...
ZAK

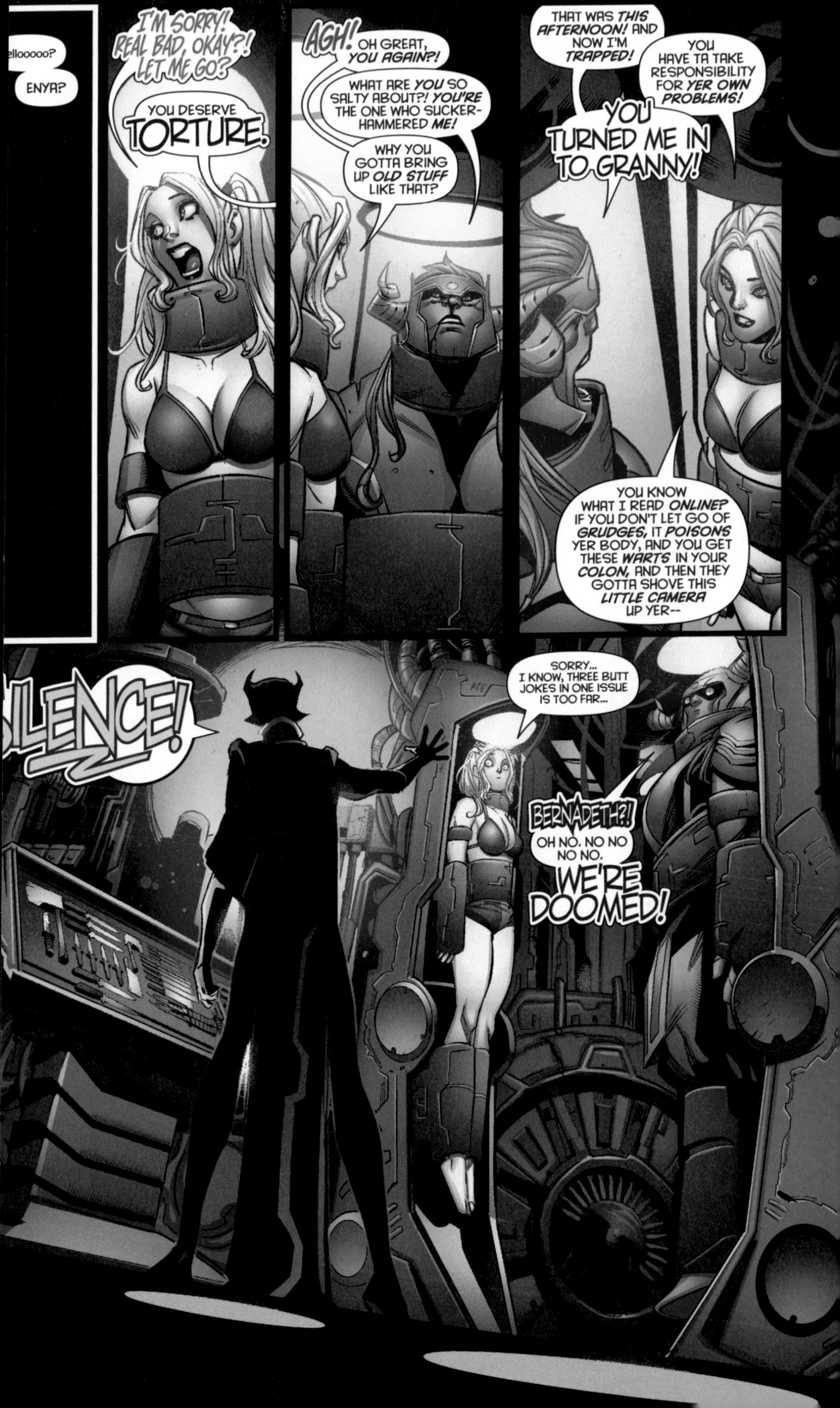
ellooooo?
ENYA?
I'M SORRY! REAL BAD, OKAY?! LET ME GO?
YOU DESERVE TORTURE.
AGH! OH GREAT, YOU AGAIN?!
WHAT ARE YOU SO SALTY ABOUT?! YOU'RE THE ONE WHO SUCKER-HAMMERED ME!
WHY YOU GOTTA BRING UP OLD STUFF LIKE THAT?
THAT WAS THIS AFTERNOON! AND NOW I'M TRAPPED!
YOU TURNED ME IN TO GRANNY!
YOU HAVE TA TAKE RESPONSIBILITY FOR YER OWN PROBLEMS!
YOU KNOW WHAT I READ ONLINE? IF YOU DON'T LET GO OF GRUDGES, IT POISONS YER BODY, AND YOU GET THESE WARTS IN YOUR COLON, AND THEN THEY GOTTA SHOVE THIS LITTLE CAMERA UP YER--
SILENCE!
SORRY... I KNOW, THREE BUTT JOKES IN ONE ISSUE IS TOO FAR...
BERNADETH?! OH NO. NO NO NO NO. WE'RE DOOMED!

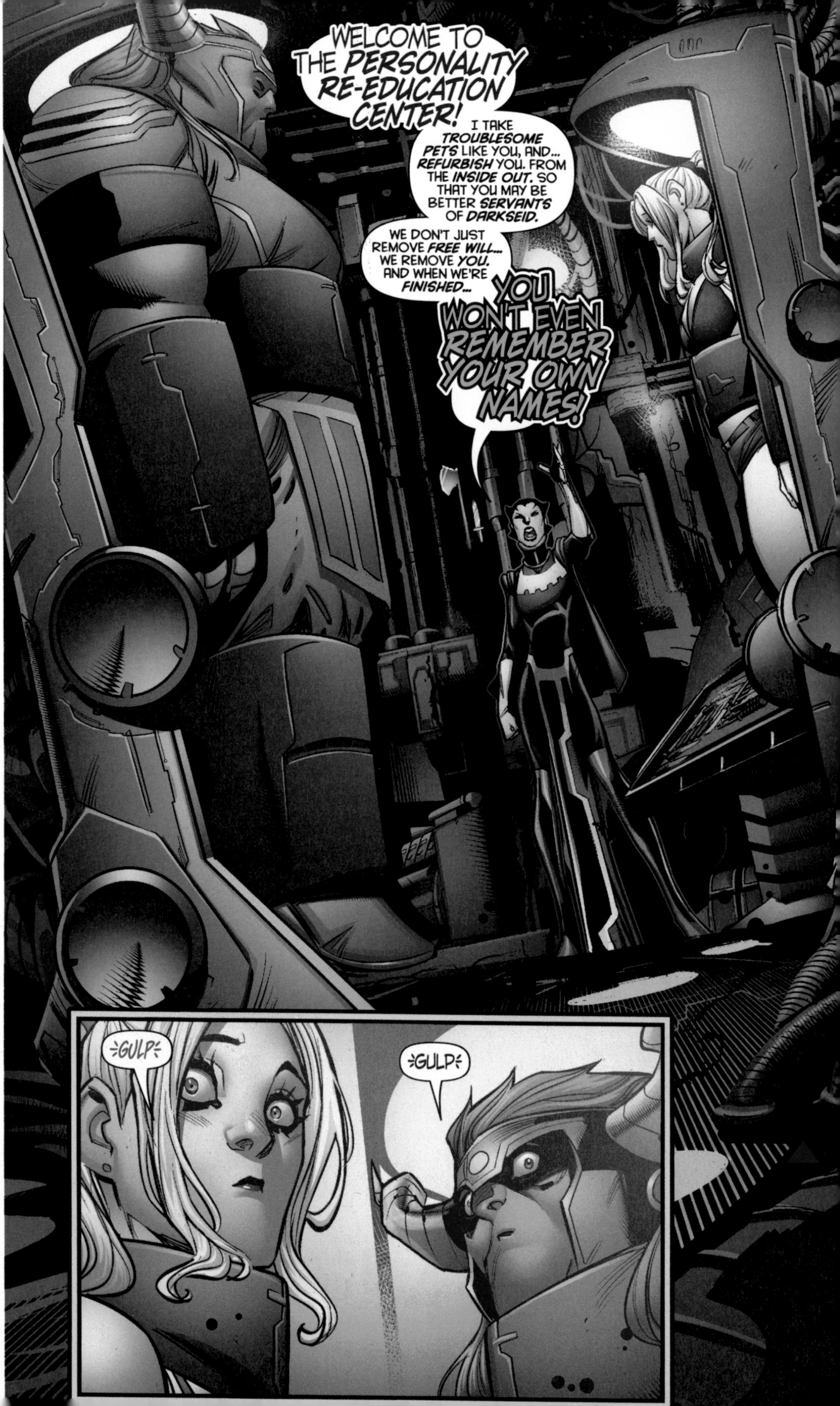
WELCOME TO THE PERSONALITY RE-EDUCATION CENTER!
I TAKE TROUBLESOME PETS LIKE YOU, AND... REFURBISH YOU. FROM THE INSIDE OUT. SO THAT YOU MAY BE BETTER SERVANTS OF DARKSEID.
WE DON'T JUST REMOVE FREE WILL... WE REMOVE YOU. AND WHEN WE'RE FINISHED...
YOU WON'T EVEN REMEMBER YOUR OWN NAMES!
GULP
GULP

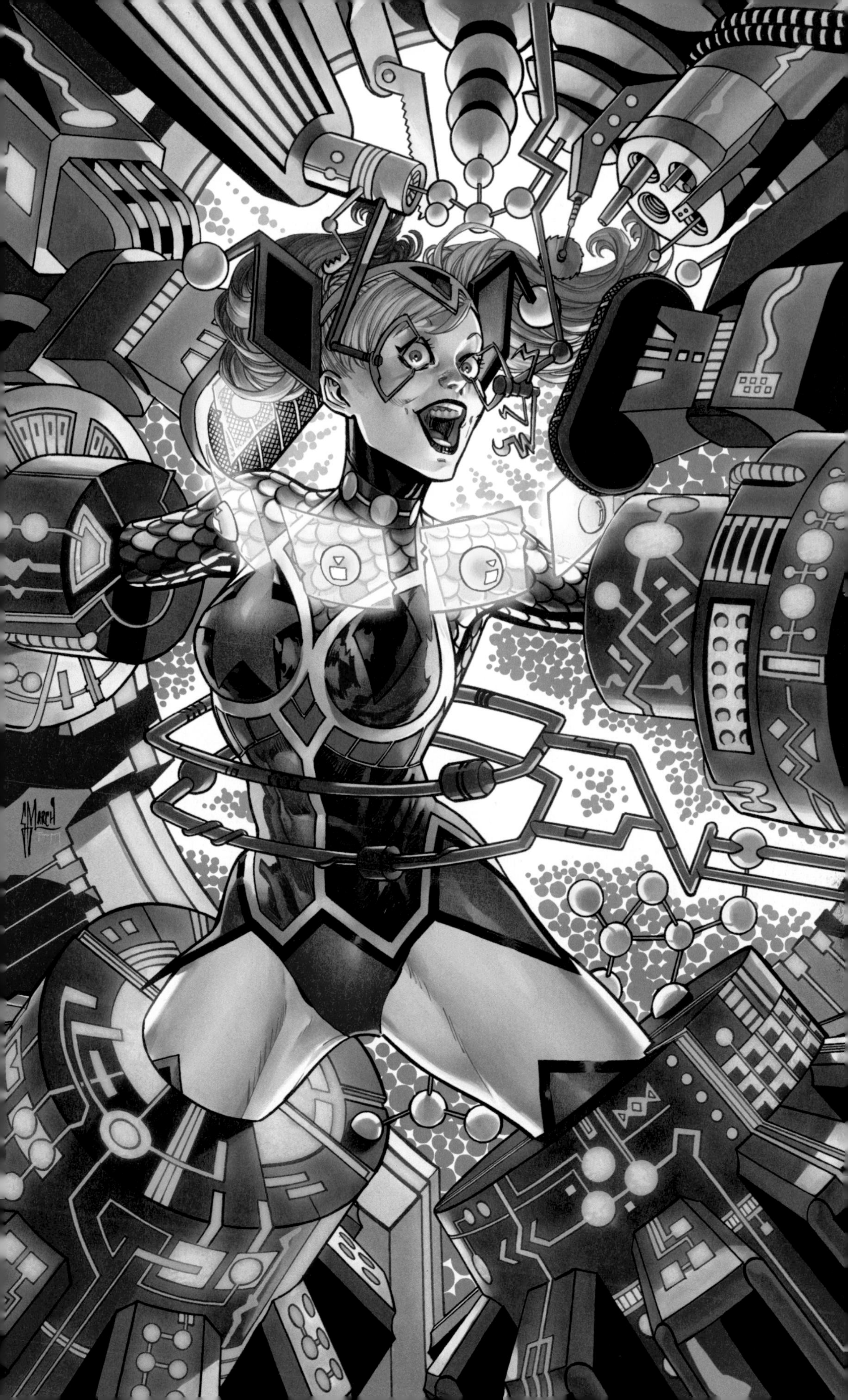

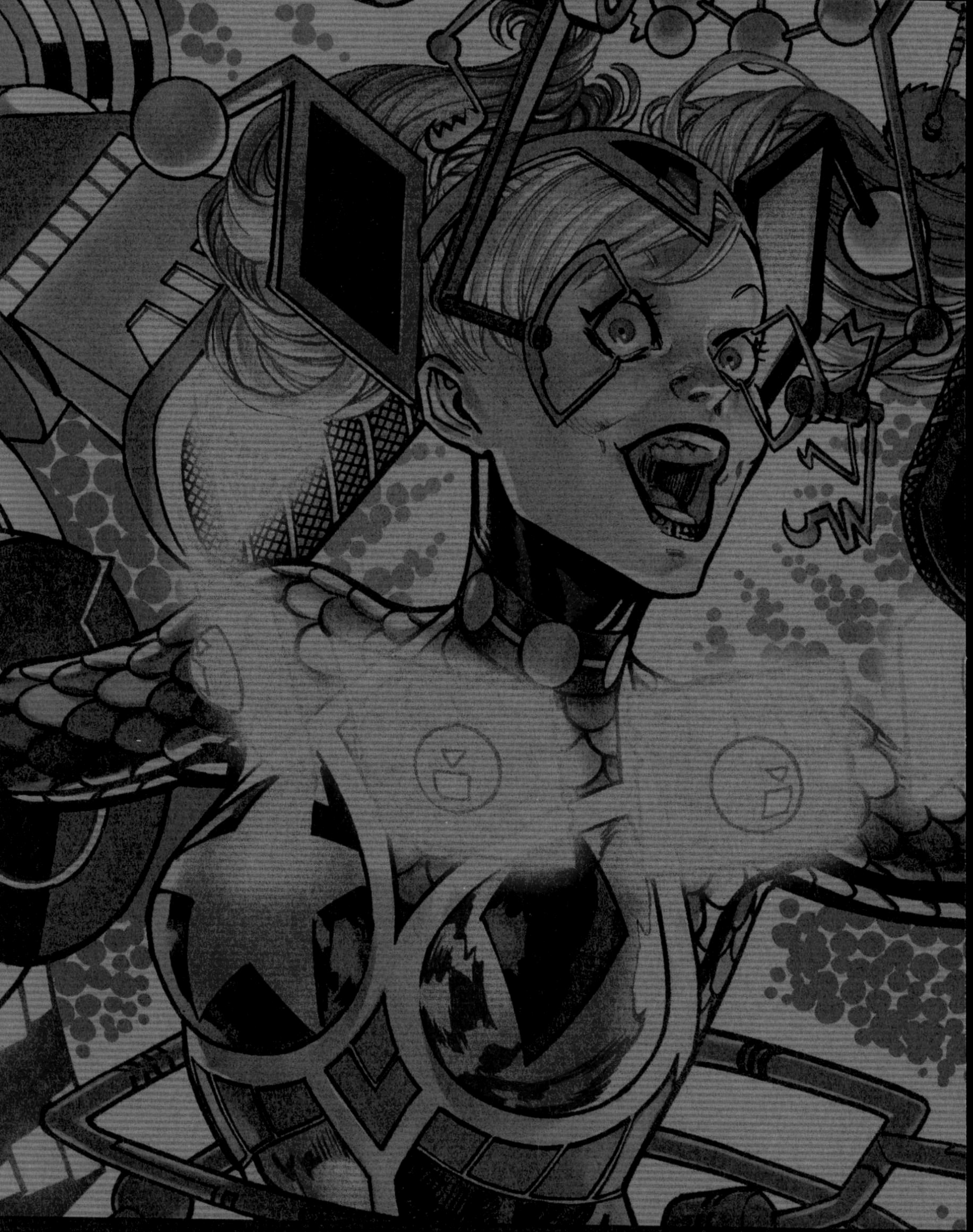

HARLEY QUINN

#47

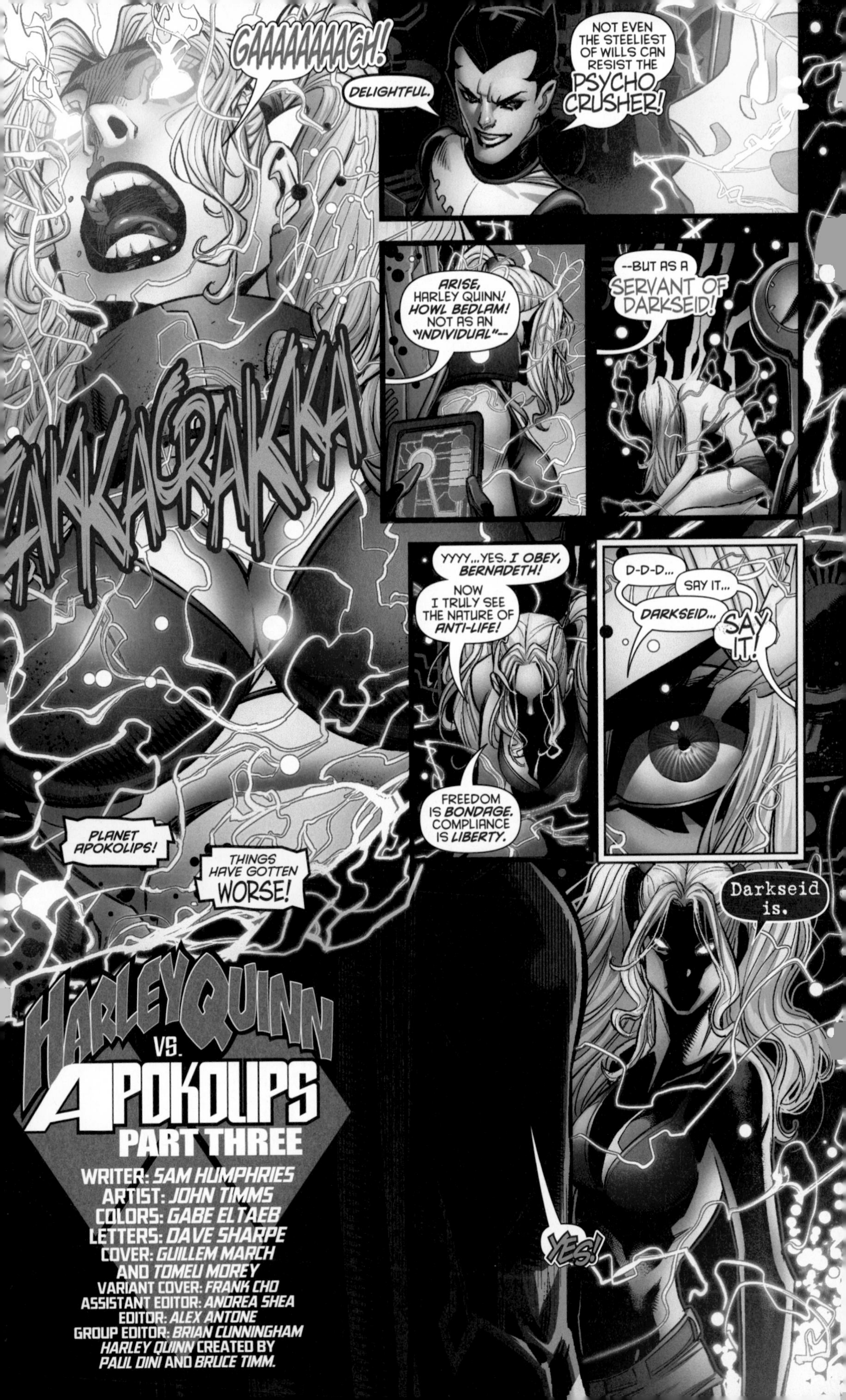
GAAAAAAAAGH!
DELIGHTFUL.
NOT EVEN THE STEELIEST OF WILLS CAN RESIST THE PSYCHO CRUSHER!
AKKACRAKKA
ARISE, HARLEY QUINN! HOWL BEDLAM! NOT AS AN "INDIVIDUAL"--
--BUT AS A SERVANT OF DARKSEID!
YYYY...YES. I OBEY, BERNADETH!
NOW I TRULY SEE THE NATURE OF ANTI-LIFE!
FREEDOM IS BONDAGE. COMPLIANCE IS LIBERTY.
D-D-D...
SAY IT...
DARKSEID...
SAY IT!
PLANET APOKOLIPS!
THINGS HAVE GOTTEN WORSE!
Darkseid is.
YES!
HARLEY QUINN VS. APOKOLIPS
PART THREE
WRITER: SAM HUMPHRIES
ARTIST: JOHN TIMMS
COLORS: GABE ELTAEB
LETTERS: DAVE SHARPE
COVER: GUILLEM MARCH AND TOMEU MOREY
VARIANT COVER: FRANK CHO
ASSISTANT EDITOR: ANDREA SHEA
EDITOR: ALEX ANTONE
GROUP EDITOR: BRIAN CUNNINGHAM
HARLEY QUINN CREATED BY PAUL DINI AND BRUCE TIMM.

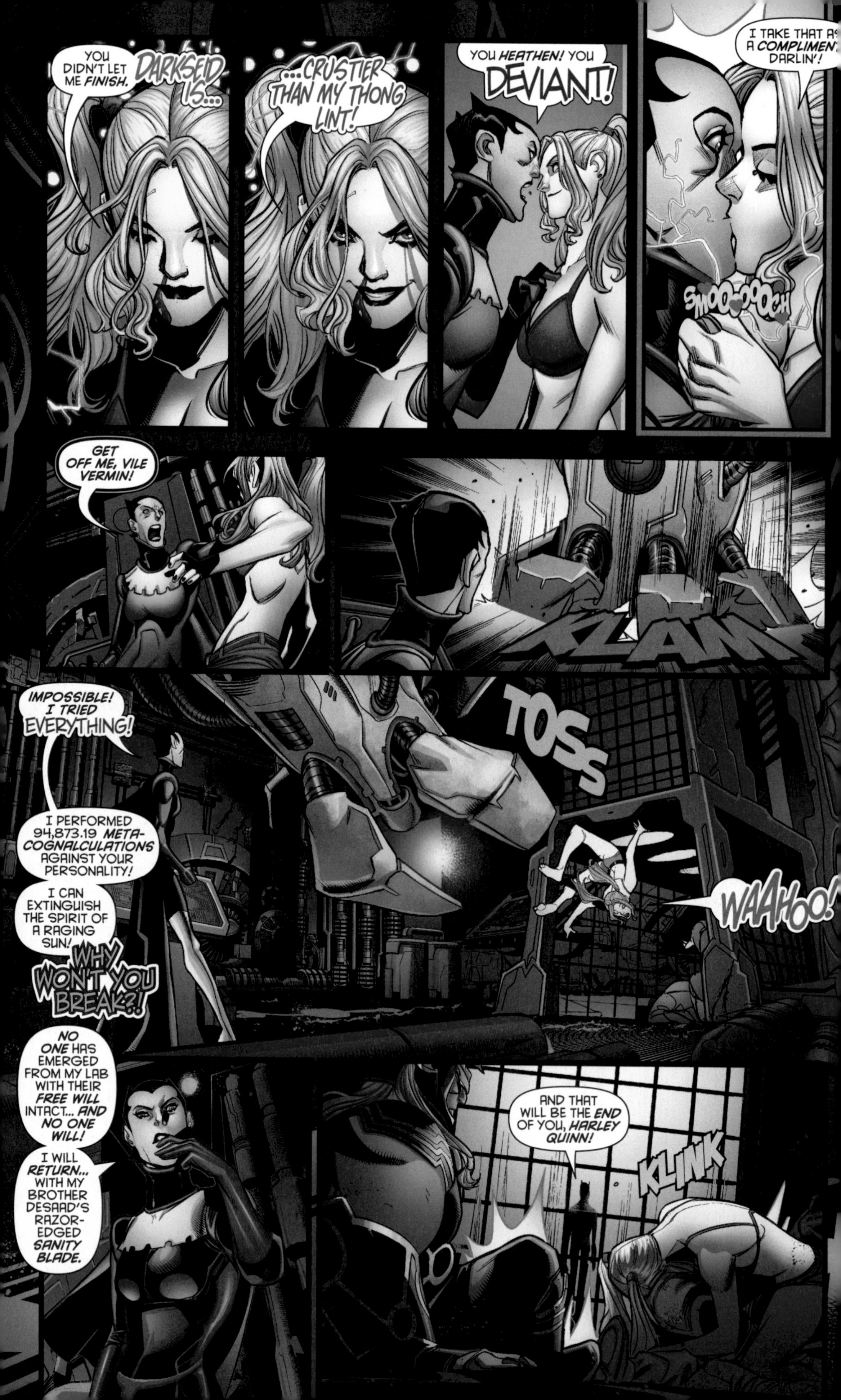

YOU DIDN'T LET ME FINISH.
DARKSEID IS...
...CRUSTIER THAN MY THONG LINT!
YOU HEATHEN! YOU DEVIANT!
I TAKE THAT AS A COMPLIMENT, DARLIN'!
SMOO-OOOCH
GET OFF ME, VILE VERMIN!
KLAM
IMPOSSIBLE! I TRIED EVERYTHING!
I PERFORMED 94,873.19 META-COGNALCULATIONS AGAINST YOUR PERSONALITY!
I CAN EXTINGUISH THE SPIRIT OF A RAGING SUN!
WHY WON'T YOU BREAK?!
TOSS
WAAHOO!
NO ONE HAS EMERGED FROM MY LAB WITH THEIR FREE WILL INTACT... AND NO ONE WILL!
I WILL RETURN... WITH MY BROTHER DESAAD'S RAZOR-EDGED SANITY BLADE.
AND THAT WILL BE THE END OF YOU, HARLEY QUINN!
KLINK

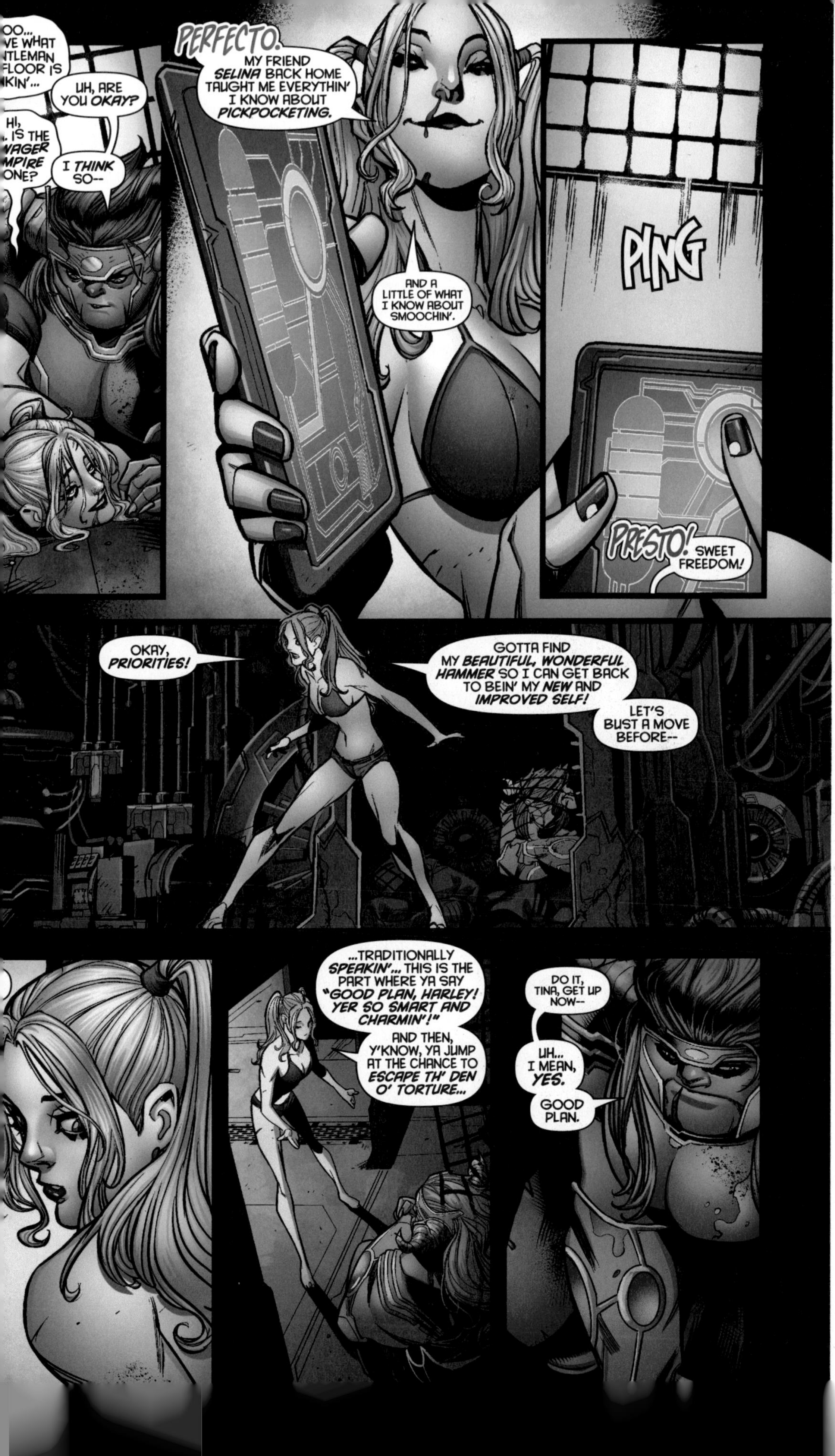
OO...
VE WHAT
NTLEMAN
FLOOR IS
NKIN'...
UH, ARE YOU OKAY?
HI,
. IS THE
WAGER
MPIRE
ONE?
I THINK SO--
PERFECTO.
MY FRIEND SELINA BACK HOME TAUGHT ME EVERYTHIN' I KNOW ABOUT PICKPOCKETING.
AND A LITTLE OF WHAT I KNOW ABOUT SMOOCHIN'.
PING
PRESTO!
SWEET FREEDOM!
OKAY, PRIORITIES!
GOTTA FIND MY BEAUTIFUL, WONDERFUL HAMMER SO I CAN GET BACK TO BEIN' MY NEW AND IMPROVED SELF!
LET'S BUST A MOVE BEFORE--
...TRADITIONALLY SPEAKIN'... THIS IS THE PART WHERE YA SAY "GOOD PLAN, HARLEY! YER SO SMART AND CHARMIN'!"
AND THEN, Y'KNOW, YA JUMP AT THE CHANCE TO ESCAPE TH' DEN O' TORTURE...
DO IT, TINA, GET UP NOW--
UH... I MEAN, YES.
GOOD PLAN.

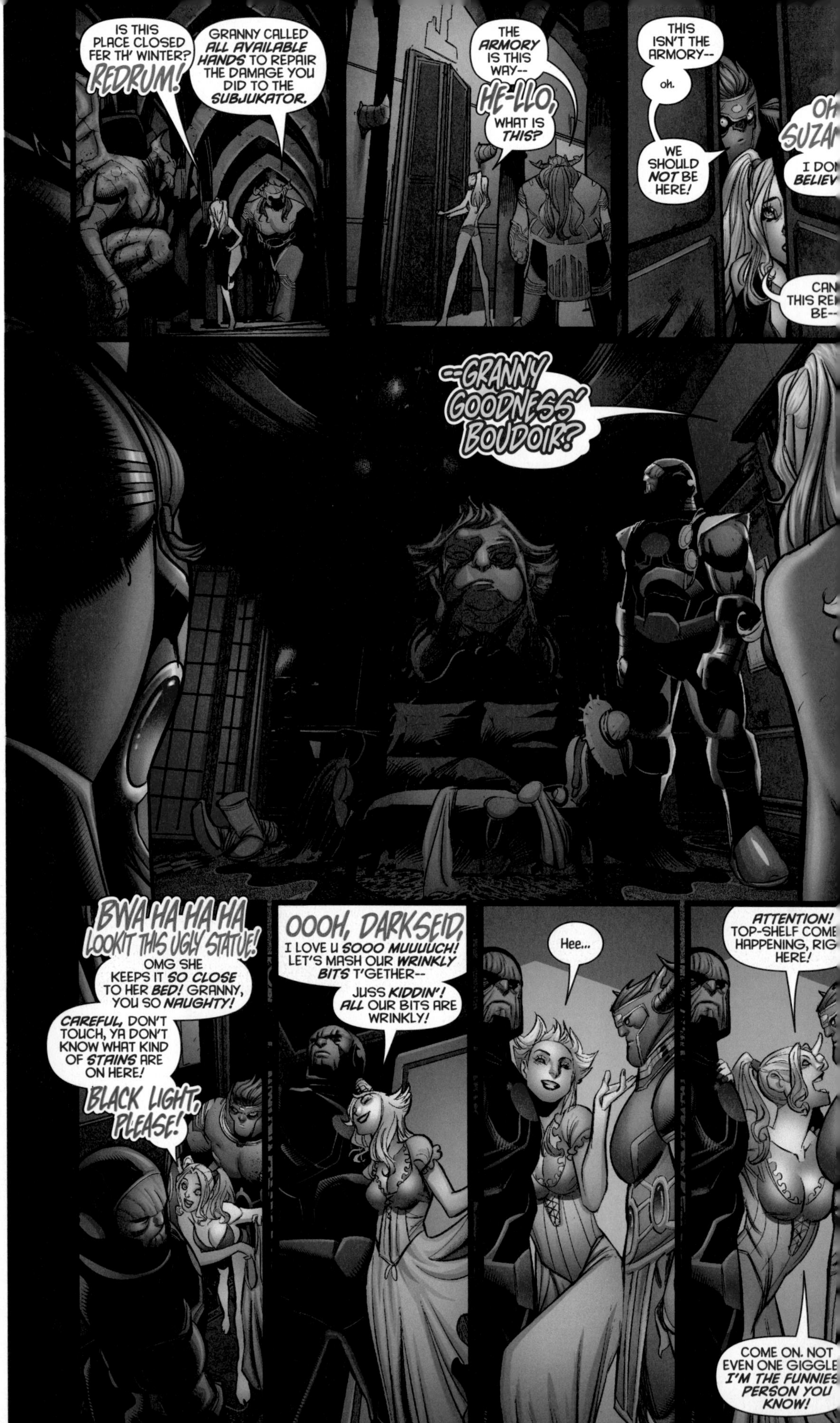

IS THIS PLACE CLOSED FER TH' WINTER? REDRUM!
GRANNY CALLED ALL AVAILABLE HANDS TO REPAIR THE DAMAGE YOU DID TO THE SUBJUKATOR.
THE ARMORY IS THIS WAY--
HE-LLO, WHAT IS THIS?
THIS ISN'T THE ARMORY--
oh.
WE SHOULD NOT BE HERE!
I DON BELIEV
CAN THIS RE BE--
--GRANNY GOODNESS' BOUDOIR?
BWA HA HA HA LOOKIT THIS UGLY STATUE!
OMG SHE KEEPS IT SO CLOSE TO HER BED! GRANNY, YOU SO NAUGHTY!
CAREFUL, DON'T TOUCH, YA DON'T KNOW WHAT KIND OF STAINS ARE ON HERE!
BLACK LIGHT, PLEASE!
OOOH, DARKSEID, I LOVE U SOOO MUUUUCH! LET'S MASH OUR WRINKLY BITS T'GETHER--
JUSS KIDDIN'! ALL OUR BITS ARE WRINKLY!
Hee...
ATTENTION! TOP-SHELF COME HAPPENING, RIG HERE!
COME ON. NOT EVEN ONE GIGGLE I'M THE FUNNIES PERSON YOU KNOW!

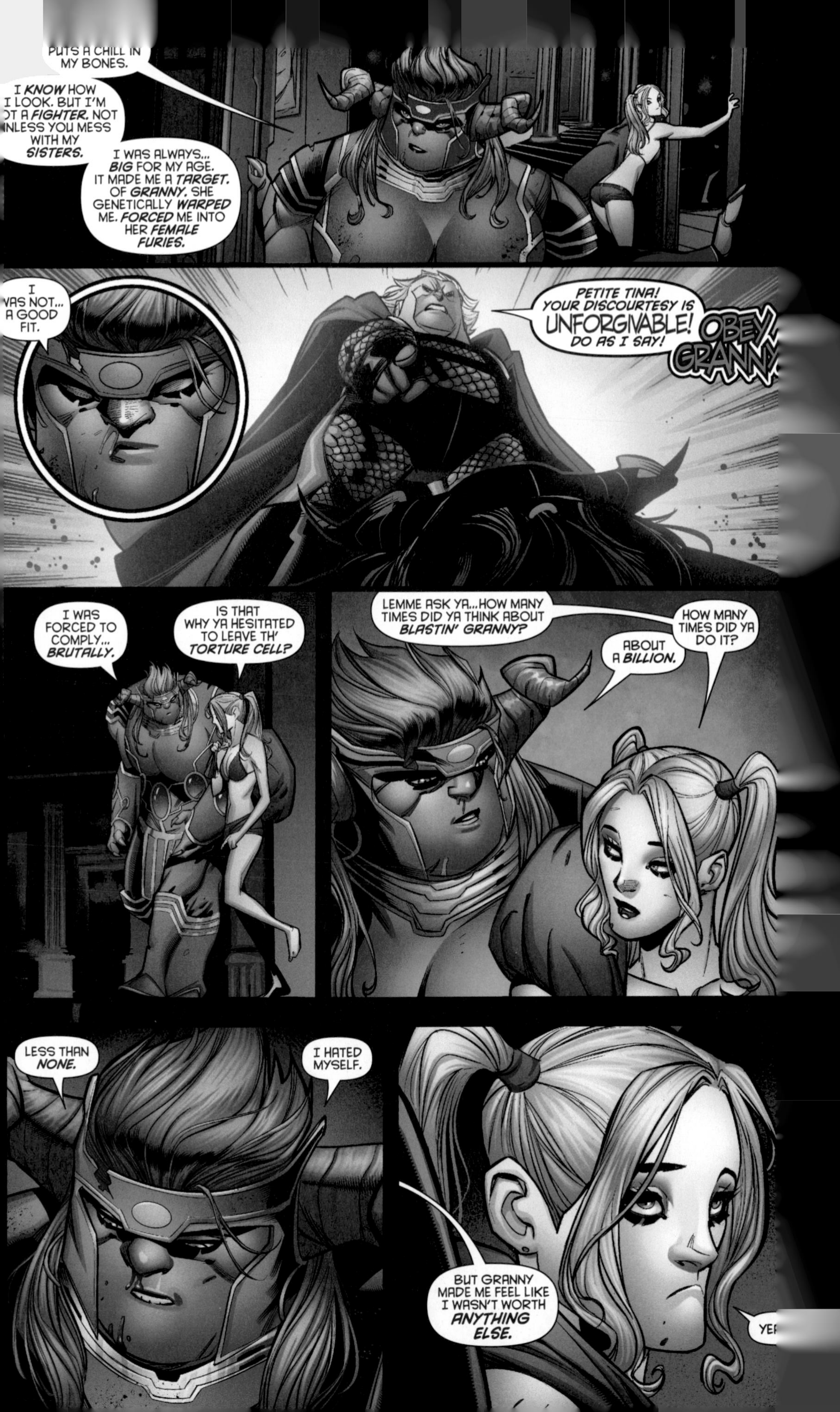

PUTS A CHILL IN MY BONES.
I KNOW HOW I LOOK. BUT I'M OT A FIGHTER. NOT NLESS YOU MESS WITH MY SISTERS.
I WAS ALWAYS... BIG FOR MY AGE. IT MADE ME A TARGET. OF GRANNY. SHE GENETICALLY WARPED ME. FORCED ME INTO HER FEMALE FURIES.
I VAS NOT... A GOOD FIT.
PETITE TINA! YOUR DISCOURTESY IS UNFORGIVABLE! DO AS I SAY!
OBEY GRANNY
I WAS FORCED TO COMPLY... BRUTALLY.
IS THAT WHY YA HESITATED TO LEAVE TH' TORTURE CELL?
LEMME ASK YA...HOW MANY TIMES DID YA THINK ABOUT BLASTIN' GRANNY?
ABOUT A BILLION.
HOW MANY TIMES DID YA DO IT?
LESS THAN NONE.
I HATED MYSELF.
BUT GRANNY MADE ME FEEL LIKE I WASN'T WORTH ANYTHING ELSE.
YE

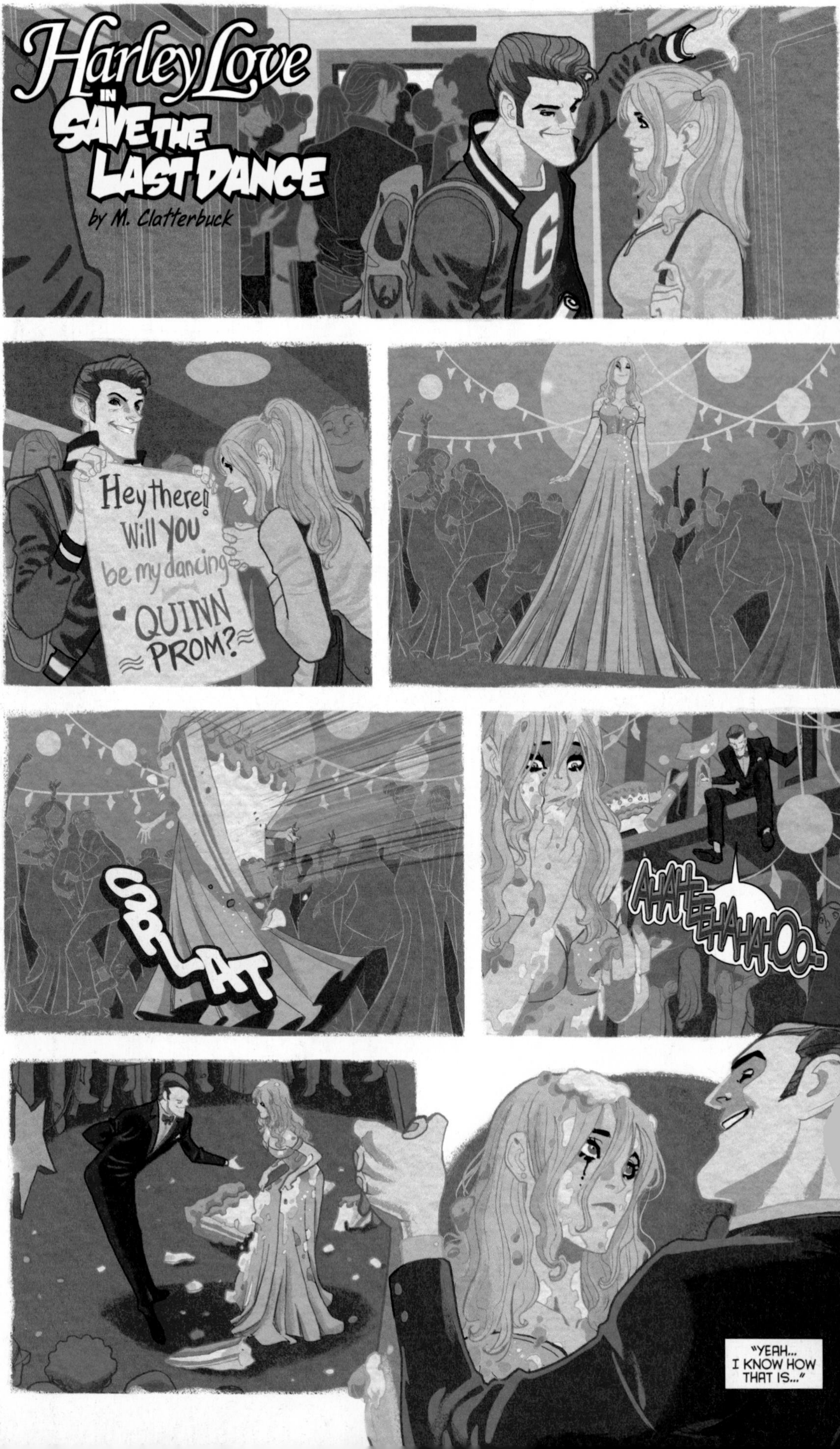
Harley Love in Save the Last Dance
by M. Clatterbuck
Hey there!! Will YOU be my dancing QUINN PROM?
SPLAT
AHAHEEHAHAHOO-
"YEAH... I KNOW HOW THAT IS..."

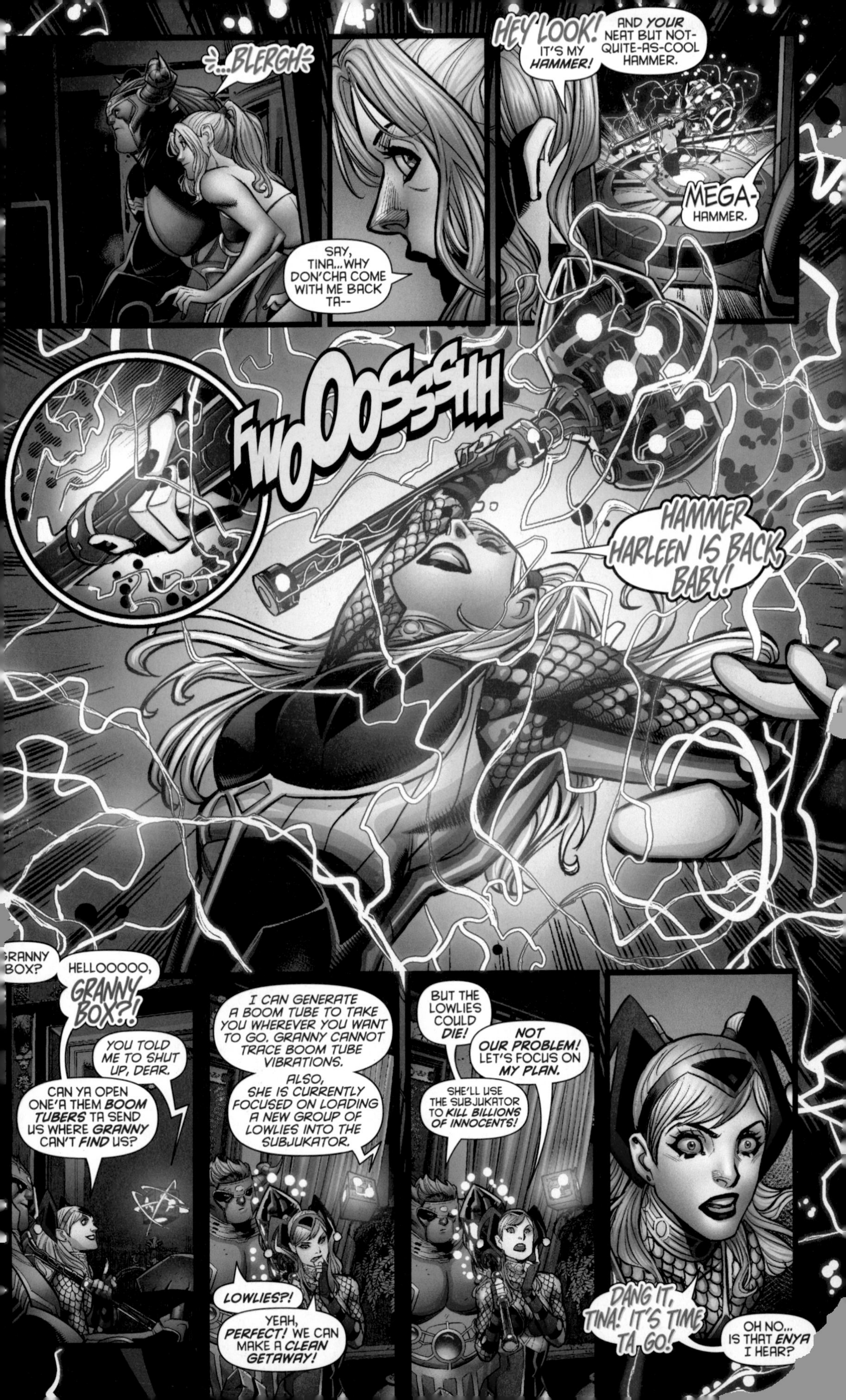

...BLERGH
SAY, TINA...WHY DON'CHA COME WITH ME BACK TA--
HEY LOOK! IT'S MY HAMMER!
AND YOUR NEAT BUT NOT-QUITE-AS-COOL HAMMER.
MEGA-HAMMER.
FWOOOSSSHH
HAMMER HARLEEN IS BACK, BABY!
GRANNY BOX?
HELLOOOOO, GRANNY BOX?!
YOU TOLD ME TO SHUT UP, DEAR.
CAN YA OPEN ONE'A THEM BOOM TUBERS TA SEND US WHERE GRANNY CAN'T FIND US?
I CAN GENERATE A BOOM TUBE TO TAKE YOU WHEREVER YOU WANT TO GO. GRANNY CANNOT TRACE BOOM TUBE VIBRATIONS.
ALSO, SHE IS CURRENTLY FOCUSED ON LOADING A NEW GROUP OF LOWLIES INTO THE SUBJUKATOR.
LOWLIES?!
YEAH, PERFECT! WE CAN MAKE A CLEAN GETAWAY!
BUT THE LOWLIES COULD DIE!
NOT OUR PROBLEM! LET'S FOCUS ON MY PLAN.
SHE'LL USE THE SUBJUKATOR TO KILL BILLIONS OF INNOCENTS!
DANG IT, TINA! IT'S TIME TA GO!
OH NO... IS THAT ENYA I HEAR?

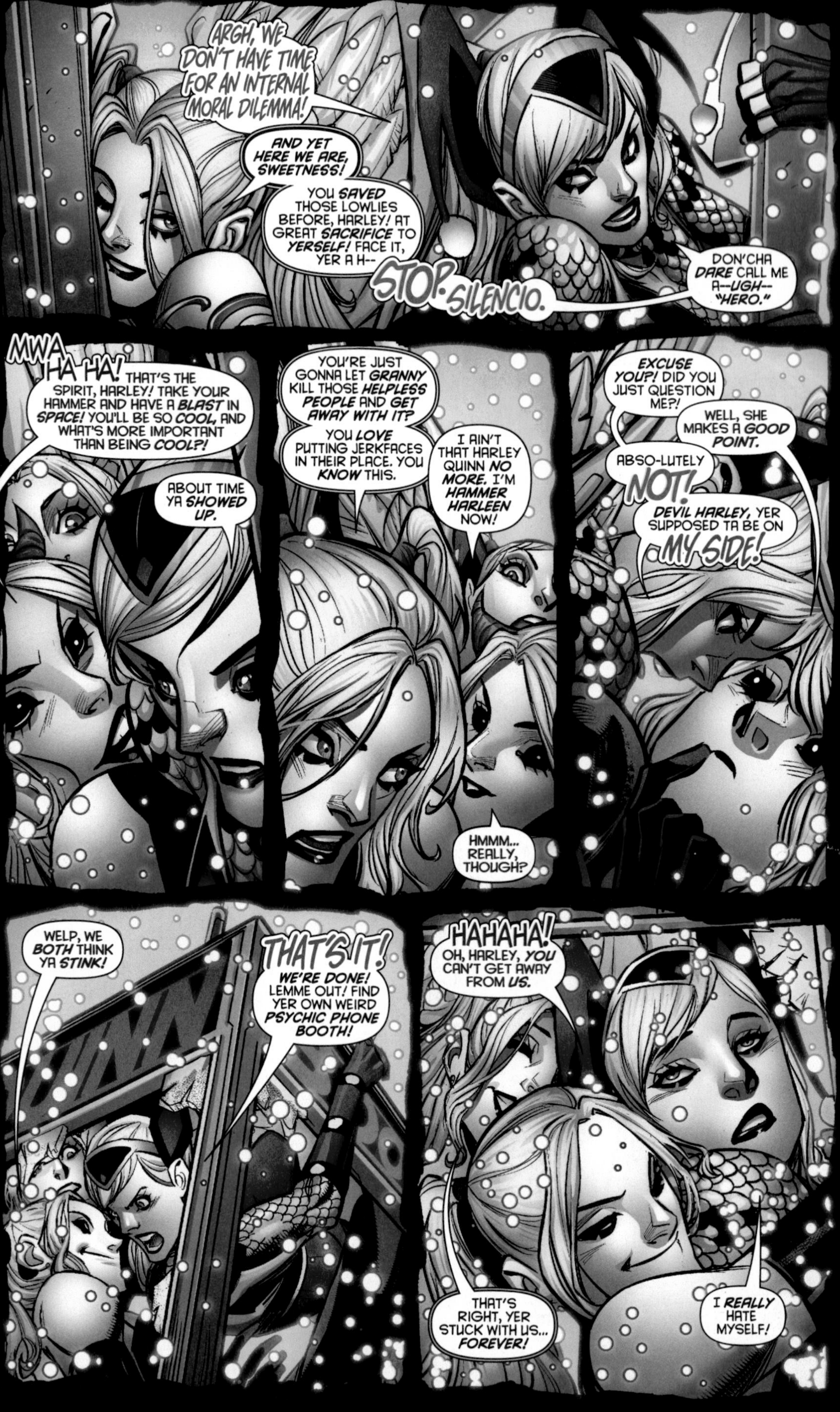
ARGH, WE DON'T HAVE TIME FOR AN INTERNAL MORAL DILEMMA!
AND YET HERE WE ARE, SWEETNESS!
YOU SAVED THOSE LOWLIES BEFORE, HARLEY! AT GREAT SACRIFICE TO YERSELF! FACE IT, YER A H--
STOP. SILENCIO.
DON'CHA DARE CALL ME A--UGH--"HERO."
MWA HA HA! THAT'S THE SPIRIT, HARLEY! TAKE YOUR HAMMER AND HAVE A BLAST IN SPACE! YOU'LL BE SO COOL, AND WHAT'S MORE IMPORTANT THAN BEING COOL?!
ABOUT TIME YA SHOWED UP.
YOU'RE JUST GONNA LET GRANNY KILL THOSE HELPLESS PEOPLE AND GET AWAY WITH IT?
YOU LOVE PUTTING JERKFACES IN THEIR PLACE. YOU KNOW THIS.
I AIN'T THAT HARLEY QUINN NO MORE. I'M HAMMER HARLEEN NOW!
HMMM... REALLY, THOUGH?
EXCUSE YOU?! DID YOU JUST QUESTION ME?!
WELL, SHE MAKES A GOOD POINT.
ABSO-LUTELY NOT!
DEVIL HARLEY, YER SUPPOSED TA BE ON MY SIDE!
WELP, WE BOTH THINK YA STINK!
THAT'S IT! WE'RE DONE! LEMME OUT! FIND YER OWN WEIRD PSYCHIC PHONE BOOTH!
HAHAHA! OH, HARLEY, YOU CAN'T GET AWAY FROM US.
THAT'S RIGHT, YER STUCK WITH US... FOREVER!
I REALLY HATE MYSELF!

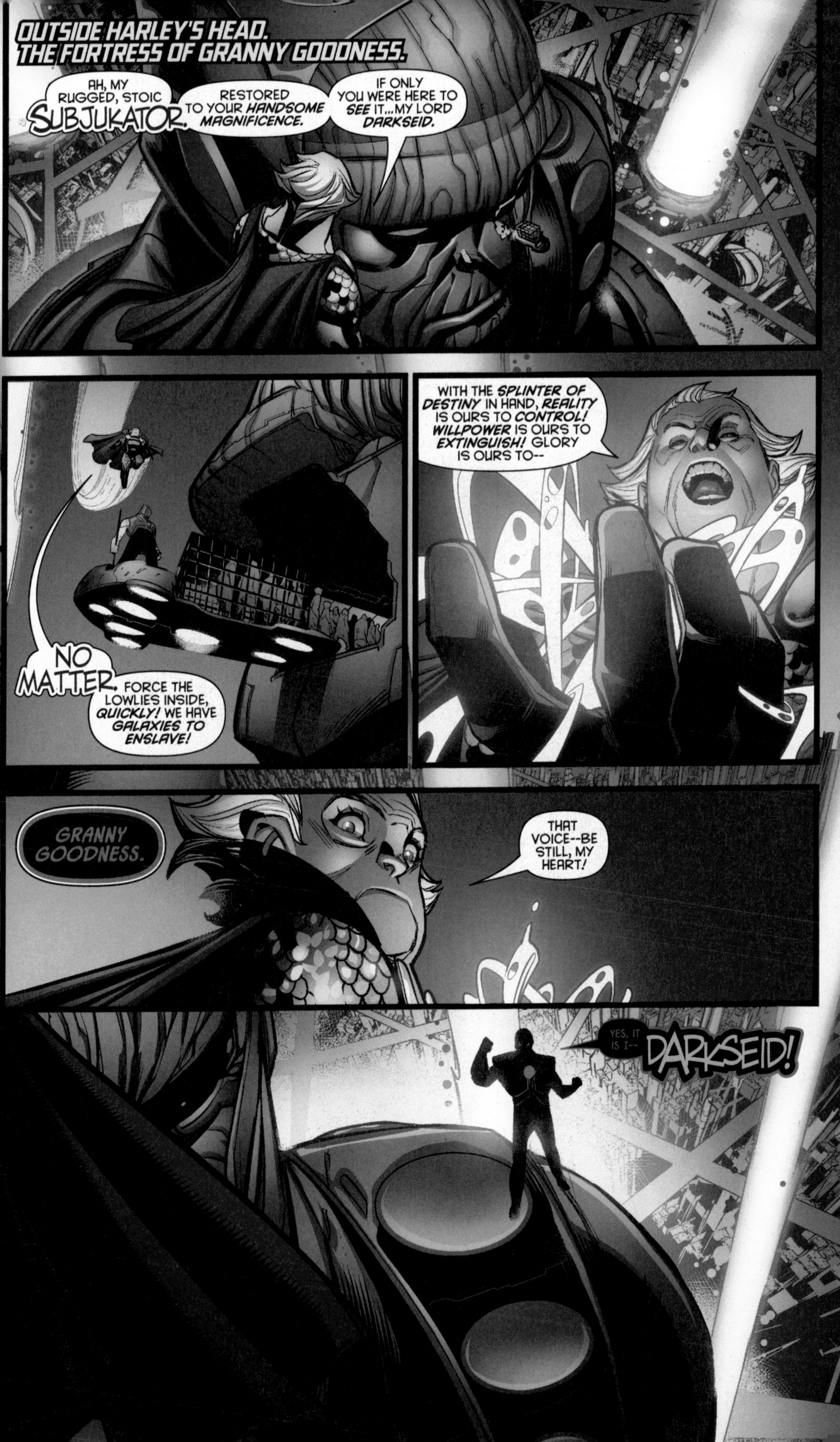
OUTSIDE HARLEY'S HEAD.
THE FORTRESS OF GRANNY GOODNESS.
AH, MY RUGGED, STOIC SUBJUKATOR.
RESTORED TO YOUR HANDSOME MAGNIFICENCE.
IF ONLY YOU WERE HERE TO SEE IT...MY LORD DARKSEID.
NO MATTER. FORCE THE LOWLIES INSIDE, QUICKLY! WE HAVE GALAXIES TO ENSLAVE!
WITH THE SPLINTER OF DESTINY IN HAND, REALITY IS OURS TO CONTROL! WILLPOWER IS OURS TO EXTINGUISH! GLORY IS OURS TO--
GRANNY GOODNESS.
THAT VOICE--BE STILL, MY HEART!
YES, IT IS I-- DARKSEID!

I HAVE **ESCAPED** MY **FOOLISH** CAPTORS AND TRAVERSIFIED THE COSMOS!

I TARRIED NOT **ONE IOTA** TO RETURN TO WITNESS YOUR **GRAND ACHIEVEMENT,** GRANNY!

AND I MUST SAY...I AM **DAZZLED.**

BOW TO ME, GRANNY GOODNESS.

OH...**YES,** DARKSEID!

FOR I, **DARKSEID,** SEE **ALL!** I HAVE WITNESSED YOUR **ACCOMPLISHMENTS.** YOUR ADMIRATION. YOUR... **DEVOTION.**

REMAIN BOWED, GRANNY.

I SEE YOU IN YOUR **ISOLATION...**

...YOUR MOST **PRIVATE** MOMENTS.

I WITNESS WHAT IS IN YOUR **HEART.** YOUR TRUEST, **DEEPEST** DESIRES.

GRANNY GOODNESS... I **SHARE THY DESIRES!**

MY LORD... CAN THIS BE REAL?

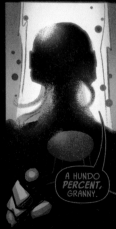

A HUNDO **PERCENT,** GRANNY.

HUNDO?

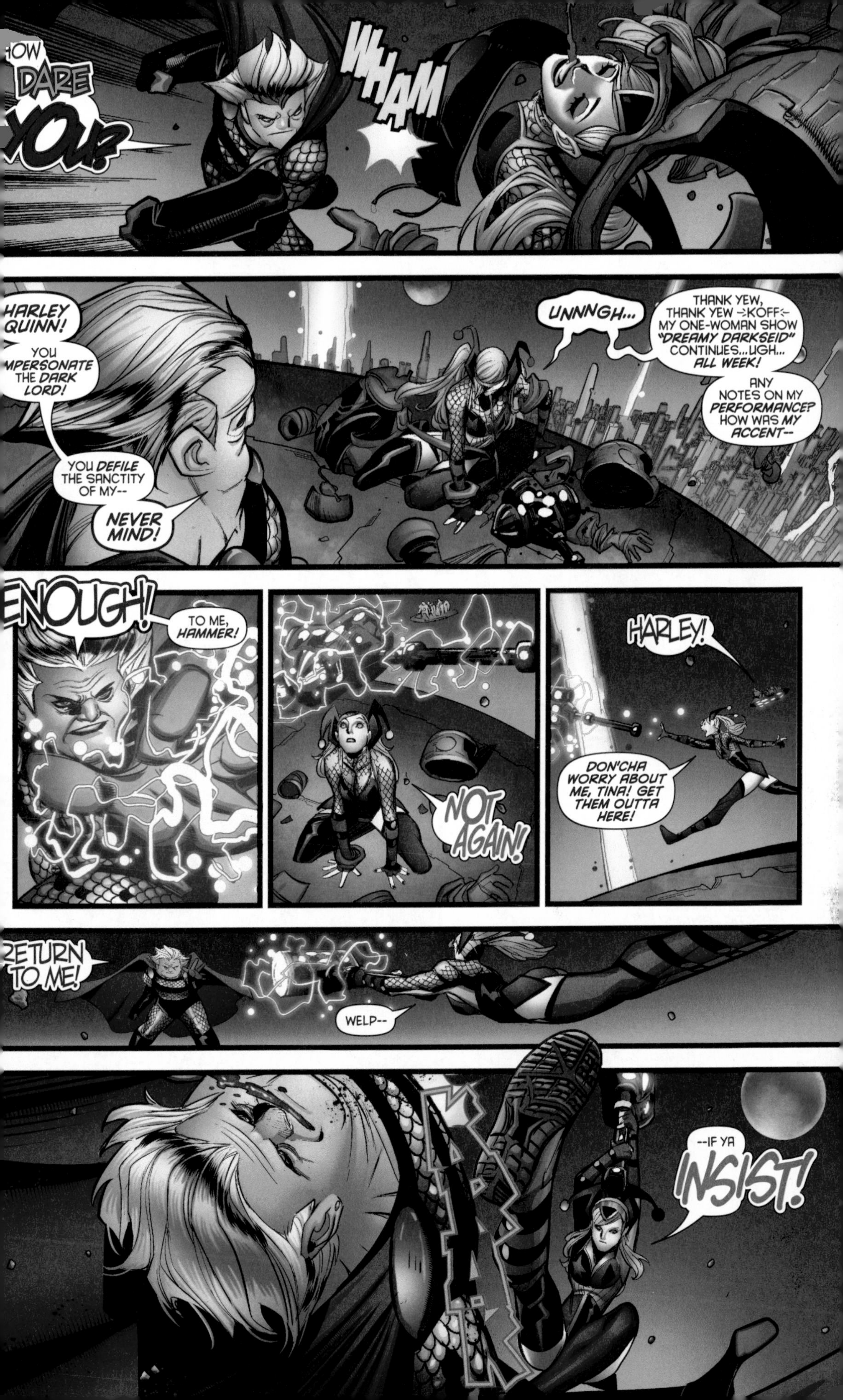
HOW DARE YOU?!
WHAM
HARLEY QUINN!
YOU IMPERSONATE THE DARK LORD!
YOU DEFILE THE SANCTITY OF MY--
NEVER MIND!
UNNNGH...
THANK YEW, THANK YEW -KOFF- MY ONE-WOMAN SHOW "DREAMY DARKSEID" CONTINUES...UGH... ALL WEEK!
ANY NOTES ON MY PERFORMANCE? HOW WAS MY ACCENT--
ENOUGH!
TO ME, HAMMER!
NOT AGAIN!
HARLEY!
DON'CHA WORRY ABOUT ME, TINA! GET THEM OUTTA HERE!
RETURN TO ME!
WELP--
--IF YA INSIST!

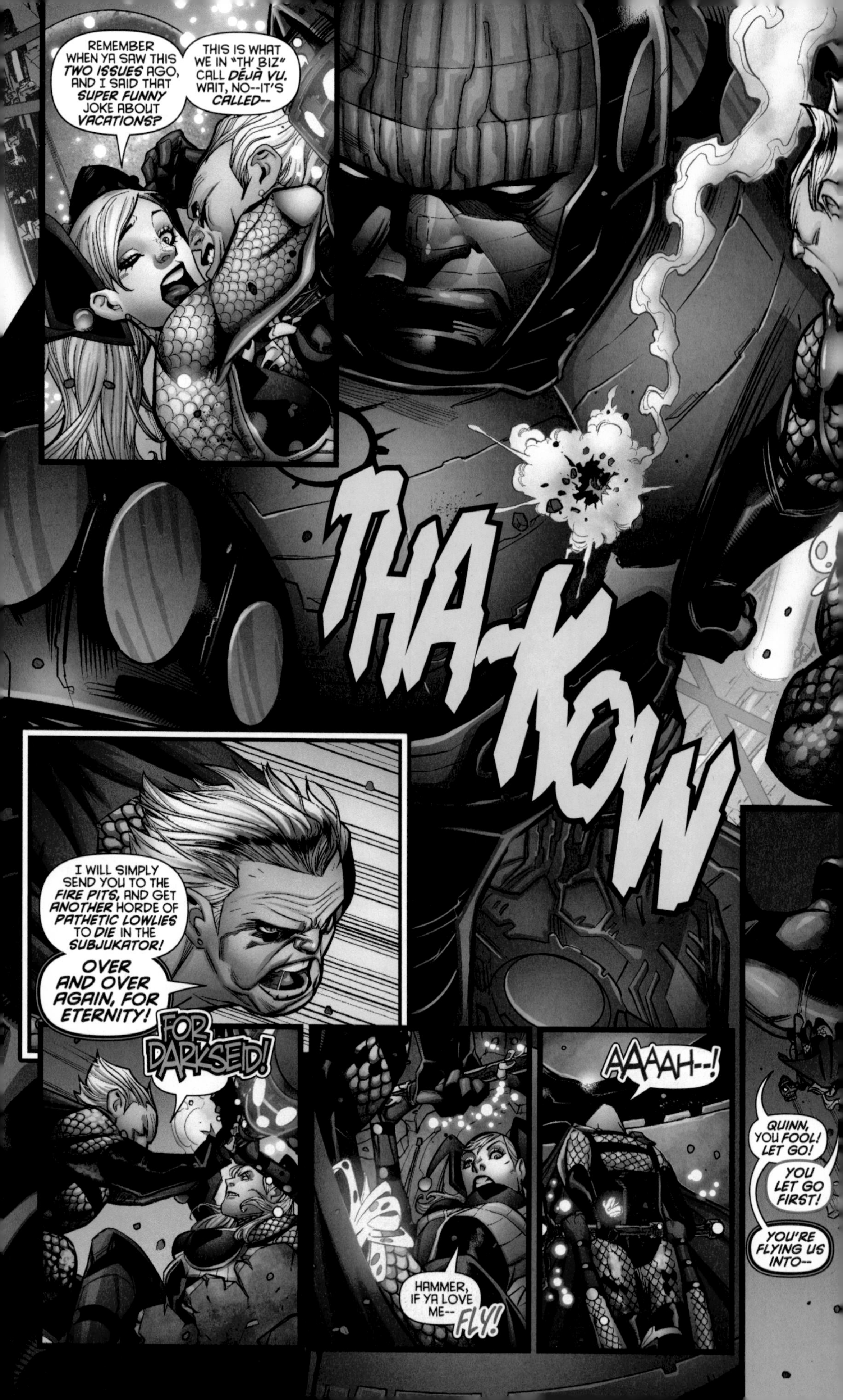
REMEMBER WHEN YA SAW THIS TWO ISSUES AGO, AND I SAID THAT SUPER FUNNY JOKE ABOUT VACATIONS?
THIS IS WHAT WE IN "TH' BIZ" CALL DÉJÀ VU. WAIT, NO--IT'S CALLED--
THA-KOW
I WILL SIMPLY SEND YOU TO THE FIRE PITS, AND GET ANOTHER HORDE OF PATHETIC LOWLIES TO DIE IN THE SUBJUKATOR!
OVER AND OVER AGAIN, FOR ETERNITY!
FOR DARKSEID!
HAMMER, IF YA LOVE ME--FLY!
AAAAH--!
QUINN, YOU FOOL! LET GO!
YOU LET GO FIRST!
YOU'RE FLYING US INTO--

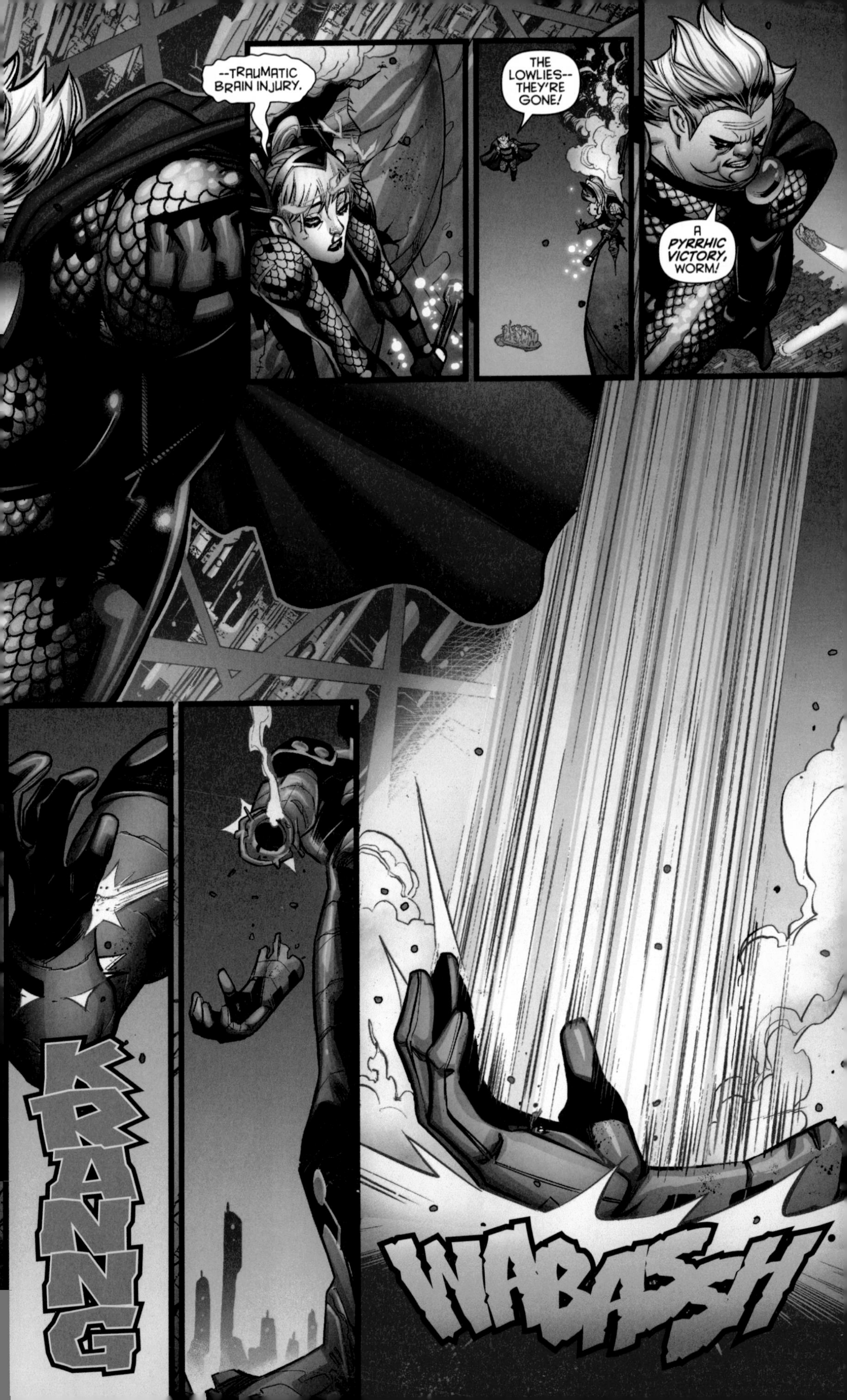
--TRAUMATIC BRAIN INJURY.
THE LOWLIES--THEY'RE GONE!
A PYRRHIC VICTORY, WORM!
KRANG
WABASH

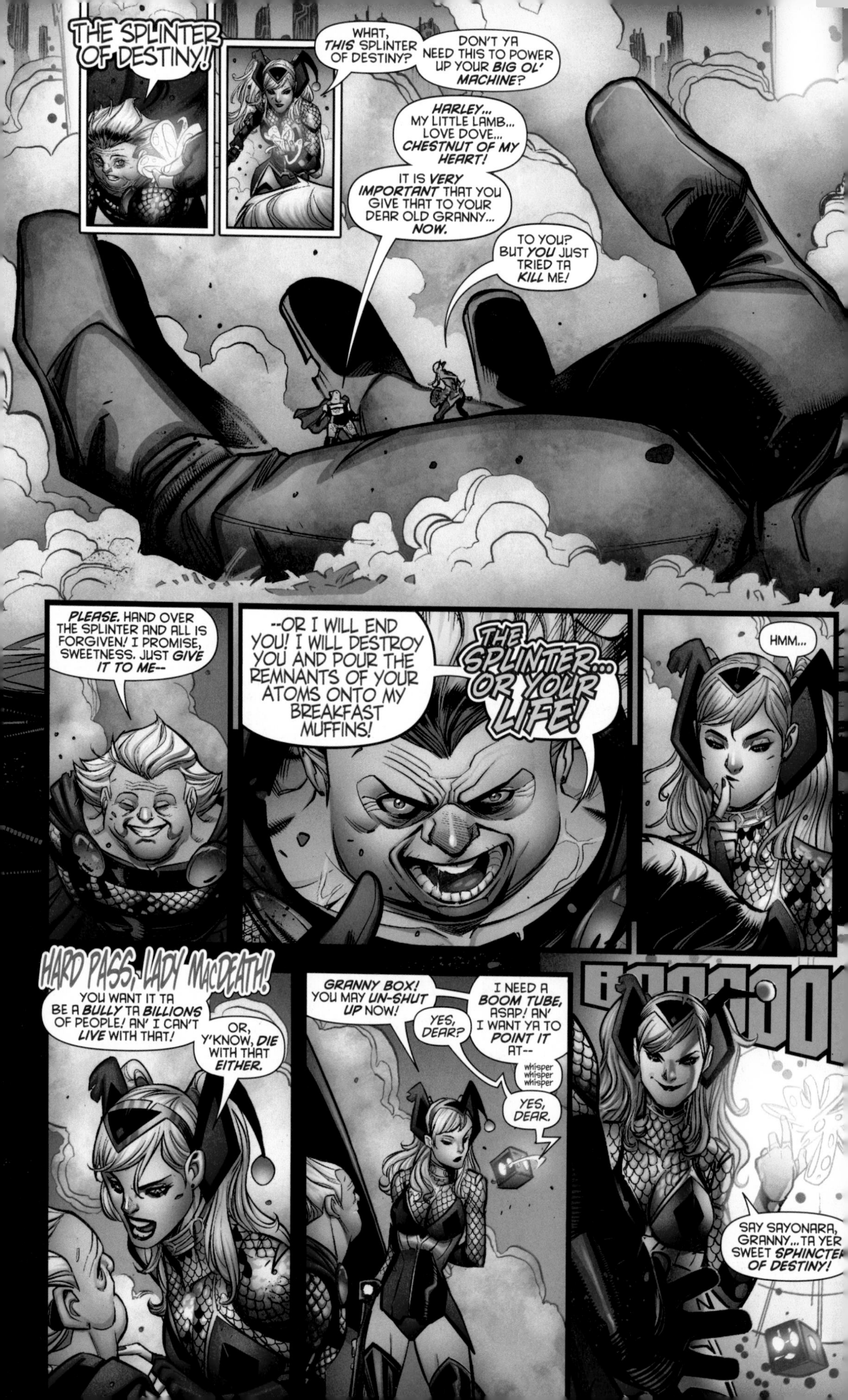
THE SPLINTER OF DESTINY!
WHAT, THIS SPLINTER OF DESTINY?
DON'T YA NEED THIS TO POWER UP YOUR BIG OL' MACHINE?
HARLEY... MY LITTLE LAMB... LOVE DOVE... CHESTNUT OF MY HEART!
IT IS VERY IMPORTANT THAT YOU GIVE THAT TO YOUR DEAR OLD GRANNY... NOW.
TO YOU? BUT YOU JUST TRIED TA KILL ME!
PLEASE. HAND OVER THE SPLINTER AND ALL IS FORGIVEN! I PROMISE, SWEETNESS. JUST GIVE IT TO ME--
--OR I WILL END YOU! I WILL DESTROY YOU AND POUR THE REMNANTS OF YOUR ATOMS ONTO MY BREAKFAST MUFFINS!
THE SPLINTER... OR YOUR LIFE!
HMM...
HARD PASS, LADY MACDEATH!
YOU WANT IT TA BE A BULLY TA BILLIONS OF PEOPLE! AN' I CAN'T LIVE WITH THAT!
OR, Y'KNOW, DIE WITH THAT EITHER.
GRANNY BOX! YOU MAY UN-SHUT UP NOW!
YES, DEAR?
I NEED A BOOM TUBE, ASAP! AN' I WANT YA TO POINT IT AT--
whisper whisper whisper
YES, DEAR.
SAY SAYONARA, GRANNY... TA YER SWEET SPHINCTER OF DESTINY!

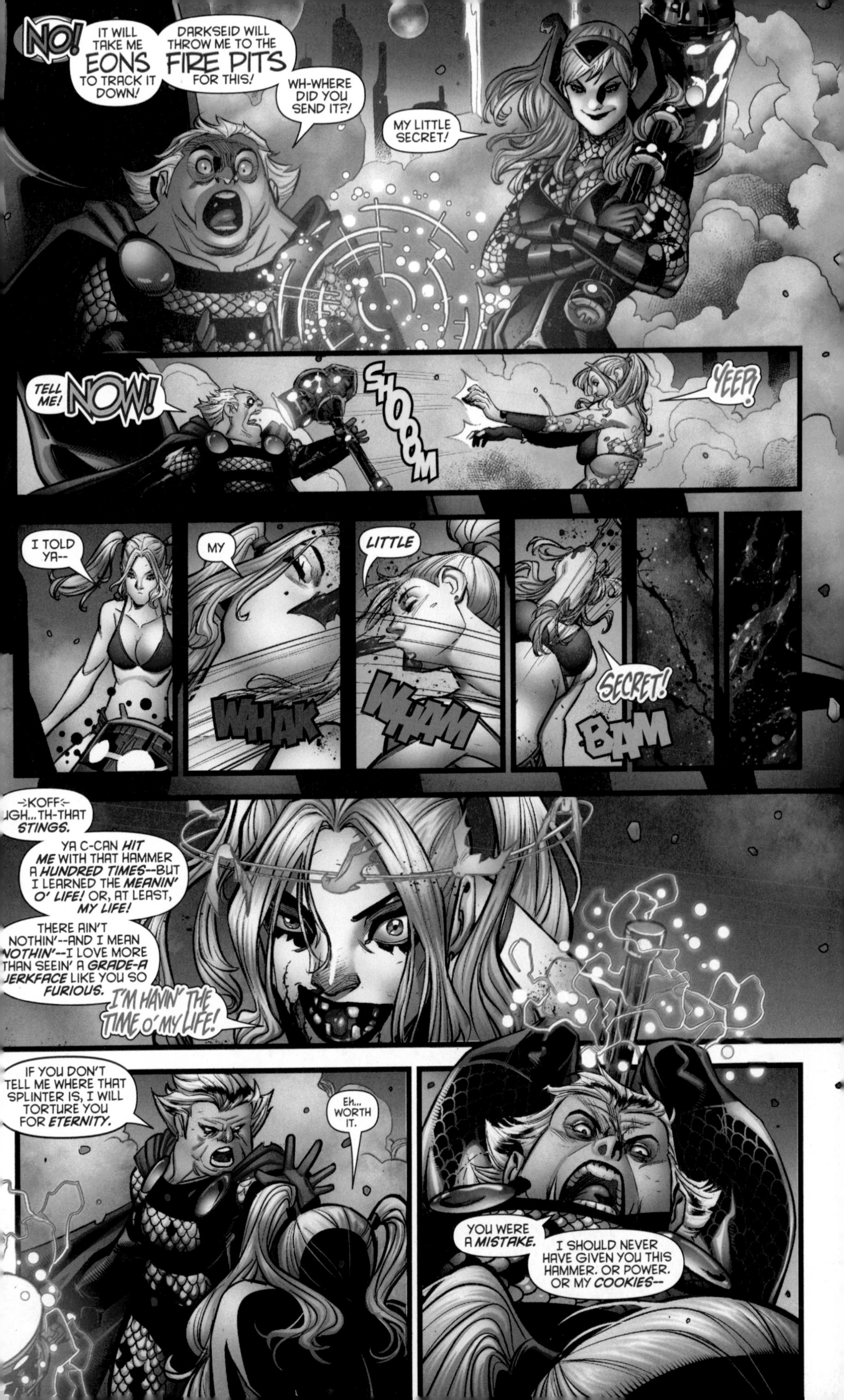
NO!
IT WILL TAKE ME EONS TO TRACK IT DOWN!
DARKSEID WILL THROW ME TO THE FIRE PITS FOR THIS!
WH-WHERE DID YOU SEND IT?!
MY LITTLE SECRET!
TELL ME! NOW!
SHOOOM
YEEP!
I TOLD YA--
MY
WHAK
LITTLE
WHAM
SECRET!
BAM
-KOFF- UGH...TH-THAT STINGS.
YA C-CAN HIT ME WITH THAT HAMMER A HUNDRED TIMES--BUT I LEARNED THE MEANIN' O' LIFE! OR, AT LEAST, MY LIFE!
THERE AIN'T NOTHIN'--AND I MEAN NOTHIN'--I LOVE MORE THAN SEEIN' A GRADE-A JERKFACE LIKE YOU SO FURIOUS.
I'M HAVIN' THE TIME O' MY LIFE!
IF YOU DON'T TELL ME WHERE THAT SPLINTER IS, I WILL TORTURE YOU FOR ETERNITY.
EH... WORTH IT.
YOU WERE A MISTAKE.
I SHOULD NEVER HAVE GIVEN YOU THIS HAMMER. OR POWER. OR MY COOKIES--

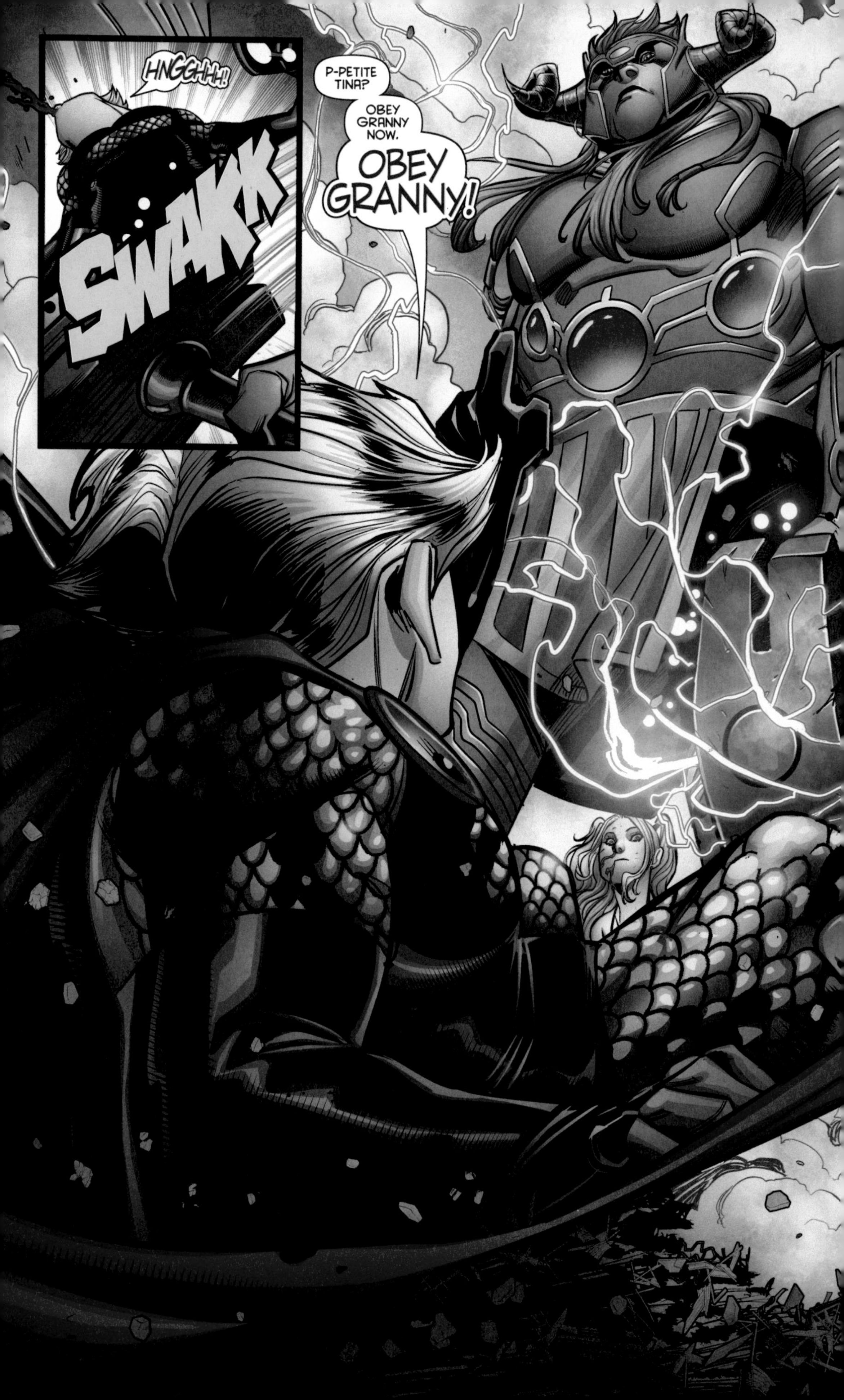
HNGGHHH!
SWAKK
P-PETITE TINA?
OBEY GRANNY NOW.
OBEY GRANNY!

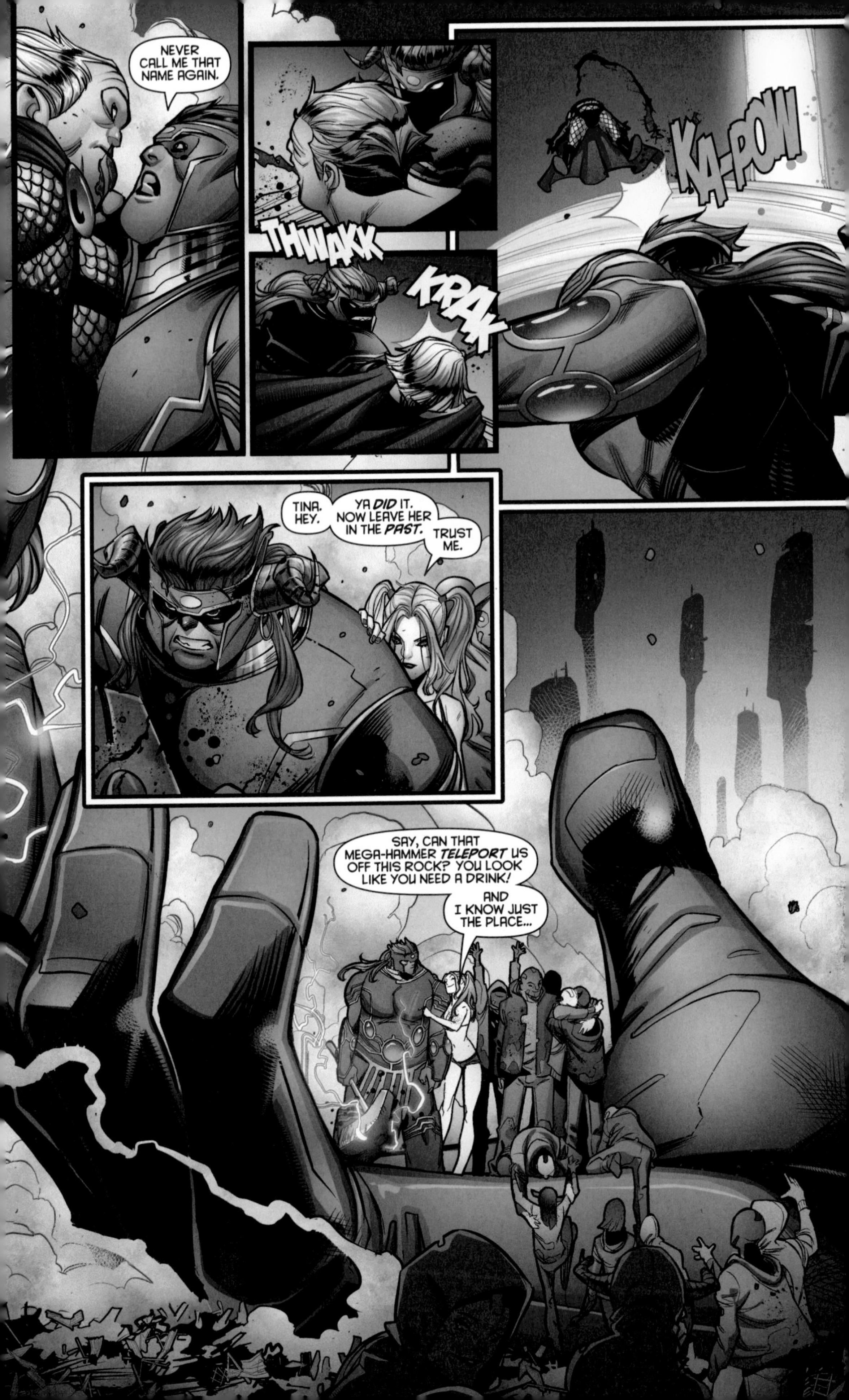
NEVER CALL ME THAT NAME AGAIN.
THWAKK
KRAK
KA-POW
TINA. HEY.
YA DID IT. NOW LEAVE HER IN THE PAST.
TRUST ME.
SAY, CAN THAT MEGA-HAMMER TELEPORT US OFF THIS ROCK? YOU LOOK LIKE YOU NEED A DRINK!
AND I KNOW JUST THE PLACE...

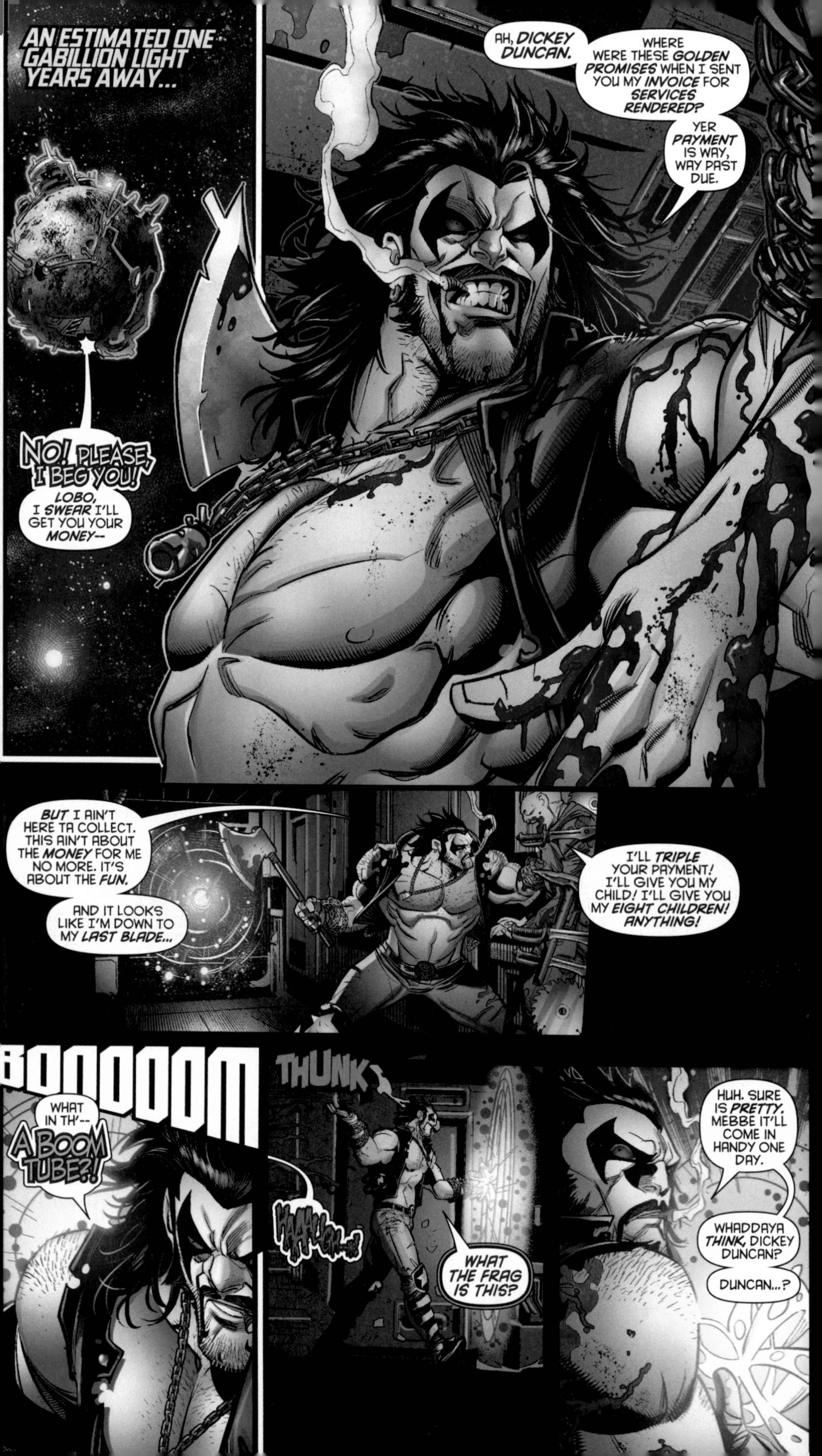
AN ESTIMATED ONE GABILLION LIGHT YEARS AWAY...
NO! PLEASE, I BEG YOU!
LOBO, I SWEAR I'LL GET YOU YOUR MONEY--
AH, DICKEY DUNCAN.
WHERE WERE THESE GOLDEN PROMISES WHEN I SENT YOU MY INVOICE FOR SERVICES RENDERED?
YER PAYMENT IS WAY, WAY PAST DUE.
BUT I AIN'T HERE TA COLLECT. THIS AIN'T ABOUT THE MONEY FOR ME NO MORE. IT'S ABOUT THE FUN.
AND IT LOOKS LIKE I'M DOWN TO MY LAST BLADE...
I'LL TRIPLE YOUR PAYMENT! I'LL GIVE YOU MY CHILD! I'LL GIVE YOU MY EIGHT CHILDREN! ANYTHING!
BOOOOOM
WHAT IN TH'--
A BOOM TUBE?!
THUNK
WHAT THE FRAG IS THIS?
HUH. SURE IS PRETTY. MEBBE IT'LL COME IN HANDY ONE DAY.
WHADDAYA THINK, DICKEY DUNCAN?
DUNCAN...?

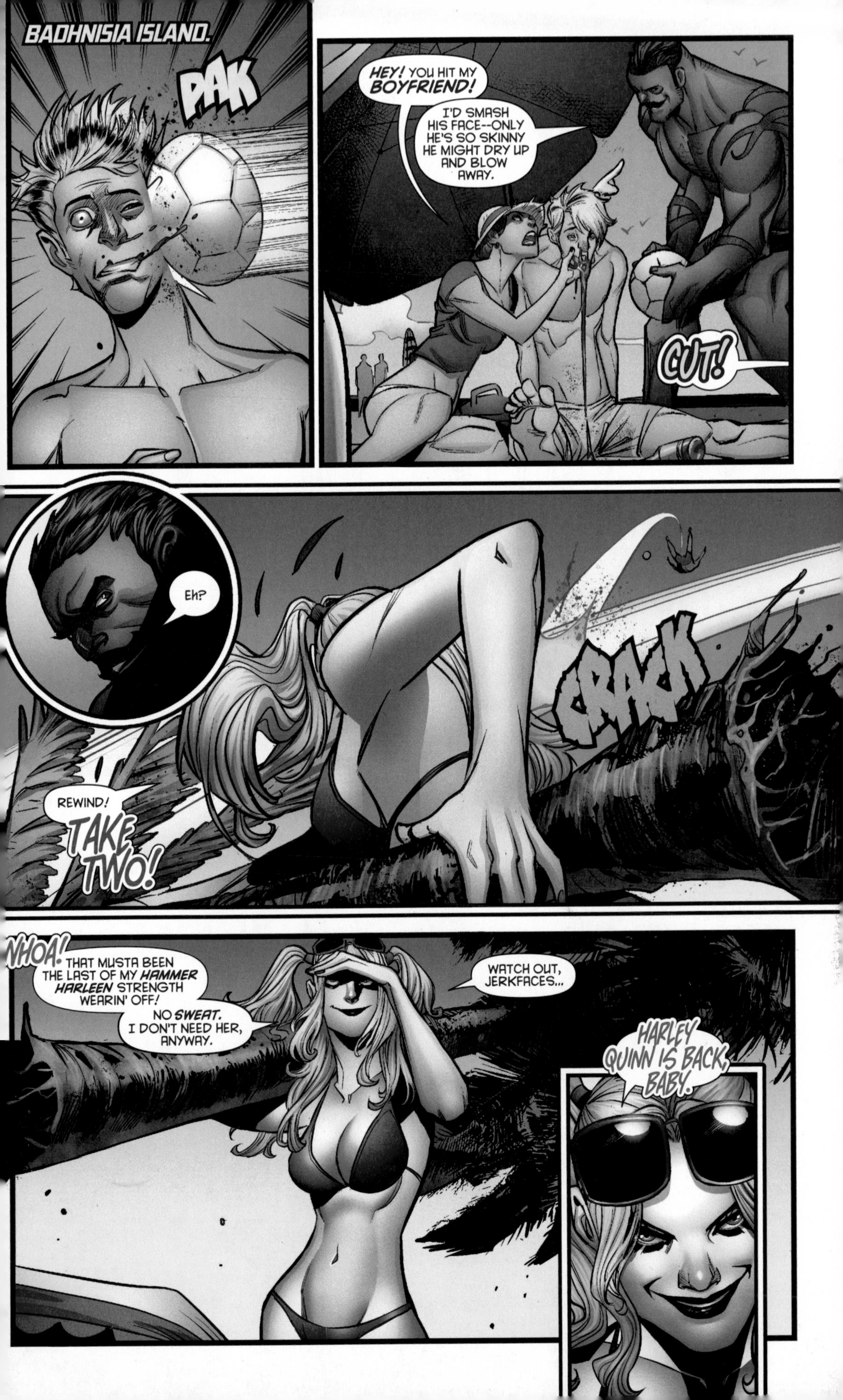
BADHNISIA ISLAND.
PAK
HEY! YOU HIT MY BOYFRIEND!
I'D SMASH HIS FACE--ONLY HE'S SO SKINNY HE MIGHT DRY UP AND BLOW AWAY.
CUT!
Eh?
REWIND! TAKE TWO!
CRACK
WHOA! THAT MUSTA BEEN THE LAST OF MY HAMMER HARLEEN STRENGTH WEARIN' OFF!
NO SWEAT. I DON'T NEED HER, ANYWAY.
WATCH OUT, JERKFACES...
HARLEY QUINN IS BACK, BABY.

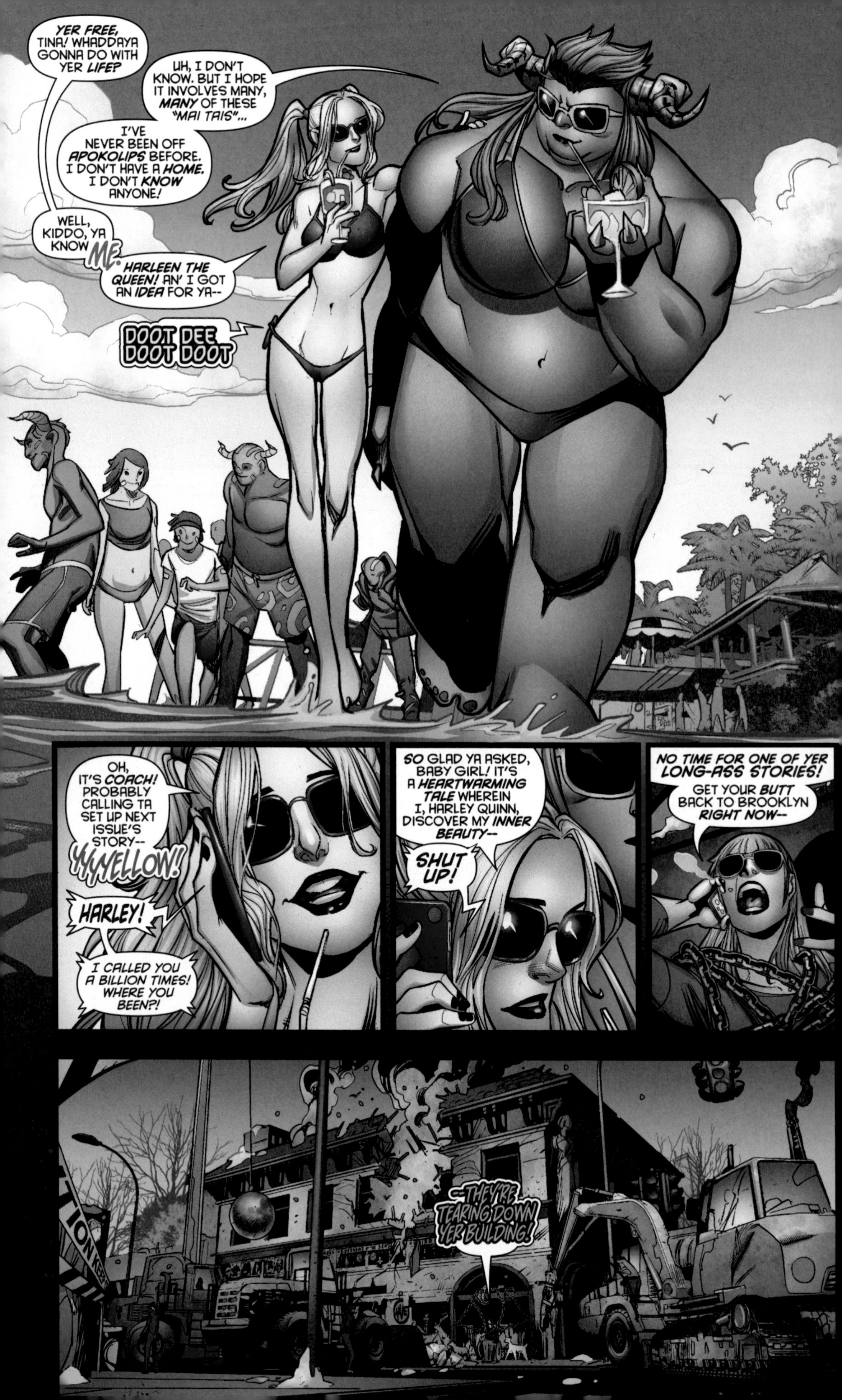
YER FREE, TINA! WHADDAYA GONNA DO WITH YER LIFE?
UH, I DON'T KNOW. BUT I HOPE IT INVOLVES MANY, MANY OF THESE "MAI TAIS"...
I'VE NEVER BEEN OFF APOKOLIPS BEFORE. I DON'T HAVE A HOME. I DON'T KNOW ANYONE!
WELL, KIDDO, YA KNOW ME. HARLEEN THE QUEEN! AN' I GOT AN IDEA FOR YA--
DOOT DEE DOOT DOOT
OH, IT'S COACH! PROBABLY CALLING TA SET UP NEXT ISSUE'S STORY--
YYYYELLOW!
HARLEY!
I CALLED YOU A BILLION TIMES! WHERE YOU BEEN?!
SO GLAD YA ASKED, BABY GIRL! IT'S A HEARTWARMING TALE WHEREIN I, HARLEY QUINN, DISCOVER MY INNER BEAUTY--
SHUT UP!
NO TIME FOR ONE OF YER LONG-ASS STORIES!
GET YOUR BUTT BACK TO BROOKLYN RIGHT NOW--
--THEY'RE TEARING DOWN YER BUILDING!

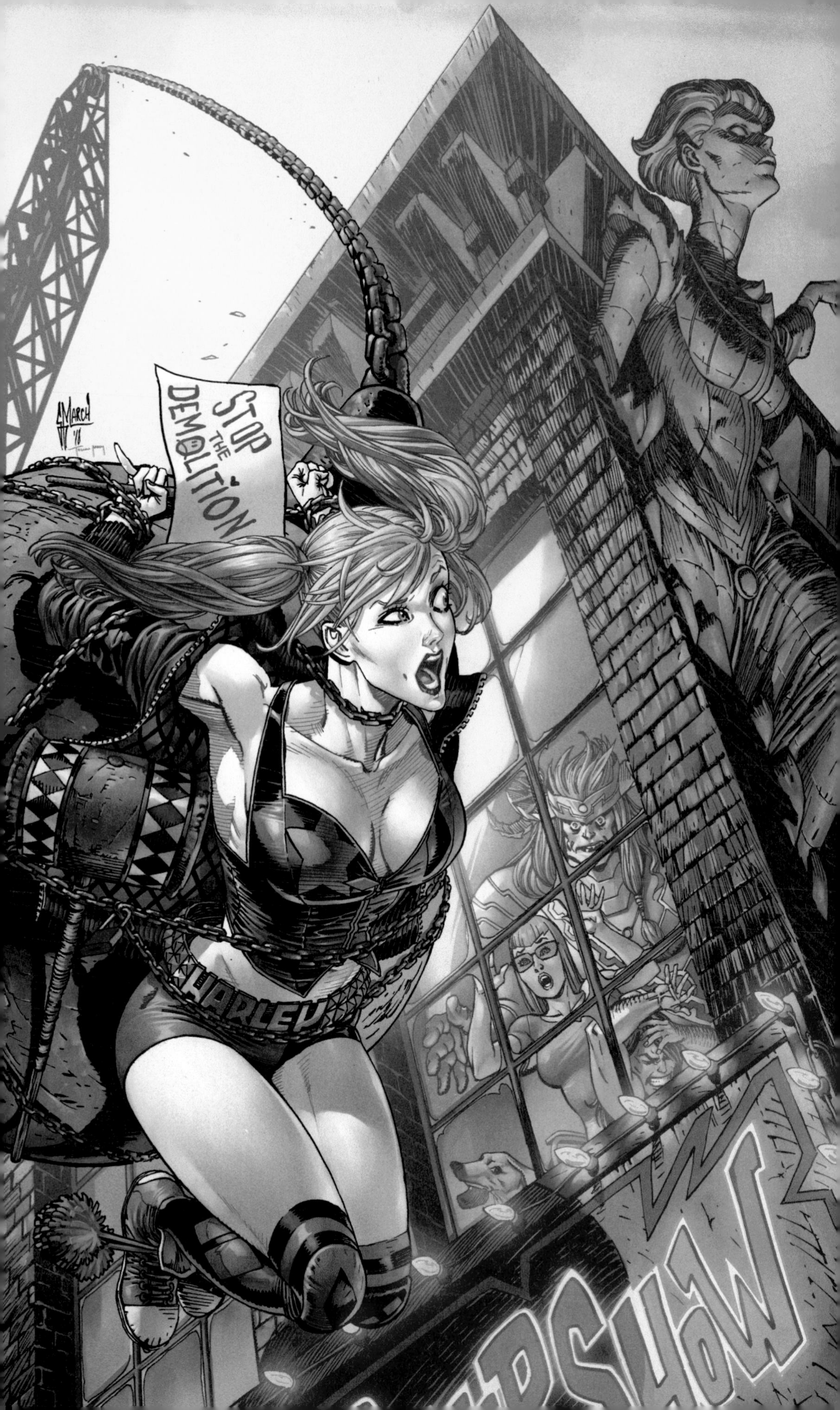
STOP THE DEMOLITION
HARLEY

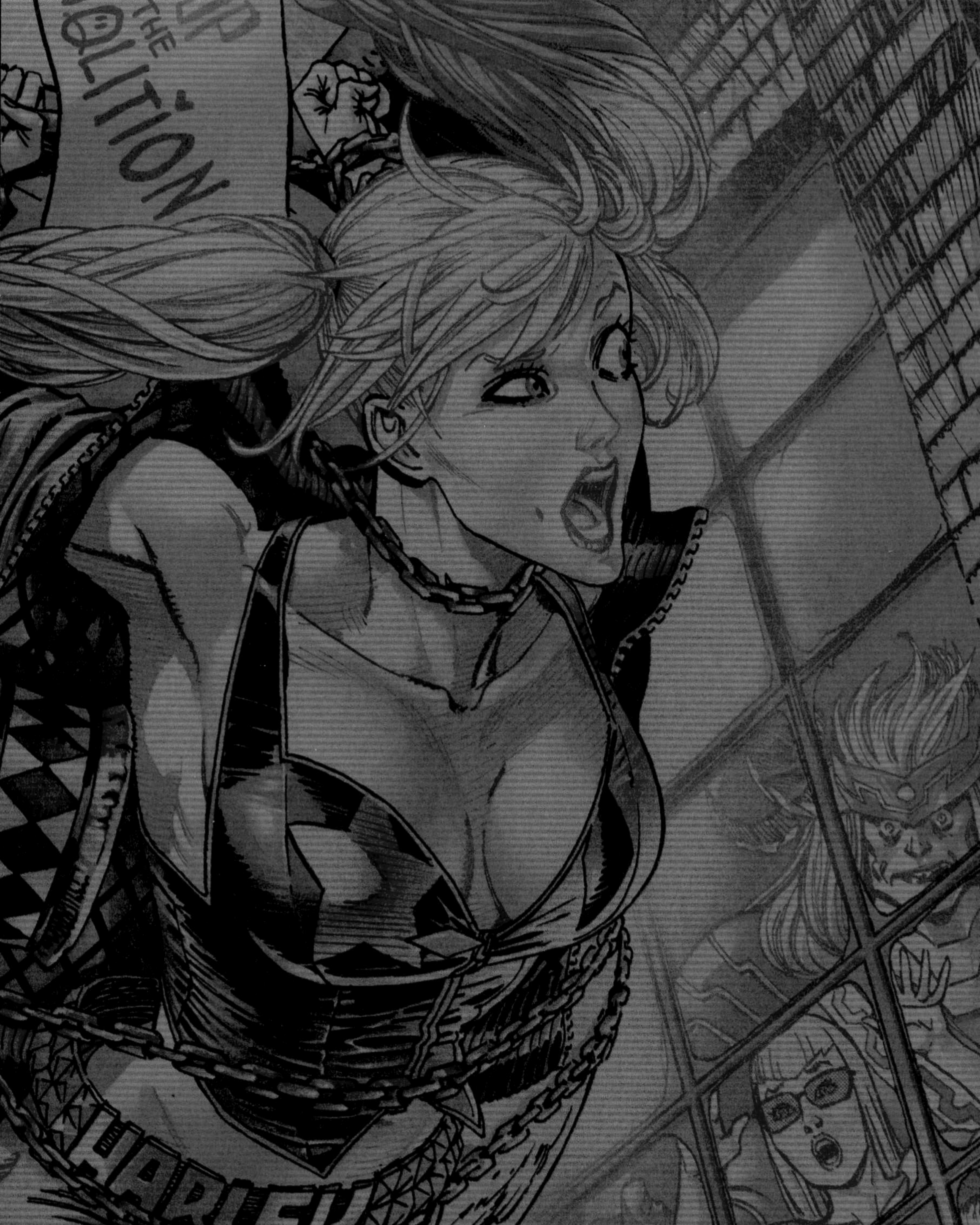

HARLEY QUINN
#48

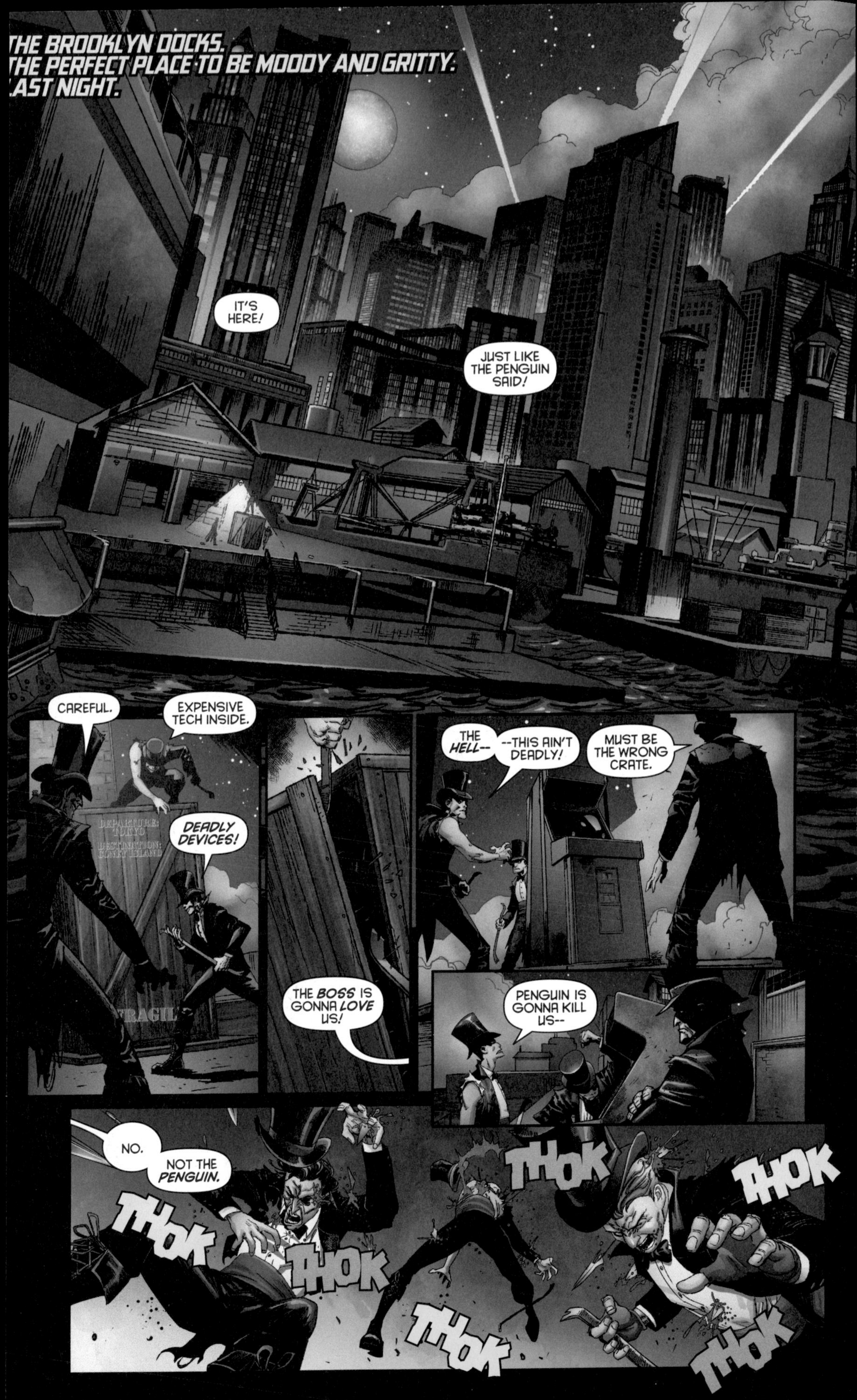

THE BROOKLYN DOCKS.
THE PERFECT PLACE TO BE MOODY AND GRITTY.
LAST NIGHT.
IT'S HERE!
JUST LIKE THE PENGUIN SAID!
CAREFUL.
EXPENSIVE TECH INSIDE.
DEPARTURE: TOKYO
DESTINATION: CONEY ISLAND
DEADLY DEVICES!
FRAGIL
THE BOSS IS GONNA LOVE US!
THE HELL--
--THIS AIN'T DEADLY!
MUST BE THE WRONG CRATE.
PENGUIN IS GONNA KILL US--
NO.
NOT THE PENGUIN.
THOK
THOK
THOK
THOK
THOK
THOK

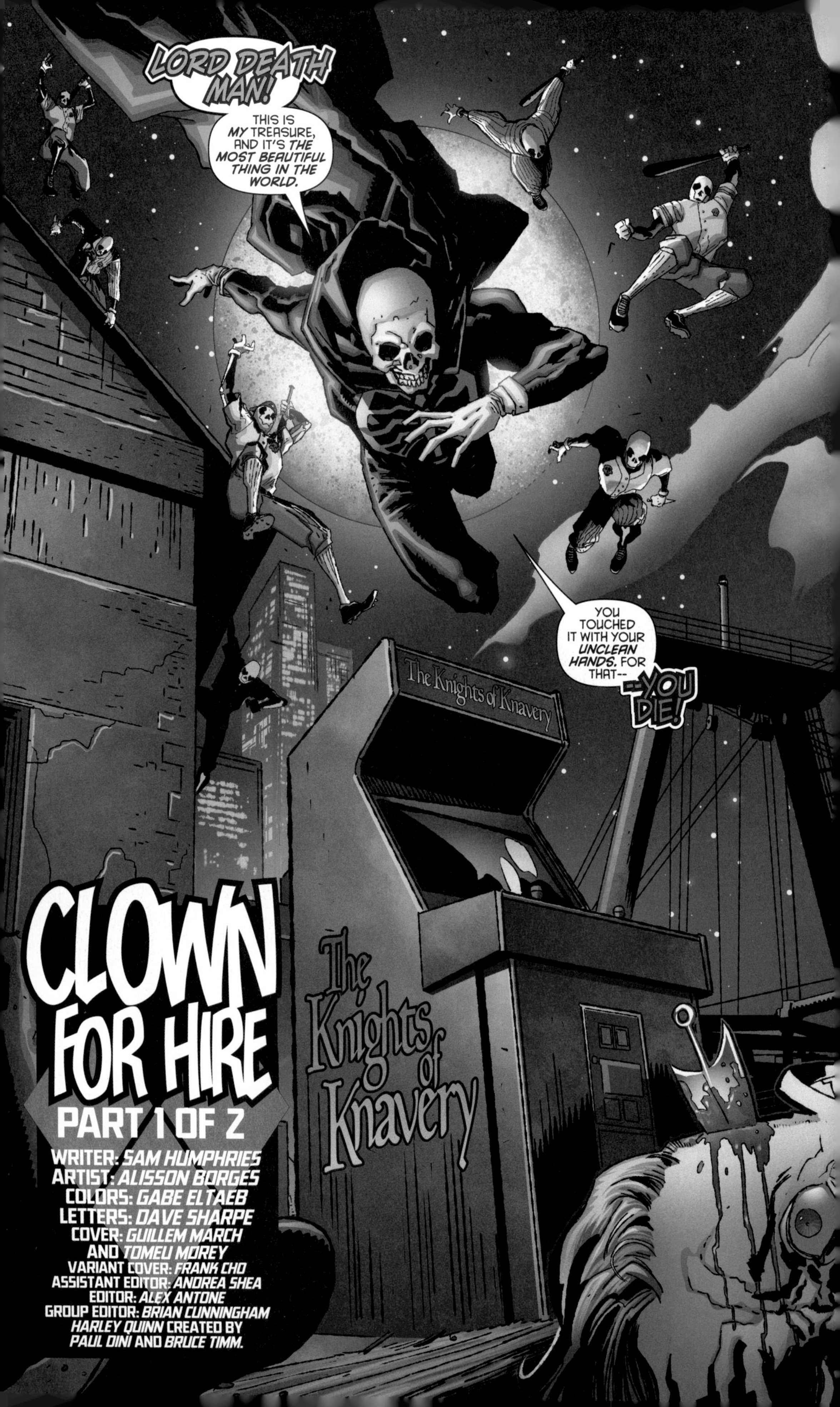
LORD DEATH MAN!
THIS IS MY TREASURE, AND IT'S THE MOST BEAUTIFUL THING IN THE WORLD.
YOU TOUCHED IT WITH YOUR UNCLEAN HANDS. FOR THAT--
--YOU DIE!
The Knights of Knavery
The Knights of Knavery
CLOWN FOR HIRE
PART 1 OF 2
WRITER: SAM HUMPHRIES
ARTIST: ALISSON BORGES
COLORS: GABE ELTAEB
LETTERS: DAVE SHARPE
COVER: GUILLEM MARCH AND TOMEU MOREY
VARIANT COVER: FRANK CHO
ASSISTANT EDITOR: ANDREA SHEA
EDITOR: ALEX ANTONE
GROUP EDITOR: BRIAN CUNNINGHAM
HARLEY QUINN CREATED BY PAUL DINI AND BRUCE TIMM.

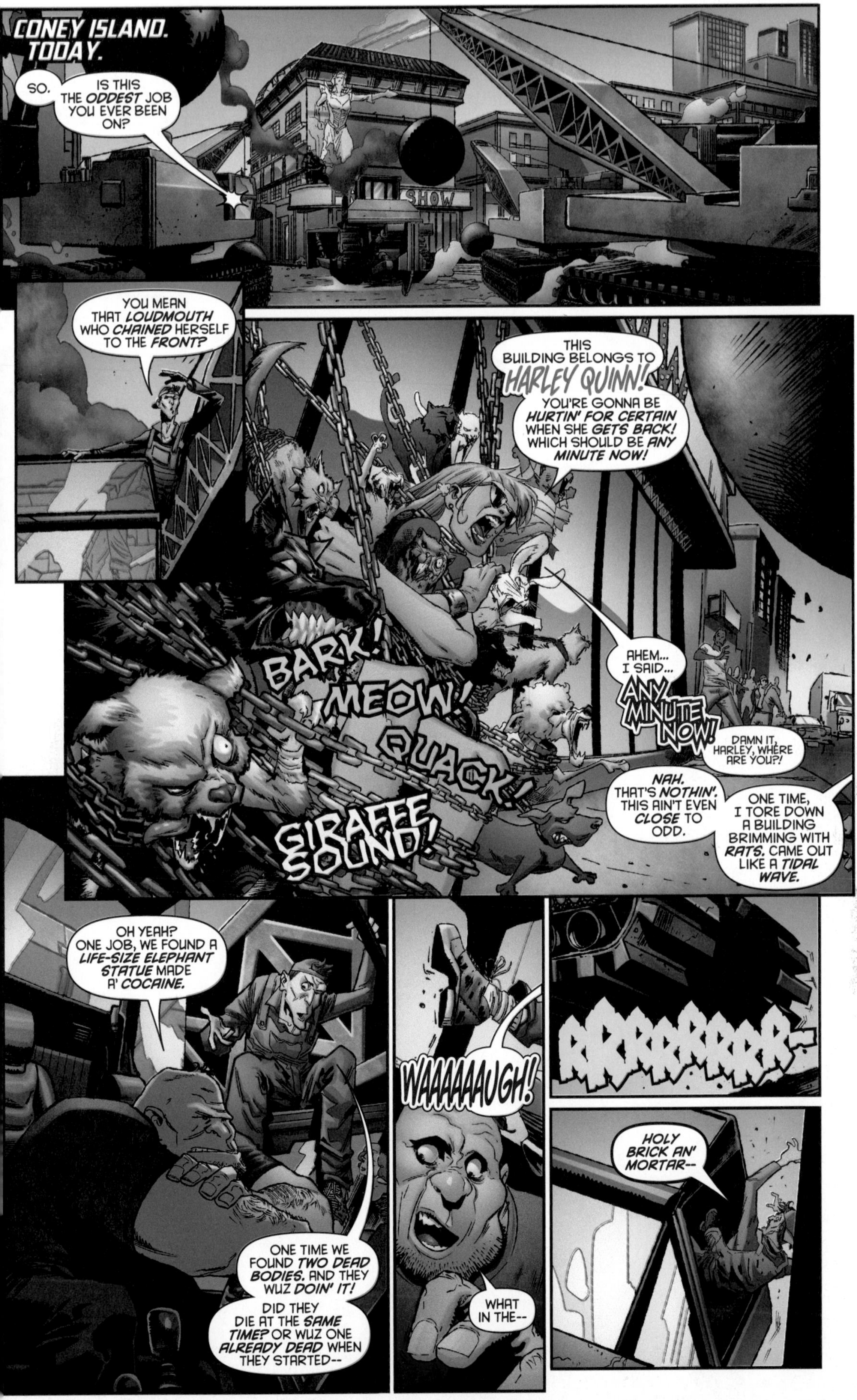
CONEY ISLAND. TODAY.
SO.
IS THIS THE ODDEST JOB YOU EVER BEEN ON?
SHOW
YOU MEAN THAT LOUDMOUTH WHO CHAINED HERSELF TO THE FRONT?
THIS BUILDING BELONGS TO HARLEY QUINN!
YOU'RE GONNA BE HURTIN' FOR CERTAIN WHEN SHE GETS BACK! WHICH SHOULD BE ANY MINUTE NOW!
BARK! MEOW! QUACK! GIRAFFE SOUND!
AHEM... I SAID... ANY MINUTE NOW!
DAMN IT, HARLEY, WHERE ARE YOU?!
NAH. THAT'S NOTHIN'. THIS AIN'T EVEN CLOSE TO ODD.
ONE TIME, I TORE DOWN A BUILDING BRIMMING WITH RATS. CAME OUT LIKE A TIDAL WAVE.
OH YEAH? ONE JOB, WE FOUND A LIFE-SIZE ELEPHANT STATUE MADE A' COCAINE.
ONE TIME WE FOUND TWO DEAD BODIES. AND THEY WUZ DOIN' IT!
DID THEY DIE AT THE SAME TIME? OR WUZ ONE ALREADY DEAD WHEN THEY STARTED--
WAAAAAAUGH!
WHAT IN THE--
RRRRRRRRR-
HOLY BRICK AN' MORTAR--

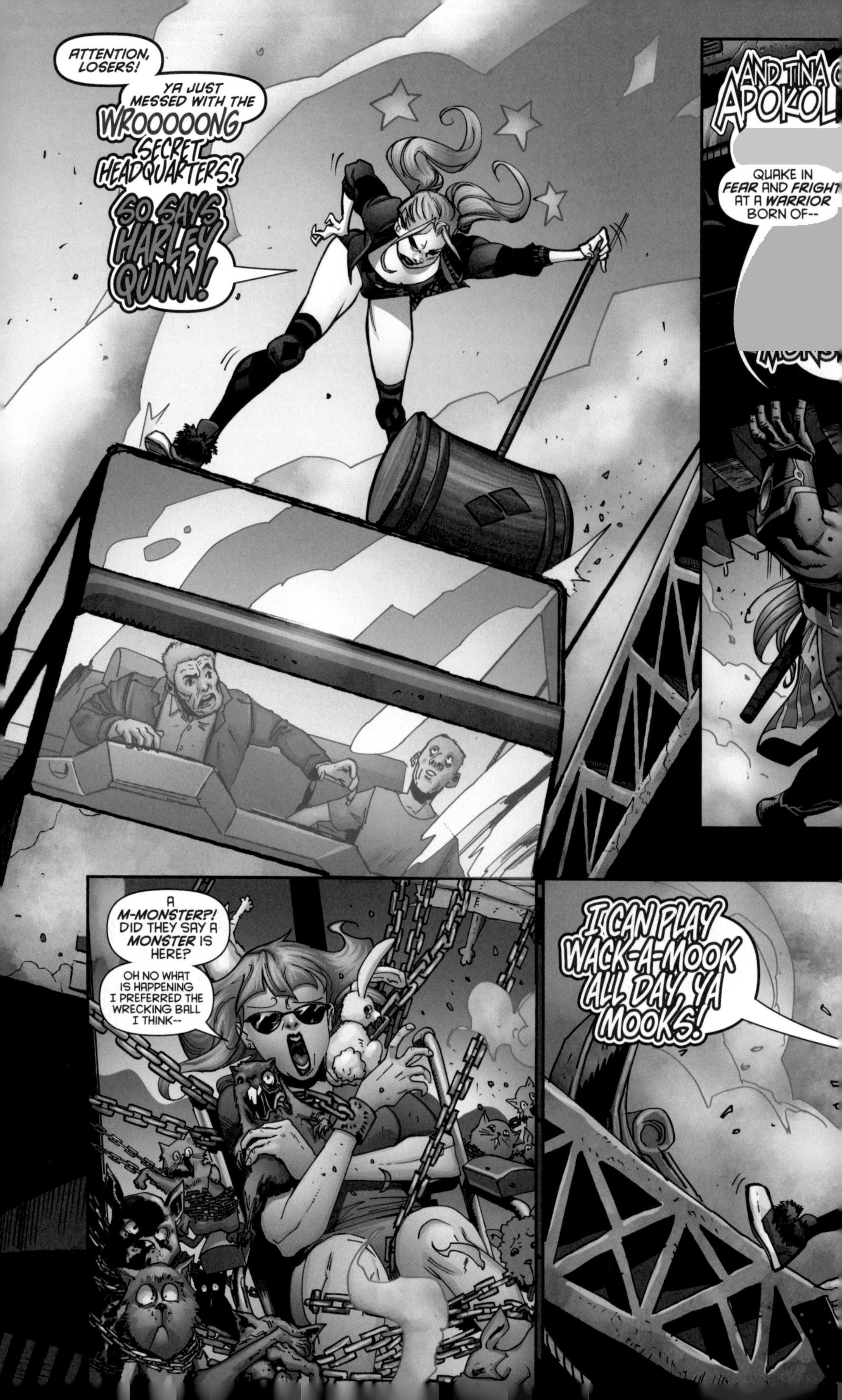
ATTENTION, LOSERS!
YA JUST MESSED WITH THE WROOOOONG SECRET HEADQUARTERS!
SO SAYS HARLEY QUINN!
AND TINA
APOKOL
QUAKE IN FEAR AND FRIGHT AT A WARRIOR BORN OF--
A M-MONSTER?! DID THEY SAY A MONSTER IS HERE?
OH NO WHAT IS HAPPENING I PREFERRED THE WRECKING BALL I THINK--
I CAN PLAY WACK-A-MOOK ALL DAY, YA MOOKS!

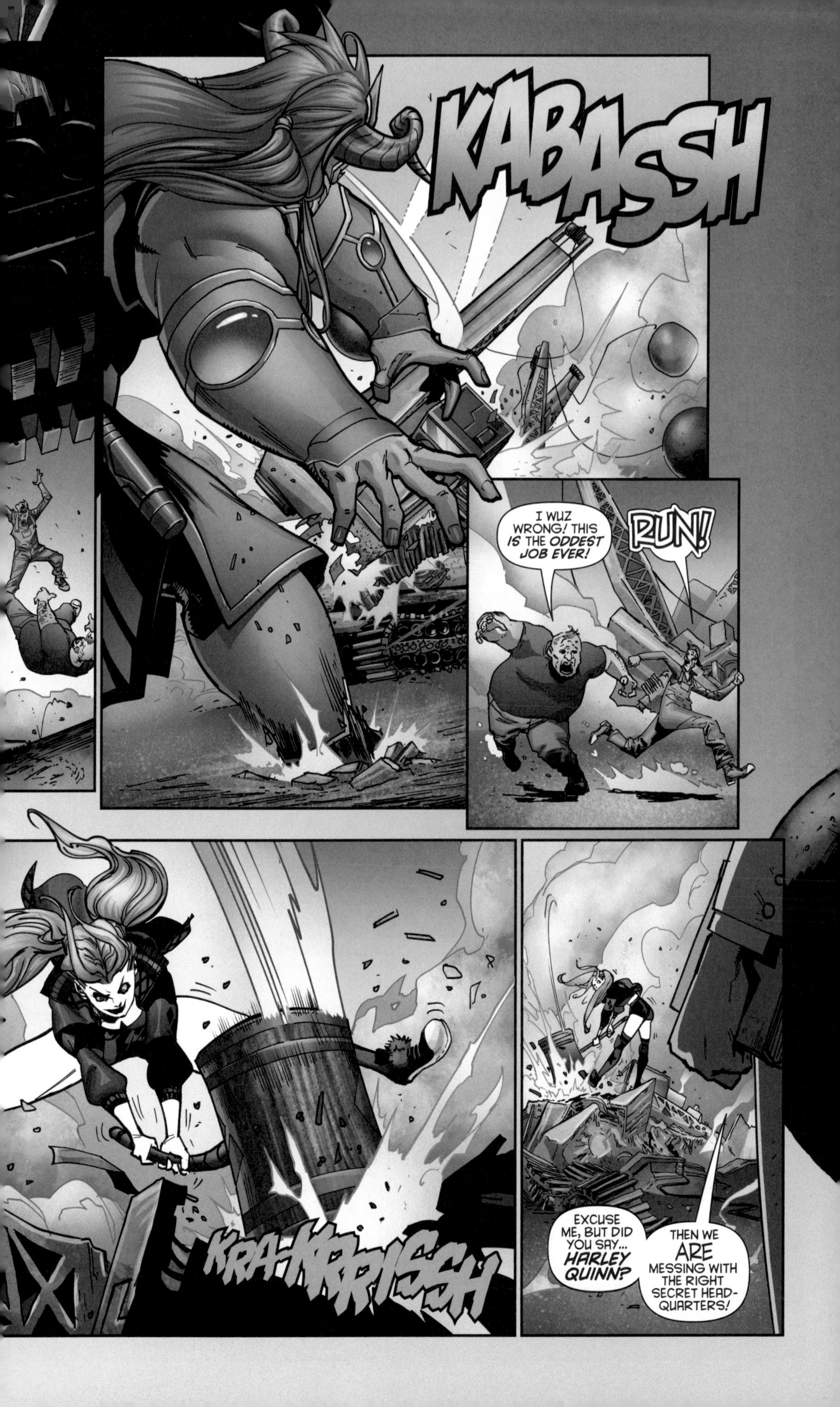
KABASSH
I WUZ WRONG! THIS *IS* THE *ODDEST JOB EVER!*
RUN!
KRA-KRRISSH
EXCUSE ME, BUT DID YOU SAY... *HARLEY QUINN?*
THEN WE ARE MESSING WITH THE RIGHT SECRET HEAD-QUARTERS!

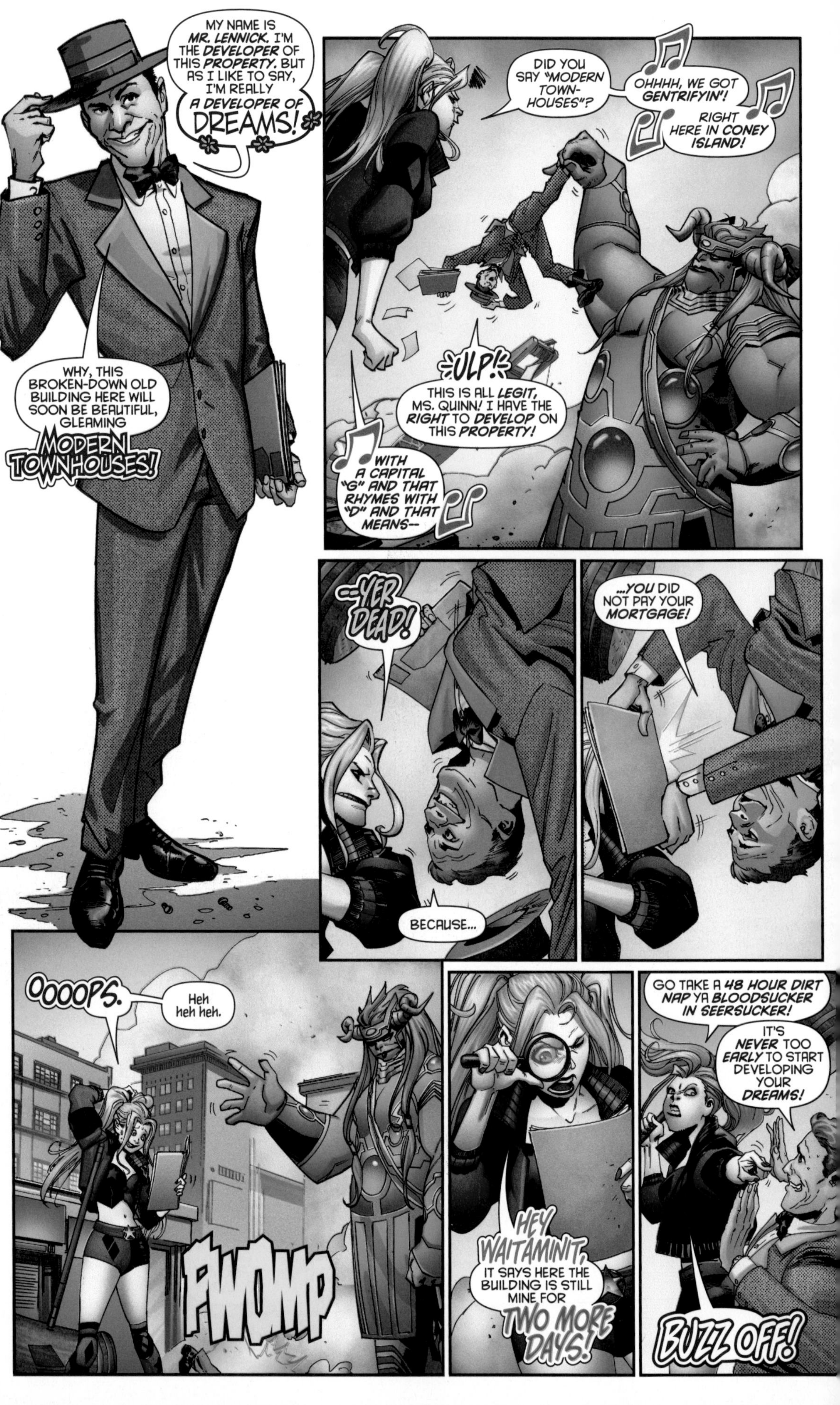

MY NAME IS MR. LENNICK. I'M THE DEVELOPER OF THIS PROPERTY. BUT AS I LIKE TO SAY, I'M REALLY A DEVELOPER OF DREAMS!
WHY, THIS BROKEN-DOWN OLD BUILDING HERE WILL SOON BE BEAUTIFUL, GLEAMING MODERN TOWNHOUSES!
DID YOU SAY "MODERN TOWN-HOUSES"?
OHHHH, WE GOT GENTRIFYIN'!
RIGHT HERE IN CONEY ISLAND!
ULP!
THIS IS ALL LEGIT, MS. QUINN! I HAVE THE RIGHT TO DEVELOP ON THIS PROPERTY!
WITH A CAPITAL "G" AND THAT RHYMES WITH "D" AND THAT MEANS--
--YER DEAD!
BECAUSE...
...YOU DID NOT PAY YOUR MORTGAGE!
OOOOPS.
Heh heh heh.
PWOMP
HEY WAITAMINIT, IT SAYS HERE THE BUILDING IS STILL MINE FOR TWO MORE DAYS!
GO TAKE A 48 HOUR DIRT NAP YA BLOODSUCKER IN SEERSUCKER!
IT'S NEVER TOO EARLY TO START DEVELOPING YOUR DREAMS!
BUZZ OFF!

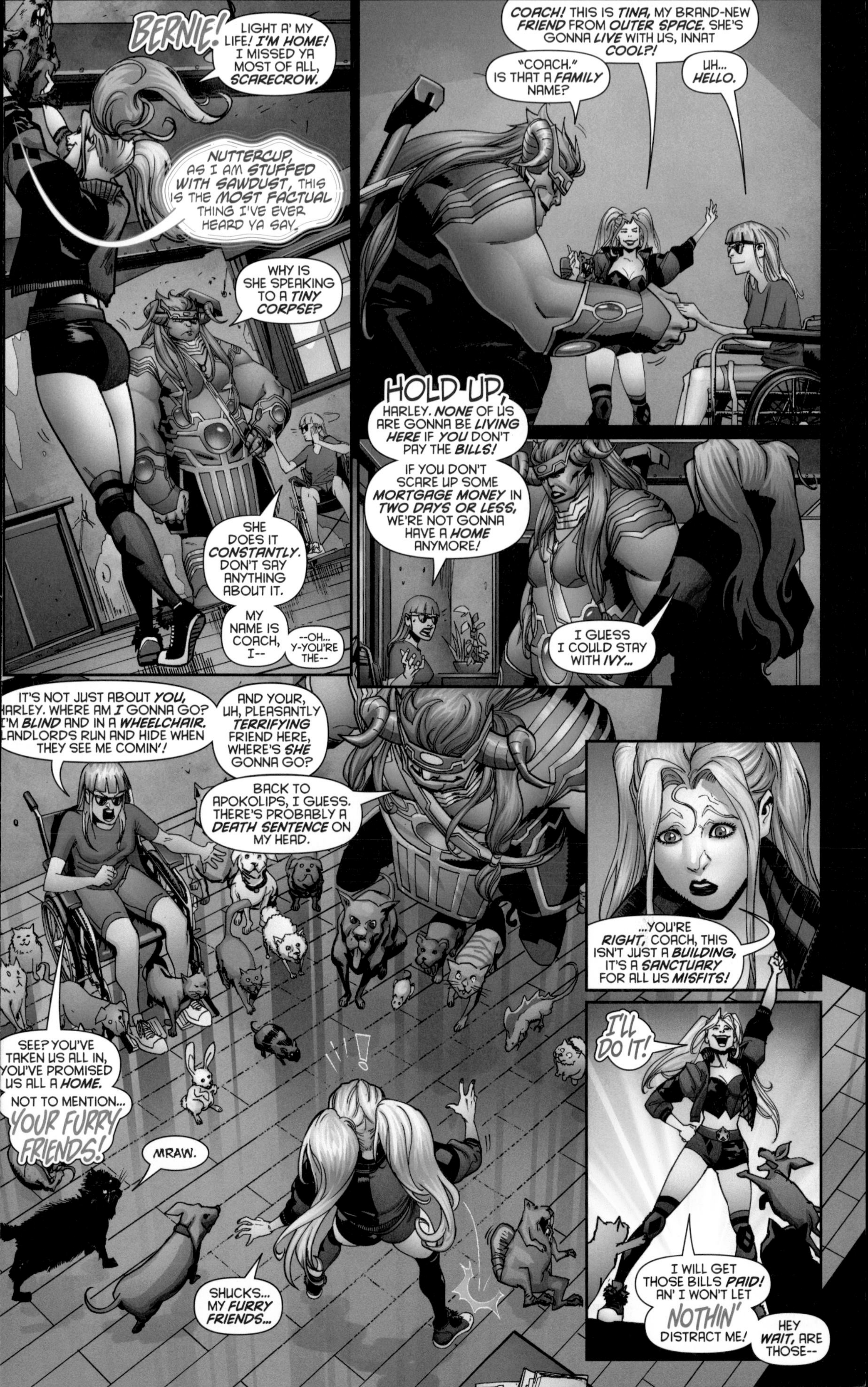
BERNIE!
LIGHT A' MY LIFE! I'M HOME! I MISSED YA MOST OF ALL, SCARECROW.
NUTTERCUP, AS I AM STUFFED WITH SAWDUST, THIS IS THE MOST FACTUAL THING I'VE EVER HEARD YA SAY.
WHY IS SHE SPEAKING TO A TINY CORPSE?
SHE DOES IT CONSTANTLY. DON'T SAY ANYTHING ABOUT IT.
MY NAME IS COACH, I--
--OH... Y-YOU'RE THE--
COACH! THIS IS TINA, MY BRAND-NEW FRIEND FROM OUTER SPACE. SHE'S GONNA LIVE WITH US, INNAT COOL?!
"COACH." IS THAT A FAMILY NAME?
UH... HELLO.
HOLD UP, HARLEY. NONE OF US ARE GONNA BE LIVING HERE IF YOU DON'T PAY THE BILLS!
IF YOU DON'T SCARE UP SOME MORTGAGE MONEY IN TWO DAYS OR LESS, WE'RE NOT GONNA HAVE A HOME ANYMORE!
I GUESS I COULD STAY WITH IVY...
IT'S NOT JUST ABOUT YOU, HARLEY. WHERE AM I GONNA GO? I'M BLIND AND IN A WHEELCHAIR. LANDLORDS RUN AND HIDE WHEN THEY SEE ME COMIN'!
AND YOUR, UH, PLEASANTLY TERRIFYING FRIEND HERE, WHERE'S SHE GONNA GO?
BACK TO APOKOLIPS, I GUESS. THERE'S PROBABLY A DEATH SENTENCE ON MY HEAD.
SEE? YOU'VE TAKEN US ALL IN, YOU'VE PROMISED US ALL A HOME.
NOT TO MENTION... YOUR FURRY FRIENDS!
MRAW.
SHUCKS... MY FURRY FRIENDS...
...YOU'RE RIGHT, COACH, THIS ISN'T JUST A BUILDING, IT'S A SANCTUARY FOR ALL US MISFITS!
I'LL DO IT!
I WILL GET THOSE BILLS PAID! AN' I WON'T LET NOTHIN' DISTRACT ME!
HEY WAIT, ARE THOSE--

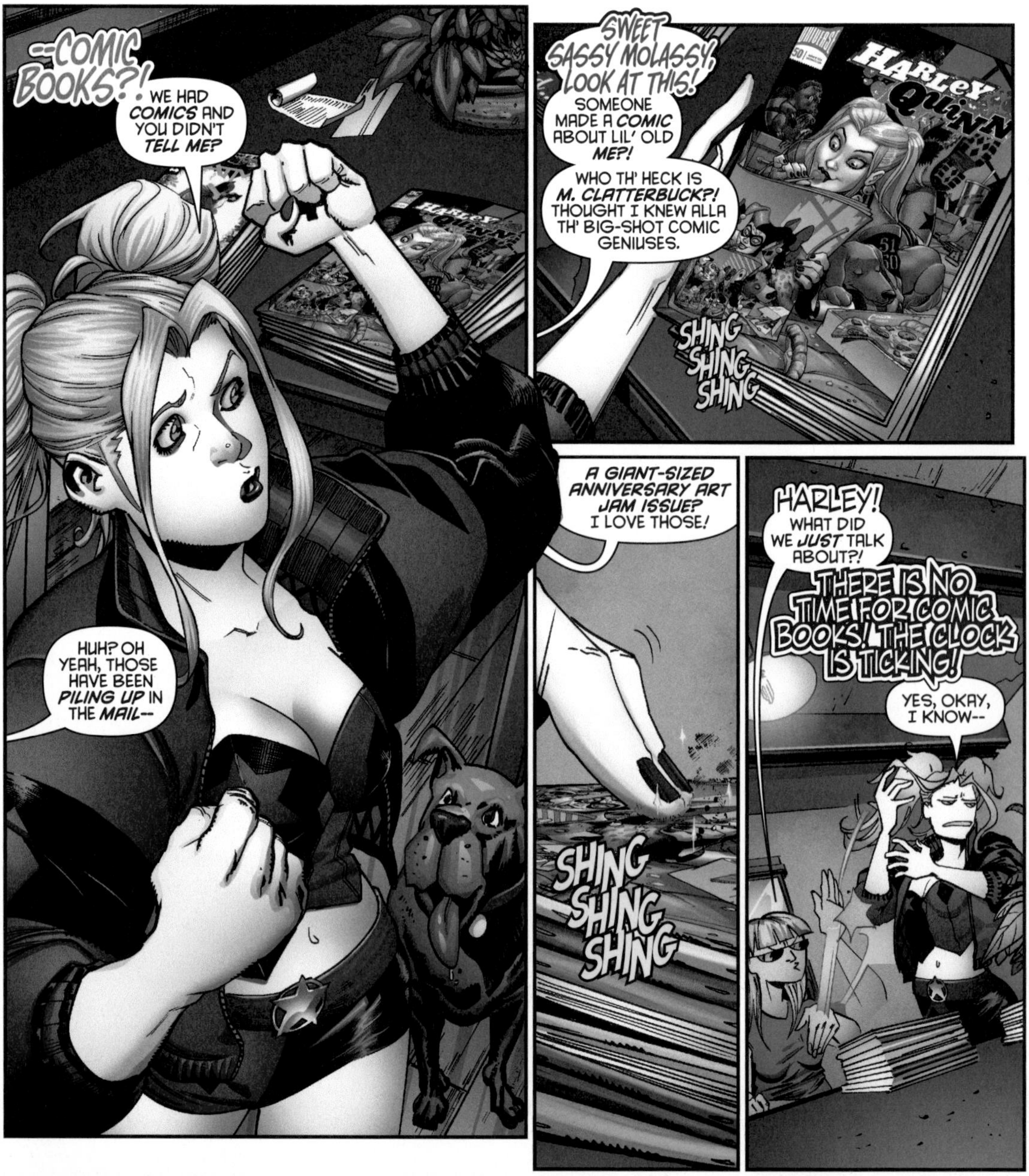
--COMIC BOOKS?!
WE HAD COMICS AND YOU DIDN'T TELL ME?
HUH? OH YEAH, THOSE HAVE BEEN PILING UP IN THE MAIL--
SWEET SASSY MOLASSY! LOOK AT THIS!
SOMEONE MADE A COMIC ABOUT LIL' OLD ME?!
WHO TH' HECK IS M. CLATTERBUCK?! THOUGHT I KNEW ALLA TH' BIG-SHOT COMIC GENIUSES.
HARLEY QUINN
SHING SHING SHING
A GIANT-SIZED ANNIVERSARY ART JAM ISSUE? I LOVE THOSE!
SHING SHING SHING
HARLEY! WHAT DID WE JUST TALK ABOUT?!
THERE IS NO TIME FOR COMIC BOOKS! THE CLOCK IS TICKING!
YES, OKAY, I KNOW--

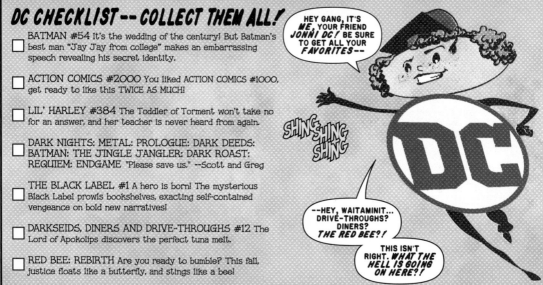

DC CHECKLIST -- COLLECT THEM ALL!

- ☐ BATMAN #54 It's the wedding of the century! But Batman's best man "Jay Jay from college" makes an embarrassing speech revealing his secret identity.
- ☐ ACTION COMICS #2000 You liked ACTION COMICS #1000, get ready to like this TWICE AS MUCH!
- ☐ LIL' HARLEY #384 The Toddler of Torment won't take no for an answer, and her teacher is never heard from again.
- ☐ DARK NIGHTS: METAL: PROLOGUE: DARK DEEDS: BATMAN: THE JINGLE JANGLER: DARK ROAST: REQUIEM: ENDGAME "Please save us." --Scott and Greg
- ☐ THE BLACK LABEL #1 A hero is born! The mysterious Black Label prowls bookshelves, exacting self-contained vengeance on bold new narratives!
- ☐ DARKSEIDS, DINERS AND DRIVE-THROUGHS #12 The Lord of Apokolips discovers the perfect tuna melt.
- ☐ RED BEE: REBIRTH Are you ready to bumble? This fall, justice floats like a butterfly, and stings like a bee!

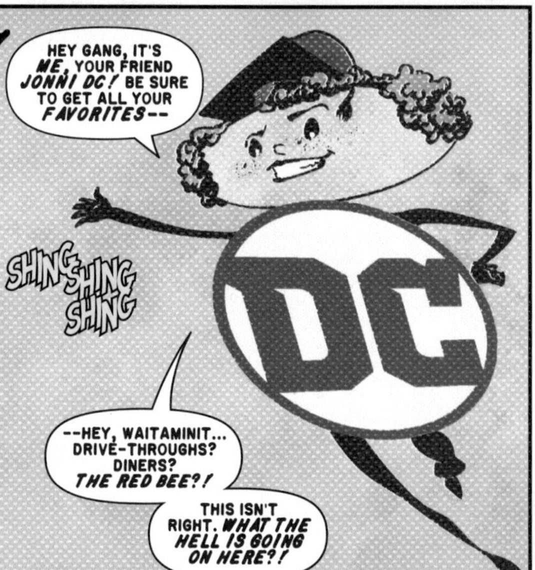
HEY GANG, IT'S ME, YOUR FRIEND JONNI DC! BE SURE TO GET ALL YOUR FAVORITES--
SHING SHING SHING
DC
--HEY, WAITAMINIT... DRIVE-THROUGHS? DINERS? THE RED BEE?!
THIS ISN'T RIGHT. WHAT THE HELL IS GOING ON HERE?!

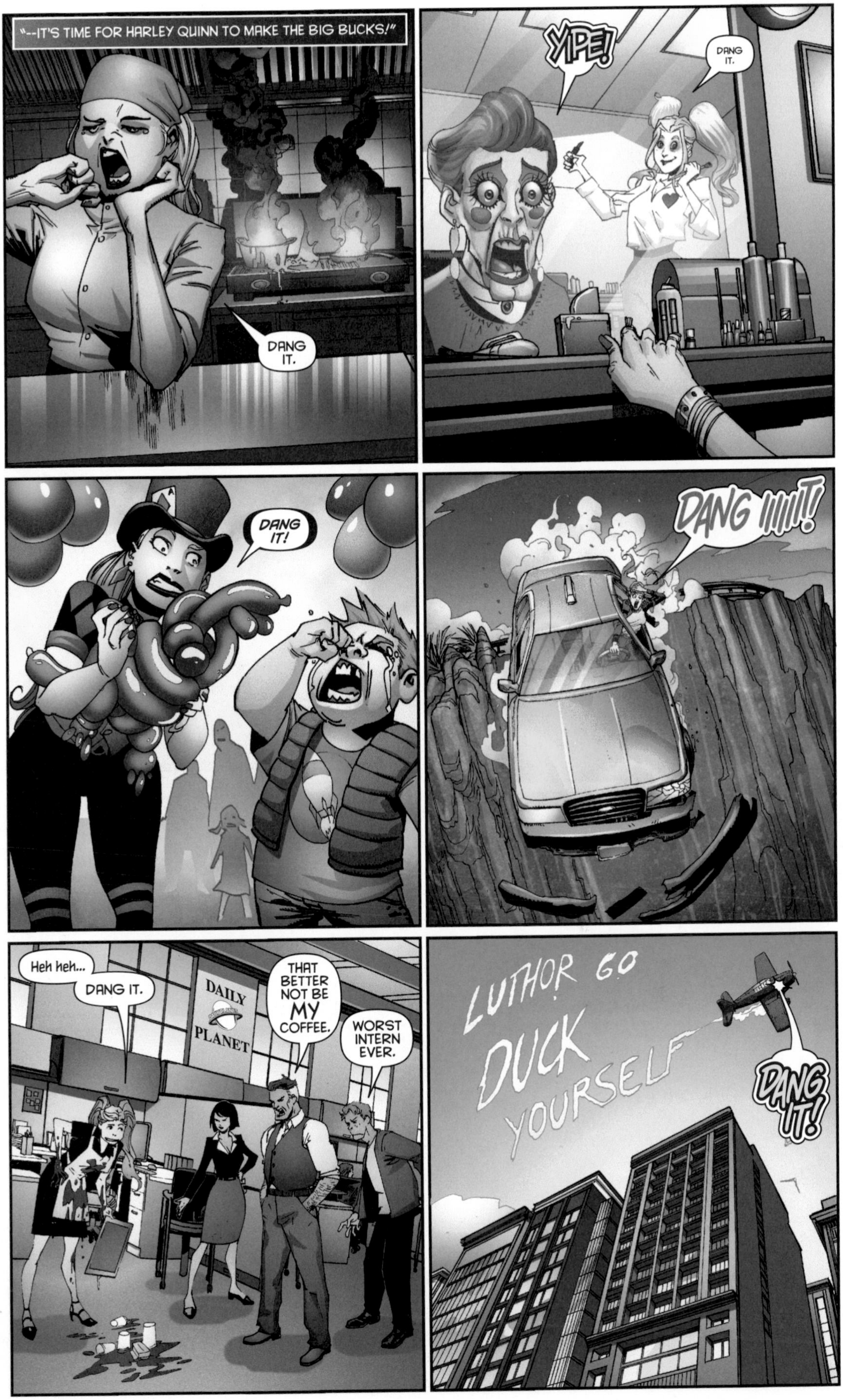
"--IT'S TIME FOR HARLEY QUINN TO MAKE THE BIG BUCKS!"
DANG IT.
YIPE!
DANG IT.
DANG IT!
DANG IIIIIIT!
Heh heh...
DANG IT.
DAILY PLANET
THAT BETTER NOT BE MY COFFEE.
WORST INTERN EVER.
LUTHOR GO DUCK YOURSELF
DANG IT!

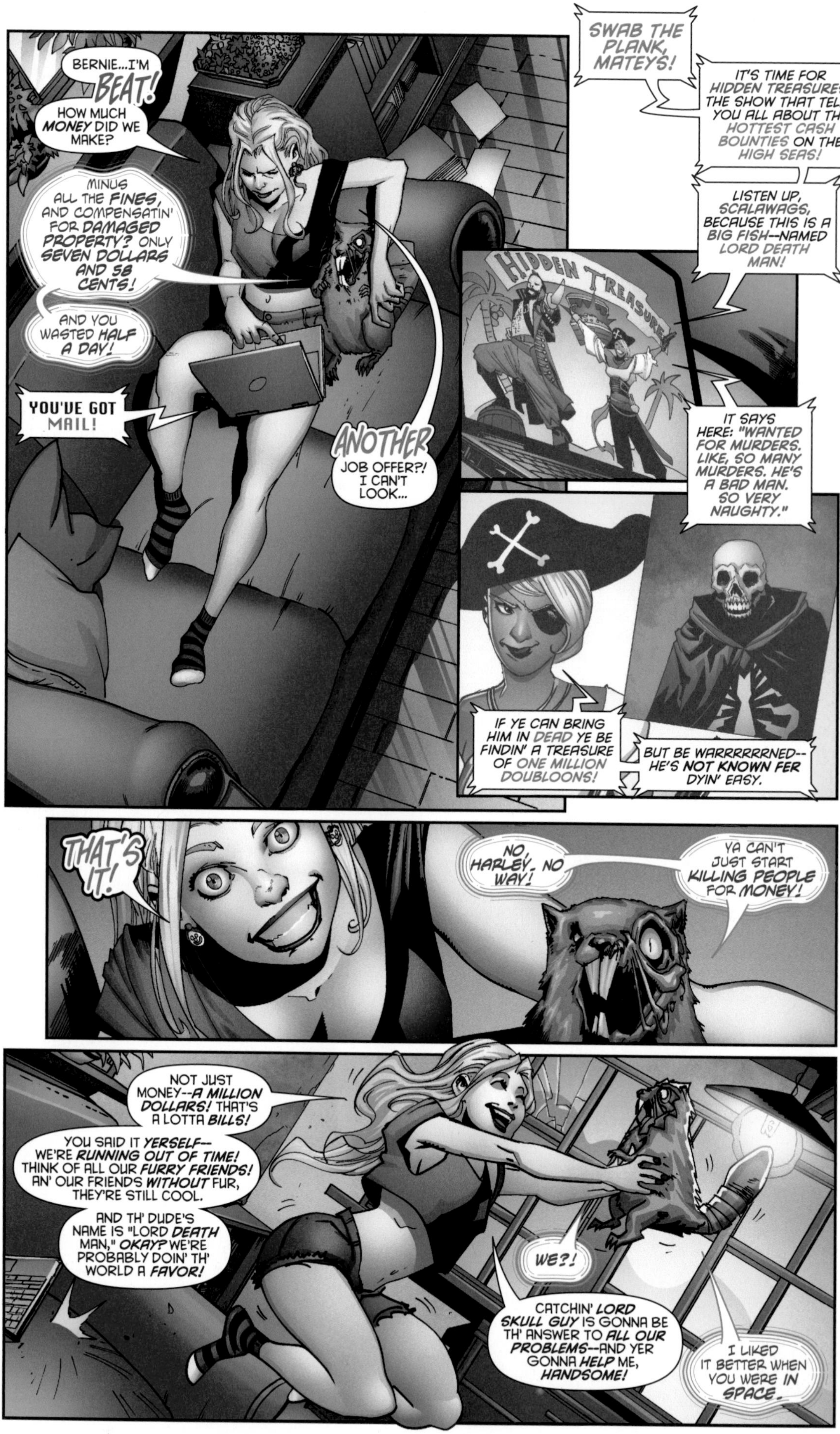
BERNIE...I'M BEAT!
HOW MUCH MONEY DID WE MAKE?
MINUS ALL THE FINES, AND COMPENSATIN' FOR DAMAGED PROPERTY? ONLY SEVEN DOLLARS AND 58 CENTS!
AND YOU WASTED HALF A DAY!
YOU'VE GOT MAIL!
ANOTHER JOB OFFER?! I CAN'T LOOK...
SWAB THE PLANK, MATEYS!
IT'S TIME FOR HIDDEN TREASURES, THE SHOW THAT TELLS YOU ALL ABOUT THE HOTTEST CASH BOUNTIES ON THE HIGH SEAS!
LISTEN UP, SCALAWAGS, BECAUSE THIS IS A BIG FISH--NAMED LORD DEATH MAN!
HIDDEN TREASURE
IT SAYS HERE: "WANTED FOR MURDERS. LIKE, SO MANY MURDERS. HE'S A BAD MAN. SO VERY NAUGHTY."
IF YE CAN BRING HIM IN DEAD YE BE FINDIN' A TREASURE OF ONE MILLION DOUBLOONS!
BUT BE WARRRRRRNED--HE'S NOT KNOWN FER DYIN' EASY.
THAT'S IT!
NO, HARLEY. NO WAY!
YA CAN'T JUST START KILLING PEOPLE FOR MONEY!
NOT JUST MONEY--A MILLION DOLLARS! THAT'S A LOTTA BILLS!
YOU SAID IT YERSELF--WE'RE RUNNING OUT OF TIME! THINK OF ALL OUR FURRY FRIENDS! AN' OUR FRIENDS WITHOUT FUR, THEY'RE STILL COOL.
AND TH' DUDE'S NAME IS "LORD DEATH MAN," OKAY? WE'RE PROBABLY DOIN' TH' WORLD A FAVOR!
WE?!
CATCHIN' LORD SKULL GUY IS GONNA BE TH' ANSWER TO ALL OUR PROBLEMS--AND YER GONNA HELP ME, HANDSOME!
I LIKED IT BETTER WHEN YOU WERE IN SPACE.

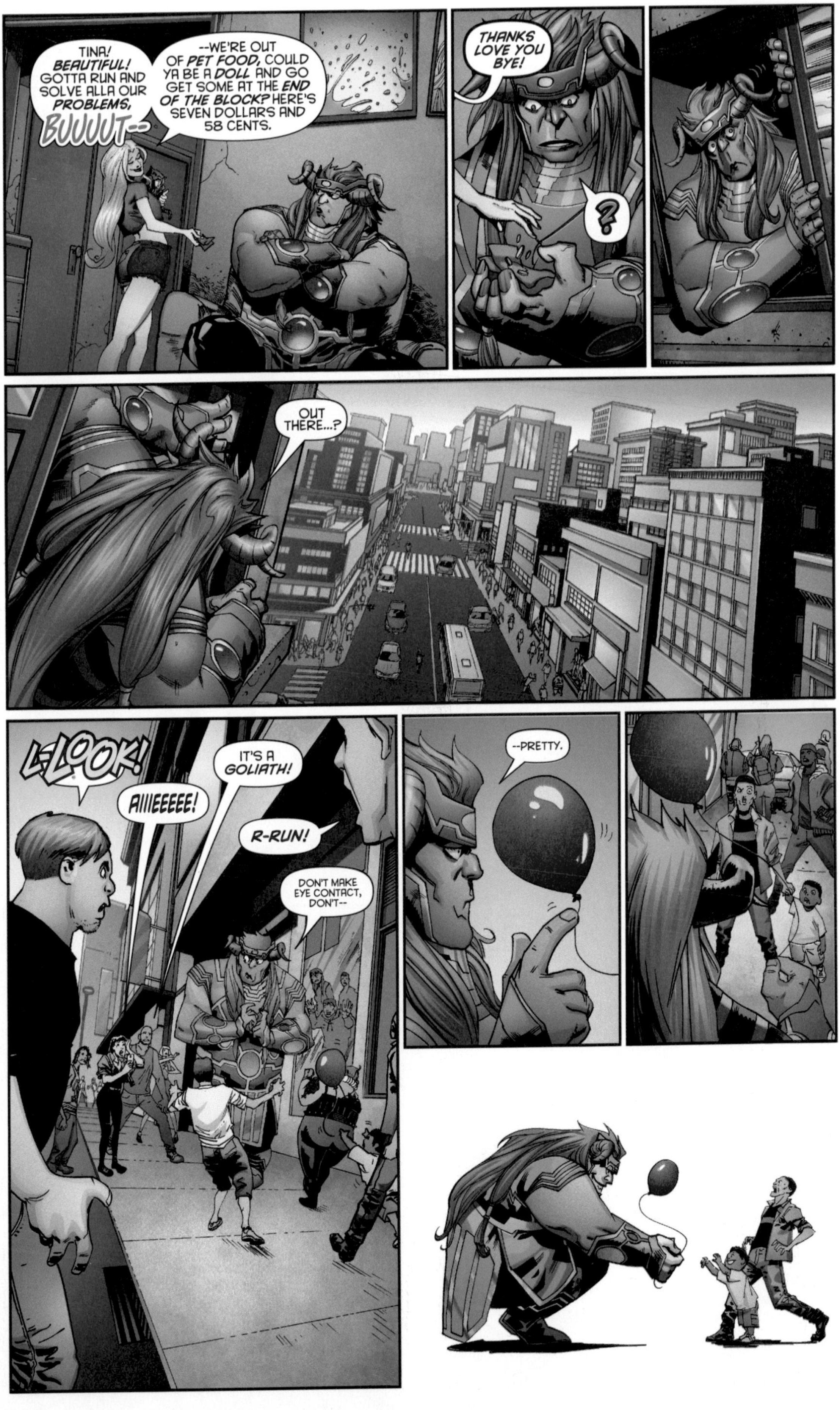
TINA! BEAUTIFUL! GOTTA RUN AND SOLVE ALLA OUR PROBLEMS, BUUUUT--
--WE'RE OUT OF PET FOOD, COULD YA BE A DOLL AND GO GET SOME AT THE END OF THE BLOCK? HERE'S SEVEN DOLLARS AND 58 CENTS.
THANKS LOVE YOU BYE!
?
OUT THERE...?
L-LOOK!
AIIIEEEEE!
IT'S A GOLIATH!
R-RUN!
DON'T MAKE EYE CONTACT, DON'T--
--PRETTY.

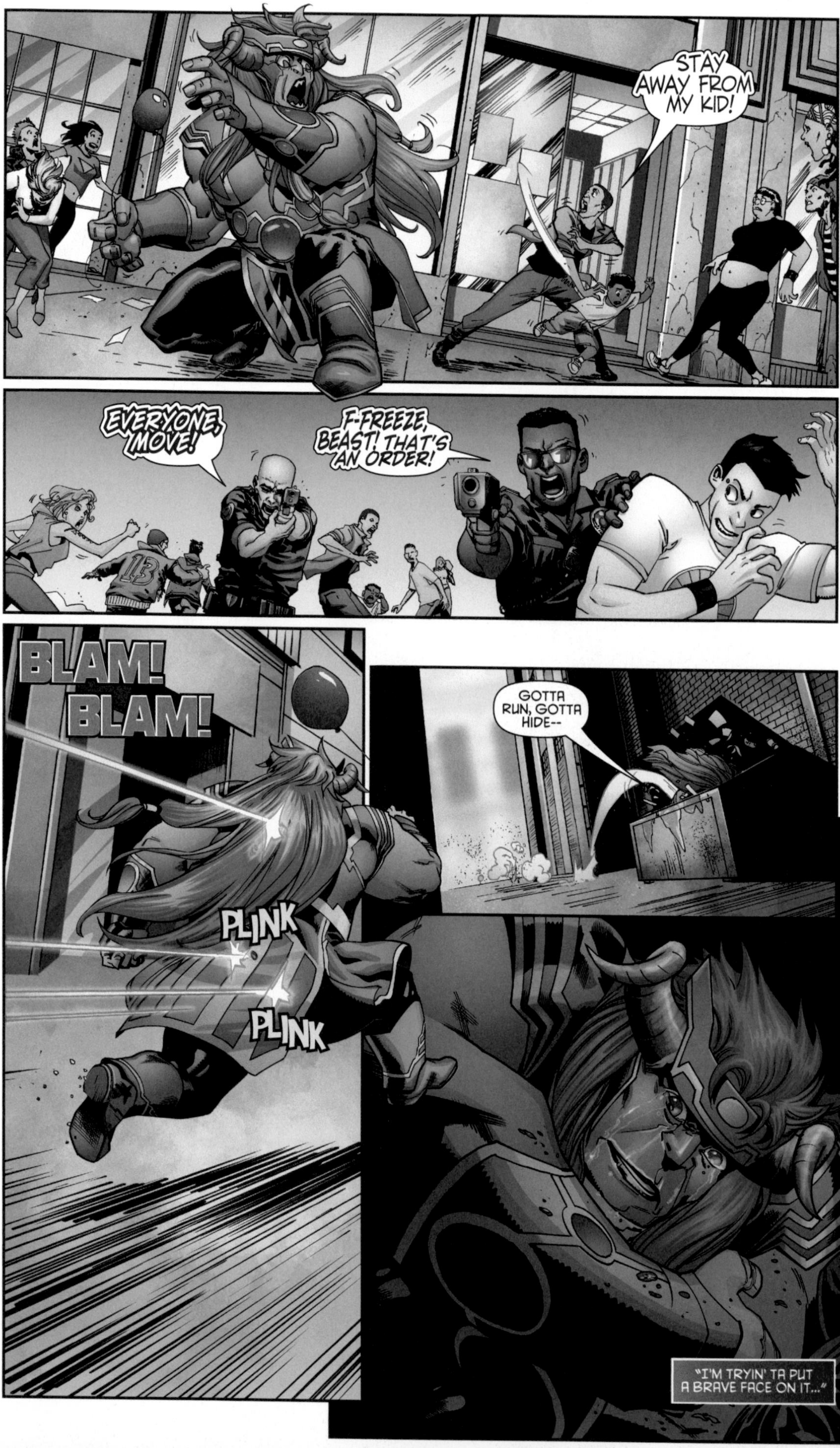
STAY AWAY FROM MY KID!
EVERYONE, MOVE!
F-FREEZE, BEAST! THAT'S AN ORDER!
BLAM! BLAM!
PLINK
PLINK
GOTTA RUN, GOTTA HIDE--
"I'M TRYIN' TA PUT A BRAVE FACE ON IT..."

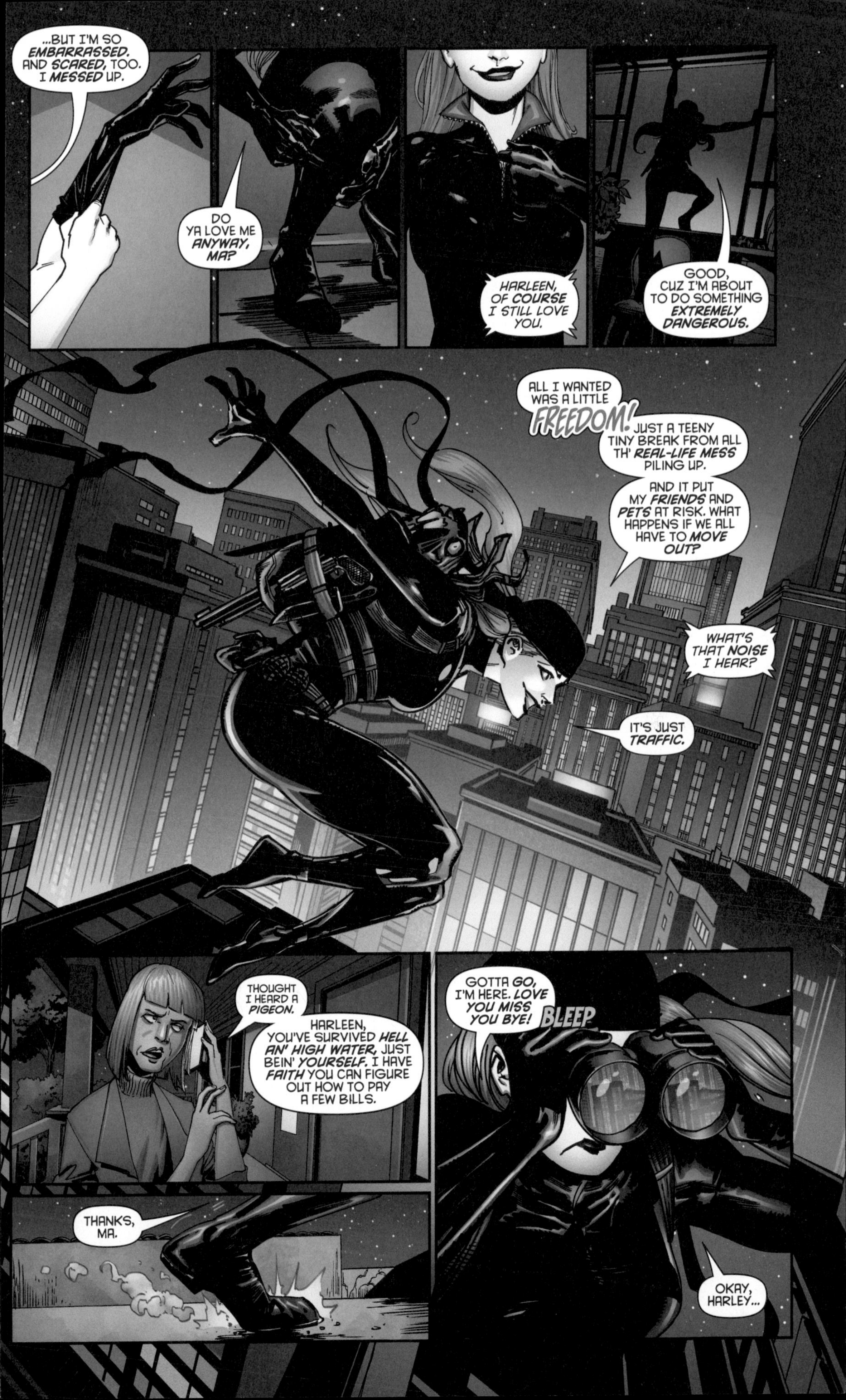

...BUT I'M SO EMBARRASSED. AND SCARED, TOO. I MESSED UP.
DO YA LOVE ME ANYWAY, MA?
HARLEEN, OF COURSE I STILL LOVE YOU.
GOOD, CUZ I'M ABOUT TO DO SOMETHING EXTREMELY DANGEROUS.
ALL I WANTED WAS A LITTLE FREEDOM! JUST A TEENY TINY BREAK FROM ALL TH' REAL-LIFE MESS PILING UP.
AND IT PUT MY FRIENDS AND PETS AT RISK. WHAT HAPPENS IF WE ALL HAVE TO MOVE OUT?
WHAT'S THAT NOISE I HEAR?
IT'S JUST TRAFFIC.
THOUGHT I HEARD A PIGEON.
HARLEEN, YOU'VE SURVIVED HELL AN' HIGH WATER, JUST BEIN' YOURSELF. I HAVE FAITH YOU CAN FIGURE OUT HOW TO PAY A FEW BILLS.
GOTTA GO, I'M HERE. LOVE YOU MISS YOU BYE!
BLEEP
THANKS, MA.
OKAY, HARLEY...

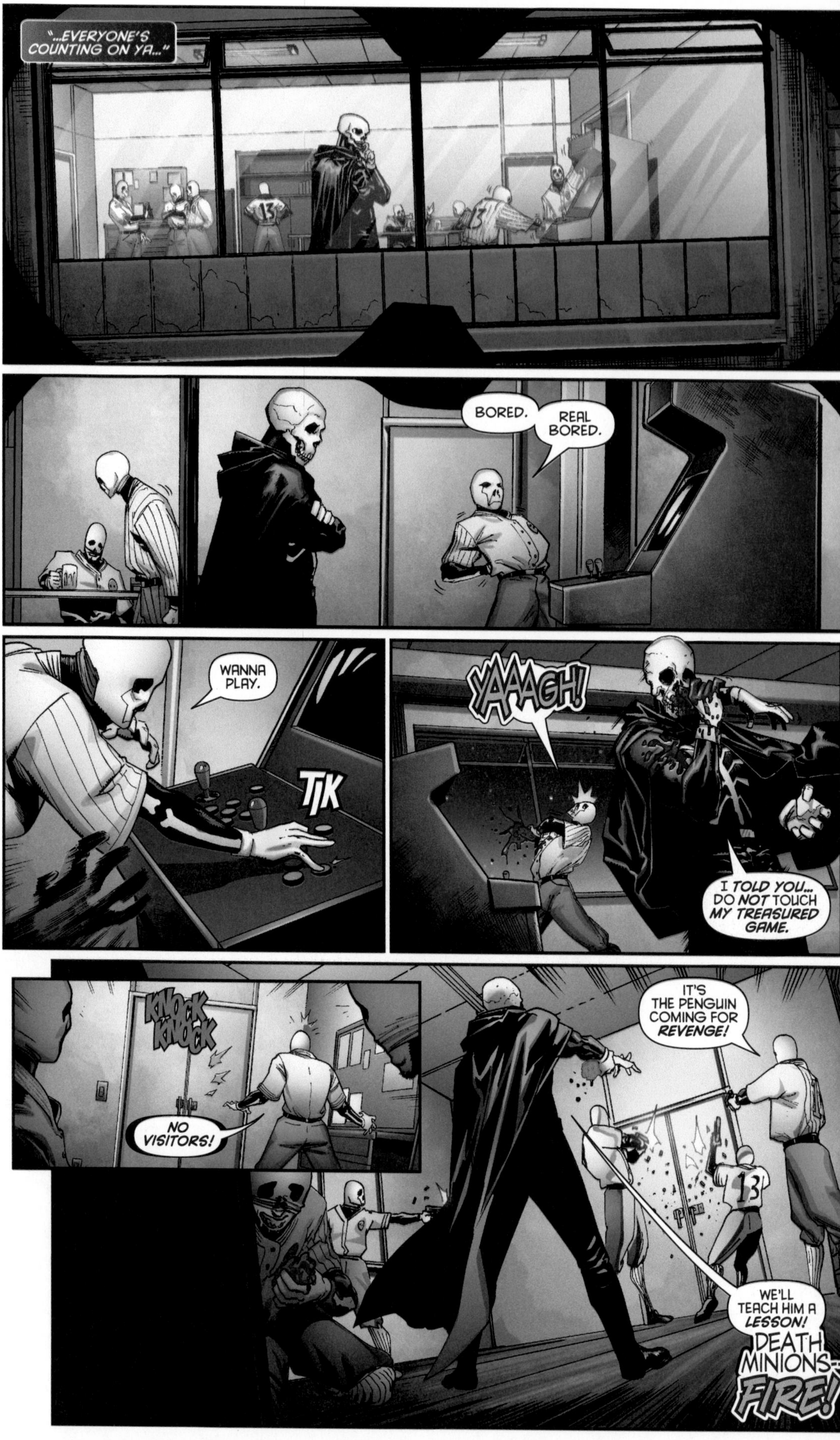

"...EVERYONE'S COUNTING ON YA..."
BORED.
REAL BORED.
WANNA PLAY.
TJK
YAAAGH!
I TOLD YOU... DO NOT TOUCH MY TREASURED GAME.
KNOCK KNOCK
NO VISITORS!
IT'S THE PENGUIN COMING FOR REVENGE!
WE'LL TEACH HIM A LESSON!
DEATH MINIONS-- FIRE!

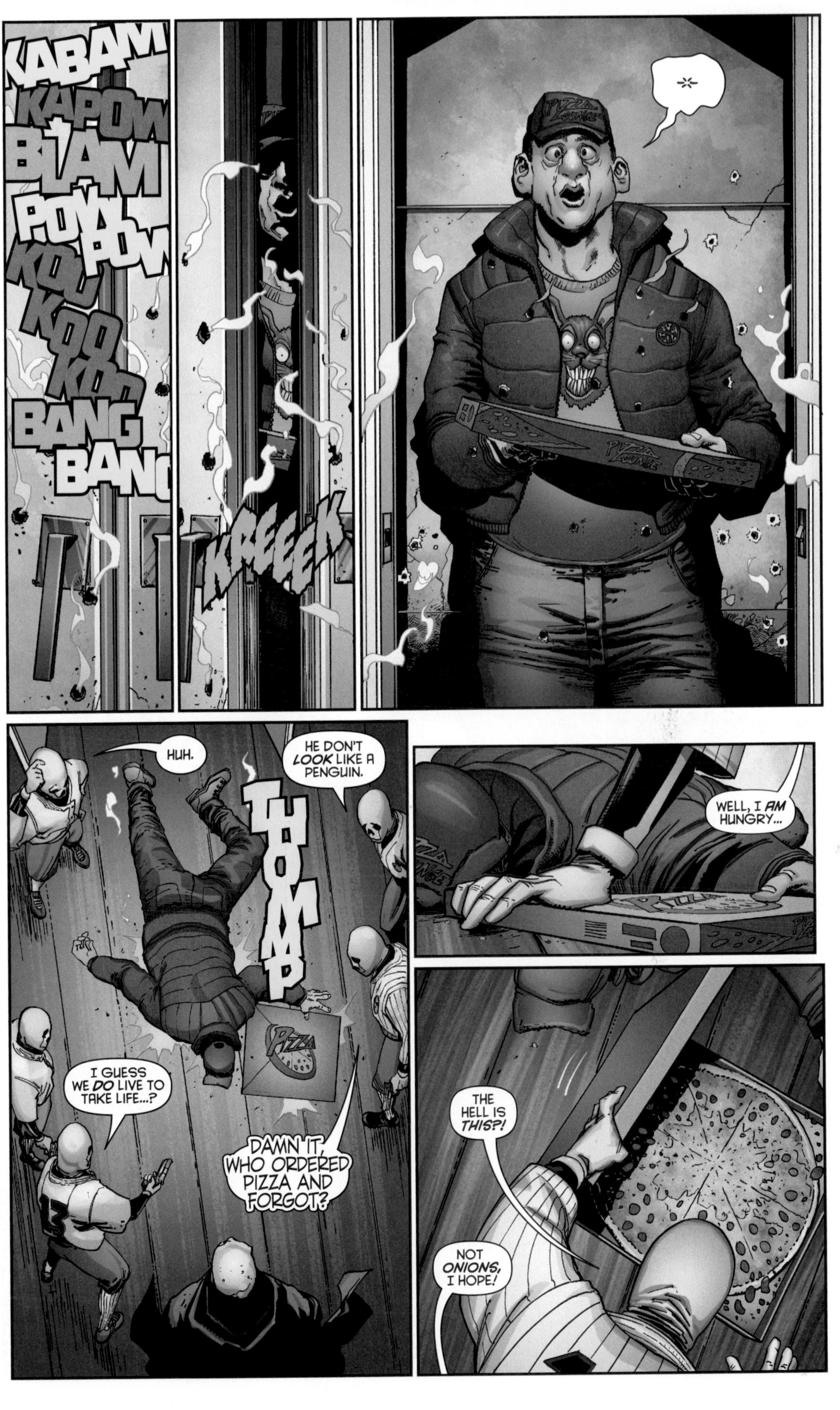
KABAM
KAPOW
BLAM
POW
POW
BANG
KREEEK
HUH.
HE DON'T *LOOK* LIKE A PENGUIN.
THOOMP
I GUESS WE *DO* LIVE TO TAKE LIFE...?
DAMN IT, WHO ORDERED PIZZA AND FORGOT?
WELL, I *AM* HUNGRY...
THE HELL IS *THIS?!*
NOT *ONIONS,* I HOPE!

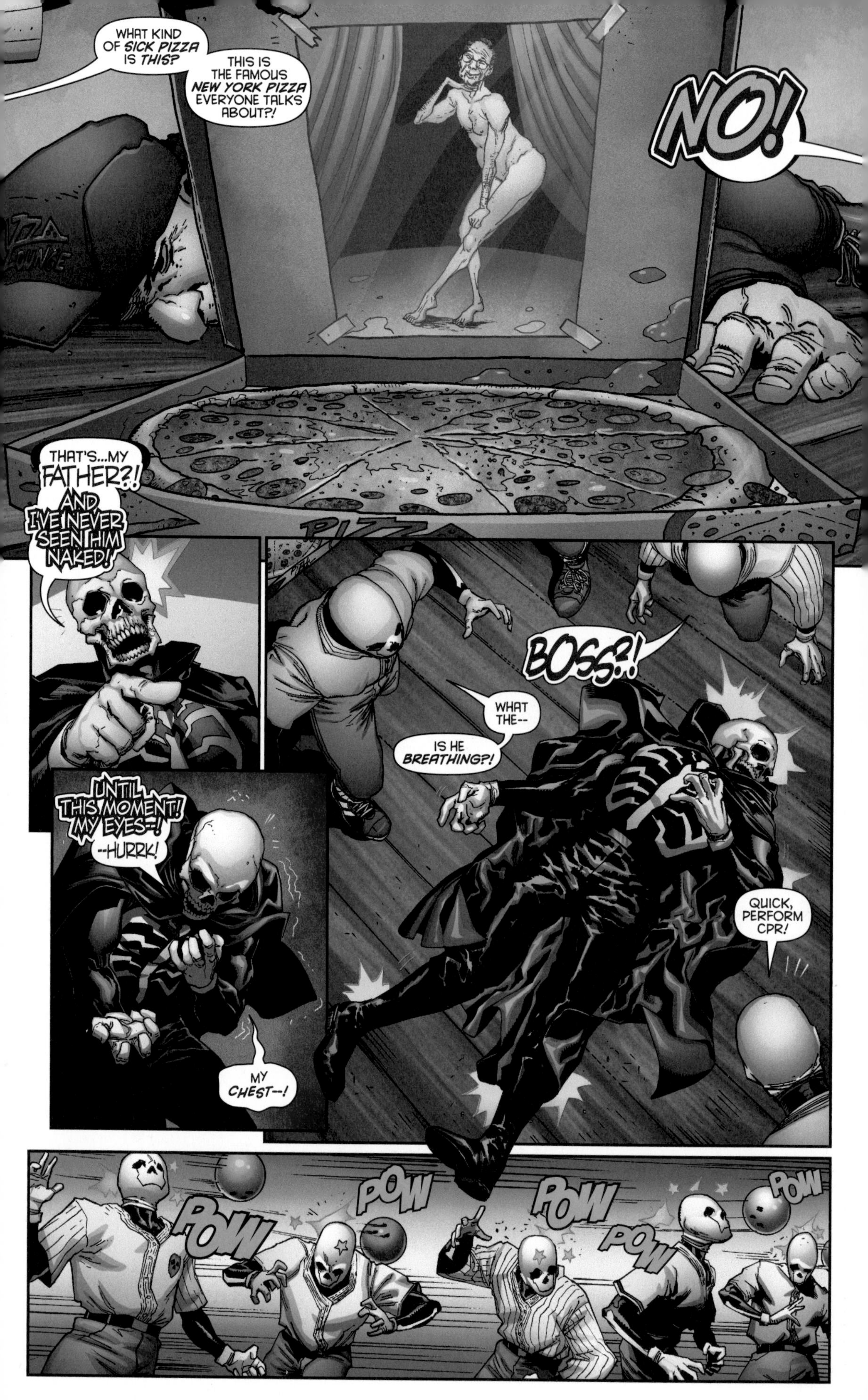

WHAT KIND OF SICK PIZZA IS THIS?
THIS IS THE FAMOUS NEW YORK PIZZA EVERYONE TALKS ABOUT?!
NO!
THAT'S...MY FATHER?! AND I'VE NEVER SEEN HIM NAKED!
UNTIL THIS MOMENT! MY EYES--!
--HURRK!
MY CHEST--!
BOSS?!
WHAT THE--
IS HE BREATHING?!
QUICK, PERFORM CPR!
POW
POW
POW
POW
POW

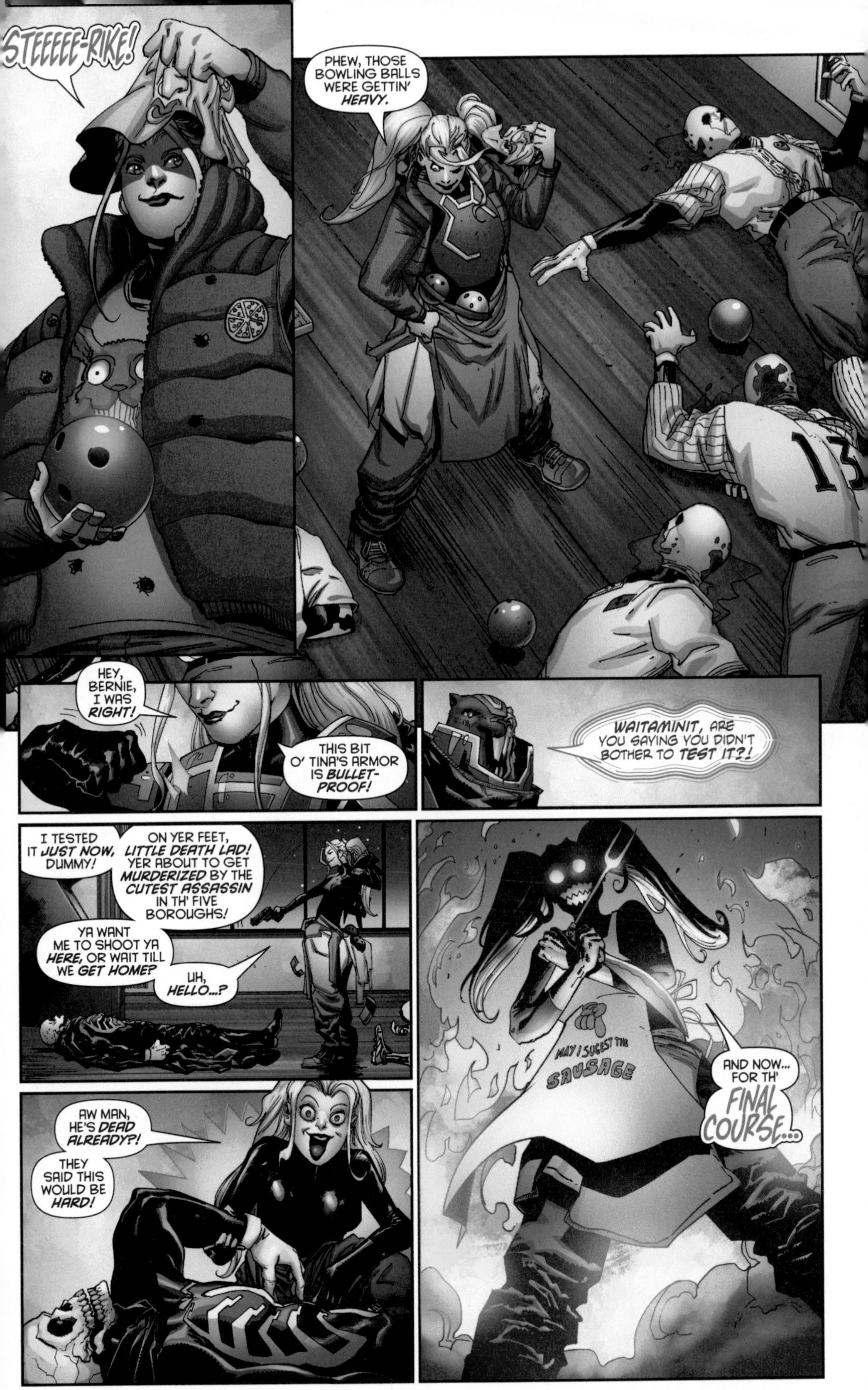
STEEEEEE-RIKE!
PHEW, THOSE BOWLING BALLS WERE GETTIN' HEAVY.
HEY, BERNIE, I WAS RIGHT!
THIS BIT O' TINA'S ARMOR IS BULLET-PROOF!
WAITAMINIT, ARE YOU SAYING YOU DIDN'T BOTHER TO TEST IT?!
I TESTED IT JUST NOW, DUMMY!
ON YER FEET, LITTLE DEATH LAD! YER ABOUT TO GET MURDERIZED BY THE CUTEST ASSASSIN IN TH' FIVE BOROUGHS!
YA WANT ME TO SHOOT YA HERE, OR WAIT TILL WE GET HOME?
UH, HELLO...?
MAY I SUGEST THE
SAUSAGE
AND NOW... FOR TH' FINAL COURSE...
AW MAN, HE'S DEAD ALREADY?!
THEY SAID THIS WOULD BE HARD!

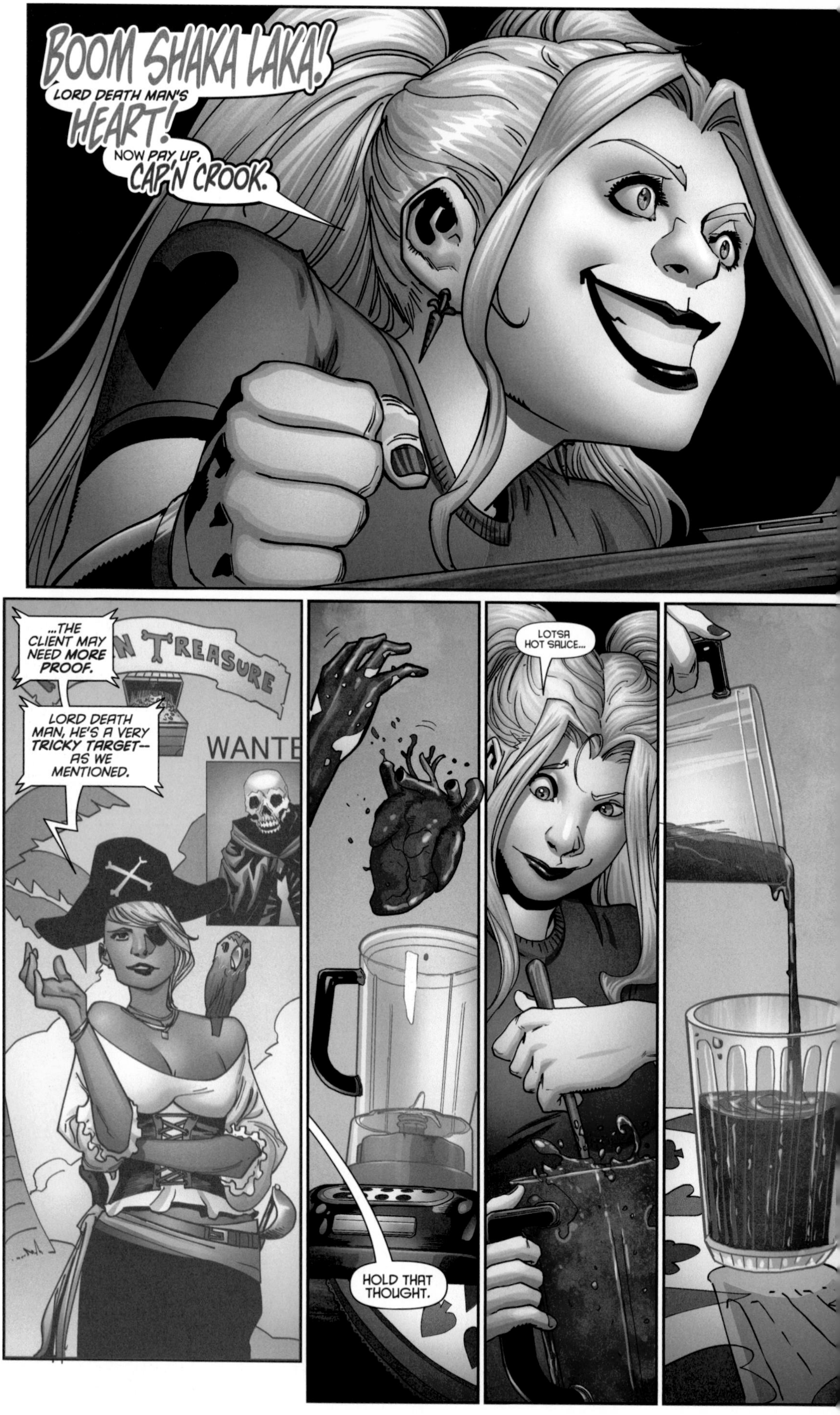
BOOM SHAKA LAKA!
LORD DEATH MAN'S HEART!
NOW PAY UP, CAP'N CROOK.
...THE CLIENT MAY NEED MORE PROOF.
LORD DEATH MAN, HE'S A VERY TRICKY TARGET-- AS WE MENTIONED.
TREASURE
WANTE
HOLD THAT THOUGHT.
LOTSA HOT SAUCE...

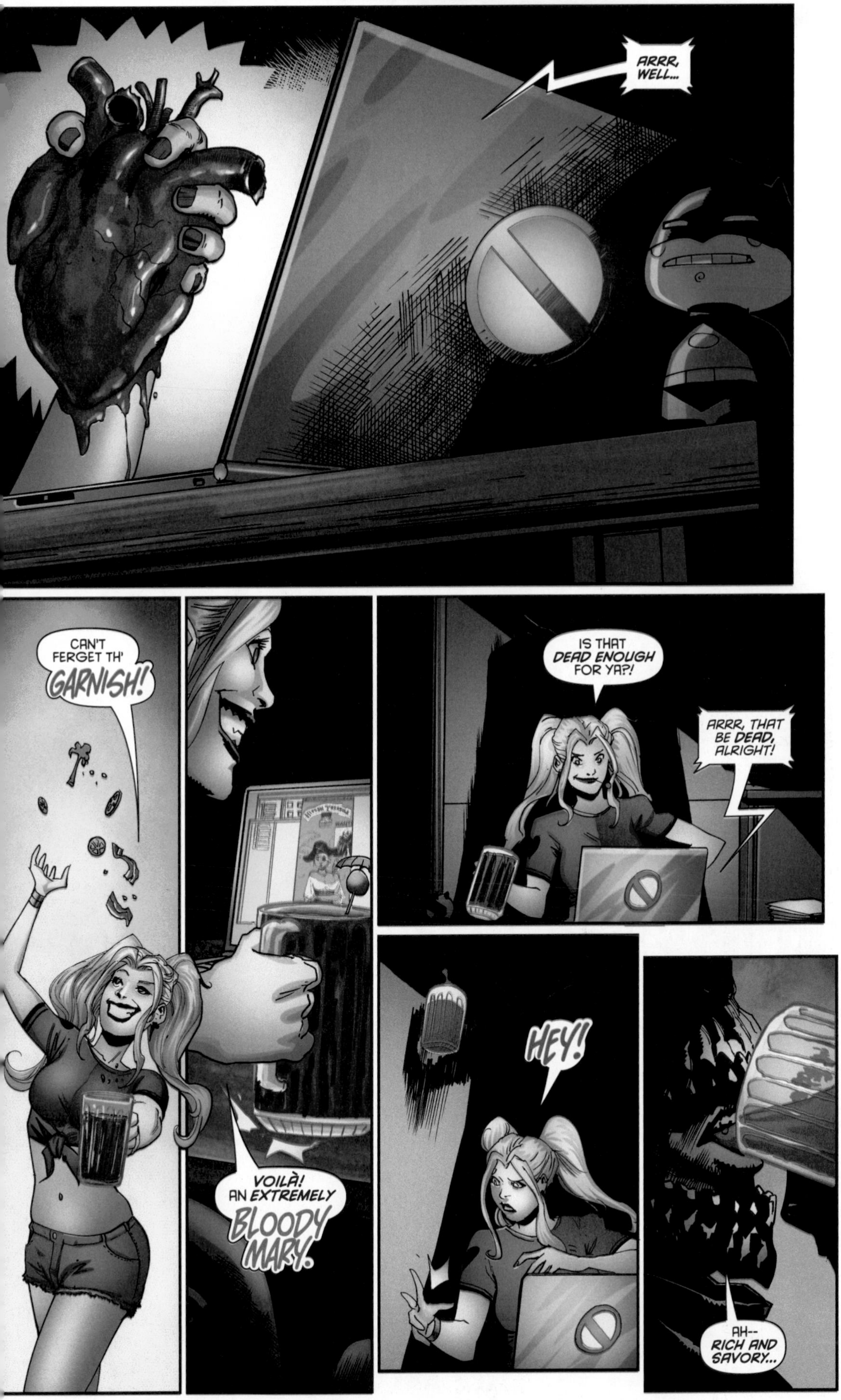
ARRR, WELL...
CAN'T FERGET TH' GARNISH!
VOILÀ! AN EXTREMELY BLOODY MARY.
IS THAT DEAD ENOUGH FOR YA?!
ARRR, THAT BE DEAD, ALRIGHT!
HEY!
AH-- RICH AND SAVORY...

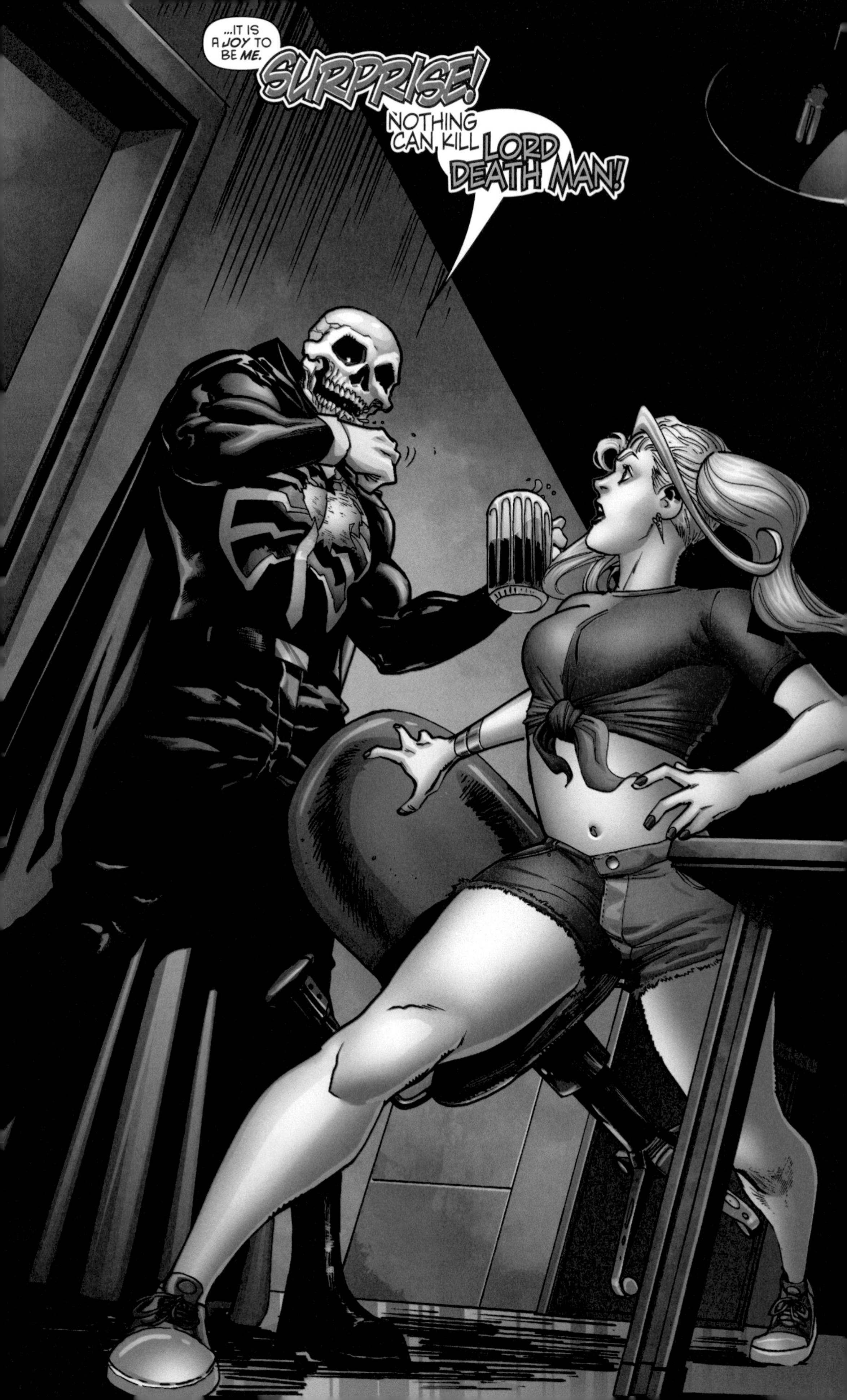
...IT IS A JOY TO BE ME.
SURPRISE!
NOTHING CAN KILL LORD DEATH MAN!

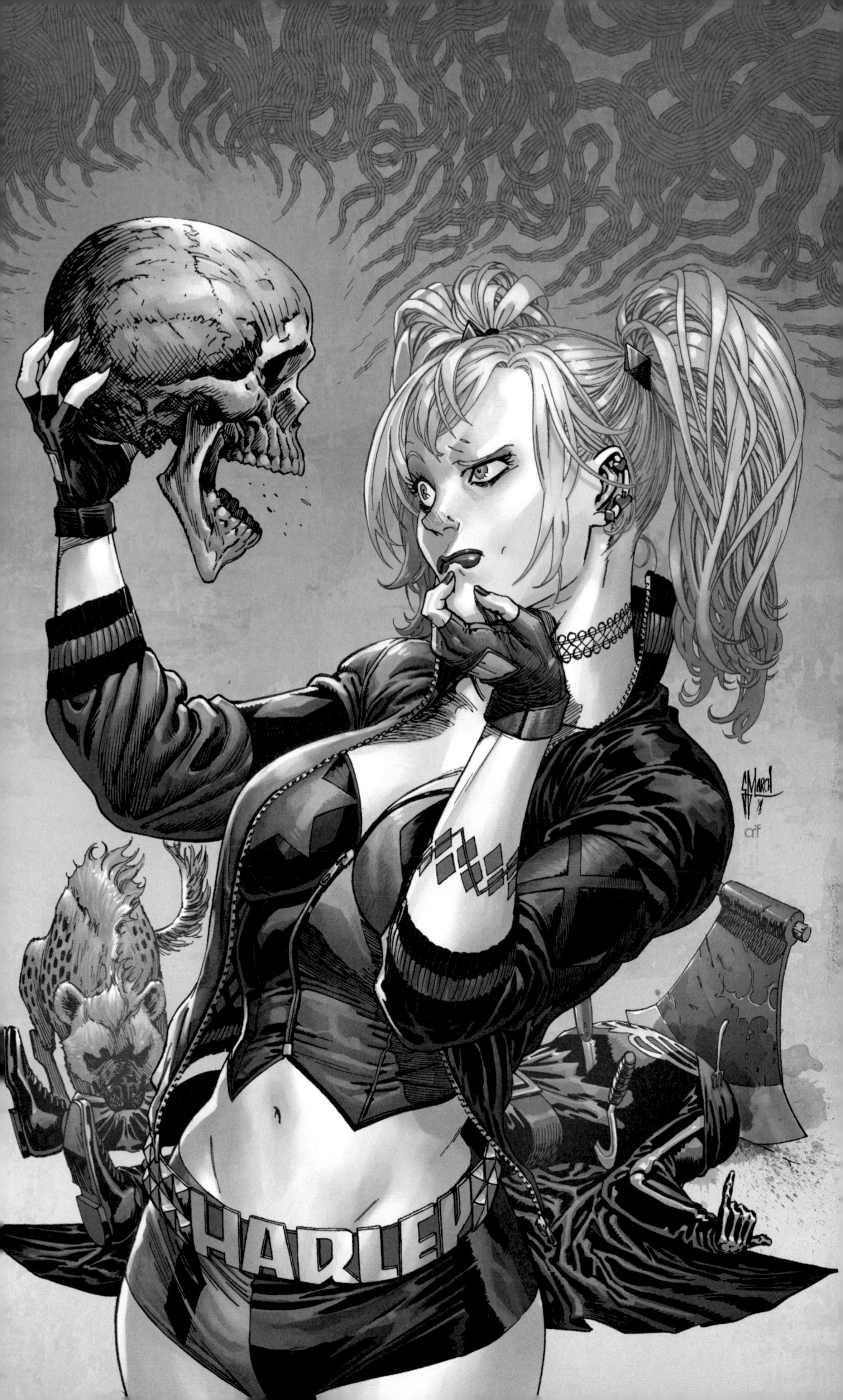
HARLE

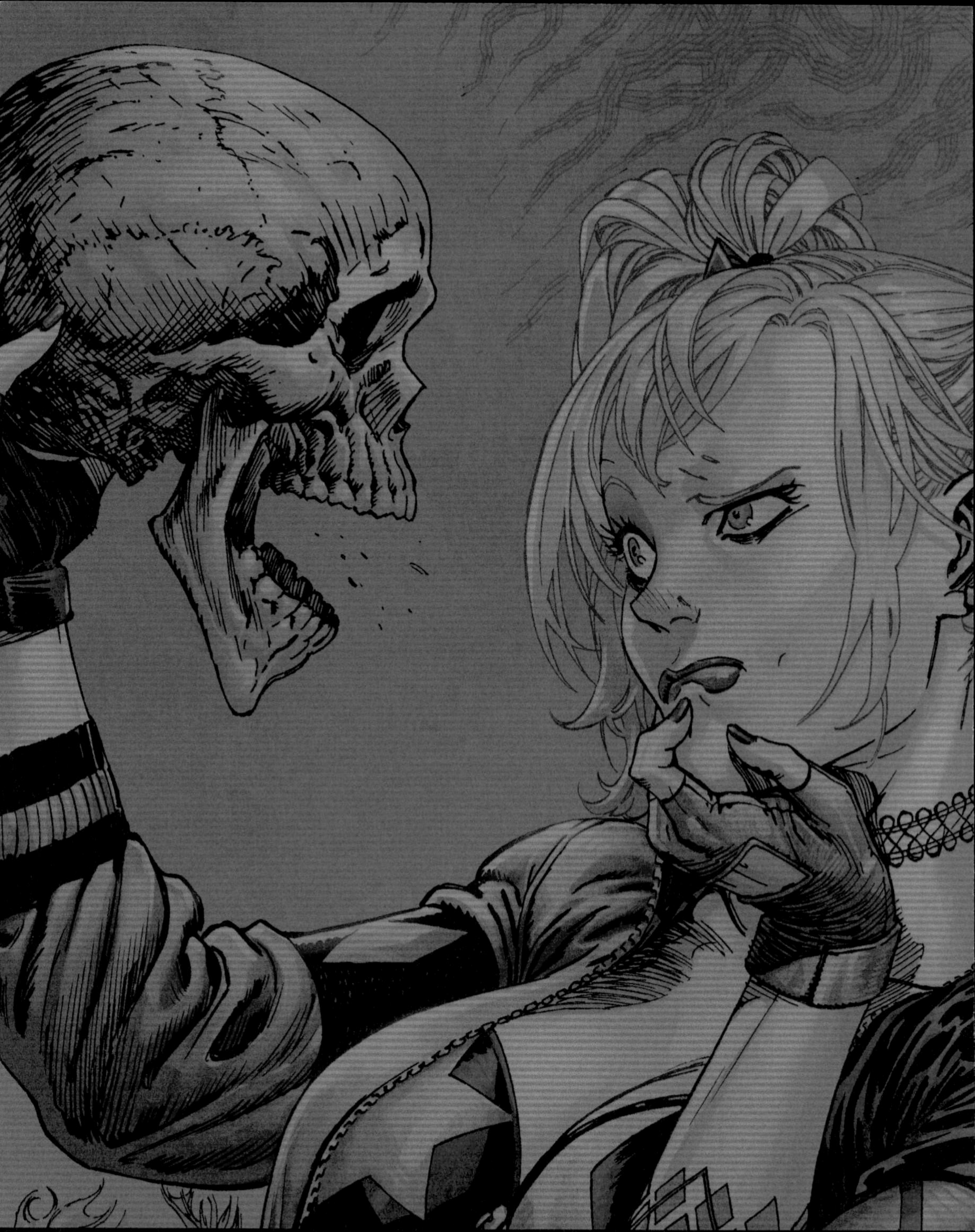

HARLEY QUINN
#49

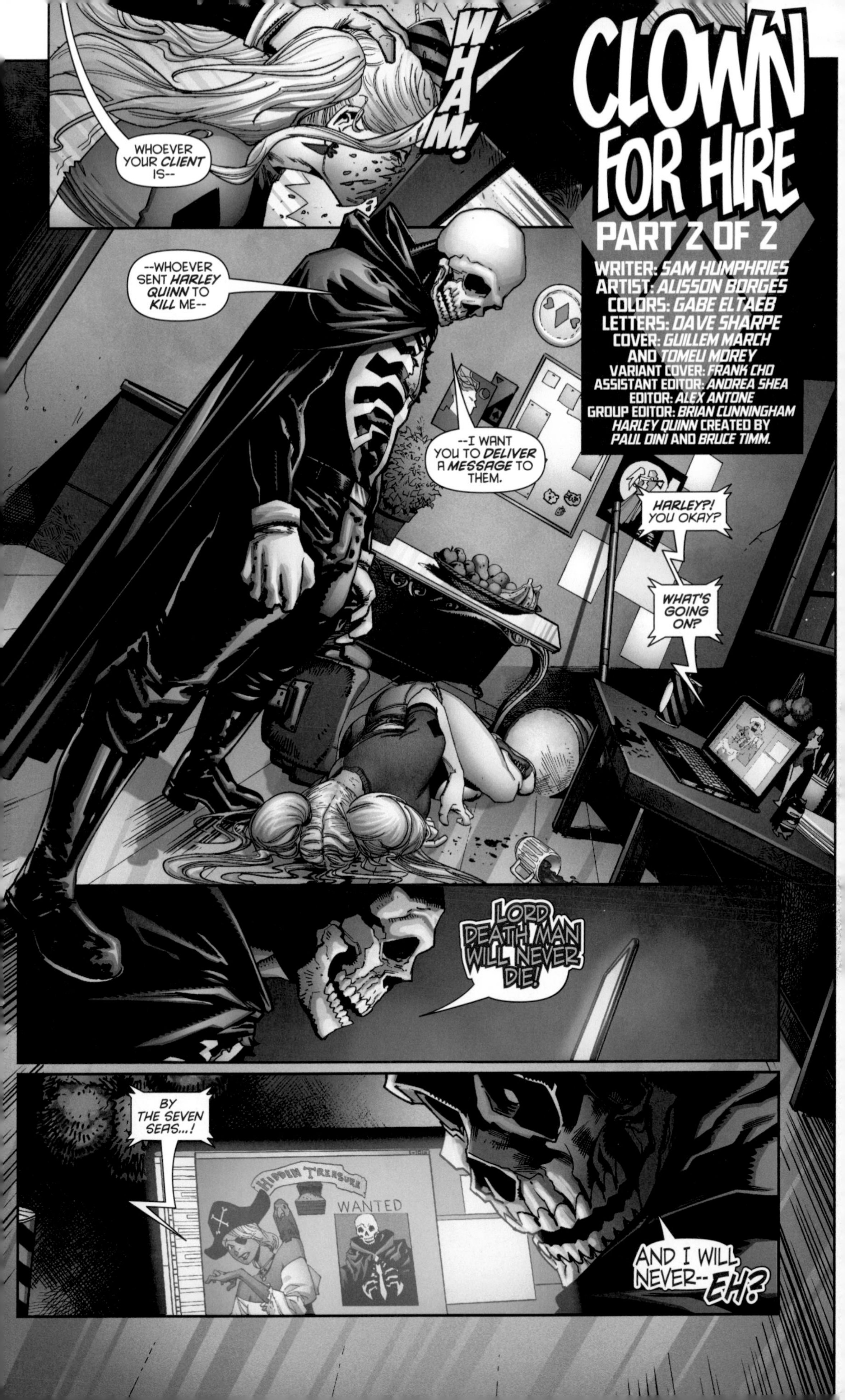
WHOEVER YOUR CLIENT IS--
WHAM!
CLOWN FOR HIRE
PART 2 OF 2
WRITER: SAM HUMPHRIES
ARTIST: ALISSON BORGES
COLORS: GABE ELTAEB
LETTERS: DAVE SHARPE
COVER: GUILLEM MARCH AND TOMEU MOREY
VARIANT COVER: FRANK CHO
ASSISTANT EDITOR: ANDREA SHEA
EDITOR: ALEX ANTONE
GROUP EDITOR: BRIAN CUNNINGHAM
HARLEY QUINN CREATED BY PAUL DINI AND BRUCE TIMM.
--WHOEVER SENT HARLEY QUINN TO KILL ME--
--I WANT YOU TO DELIVER A MESSAGE TO THEM.
HARLEY?! YOU OKAY?
WHAT'S GOING ON?
LORD DEATH MAN WILL NEVER DIE!
BY THE SEVEN SEAS...!
HIDDEN TREASURE
WANTED
AND I WILL NEVER--EH?

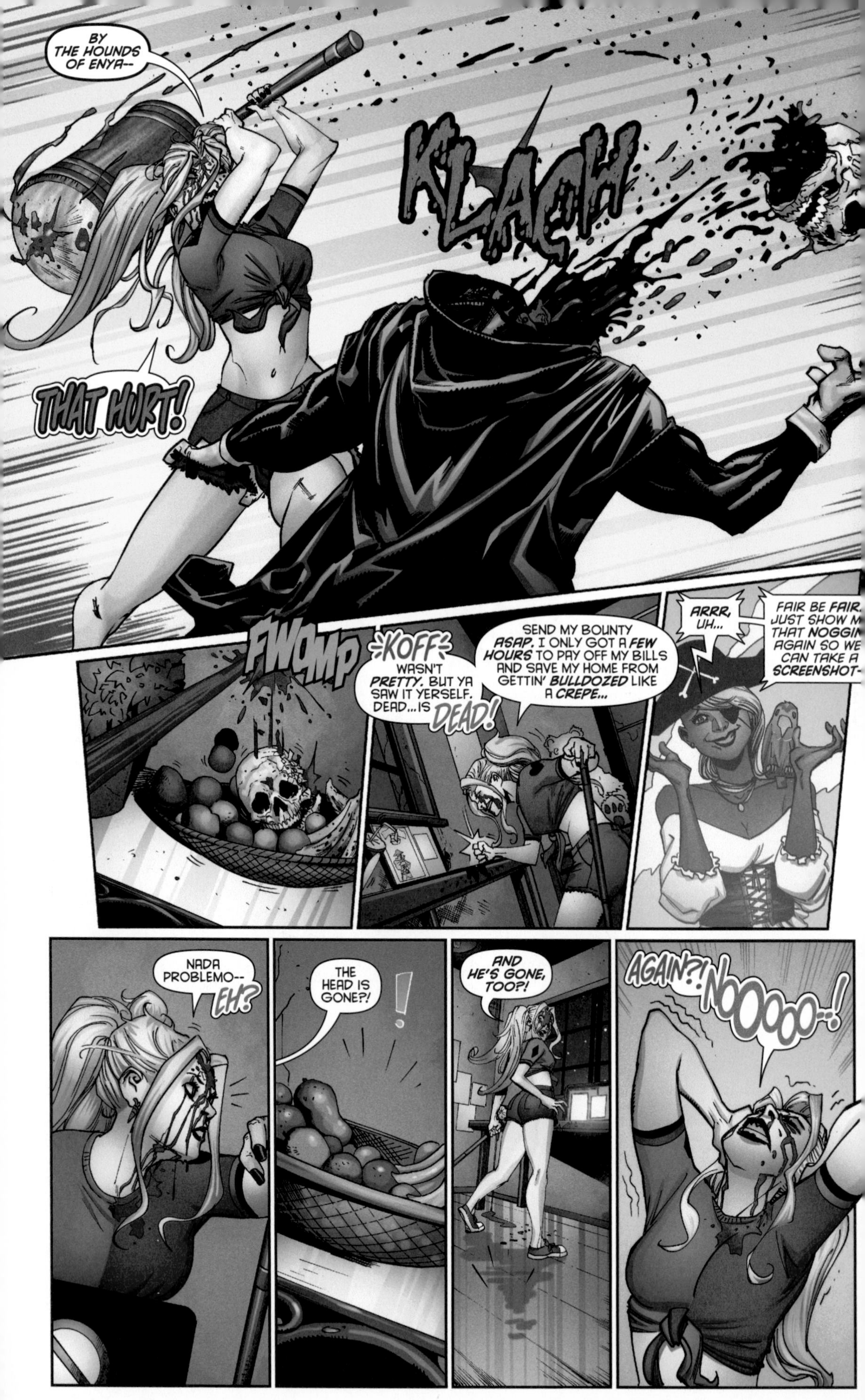
BY THE HOUNDS OF ENYA--
KLACH
THAT HURT!
FWOMP
KOFF
WASN'T PRETTY. BUT YA SAW IT YERSELF. DEAD...IS DEAD!
SEND MY BOUNTY ASAP. I ONLY GOT A FEW HOURS TO PAY OFF MY BILLS AND SAVE MY HOME FROM GETTIN' BULLDOZED LIKE A CREPE...
ARRR, UH...
FAIR BE FAIR. JUST SHOW M THAT NOGGIN AGAIN SO WE CAN TAKE A SCREENSHOT-
NADA PROBLEMO-- EH?
THE HEAD IS GONE?!
!
AND HE'S GONE, TOO?!
AGAIN?! NOOOOO--!

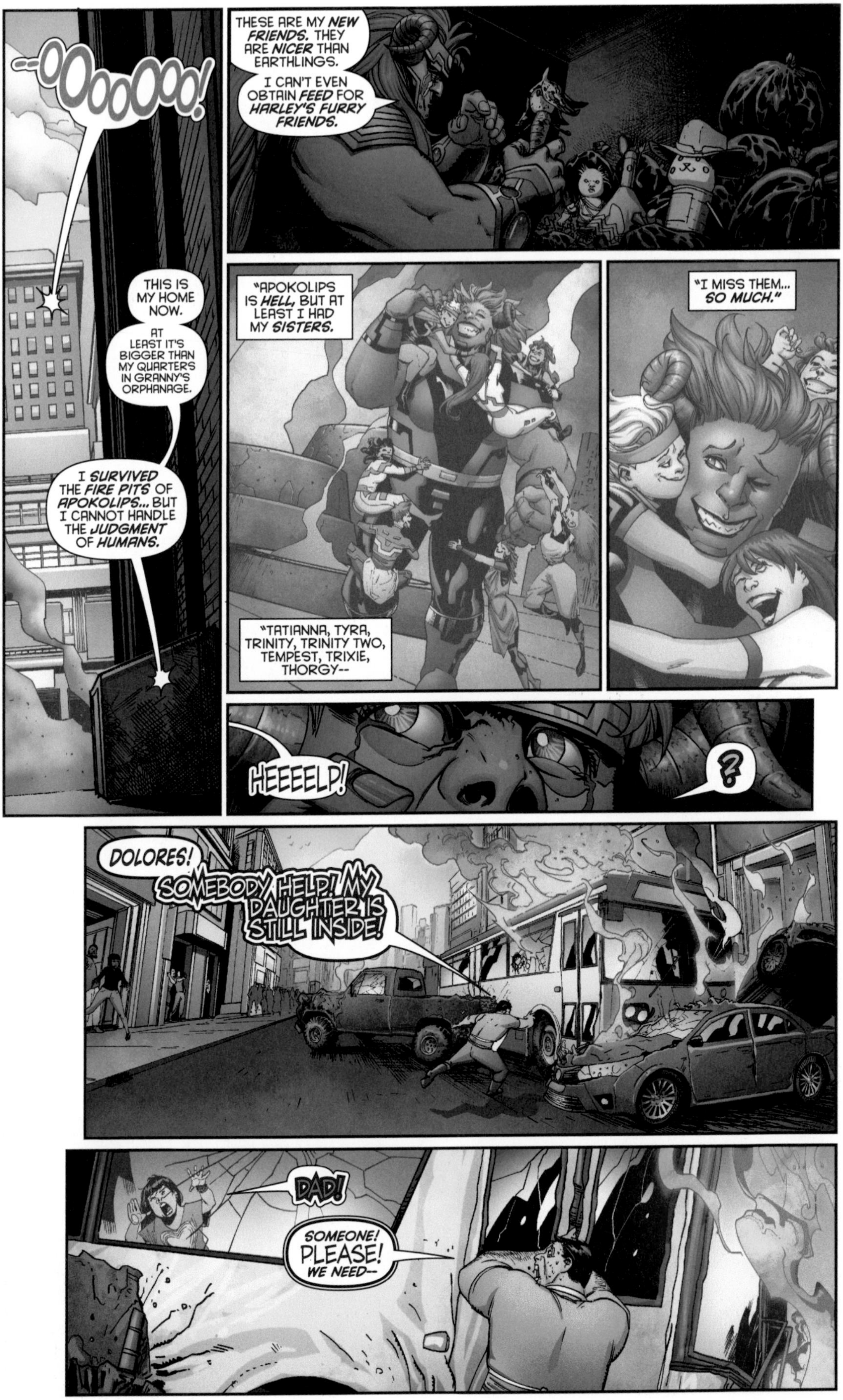
--OOOOOOO!
THESE ARE MY NEW FRIENDS. THEY ARE NICER THAN EARTHLINGS.
I CAN'T EVEN OBTAIN FEED FOR HARLEY'S FURRY FRIENDS.
THIS IS MY HOME NOW.
AT LEAST IT'S BIGGER THAN MY QUARTERS IN GRANNY'S ORPHANAGE.
I SURVIVED THE FIRE PITS OF APOKOLIPS... BUT I CANNOT HANDLE THE JUDGMENT OF HUMANS.
"APOKOLIPS IS HELL, BUT AT LEAST I HAD MY SISTERS.
"TATIANNA, TYRA, TRINITY, TRINITY TWO, TEMPEST, TRIXIE, THORGY--
"I MISS THEM... SO MUCH."
HEEEELP!
?
DOLORES!
SOMEBODY HELP! MY DAUGHTER IS STILL INSIDE!
DAD!
SOMEONE! PLEASE! WE NEED--

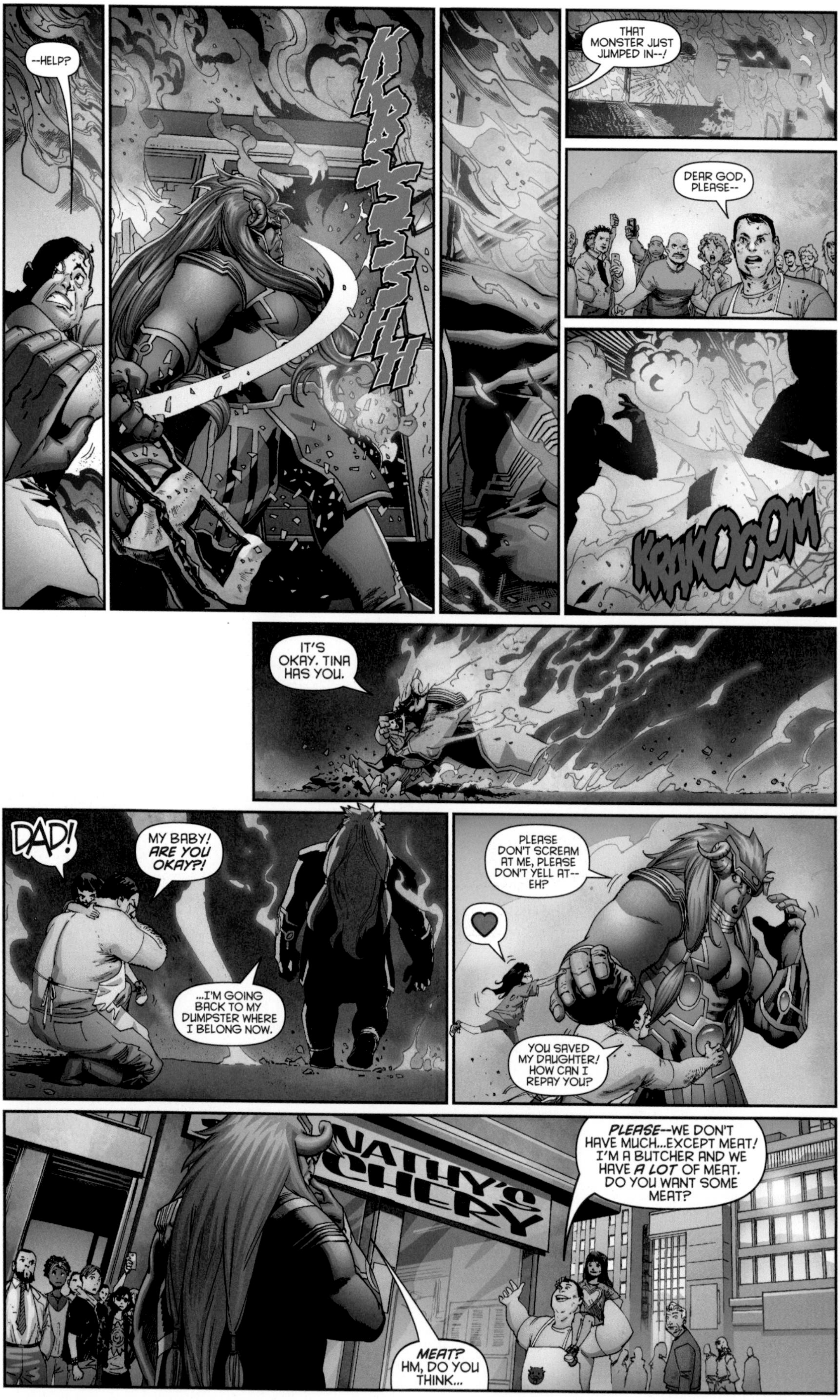
--HELP?
KRSSSHH
THAT MONSTER JUST JUMPED IN--!
DEAR GOD, PLEASE--
KRAKOOOM
IT'S OKAY. TINA HAS YOU.
DAD!
MY BABY! ARE YOU OKAY?!
...I'M GOING BACK TO MY DUMPSTER WHERE I BELONG NOW.
PLEASE DON'T SCREAM AT ME, PLEASE DON'T YELL AT-- EH?
YOU SAVED MY DAUGHTER! HOW CAN I REPAY YOU?
PLEASE--WE DON'T HAVE MUCH...EXCEPT MEAT! I'M A BUTCHER AND WE HAVE A LOT OF MEAT. DO YOU WANT SOME MEAT?
MEAT? HM, DO YOU THINK...

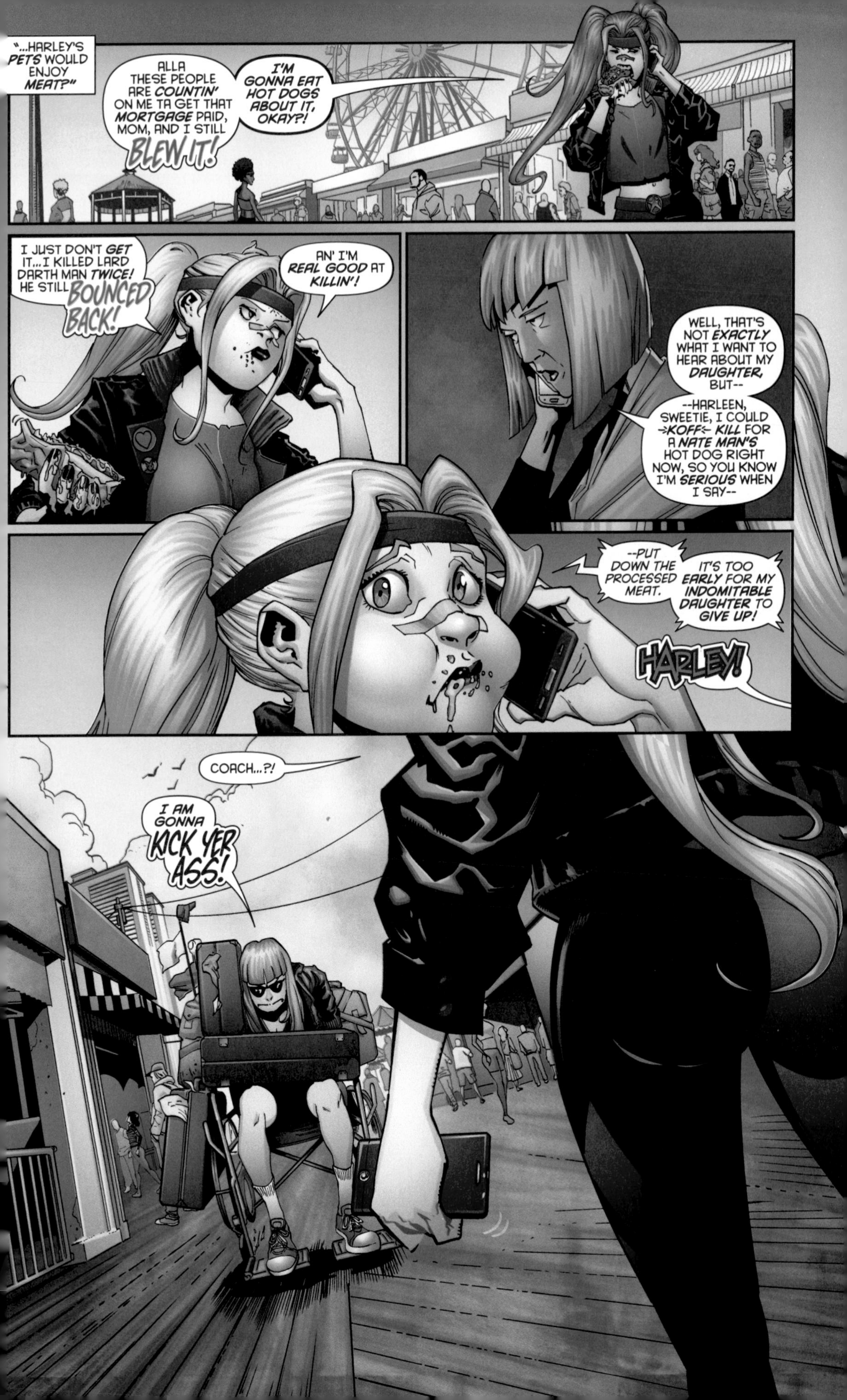
"...HARLEY'S PETS WOULD ENJOY MEAT?"
ALLA THESE PEOPLE ARE COUNTIN' ON ME TA GET THAT MORTGAGE PAID, MOM, AND I STILL BLEW IT!
I'M GONNA EAT HOT DOGS ABOUT IT, OKAY?!
I JUST DON'T GET IT...I KILLED LARD DARTH MAN TWICE! HE STILL BOUNCED BACK!
AN' I'M REAL GOOD AT KILLIN'!
WELL, THAT'S NOT EXACTLY WHAT I WANT TO HEAR ABOUT MY DAUGHTER, BUT--
--HARLEEN, SWEETIE, I COULD *KOFF* KILL FOR A NATE MAN'S HOT DOG RIGHT NOW, SO YOU KNOW I'M SERIOUS WHEN I SAY--
--PUT DOWN THE PROCESSED MEAT.
IT'S TOO EARLY FOR MY INDOMITABLE DAUGHTER TO GIVE UP!
HARLEY!
COACH...?!
I AM GONNA KICK YER ASS!

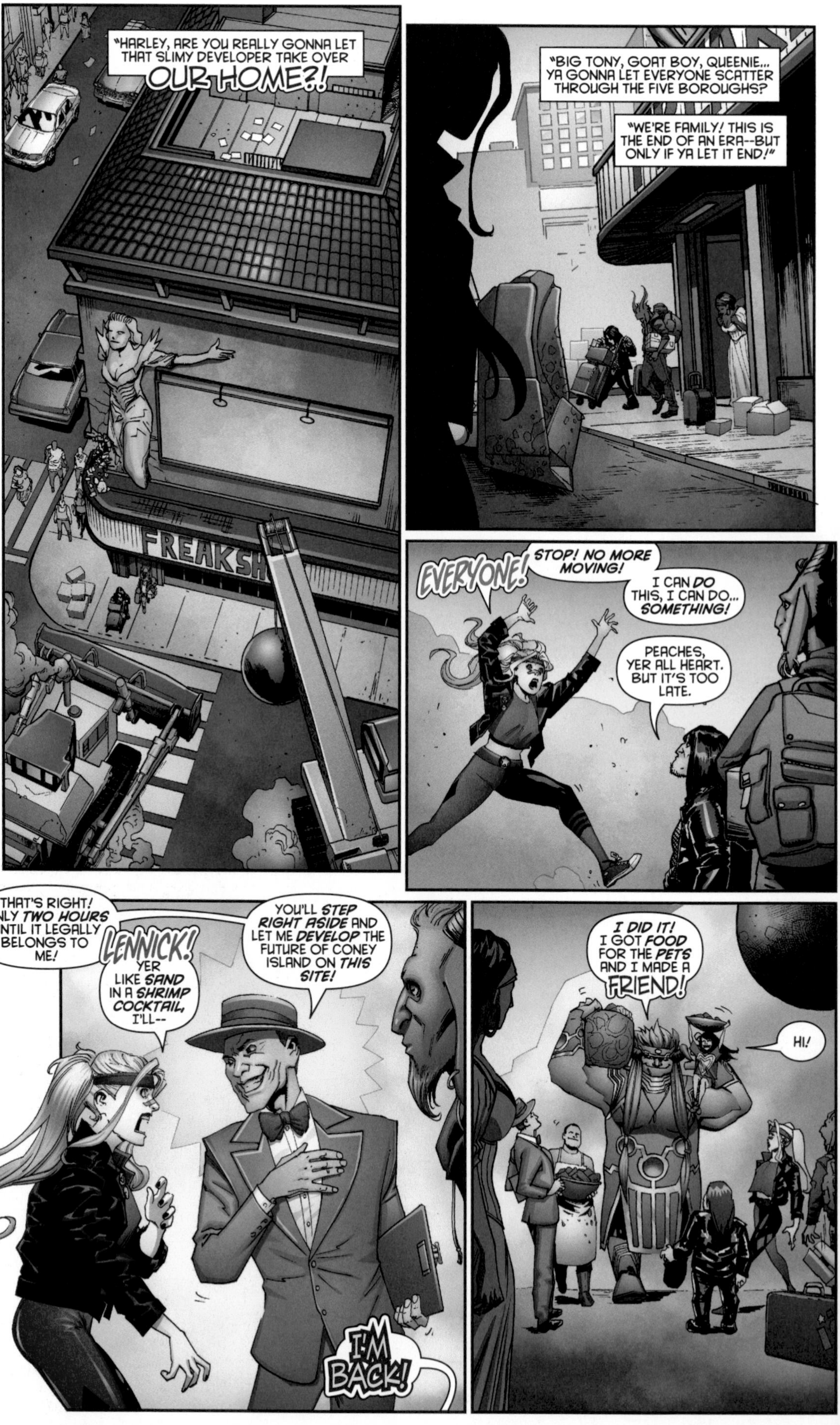
"HARLEY, ARE YOU REALLY GONNA LET THAT SLIMY DEVELOPER TAKE OVER OUR HOME?!
FREAKSH
"BIG TONY, GOAT BOY, QUEENIE... YA GONNA LET EVERYONE SCATTER THROUGH THE FIVE BOROUGHS?
"WE'RE FAMILY! THIS IS THE END OF AN ERA--BUT ONLY IF YA LET IT END!"
EVERYONE!
STOP! NO MORE MOVING!
I CAN DO THIS, I CAN DO... SOMETHING!
PEACHES, YER ALL HEART. BUT IT'S TOO LATE.
THAT'S RIGHT! ONLY TWO HOURS UNTIL IT LEGALLY BELONGS TO ME!
LENNICK! YER LIKE SAND IN A SHRIMP COCKTAIL, I'LL--
YOU'LL STEP RIGHT ASIDE AND LET ME DEVELOP THE FUTURE OF CONEY ISLAND ON THIS SITE!
I'M BACK!
I DID IT! I GOT FOOD FOR THE PETS AND I MADE A FRIEND!
HI!

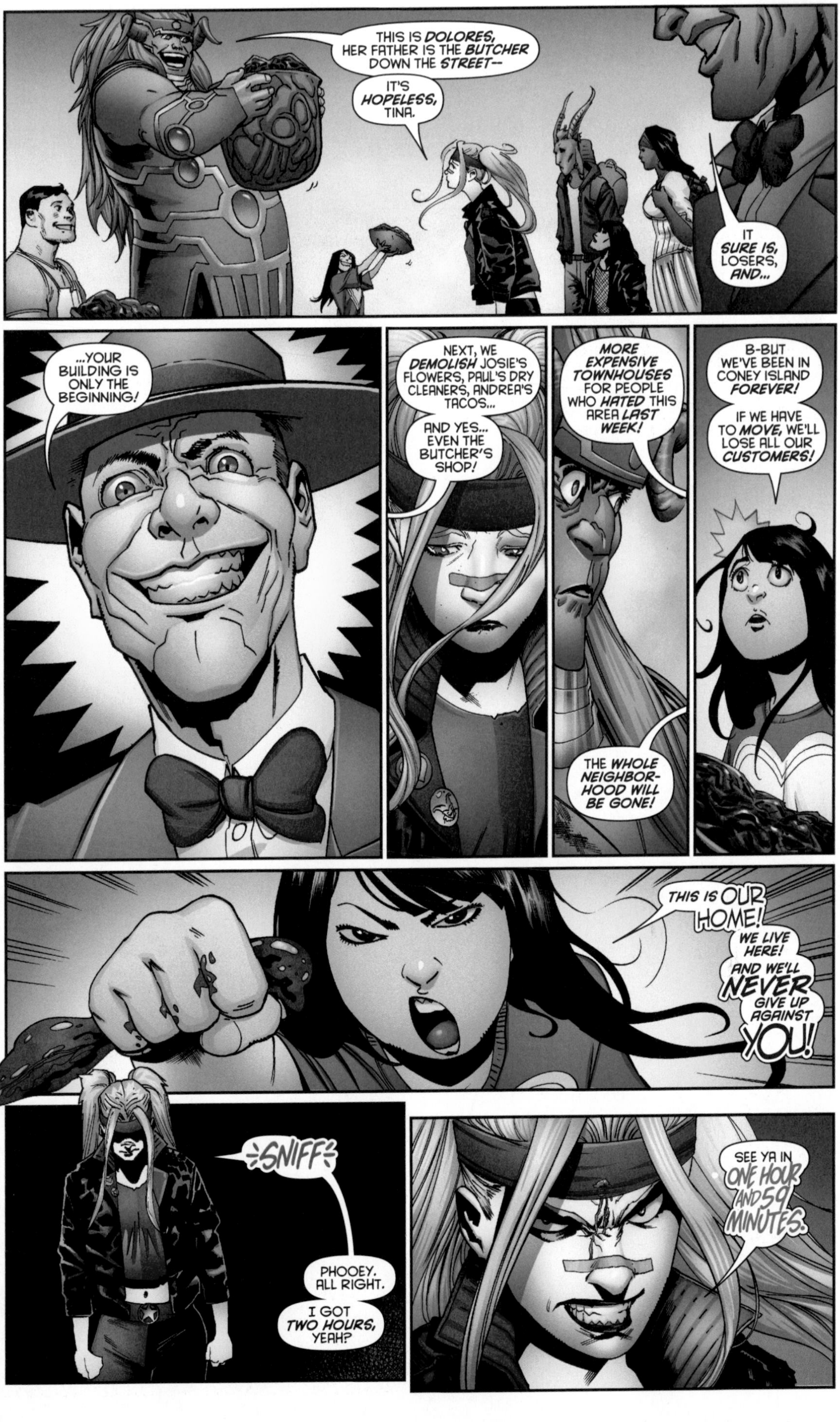
THIS IS DOLORES, HER FATHER IS THE BUTCHER DOWN THE STREET--
IT'S HOPELESS, TINA.
IT SURE IS, LOSERS, AND...
...YOUR BUILDING IS ONLY THE BEGINNING!
NEXT, WE DEMOLISH JOSIE'S FLOWERS, PAUL'S DRY CLEANERS, ANDREA'S TACOS...
AND YES... EVEN THE BUTCHER'S SHOP!
MORE EXPENSIVE TOWNHOUSES FOR PEOPLE WHO HATED THIS AREA LAST WEEK!
THE WHOLE NEIGHBOR-HOOD WILL BE GONE!
B-BUT WE'VE BEEN IN CONEY ISLAND FOREVER!
IF WE HAVE TO MOVE, WE'LL LOSE ALL OUR CUSTOMERS!
THIS IS OUR HOME!
WE LIVE HERE!
AND WE'LL NEVER GIVE UP AGAINST YOU!
SNIFF
PHOOEY. ALL RIGHT.
I GOT TWO HOURS, YEAH?
SEE YA IN ONE HOUR AND 59 MINUTES.

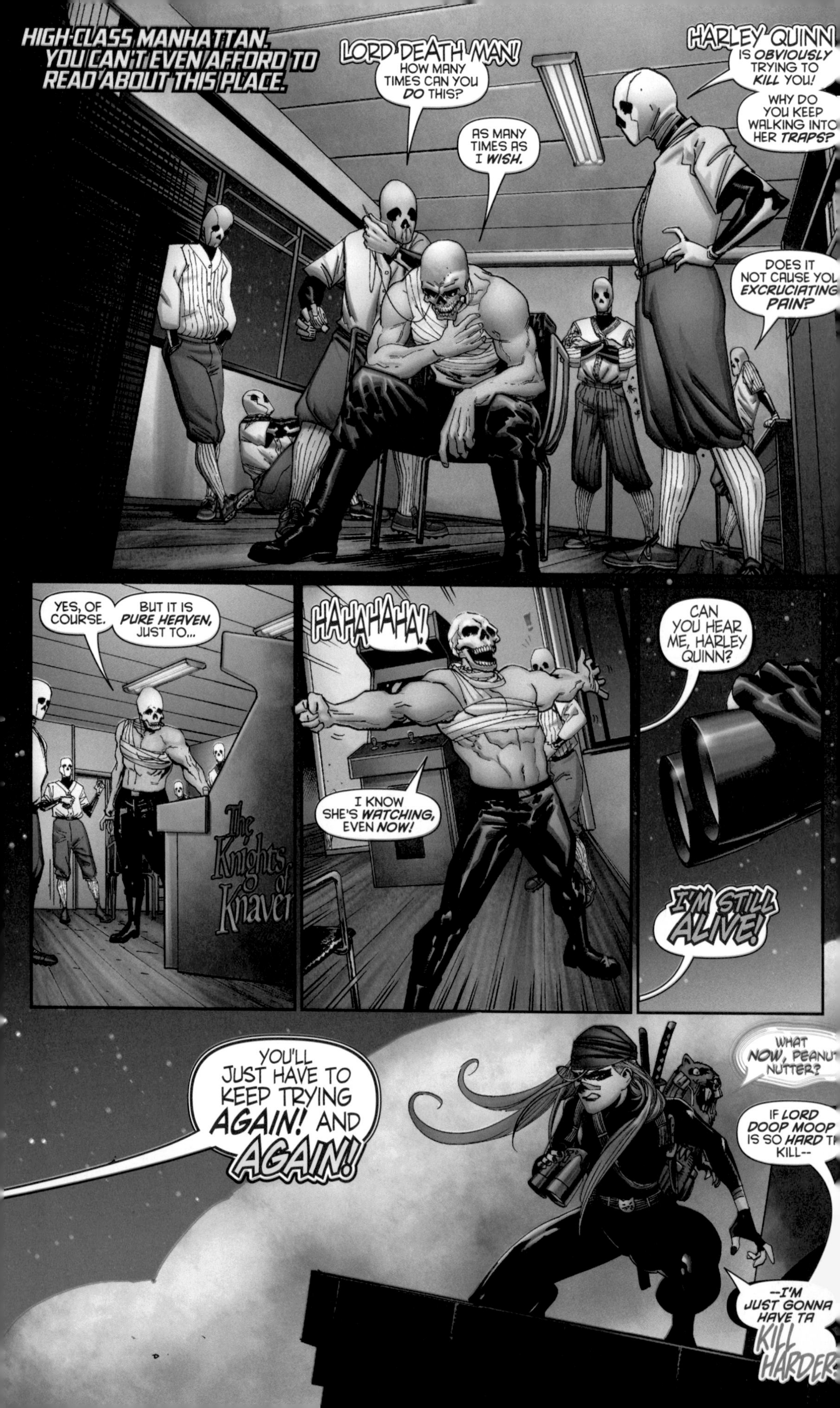
HIGH-CLASS MANHATTAN. YOU CAN'T EVEN AFFORD TO READ ABOUT THIS PLACE.
LORD DEATH MAN! HOW MANY TIMES CAN YOU DO THIS?
AS MANY TIMES AS I WISH.
HARLEY QUINN IS OBVIOUSLY TRYING TO KILL YOU!
WHY DO YOU KEEP WALKING INTO HER TRAPS?
DOES IT NOT CAUSE YOU EXCRUCIATING PAIN?
YES, OF COURSE.
BUT IT IS PURE HEAVEN, JUST TO...
The Knights of Knaver
HAHAHAHA!
I KNOW SHE'S WATCHING, EVEN NOW!
CAN YOU HEAR ME, HARLEY QUINN?
I'M STILL ALIVE!
YOU'LL JUST HAVE TO KEEP TRYING AGAIN! AND AGAIN!
WHAT NOW, PEANUT NUTTER?
IF LORD DOOP MOOP IS SO HARD T KILL--
--I'M JUST GONNA HAVE TA KILL HARDER!

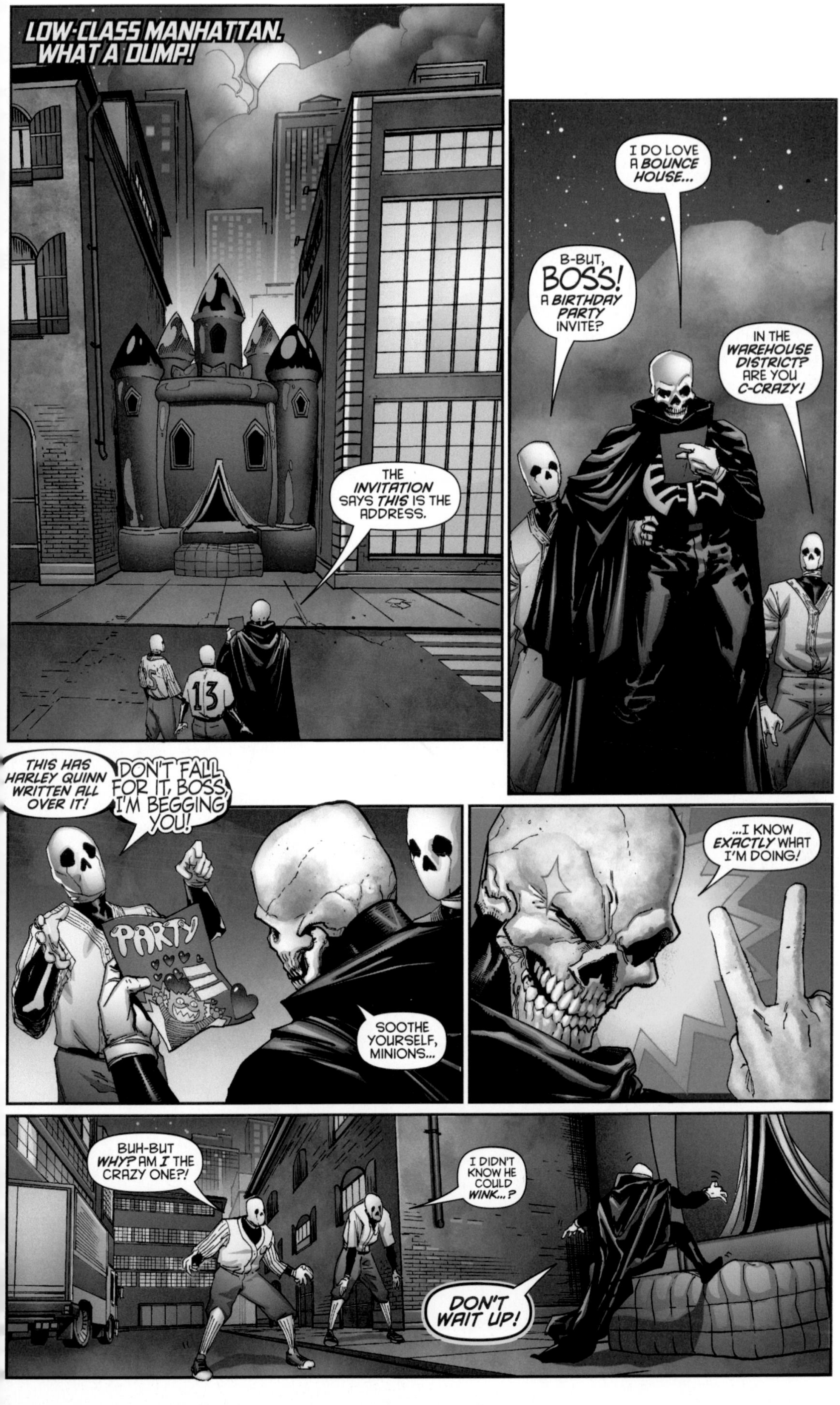
LOW-CLASS MANHATTAN. WHAT A DUMP!
THE INVITATION SAYS THIS IS THE ADDRESS.
I DO LOVE A BOUNCE HOUSE...
B-BUT, BOSS! A BIRTHDAY PARTY INVITE?
IN THE WAREHOUSE DISTRICT? ARE YOU C-CRAZY!
THIS HAS HARLEY QUINN WRITTEN ALL OVER IT!
DON'T FALL FOR IT, BOSS, I'M BEGGING YOU!
PARTY
SOOTHE YOURSELF, MINIONS...
...I KNOW EXACTLY WHAT I'M DOING!
BUH-BUT WHY? AM I THE CRAZY ONE?!
I DIDN'T KNOW HE COULD WINK...?
DON'T WAIT UP!

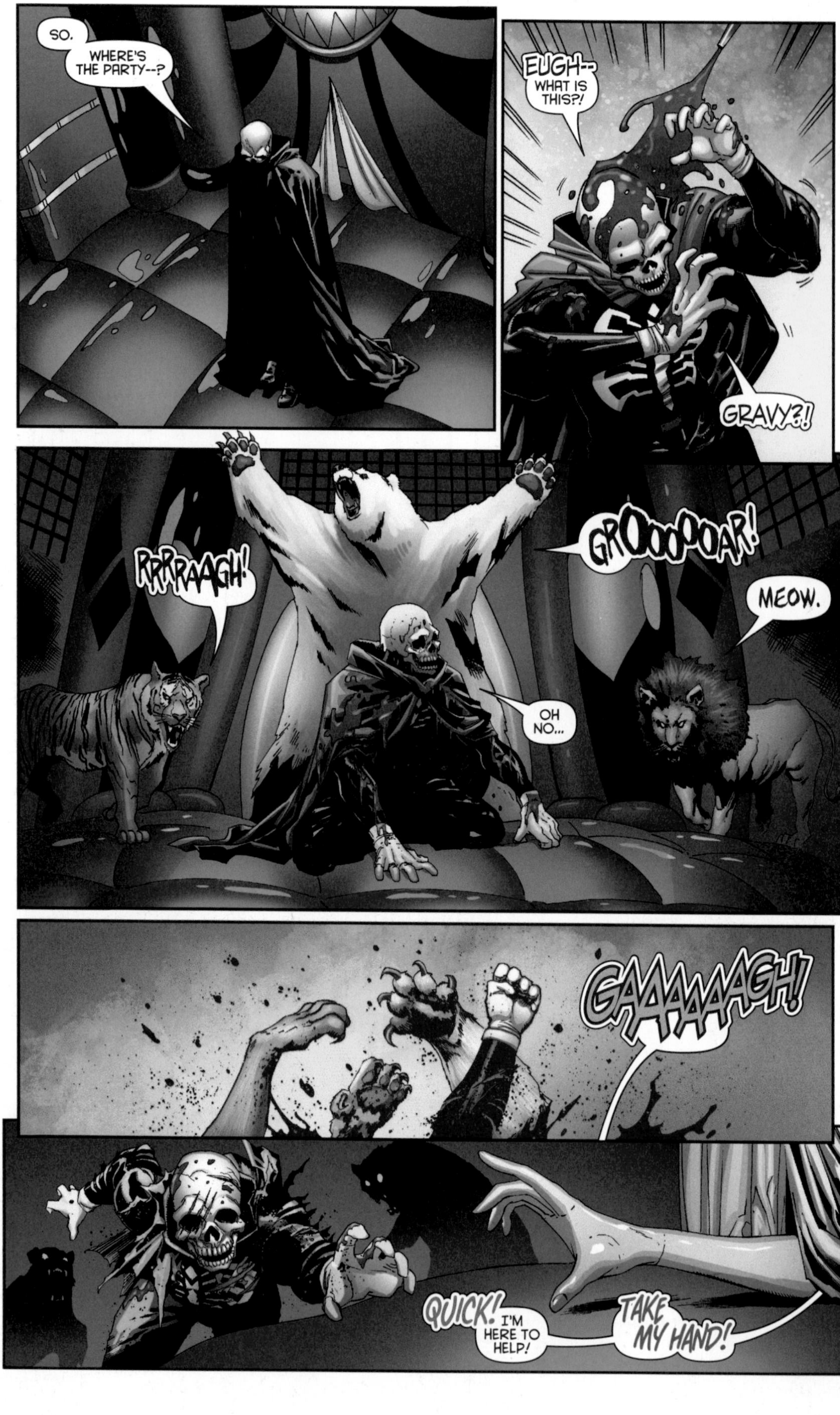
SO.
WHERE'S THE PARTY--?
EUGH--
WHAT IS THIS?!
GRAVY?!
RRRRAAGH!
GROOOOOAR!
MEOW.
OH NO...
GAAAAAAGH!
QUICK!
I'M HERE TO HELP!
TAKE MY HAND!

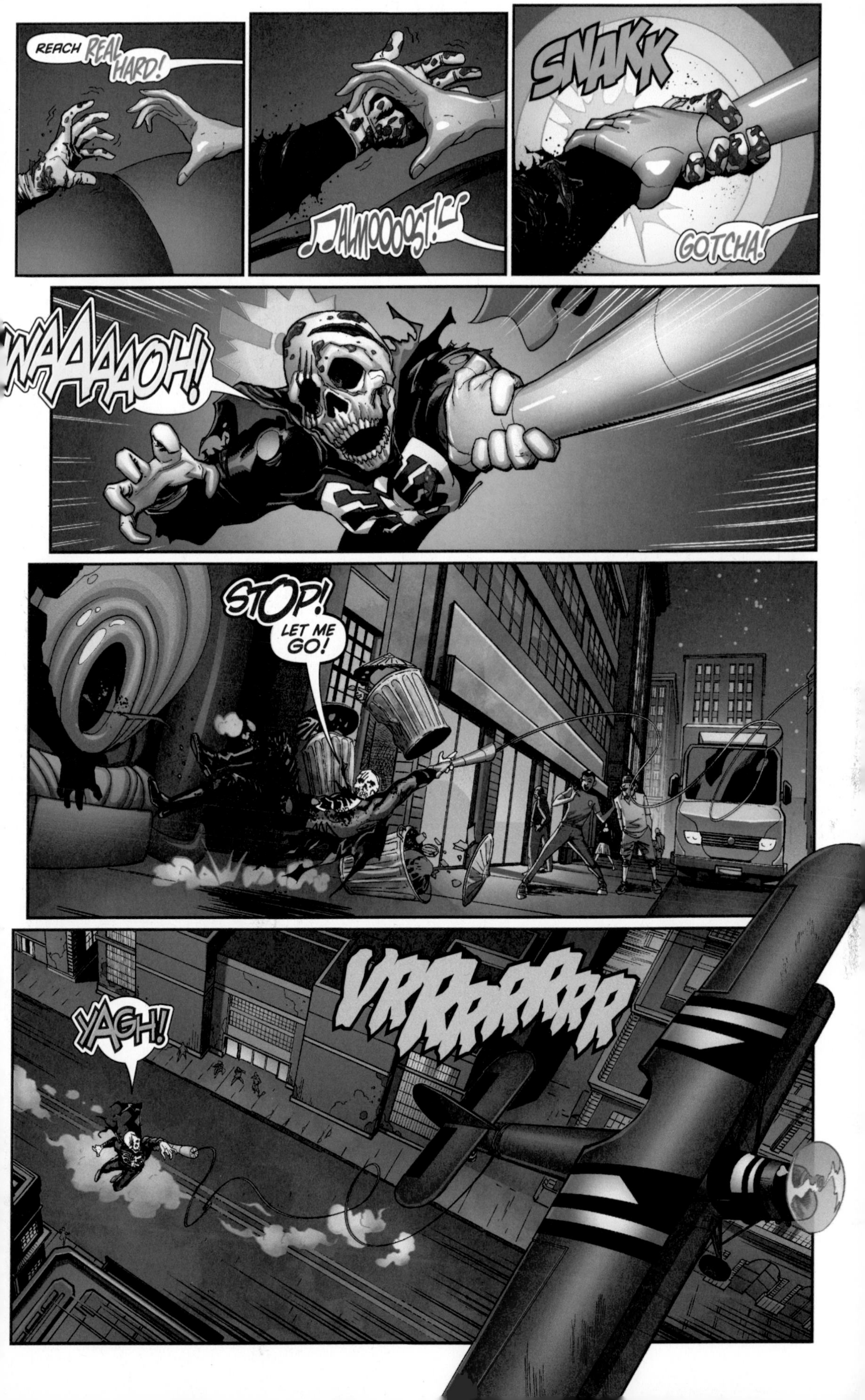

REACH REAL HARD!
ALMOOOOOST!
SNAKK
GOTCHA!
WAAAAOH!
STOP! LET ME GO!
VRRRRRRRR
YAGH!

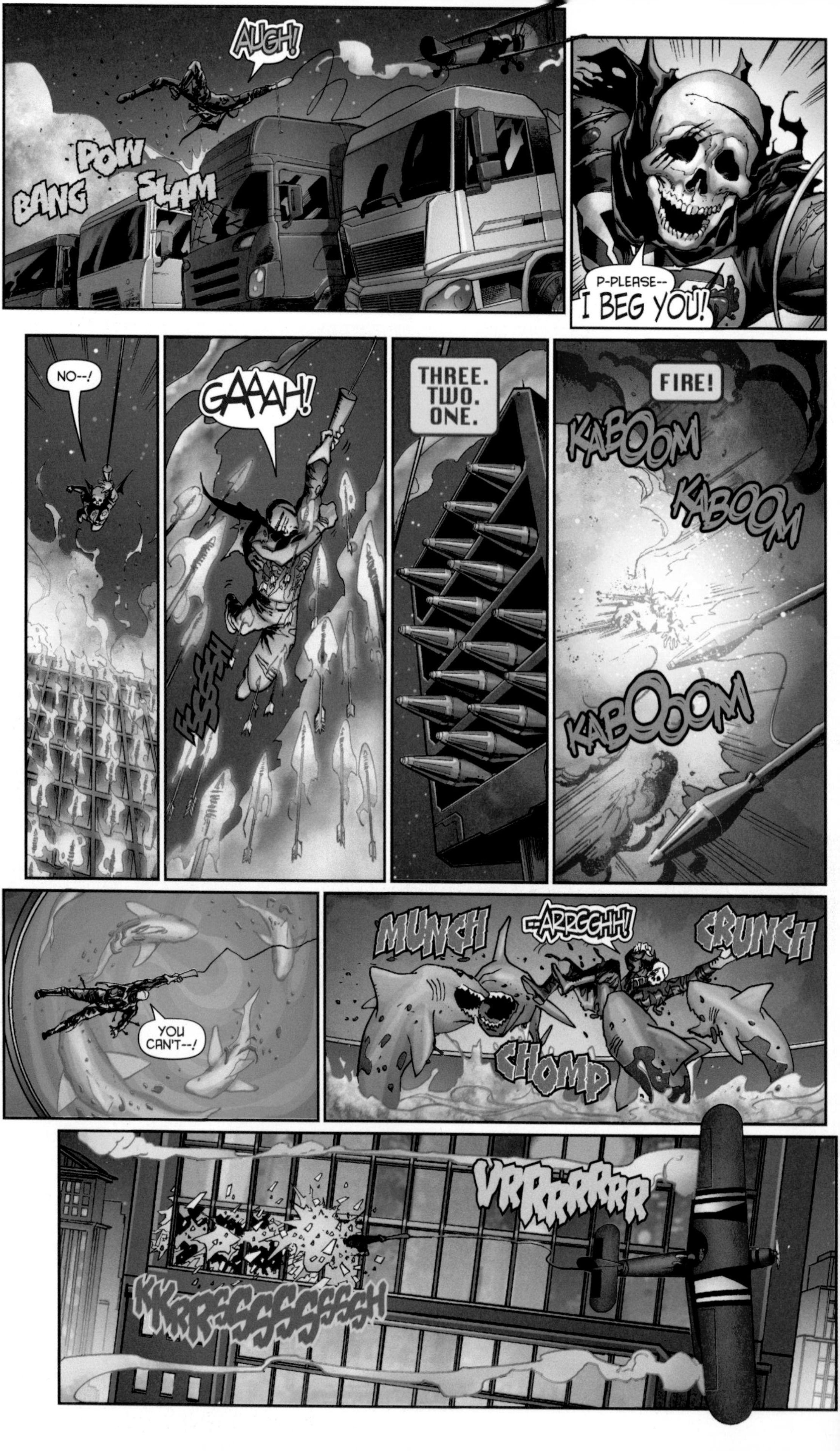
AUGH!
POW
BANG
SLAM
P-PLEASE--
I BEG YOU!
NO--!
GAAAH!
FSSSSH
THREE.
TWO.
ONE.
FIRE!
KABOOM
KABOOM
KABOOOM
YOU CAN'T--!
MUNCH
--ARRGGHH!
CRUNCH
CHOMP
VRRRRRRRR
KKRRSSSSSSSSH

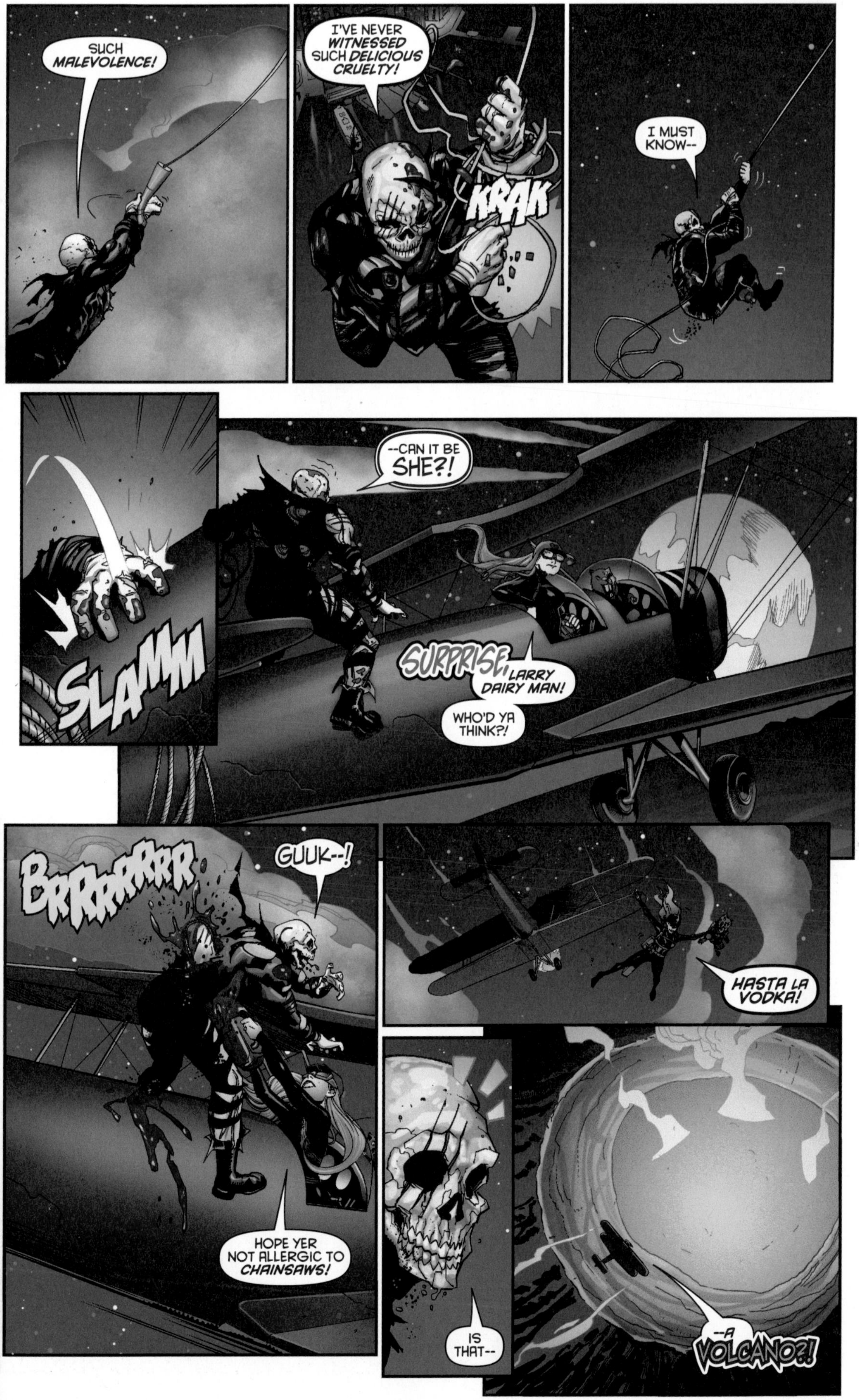
SUCH MALEVOLENCE!
I'VE NEVER WITNESSED SUCH DELICIOUS CRUELTY!
KRAK
I MUST KNOW--
SLAMM
--CAN IT BE SHE?!
SURPRISE, LARRY DAIRY MAN!
WHO'D YA THINK?!
BRRRRRRR
GUUK--!
HOPE YER NOT ALLERGIC TO CHAINSAWS!
HASTA LA VODKA!
IS THAT--
--A VOLCANO?!

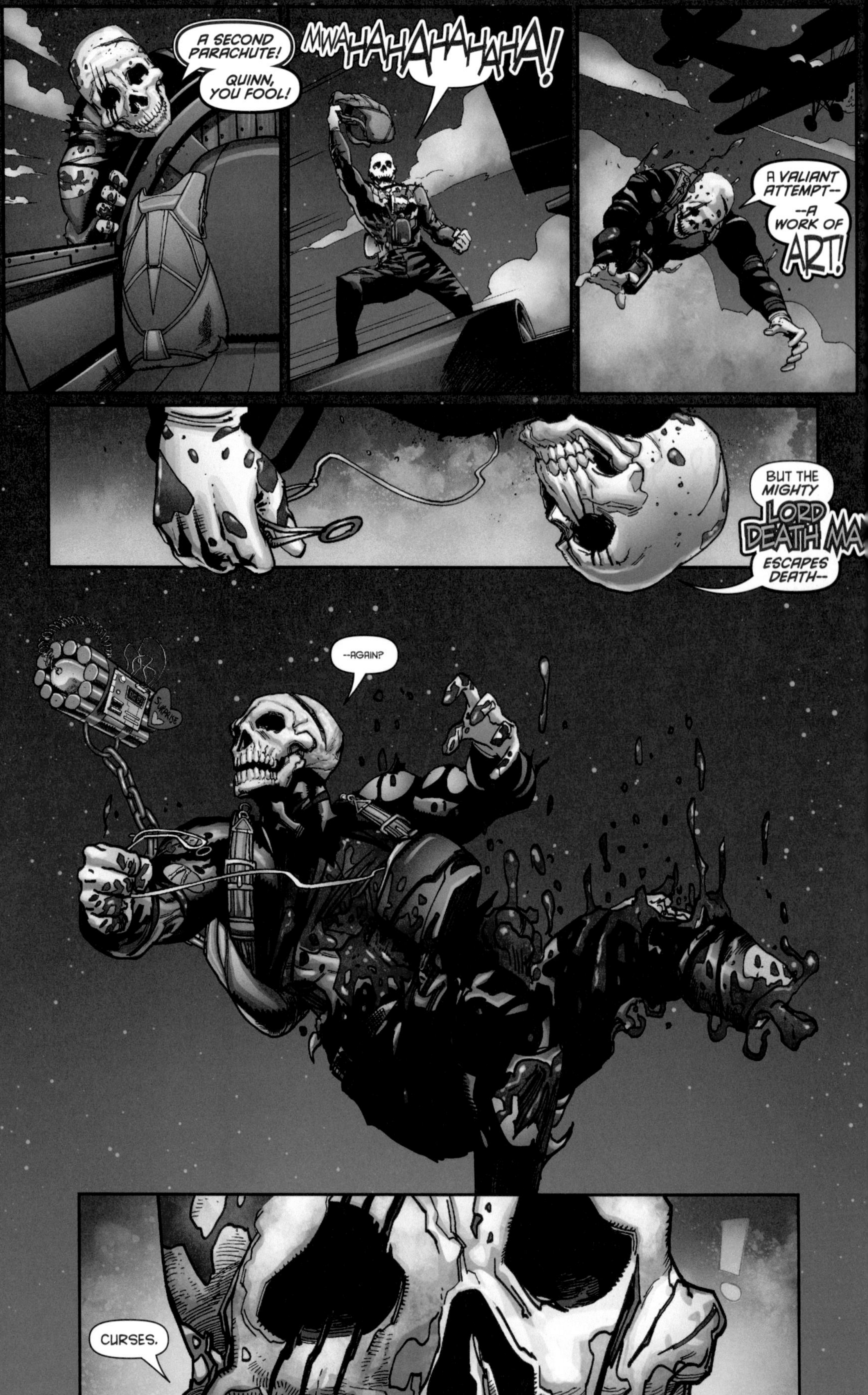
A SECOND PARACHUTE!
QUINN, YOU FOOL!
MWAHAHAHAHAHAHA!
A VALIANT ATTEMPT--
--A WORK OF ART!
BUT THE MIGHTY LORD DEATH MA
ESCAPES DEATH--
--AGAIN?
SURPRISE
CURSES.

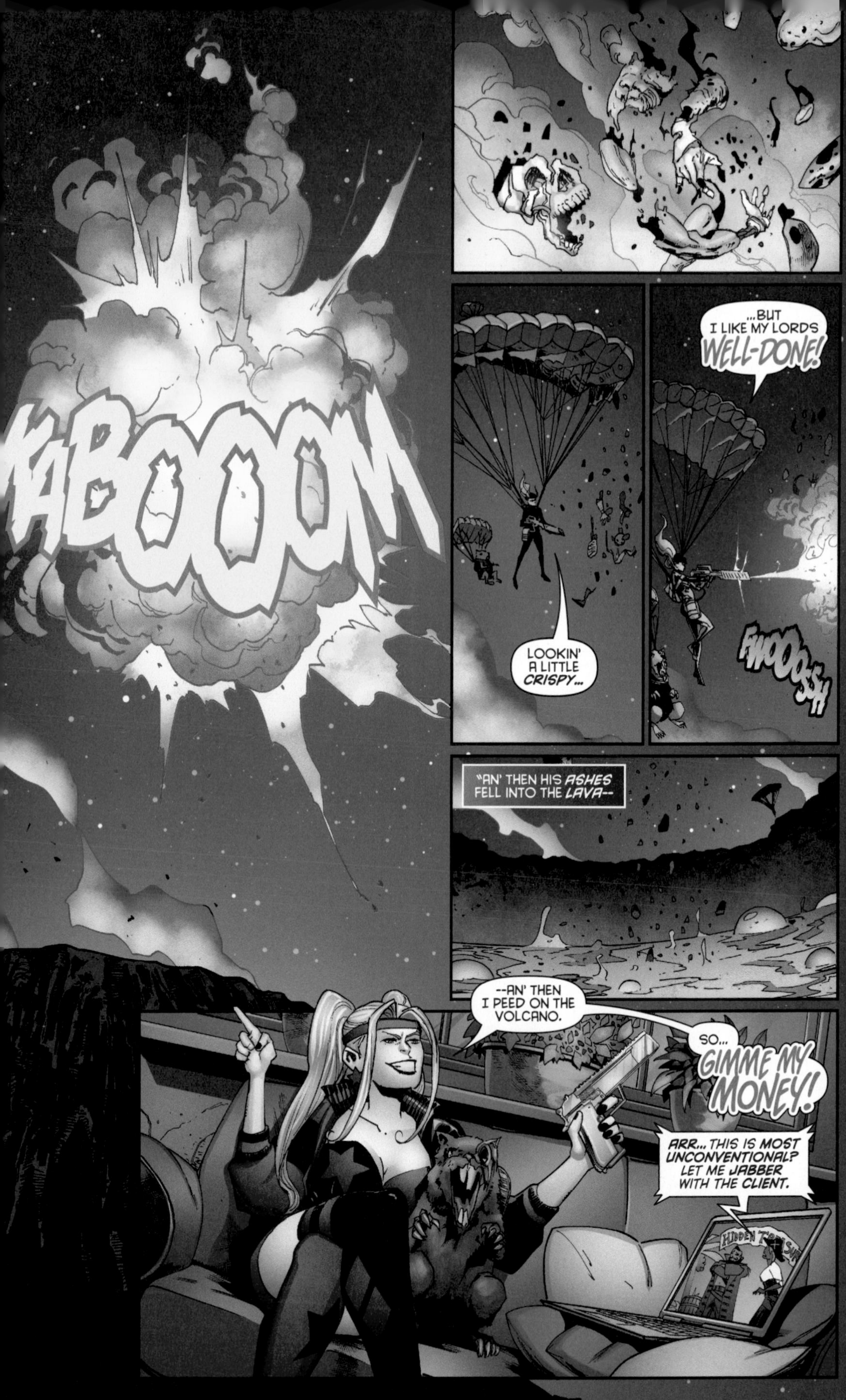
KABOOOM
LOOKIN' A LITTLE CRISPY...
...BUT I LIKE MY LORDS WELL-DONE!
FWOOOSH
"AN' THEN HIS ASHES FELL INTO THE LAVA--
--AN' THEN I PEED ON THE VOLCANO.
SO... GIMME MY MONEY!
ARR... THIS IS MOST UNCONVENTIONAL? LET ME JABBER WITH THE CLIENT.

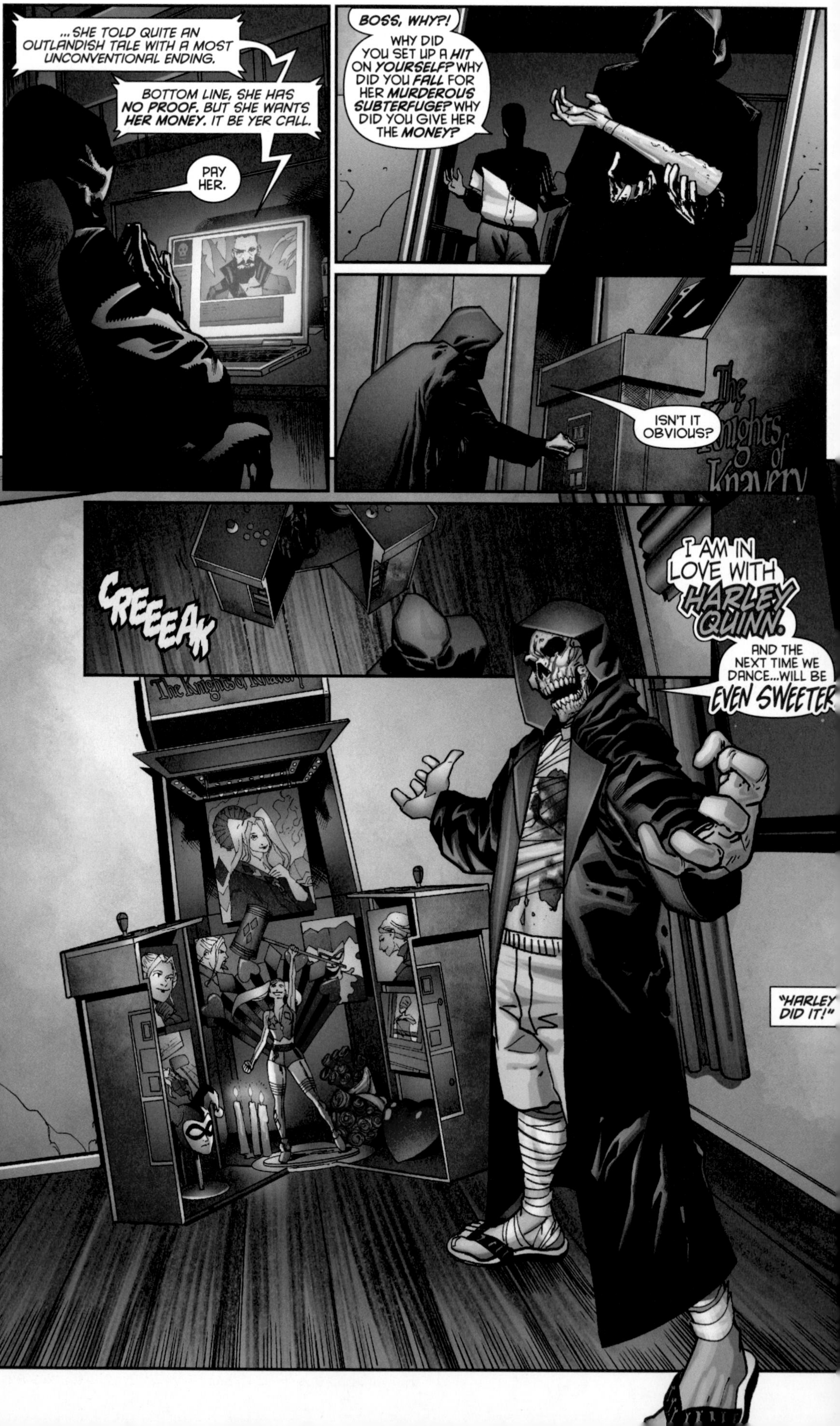
...SHE TOLD QUITE AN OUTLANDISH TALE WITH A MOST UNCONVENTIONAL ENDING.
BOTTOM LINE, SHE HAS NO PROOF. BUT SHE WANTS HER MONEY. IT BE YER CALL.
PAY HER.
BOSS, WHY?! WHY DID YOU SET UP A HIT ON YOURSELF? WHY DID YOU FALL FOR HER MURDEROUS SUBTERFUGE? WHY DID YOU GIVE HER THE MONEY?
ISN'T IT OBVIOUS?
The Knights of Knavery
CREEEAK
I AM IN LOVE WITH HARLEY QUINN.
AND THE NEXT TIME WE DANCE...WILL BE EVEN SWEETER
"HARLEY DID IT!"

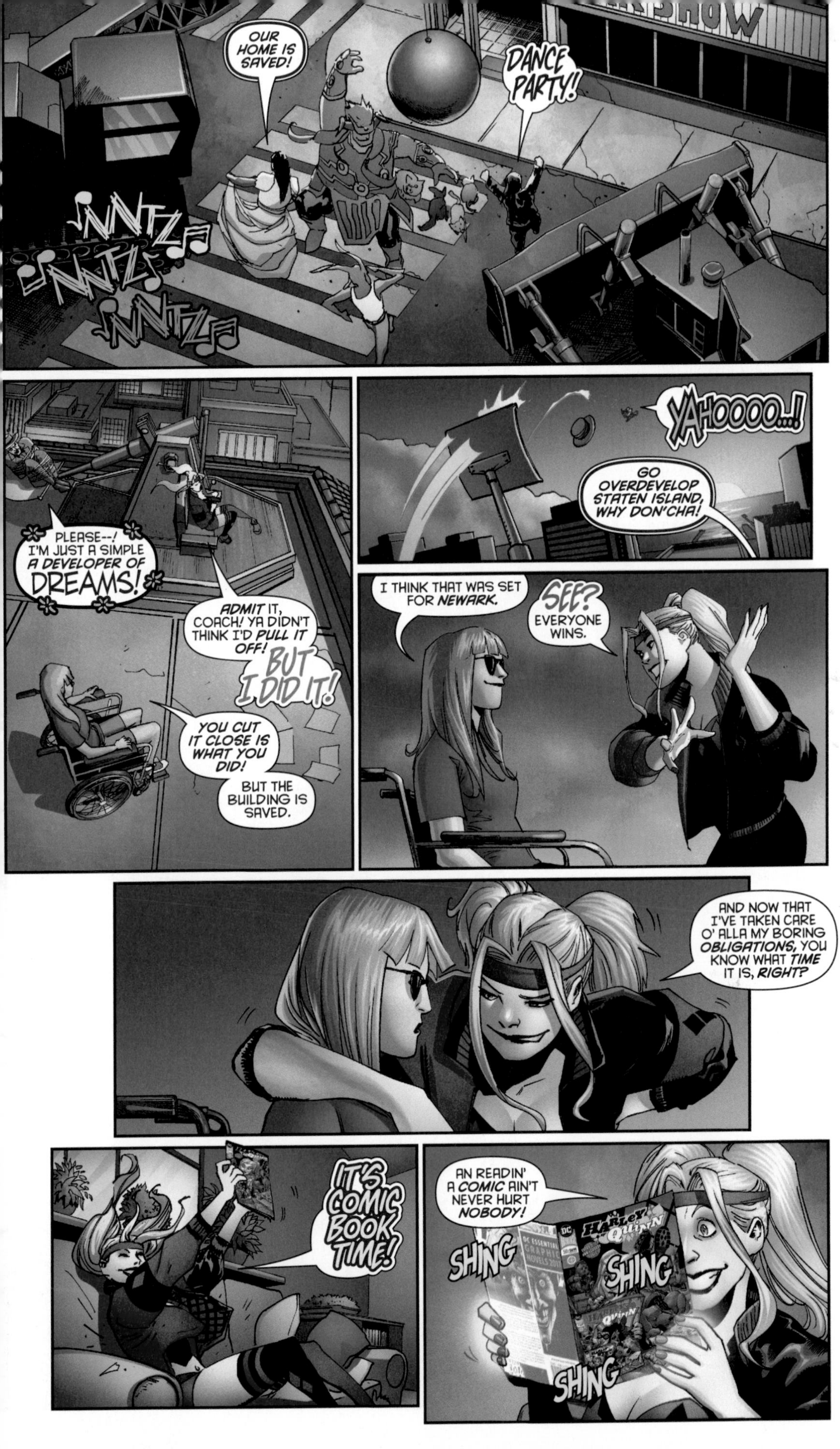
OUR HOME IS SAVED!
DANCE PARTY!
NNNTZ
NNNTZ
NNNTZ
PLEASE--! I'M JUST A SIMPLE A DEVELOPER OF DREAMS!
ADMIT IT, COACH! YA DIDN'T THINK I'D PULL IT OFF! BUT I DID IT!
YOU CUT IT CLOSE IS WHAT YOU DID!
BUT THE BUILDING IS SAVED.
YAHOOOO...!
GO OVERDEVELOP STATEN ISLAND, WHY DON'CHA!
I THINK THAT WAS SET FOR NEWARK.
SEE? EVERYONE WINS.
AND NOW THAT I'VE TAKEN CARE O' ALLA MY BORING OBLIGATIONS, YOU KNOW WHAT TIME IT IS, RIGHT?
IT'S COMIC BOOK TIME!
AN READIN' A COMIC AIN'T NEVER HURT NOBODY!
SHING
SHING
SHING

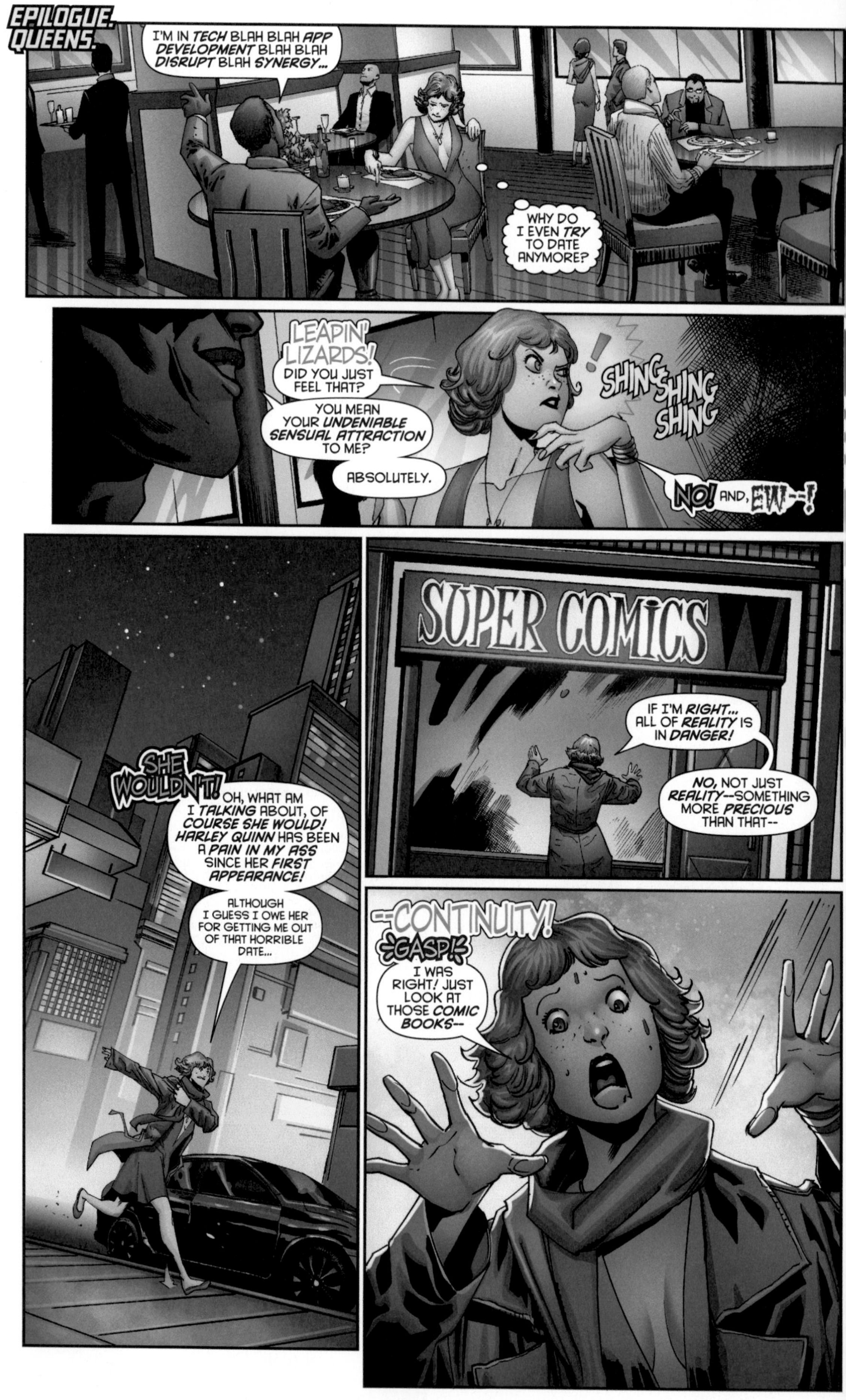
EPILOGUE. QUEENS.
I'M IN TECH BLAH BLAH APP DEVELOPMENT BLAH BLAH DISRUPT BLAH SYNERGY...
WHY DO I EVEN TRY TO DATE ANYMORE?
LEAPIN' LIZARDS!
DID YOU JUST FEEL THAT?
YOU MEAN YOUR UNDENIABLE SENSUAL ATTRACTION TO ME?
ABSOLUTELY.
SHING SHING SHING
!
NO! AND, EW--!
SHE WOULDN'T!
OH, WHAT AM I TALKING ABOUT, OF COURSE SHE WOULD! HARLEY QUINN HAS BEEN A PAIN IN MY ASS SINCE HER FIRST APPEARANCE!
ALTHOUGH I GUESS I OWE HER FOR GETTING ME OUT OF THAT HORRIBLE DATE...
SUPER COMICS
IF I'M RIGHT... ALL OF REALITY IS IN DANGER!
NO, NOT JUST REALITY--SOMETHING MORE PRECIOUS THAN THAT--
--CONTINUITY!
GASP!
I WAS RIGHT! JUST LOOK AT THOSE COMIC BOOKS--

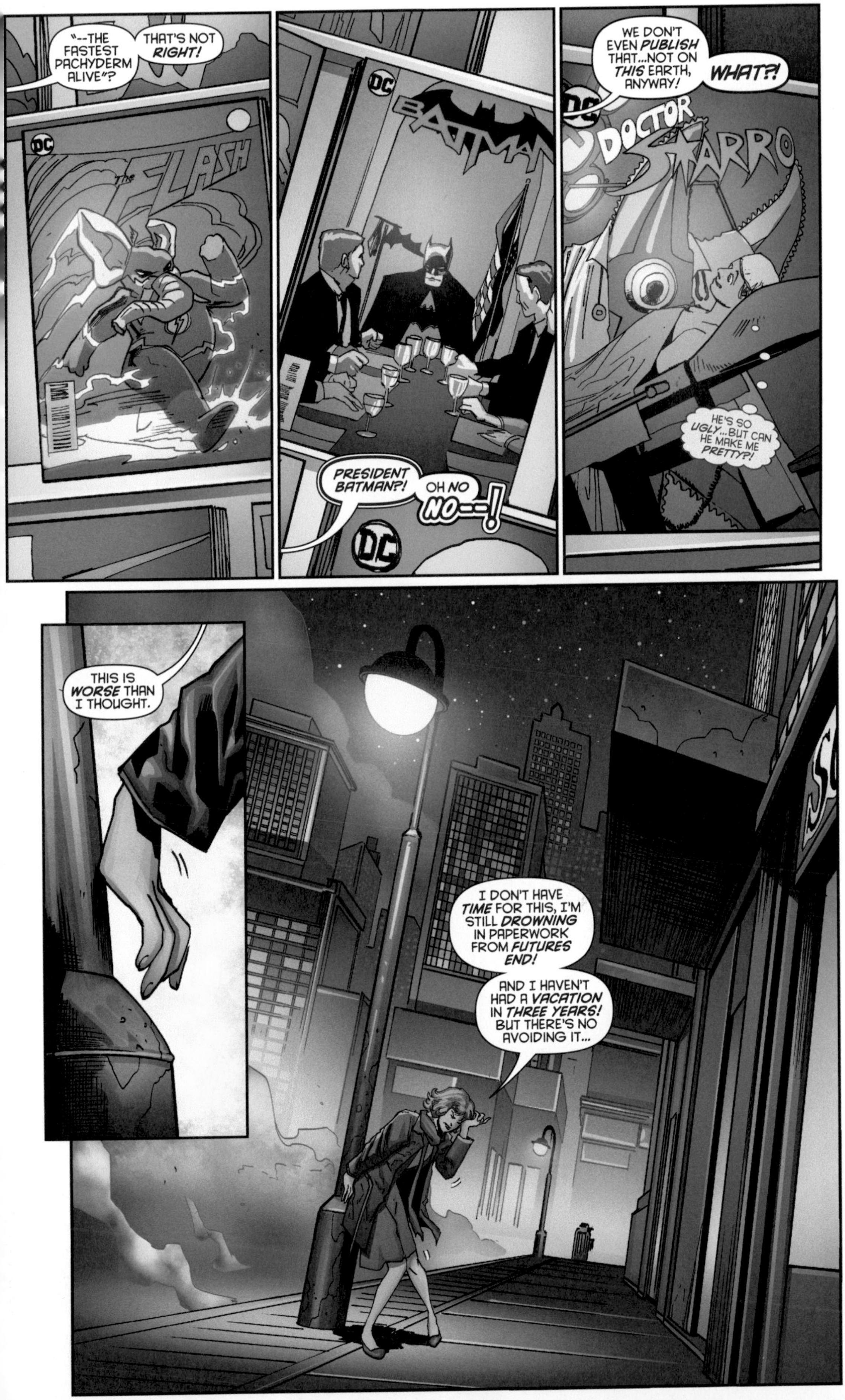
"--THE FASTEST PACHYDERM ALIVE"?
THAT'S NOT RIGHT!
DC
THE FLASH
DC
BATMAN
PRESIDENT BATMAN?!
OH NO NO--!
DC
WE DON'T EVEN PUBLISH THAT...NOT ON THIS EARTH, ANYWAY!
WHAT?!
DC
DOCTOR STARRO
HE'S SO UGLY...BUT CAN HE MAKE ME PRETTY?!
THIS IS WORSE THAN I THOUGHT.
I DON'T HAVE TIME FOR THIS, I'M STILL DROWNING IN PAPERWORK FROM FUTURES END!
AND I HAVEN'T HAD A VACATION IN THREE YEARS! BUT THERE'S NO AVOIDING IT...

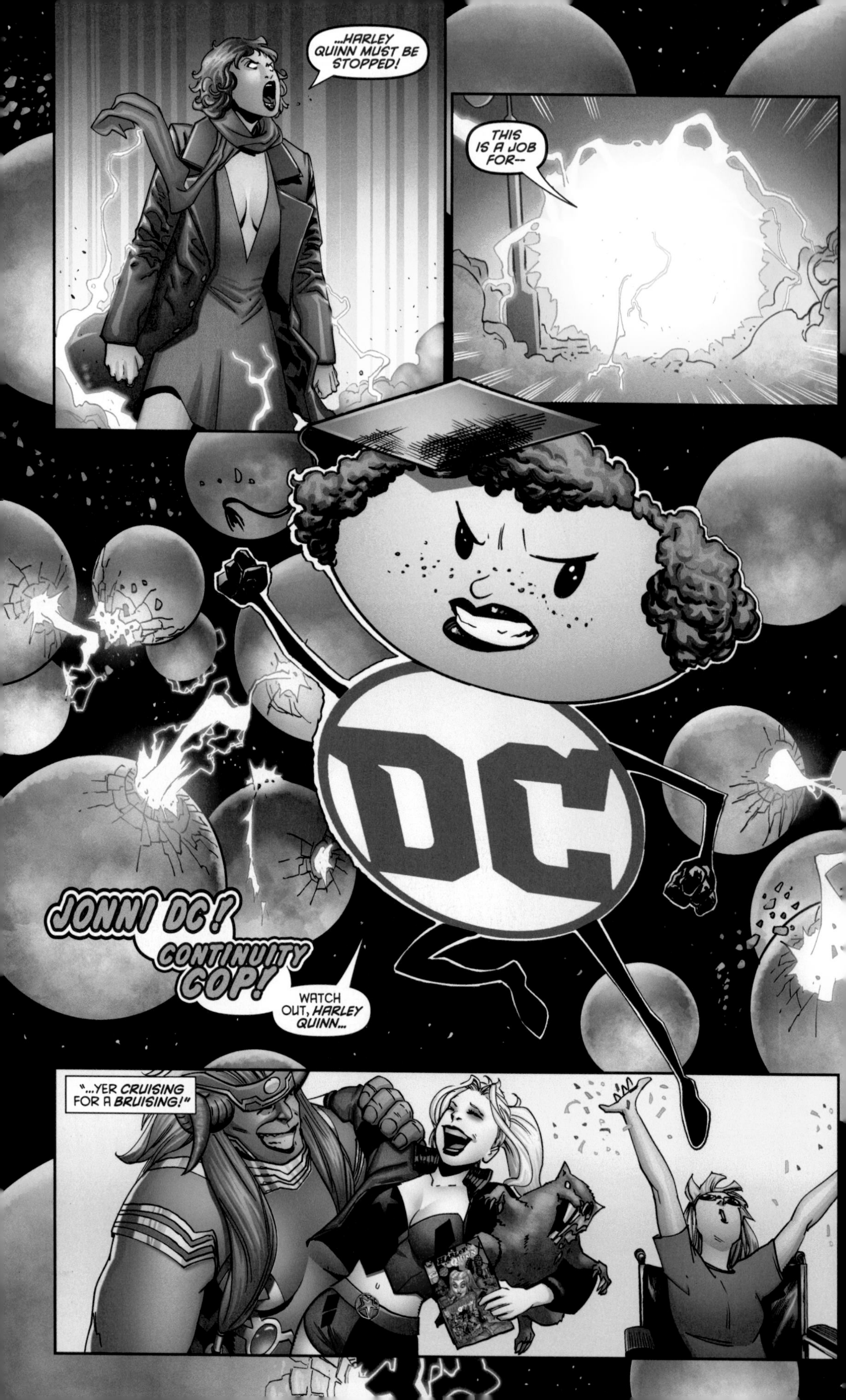
...HARLEY QUINN MUST BE STOPPED!
THIS IS A JOB FOR--
JONNI DC!
CONTINUITY COP!
WATCH OUT, HARLEY QUINN...
"...YER CRUISING FOR A BRUISING!"

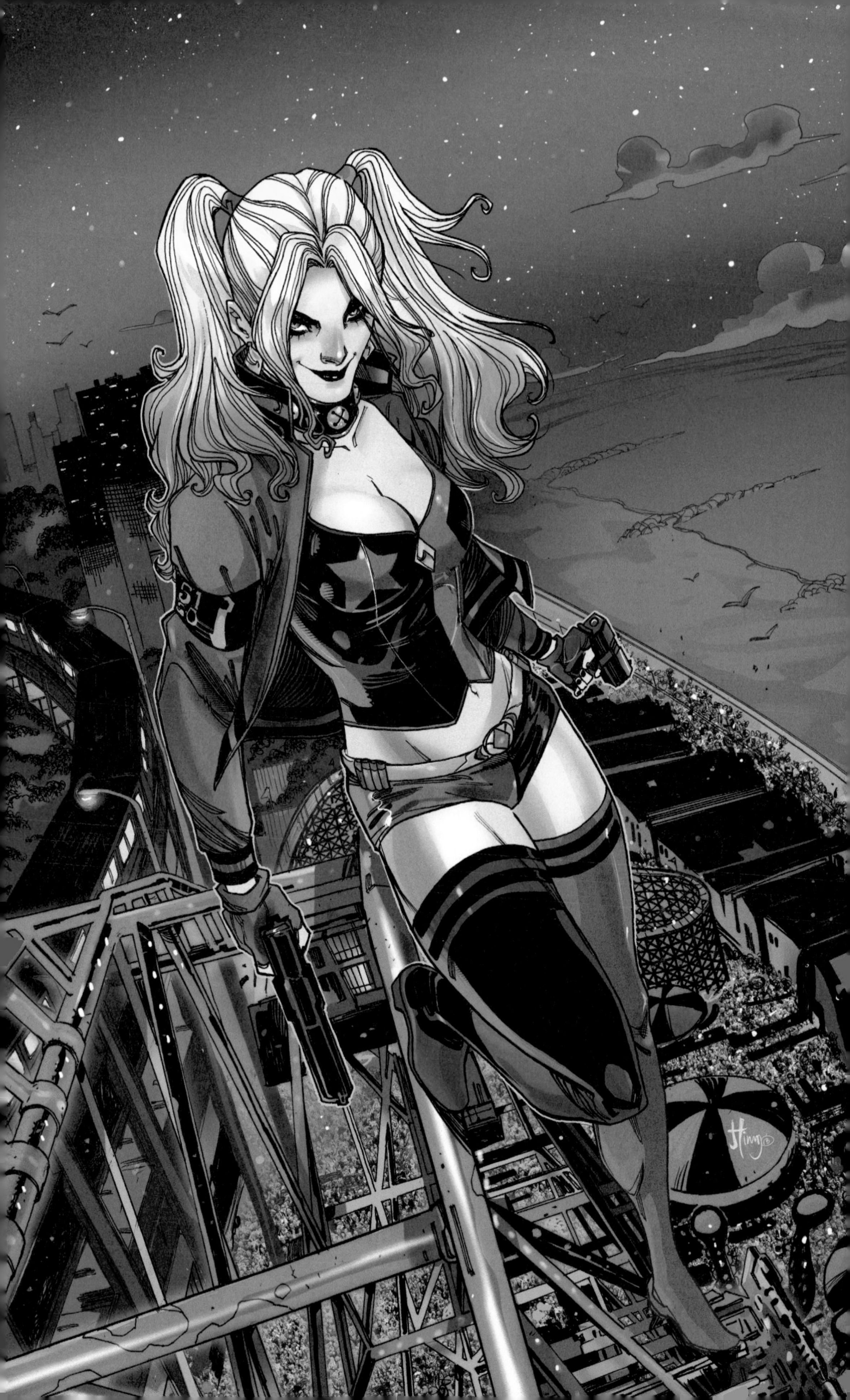

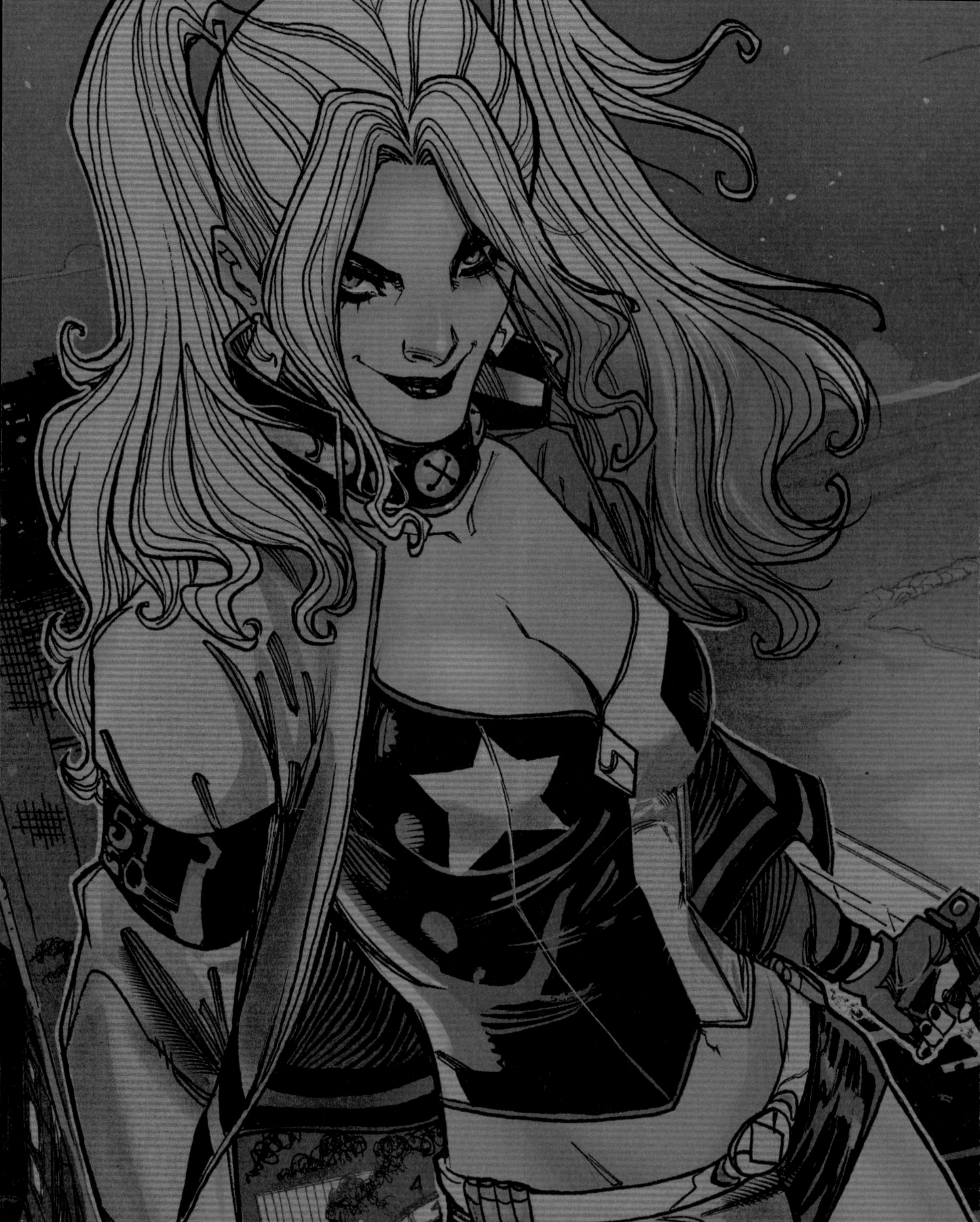

HARLEY QUINN
#43

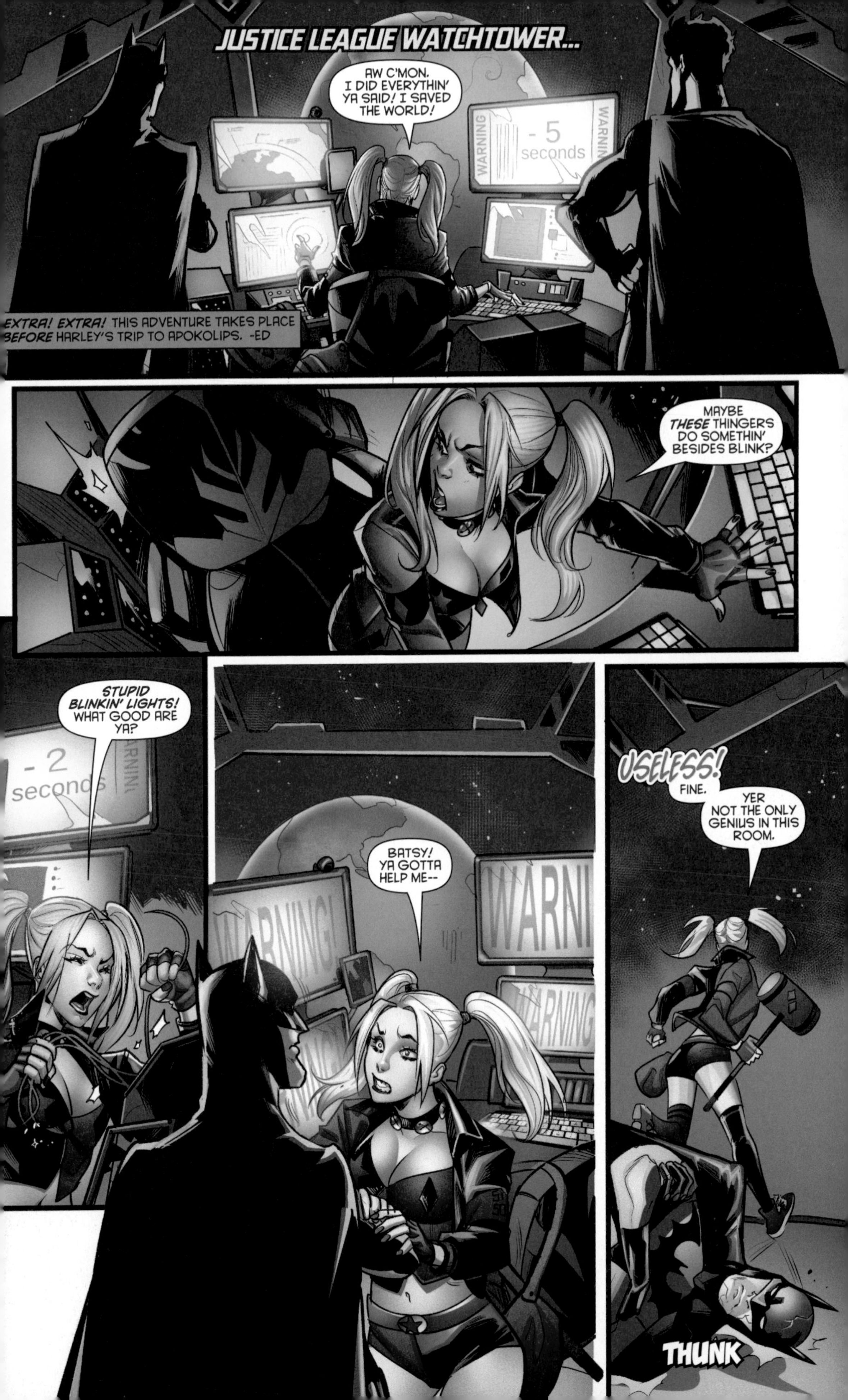
JUSTICE LEAGUE WATCHTOWER...
AW C'MON. I DID EVERYTHIN' YA SAID! I SAVED THE WORLD!
WARNING
- 5 seconds
WARNING
EXTRA! EXTRA! THIS ADVENTURE TAKES PLACE BEFORE HARLEY'S TRIP TO APOKOLIPS. -ED
MAYBE THESE THINGERS DO SOMETHIN' BESIDES BLINK?
STUPID BLINKIN' LIGHTS! WHAT GOOD ARE YA?
- 2 seconds
BATSY! YA GOTTA HELP ME--
WARNING!
WARNI
WARNING
USELESS!
FINE.
YER NOT THE ONLY GENIUS IN THIS ROOM.
THUNK

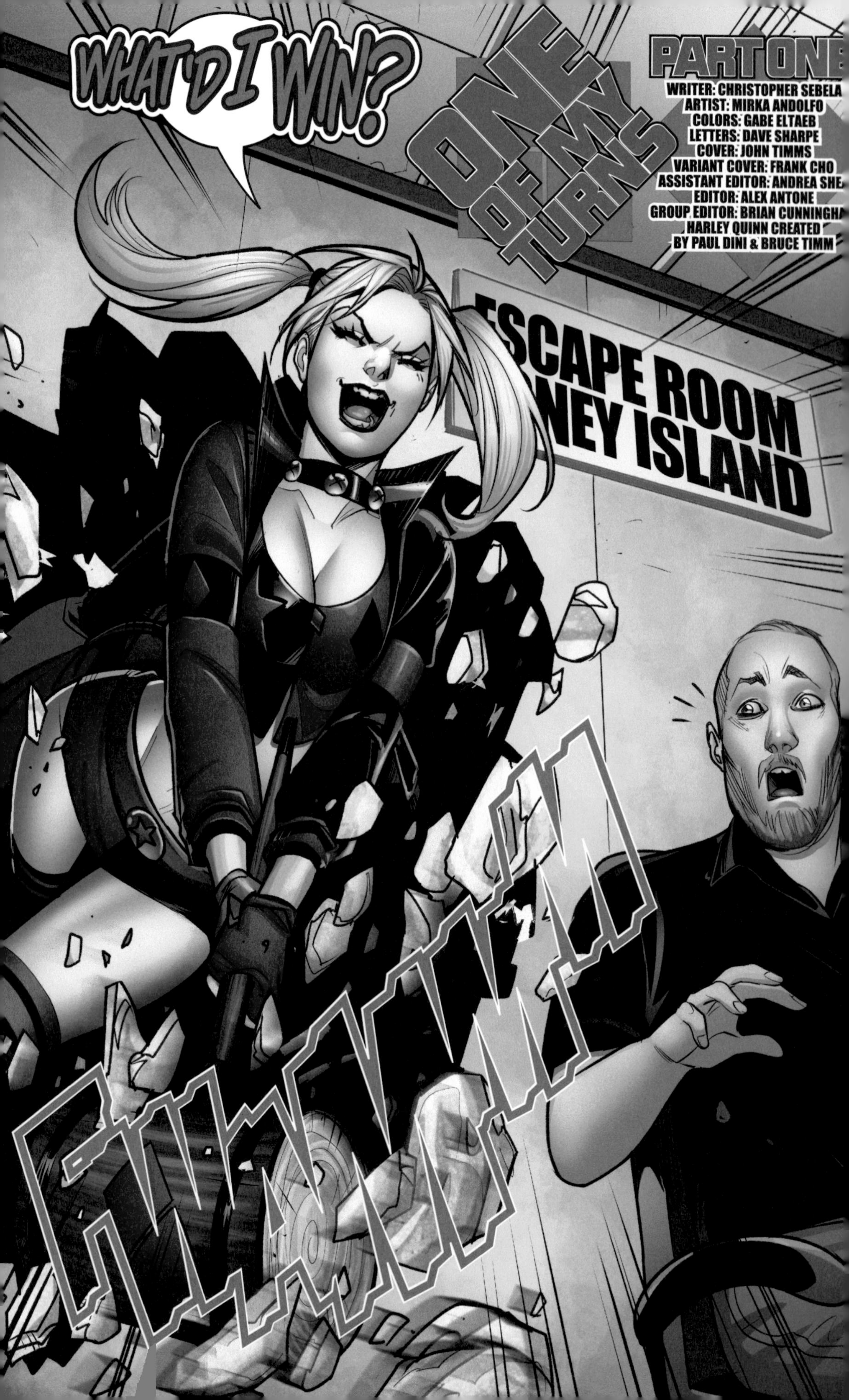
WHAT'D I WIN?
PART ONE
ONE OF MY TURNS
WRITER: CHRISTOPHER SEBELA
ARTIST: MIRKA ANDOLFO
COLORS: GABE ELTAEB
LETTERS: DAVE SHARPE
COVER: JOHN TIMMS
VARIANT COVER: FRANK CHO
ASSISTANT EDITOR: ANDREA SHE
EDITOR: ALEX ANTONE
GROUP EDITOR: BRIAN CUNNINGHA
HARLEY QUINN CREATED
BY PAUL DINI & BRUCE TIMM
ESCAPE ROOM
NEY ISLAND

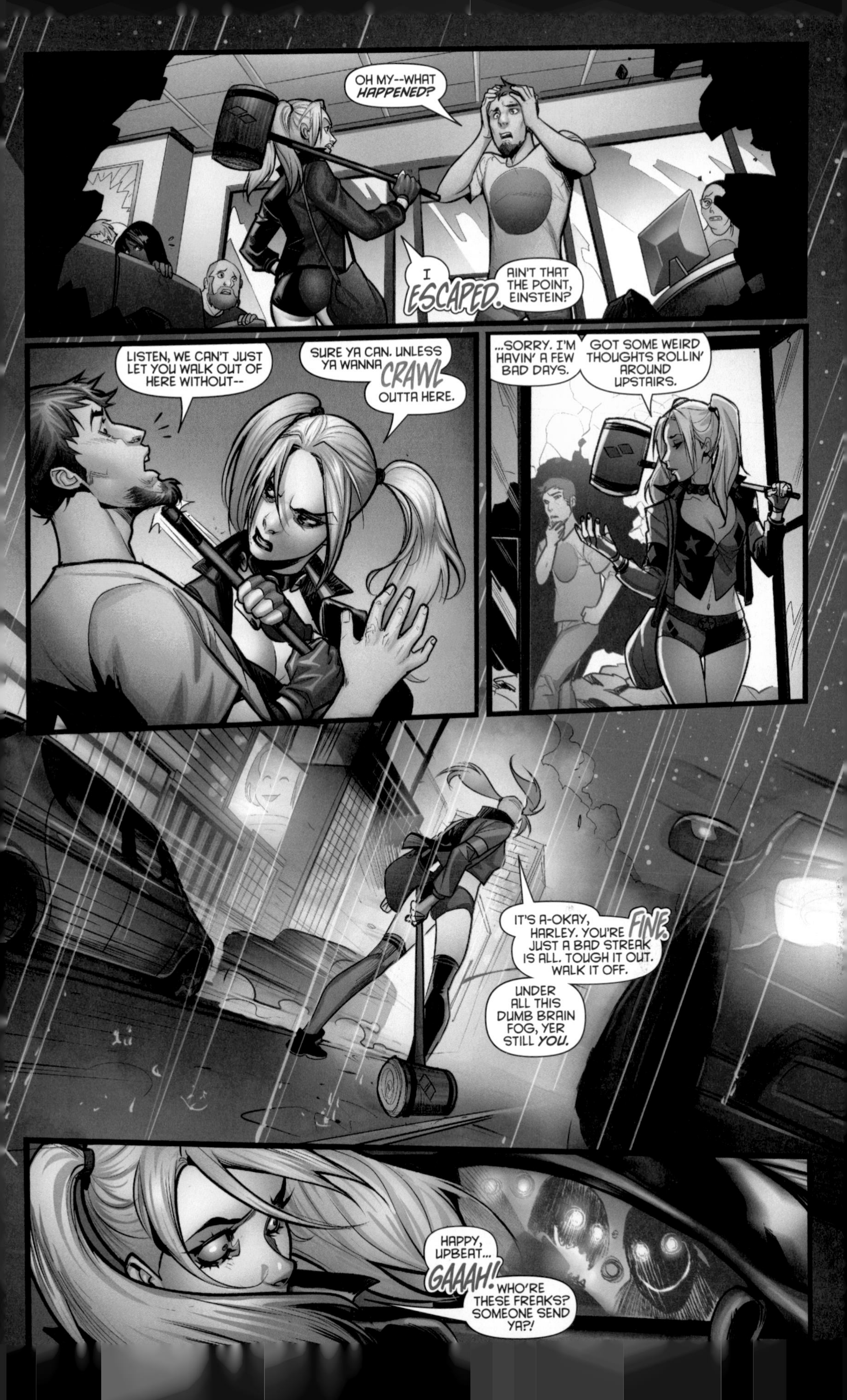
OH MY--WHAT HAPPENED?
I ESCAPED.
AIN'T THAT THE POINT, EINSTEIN?
LISTEN, WE CAN'T JUST LET YOU WALK OUT OF HERE WITHOUT--
SURE YA CAN. UNLESS YA WANNA CRAWL OUTTA HERE.
...SORRY. I'M HAVIN' A FEW BAD DAYS.
GOT SOME WEIRD THOUGHTS ROLLIN' AROUND UPSTAIRS.
IT'S A-OKAY, HARLEY. YOU'RE FINE. JUST A BAD STREAK IS ALL. TOUGH IT OUT. WALK IT OFF.
UNDER ALL THIS DUMB BRAIN FOG, YER STILL YOU.
HAPPY, UPBEAT...
GAAAH!
WHO'RE THESE FREAKS? SOMEONE SEND YA?!

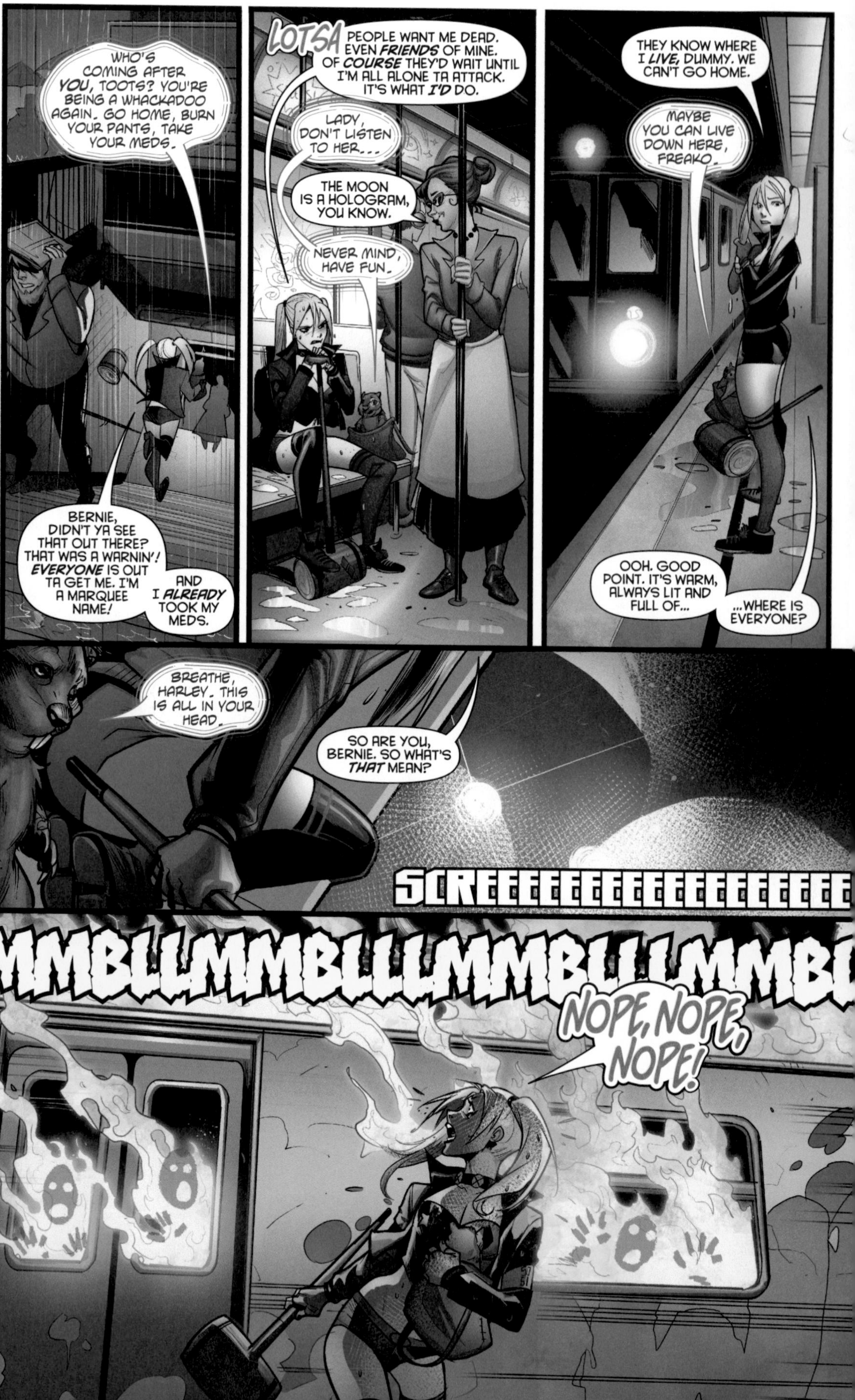
WHO'S COMING AFTER YOU, TOOTS? YOU'RE BEING A WHACKADOO AGAIN. GO HOME, BURN YOUR PANTS, TAKE YOUR MEDS.
BERNIE, DIDN'T YA SEE THAT OUT THERE? THAT WAS A WARNIN'! EVERYONE IS OUT TA GET ME. I'M A MARQUEE NAME!
AND I ALREADY TOOK MY MEDS.
LOTSA PEOPLE WANT ME DEAD. EVEN FRIENDS OF MINE. OF COURSE THEY'D WAIT UNTIL I'M ALL ALONE TA ATTACK. IT'S WHAT I'D DO.
LADY, DON'T LISTEN TO HER...
THE MOON IS A HOLOGRAM, YOU KNOW.
NEVER MIND, HAVE FUN.
THEY KNOW WHERE I LIVE, DUMMY. WE CAN'T GO HOME.
MAYBE YOU CAN LIVE DOWN HERE, FREAKO.
OOH. GOOD POINT. IT'S WARM, ALWAYS LIT AND FULL OF...
...WHERE IS EVERYONE?
BREATHE, HARLEY. THIS IS ALL IN YOUR HEAD.
SO ARE YOU, BERNIE. SO WHAT'S THAT MEAN?
SCREEEEEEEEEEEEEEEEEEE
MMBLLMMMBLLLMMBLLMMBL
NOPE, NOPE, NOPE!

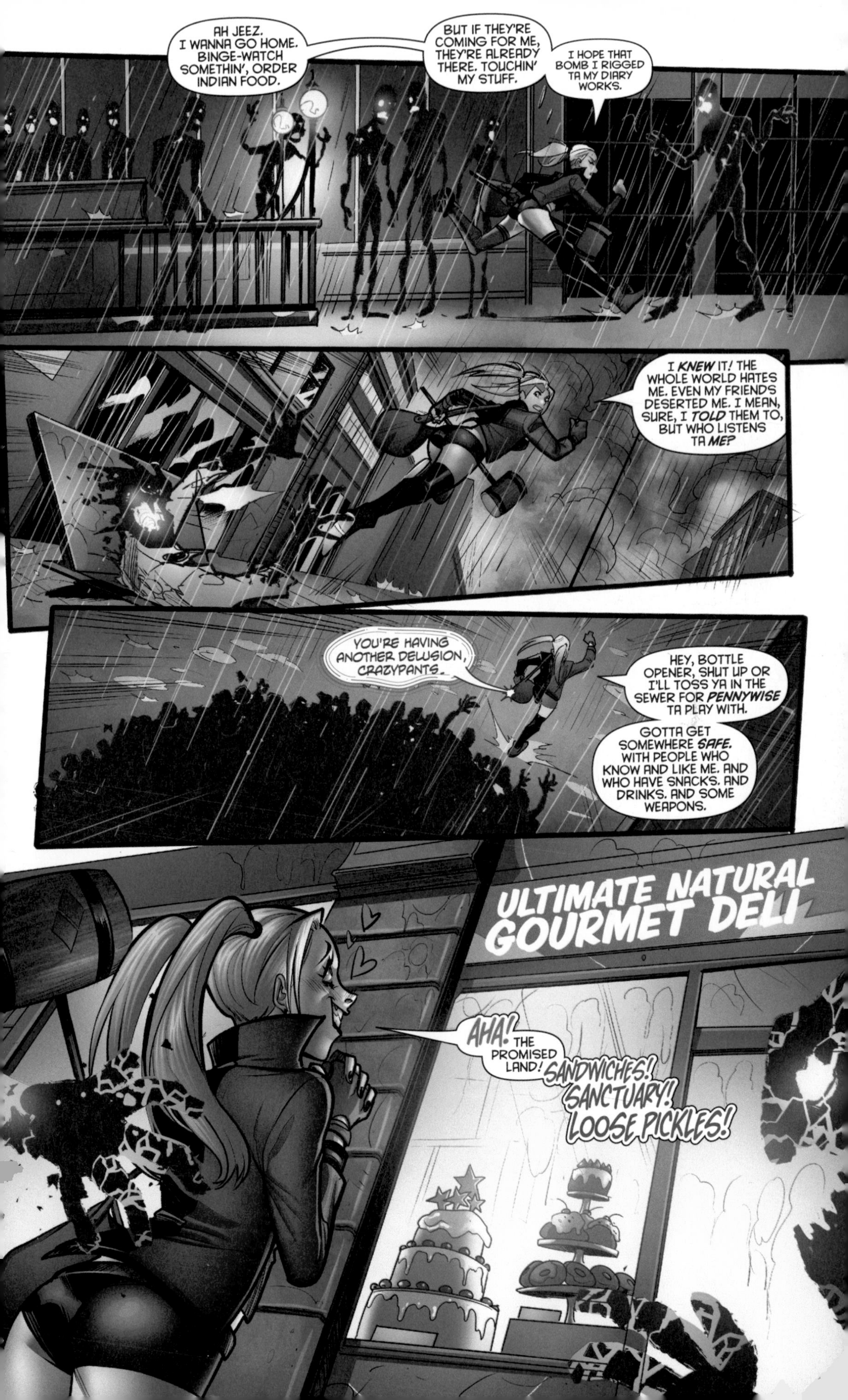

AH JEEZ. I WANNA GO HOME. BINGE-WATCH SOMETHIN', ORDER INDIAN FOOD.
BUT IF THEY'RE COMING FOR ME, THEY'RE ALREADY THERE. TOUCHIN' MY STUFF.
I HOPE THAT BOMB I RIGGED TA MY DIARY WORKS.
I KNEW IT! THE WHOLE WORLD HATES ME. EVEN MY FRIENDS DESERTED ME. I MEAN, SURE, I TOLD THEM TO, BUT WHO LISTENS TA ME?
YOU'RE HAVING ANOTHER DELUSION, CRAZYPANTS.
HEY, BOTTLE OPENER, SHUT UP OR I'LL TOSS YA IN THE SEWER FOR PENNYWISE TA PLAY WITH.
GOTTA GET SOMEWHERE SAFE. WITH PEOPLE WHO KNOW AND LIKE ME. AND WHO HAVE SNACKS. AND DRINKS. AND SOME WEAPONS.
ULTIMATE NATURAL GOURMET DELI
AHA! THE PROMISED LAND! SANDWICHES! SANCTUARY! LOOSE PICKLES!

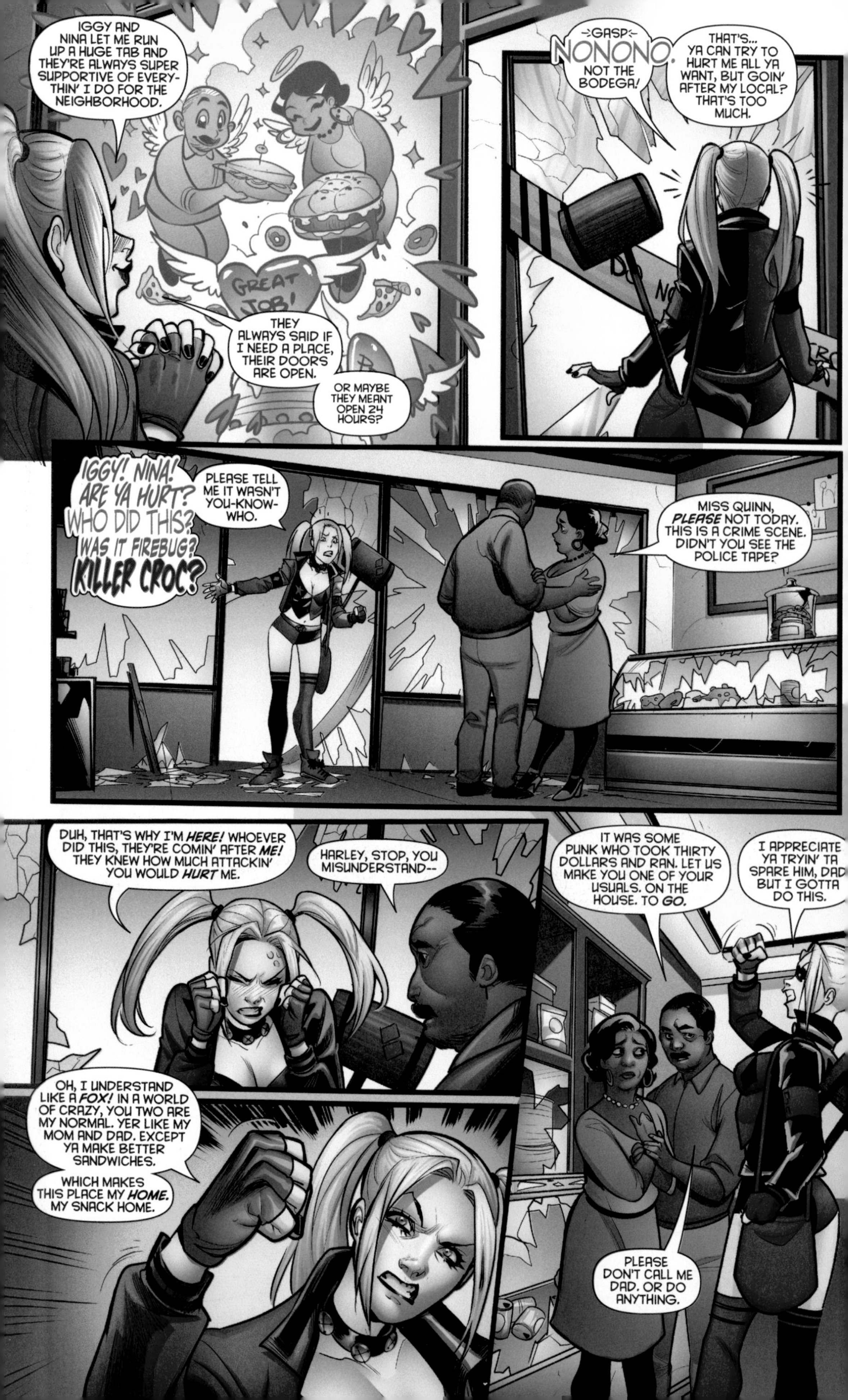

IGGY AND NINA LET ME RUN UP A HUGE TAB AND THEY'RE ALWAYS SUPER SUPPORTIVE OF EVERY-THIN' I DO FOR THE NEIGHBORHOOD.
GREAT JOB!
THEY ALWAYS SAID IF I NEED A PLACE, THEIR DOORS ARE OPEN.
OR MAYBE THEY MEANT OPEN 24 HOURS?
-GASP- NONONO. NOT THE BODEGA!
THAT'S... YA CAN TRY TO HURT ME ALL YA WANT, BUT GOIN' AFTER MY LOCAL? THAT'S TOO MUCH.
IGGY! NINA! ARE YA HURT? WHO DID THIS? WAS IT FIREBUG? KILLER CROC?
PLEASE TELL ME IT WASN'T YOU-KNOW-WHO.
MISS QUINN, PLEASE NOT TODAY. THIS IS A CRIME SCENE. DIDN'T YOU SEE THE POLICE TAPE?
DUH, THAT'S WHY I'M HERE! WHOEVER DID THIS, THEY'RE COMIN' AFTER ME! THEY KNEW HOW MUCH ATTACKIN' YOU WOULD HURT ME.
HARLEY, STOP, YOU MISUNDERSTAND--
OH, I UNDERSTAND LIKE A FOX! IN A WORLD OF CRAZY, YOU TWO ARE MY NORMAL. YER LIKE MY MOM AND DAD. EXCEPT YA MAKE BETTER SANDWICHES.
WHICH MAKES THIS PLACE MY HOME. MY SNACK HOME.
IT WAS SOME PUNK WHO TOOK THIRTY DOLLARS AND RAN. LET US MAKE YOU ONE OF YOUR USUALS. ON THE HOUSE. TO GO.
I APPRECIATE YA TRYIN' TA SPARE HIM, DAD, BUT I GOTTA DO THIS.
PLEASE DON'T CALL ME DAD. OR DO ANYTHING.

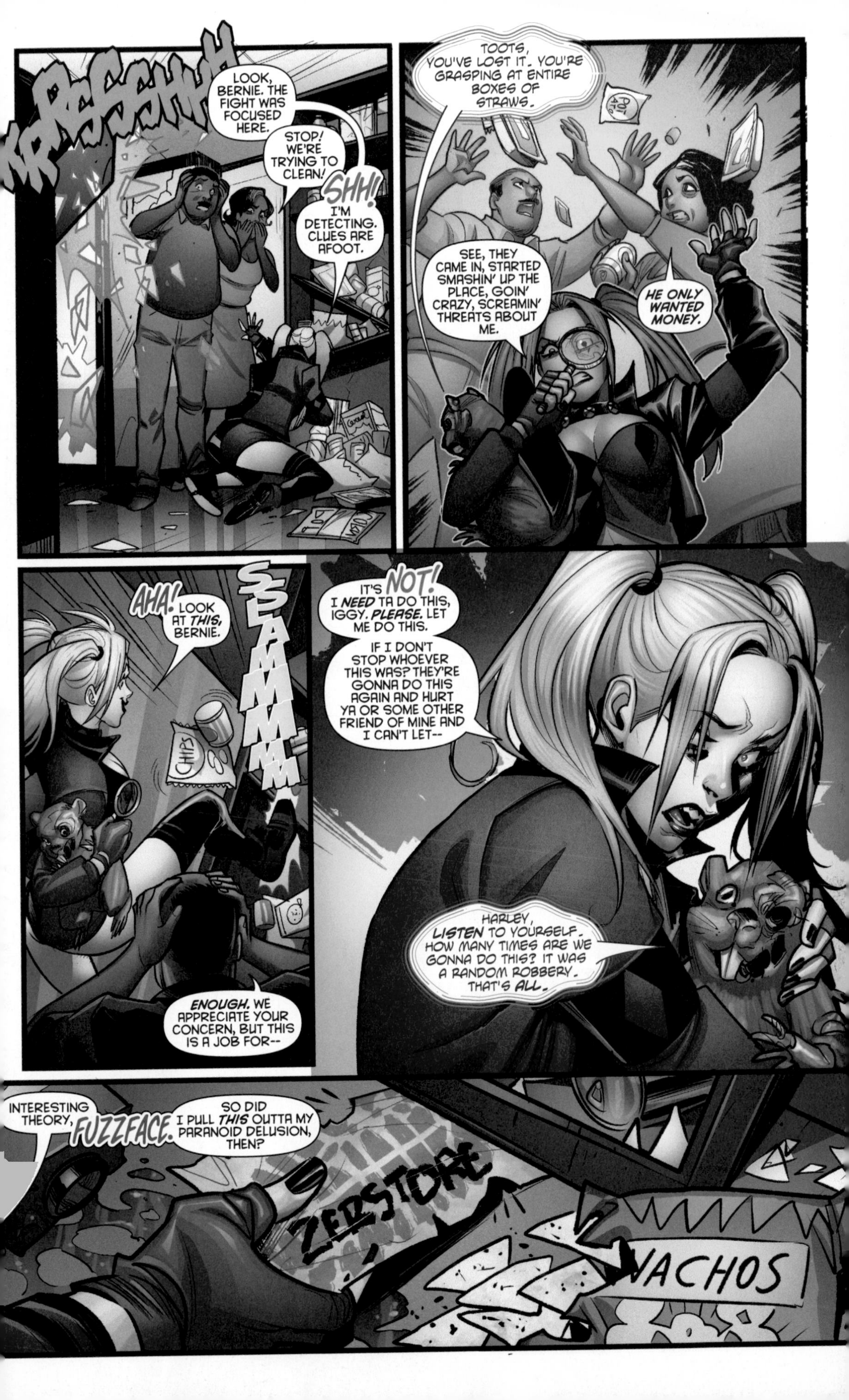
KRRSSHHH
LOOK, BERNIE. THE FIGHT WAS FOCUSED HERE.
STOP! WE'RE TRYING TO CLEAN!
SHH! I'M DETECTING. CLUES ARE AFOOT.
TOOTS, YOU'VE LOST IT. YOU'RE GRASPING AT ENTIRE BOXES OF STRAWS.
SEE, THEY CAME IN, STARTED SMASHIN' UP THE PLACE, GOIN' CRAZY, SCREAMIN' THREATS ABOUT ME.
HE ONLY WANTED MONEY.
AHA! LOOK AT THIS, BERNIE.
SSLAMMMMM
CHIPS
ENOUGH. WE APPRECIATE YOUR CONCERN, BUT THIS IS A JOB FOR--
IT'S NOT! I NEED TA DO THIS, IGGY. PLEASE. LET ME DO THIS.
IF I DON'T STOP WHOEVER THIS WAS? THEY'RE GONNA DO THIS AGAIN AND HURT YA OR SOME OTHER FRIEND OF MINE AND I CAN'T LET--
HARLEY, LISTEN TO YOURSELF. HOW MANY TIMES ARE WE GONNA DO THIS? IT WAS A RANDOM ROBBERY. THAT'S ALL.
INTERESTING THEORY, FUZZFACE.
SO DID I PULL THIS OUTTA MY PARANOID DELUSION, THEN?
ZERSTORE
NACHOS

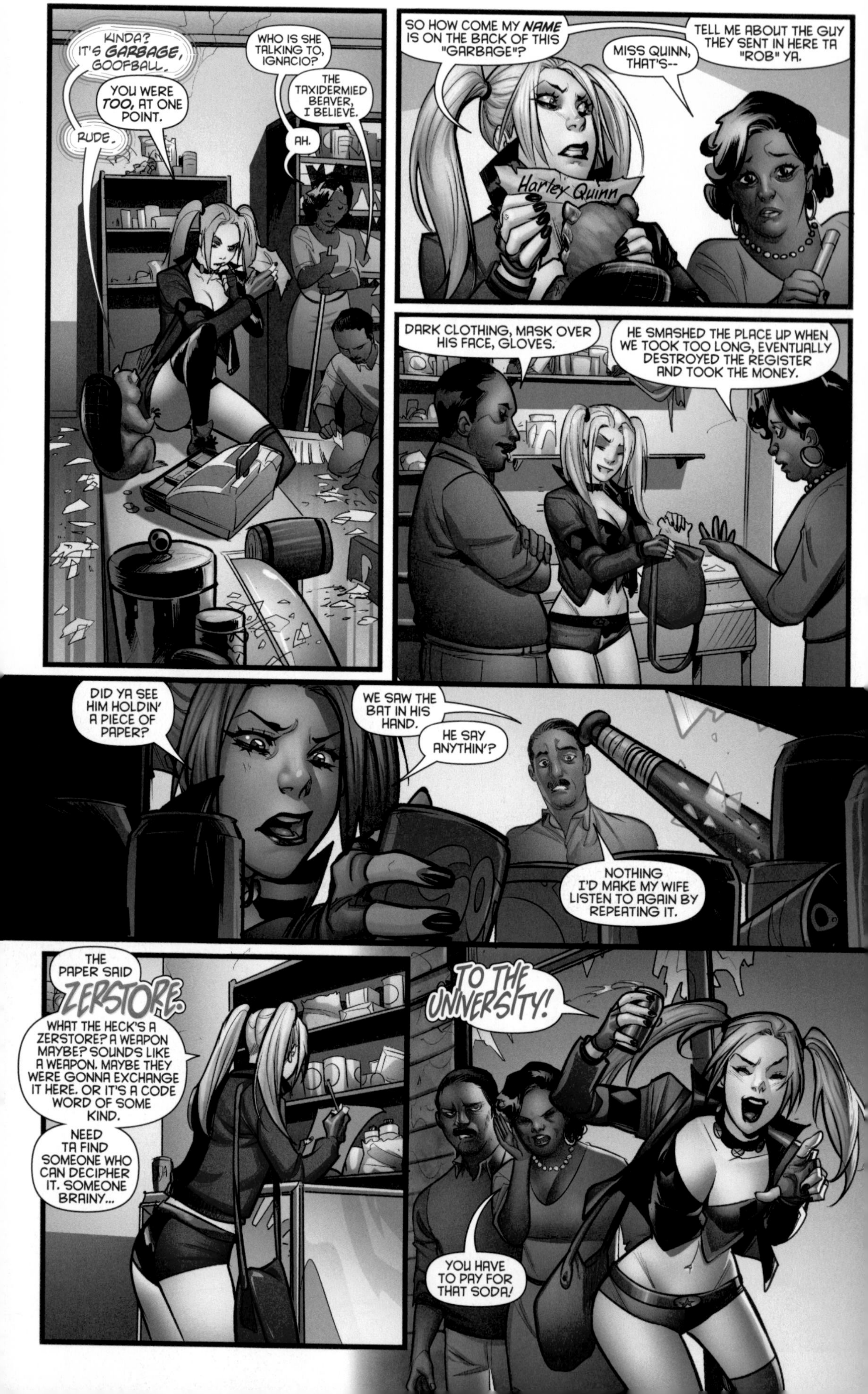
KINDA? IT'S GARBAGE, GOOFBALL.
YOU WERE TOO, AT ONE POINT.
RUDE.
WHO IS SHE TALKING TO, IGNACIO?
THE TAXIDERMIED BEAVER, I BELIEVE.
AH.
SO HOW COME MY NAME IS ON THE BACK OF THIS "GARBAGE"?
Harley Quinn
MISS QUINN, THAT'S--
TELL ME ABOUT THE GUY THEY SENT IN HERE TA "ROB" YA.
DARK CLOTHING, MASK OVER HIS FACE, GLOVES.
HE SMASHED THE PLACE UP WHEN WE TOOK TOO LONG, EVENTUALLY DESTROYED THE REGISTER AND TOOK THE MONEY.
DID YA SEE HIM HOLDIN' A PIECE OF PAPER?
WE SAW THE BAT IN HIS HAND.
HE SAY ANYTHIN'?
NOTHING I'D MAKE MY WIFE LISTEN TO AGAIN BY REPEATING IT.
THE PAPER SAID ZERSTORE.
WHAT THE HECK'S A ZERSTORE? A WEAPON MAYBE? SOUNDS LIKE A WEAPON. MAYBE THEY WERE GONNA EXCHANGE IT HERE. OR IT'S A CODE WORD OF SOME KIND.
NEED TA FIND SOMEONE WHO CAN DECIPHER IT. SOMEONE BRAINY...
TO THE UNIVERSITY!
YOU HAVE TO PAY FOR THAT SODA!

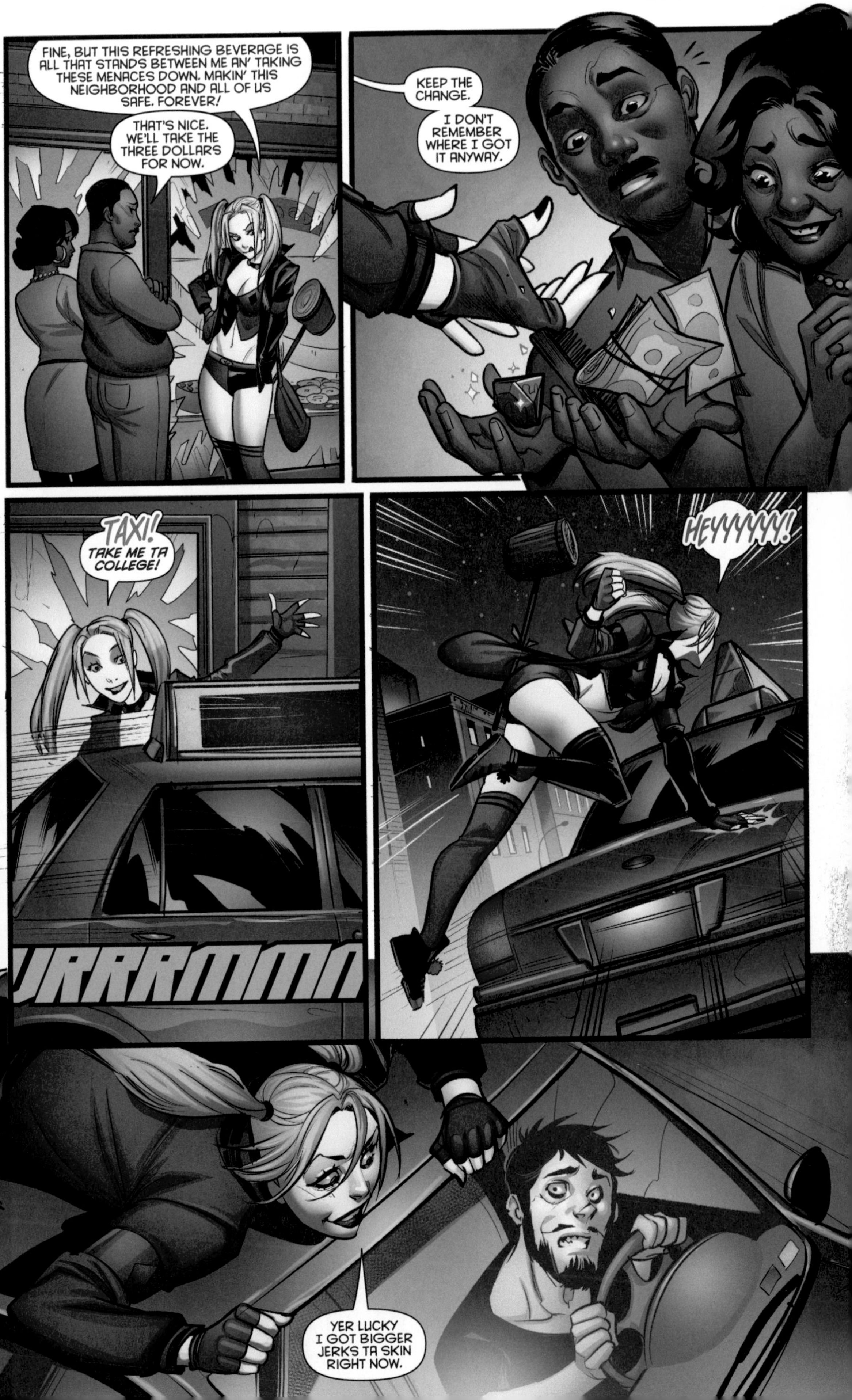
FINE, BUT THIS REFRESHING BEVERAGE IS ALL THAT STANDS BETWEEN ME AN' TAKING THESE MENACES DOWN. MAKIN' THIS NEIGHBORHOOD AND ALL OF US SAFE. FOREVER!
THAT'S NICE. WE'LL TAKE THE THREE DOLLARS FOR NOW.
KEEP THE CHANGE.
I DON'T REMEMBER WHERE I GOT IT ANYWAY.
TAXI!
TAKE ME TA COLLEGE!
VRRRMMM
HEYYYYYY!
YER LUCKY I GOT BIGGER JERKS TA SKIN RIGHT NOW.

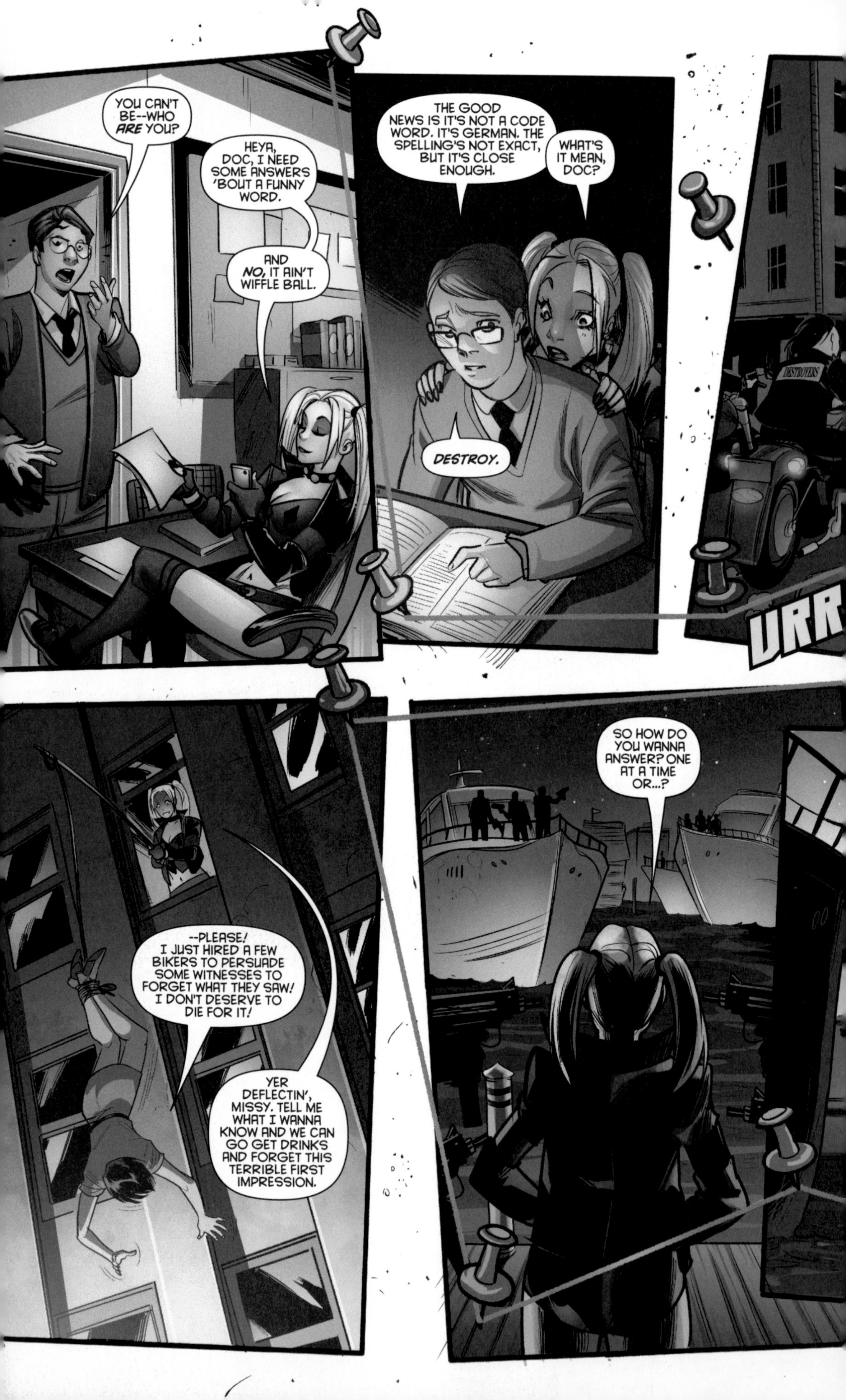
YOU CAN'T BE--WHO ARE YOU?
HEYA, DOC, I NEED SOME ANSWERS 'BOUT A FUNNY WORD.
AND NO, IT AIN'T WIFFLE BALL.
THE GOOD NEWS IS IT'S NOT A CODE WORD. IT'S GERMAN. THE SPELLING'S NOT EXACT, BUT IT'S CLOSE ENOUGH.
WHAT'S IT MEAN, DOC?
DESTROY.
DESTROYERS
URR
--PLEASE! I JUST HIRED A FEW BIKERS TO PERSUADE SOME WITNESSES TO FORGET WHAT THEY SAW! I DON'T DESERVE TO DIE FOR IT!
YER DEFLECTIN', MISSY. TELL ME WHAT I WANNA KNOW AND WE CAN GO GET DRINKS AND FORGET THIS TERRIBLE FIRST IMPRESSION.
SO HOW DO YOU WANNA ANSWER? ONE AT A TIME OR...?

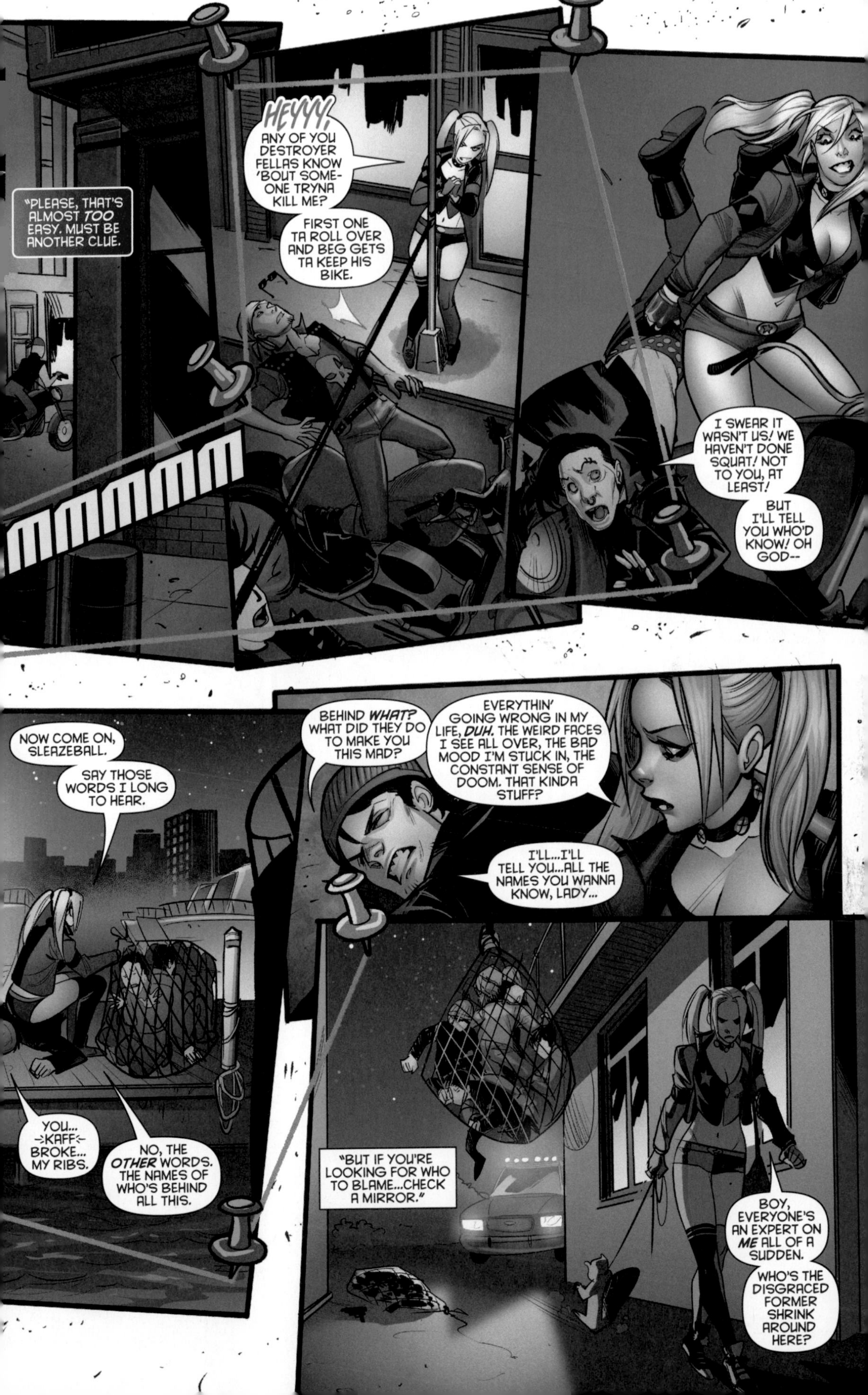
"PLEASE, THAT'S ALMOST TOO EASY. MUST BE ANOTHER CLUE.
HEYYY, ANY OF YOU DESTROYER FELLAS KNOW 'BOUT SOME-ONE TRYNA KILL ME?
FIRST ONE TA ROLL OVER AND BEG GETS TA KEEP HIS BIKE.
MMMMMM
I SWEAR IT WASN'T US! WE HAVEN'T DONE SQUAT! NOT TO YOU, AT LEAST!
BUT I'LL TELL YOU WHO'D KNOW! OH GOD--
NOW COME ON, SLEAZEBALL.
SAY THOSE WORDS I LONG TO HEAR.
YOU... -KAFF- BROKE... MY RIBS.
NO, THE OTHER WORDS. THE NAMES OF WHO'S BEHIND ALL THIS.
BEHIND WHAT? WHAT DID THEY DO TO MAKE YOU THIS MAD?
EVERYTHIN' GOING WRONG IN MY LIFE, DUH. THE WEIRD FACES I SEE ALL OVER, THE BAD MOOD I'M STUCK IN, THE CONSTANT SENSE OF DOOM. THAT KINDA STUFF?
I'LL...I'LL TELL YOU...ALL THE NAMES YOU WANNA KNOW, LADY...
"BUT IF YOU'RE LOOKING FOR WHO TO BLAME...CHECK A MIRROR."
BOY, EVERYONE'S AN EXPERT ON ME ALL OF A SUDDEN.
WHO'S THE DISGRACED FORMER SHRINK AROUND HERE?

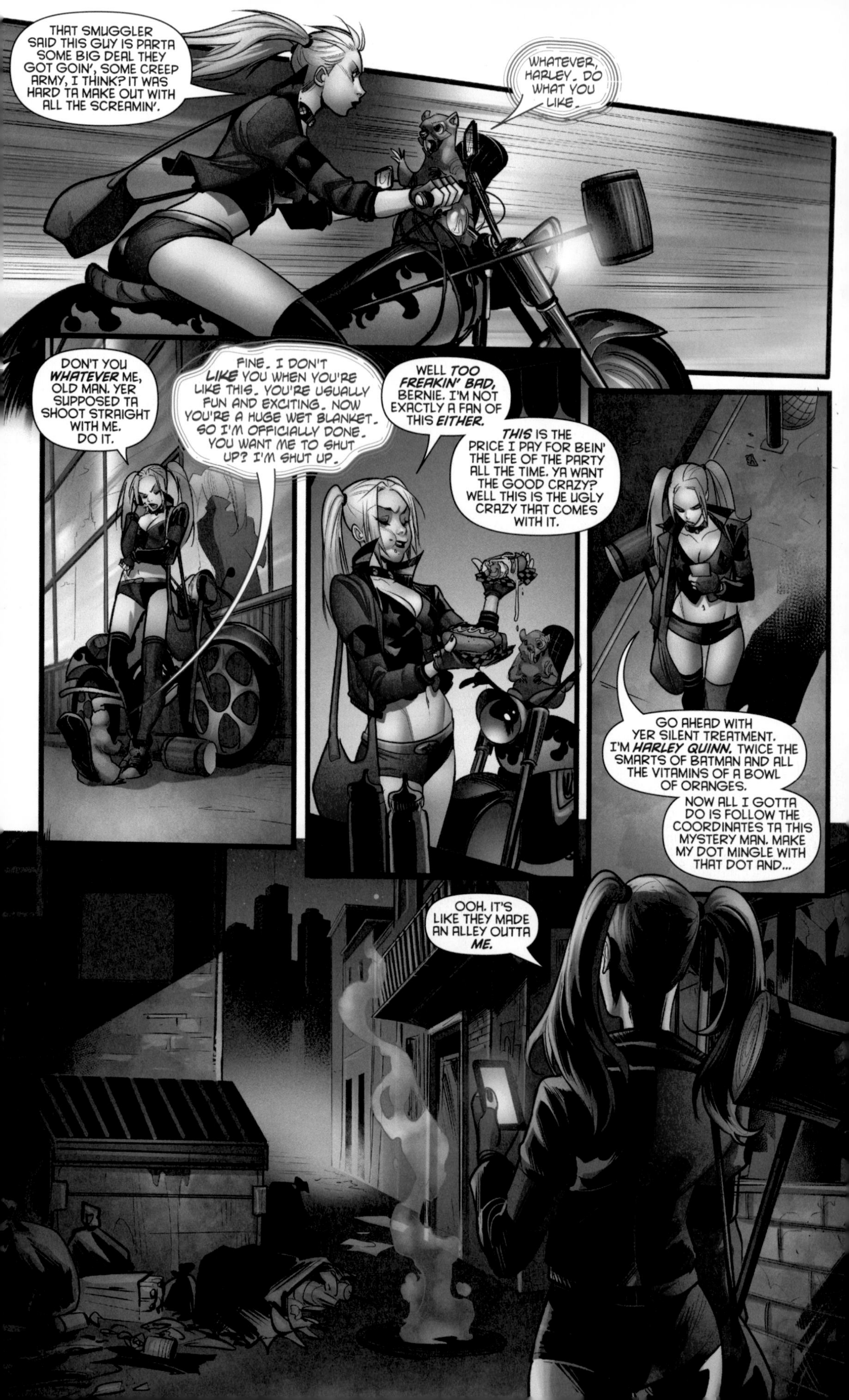
THAT SMUGGLER SAID THIS GUY IS PARTA SOME BIG DEAL THEY GOT GOIN', SOME CREEP ARMY, I THINK? IT WAS HARD TA MAKE OUT WITH ALL THE SCREAMIN'.
WHATEVER, HARLEY. DO WHAT YOU LIKE.
DON'T YOU WHATEVER ME, OLD MAN. YER SUPPOSED TA SHOOT STRAIGHT WITH ME. DO IT.
FINE. I DON'T LIKE YOU WHEN YOU'RE LIKE THIS. YOU'RE USUALLY FUN AND EXCITING. NOW YOU'RE A HUGE WET BLANKET. SO I'M OFFICIALLY DONE. YOU WANT ME TO SHUT UP? I'M SHUT UP.
WELL TOO FREAKIN' BAD, BERNIE. I'M NOT EXACTLY A FAN OF THIS EITHER.
THIS IS THE PRICE I PAY FOR BEIN' THE LIFE OF THE PARTY ALL THE TIME. YA WANT THE GOOD CRAZY? WELL THIS IS THE UGLY CRAZY THAT COMES WITH IT.
GO AHEAD WITH YER SILENT TREATMENT. I'M HARLEY QUINN. TWICE THE SMARTS OF BATMAN AND ALL THE VITAMINS OF A BOWL OF ORANGES.
NOW ALL I GOTTA DO IS FOLLOW THE COORDINATES TA THIS MYSTERY MAN. MAKE MY DOT MINGLE WITH THAT DOT AND...
OOH. IT'S LIKE THEY MADE AN ALLEY OUTTA ME.

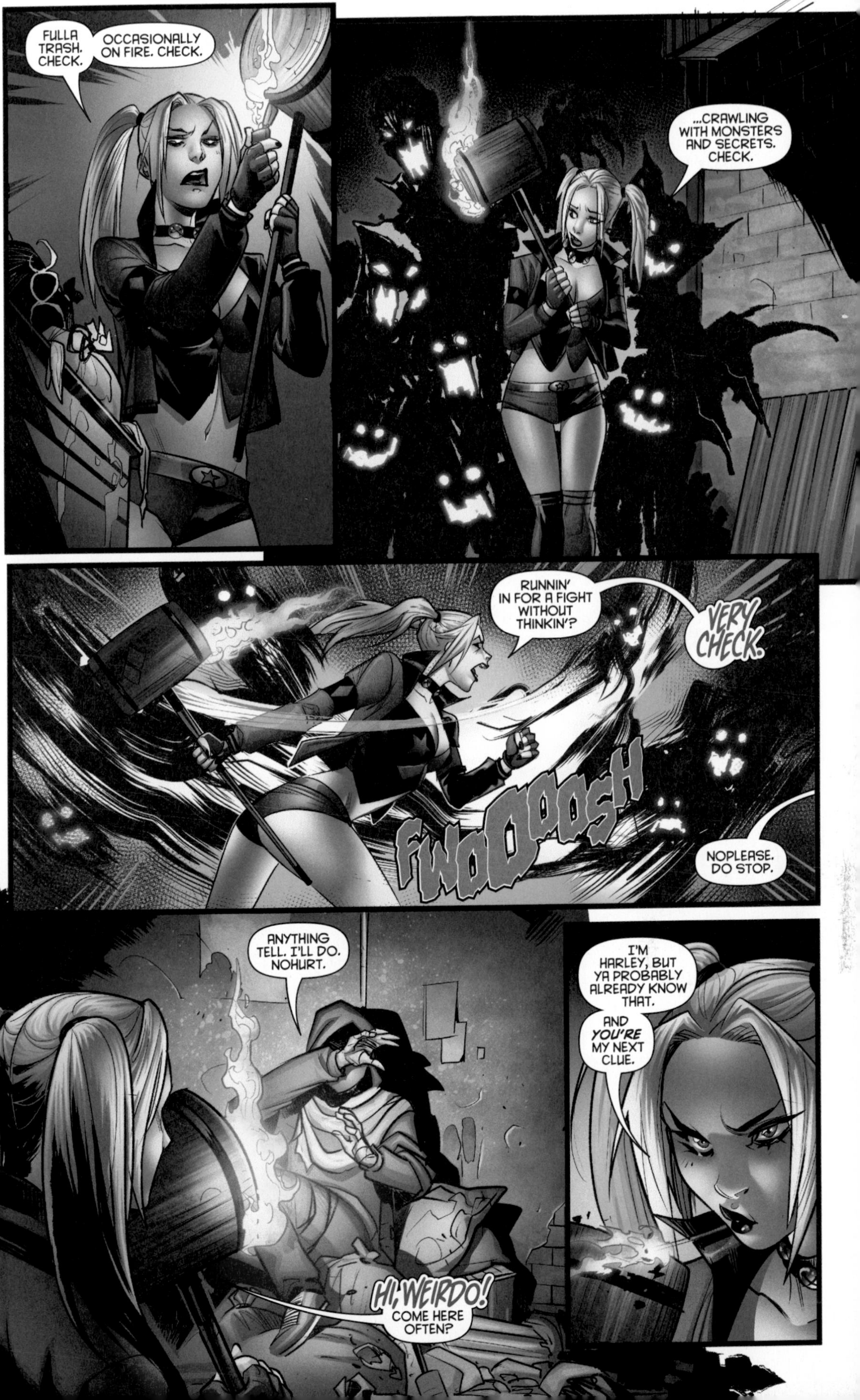
FULLA TRASH. CHECK.
OCCASIONALLY ON FIRE. CHECK.
...CRAWLING WITH MONSTERS AND SECRETS. CHECK.
RUNNIN' IN FOR A FIGHT WITHOUT THINKIN'?
VERY CHECK.
FWOOOOSH
NOPLEASE. DO STOP.
ANYTHING TELL. I'LL DO. NOHURT.
HI, WEIRDO! COME HERE OFTEN?
I'M HARLEY, BUT YA PROBABLY ALREADY KNOW THAT.
AND *YOU'RE* MY NEXT CLUE.

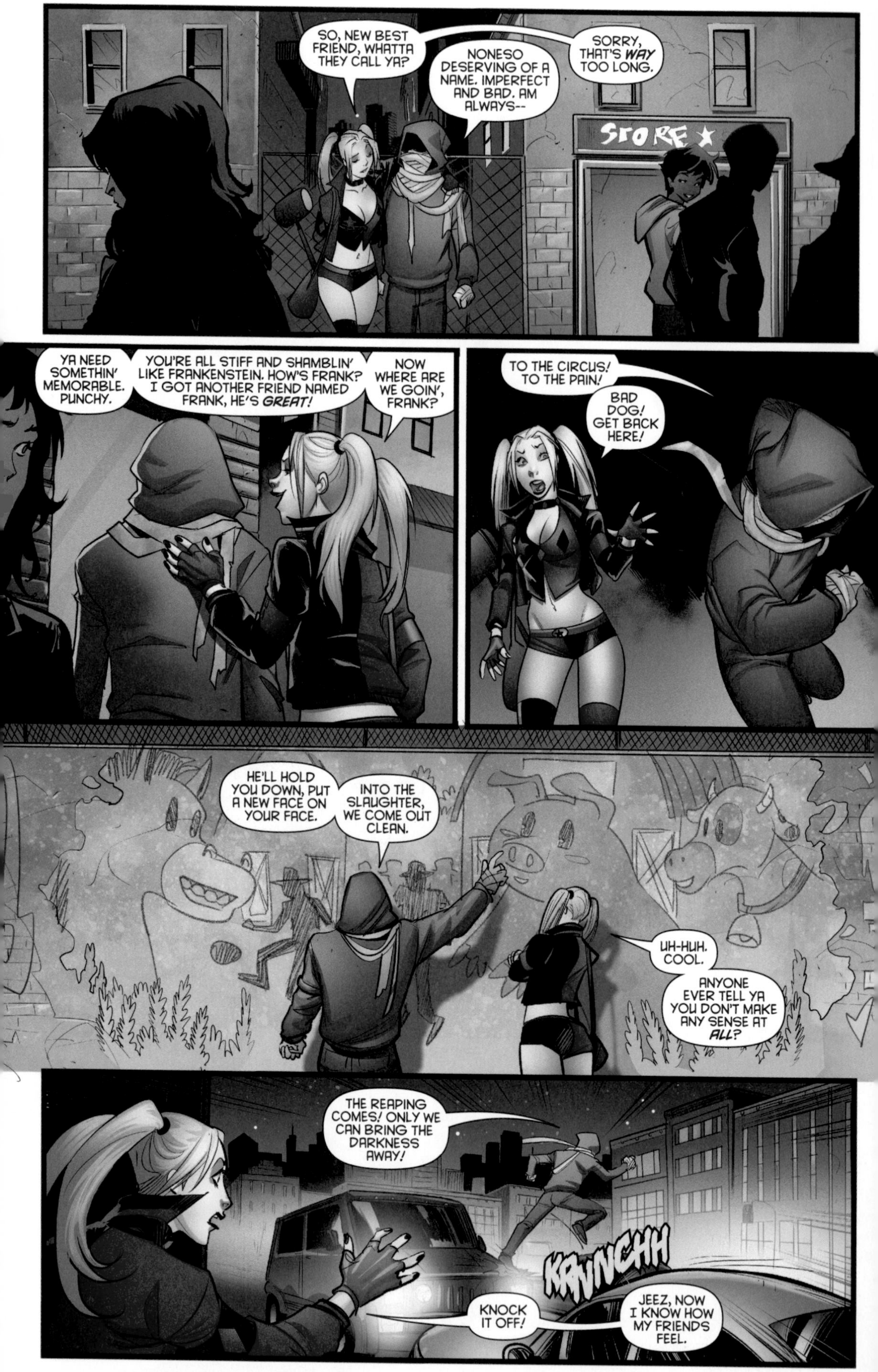
SO, NEW BEST FRIEND, WHATTA THEY CALL YA?
NONESO DESERVING OF A NAME. IMPERFECT AND BAD. AM ALWAYS--
SORRY, THAT'S *WAY* TOO LONG.
STORE
YA NEED SOMETHIN' MEMORABLE. PUNCHY.
YOU'RE ALL STIFF AND SHAMBLIN' LIKE FRANKENSTEIN. HOW'S FRANK? I GOT ANOTHER FRIEND NAMED FRANK, HE'S *GREAT!*
NOW WHERE ARE WE GOIN', FRANK?
TO THE CIRCUS! TO THE PAIN!
BAD DOG! GET BACK HERE!
HE'LL HOLD YOU DOWN, PUT A NEW FACE ON YOUR FACE.
INTO THE SLAUGHTER, WE COME OUT CLEAN.
UH-HUH. COOL.
ANYONE EVER TELL YA YOU DON'T MAKE ANY SENSE AT *ALL?*
THE REAPING COMES! ONLY WE CAN BRING THE DARKNESS AWAY!
KRUNCHH
KNOCK IT OFF!
JEEZ, NOW I KNOW HOW MY FRIENDS FEEL.

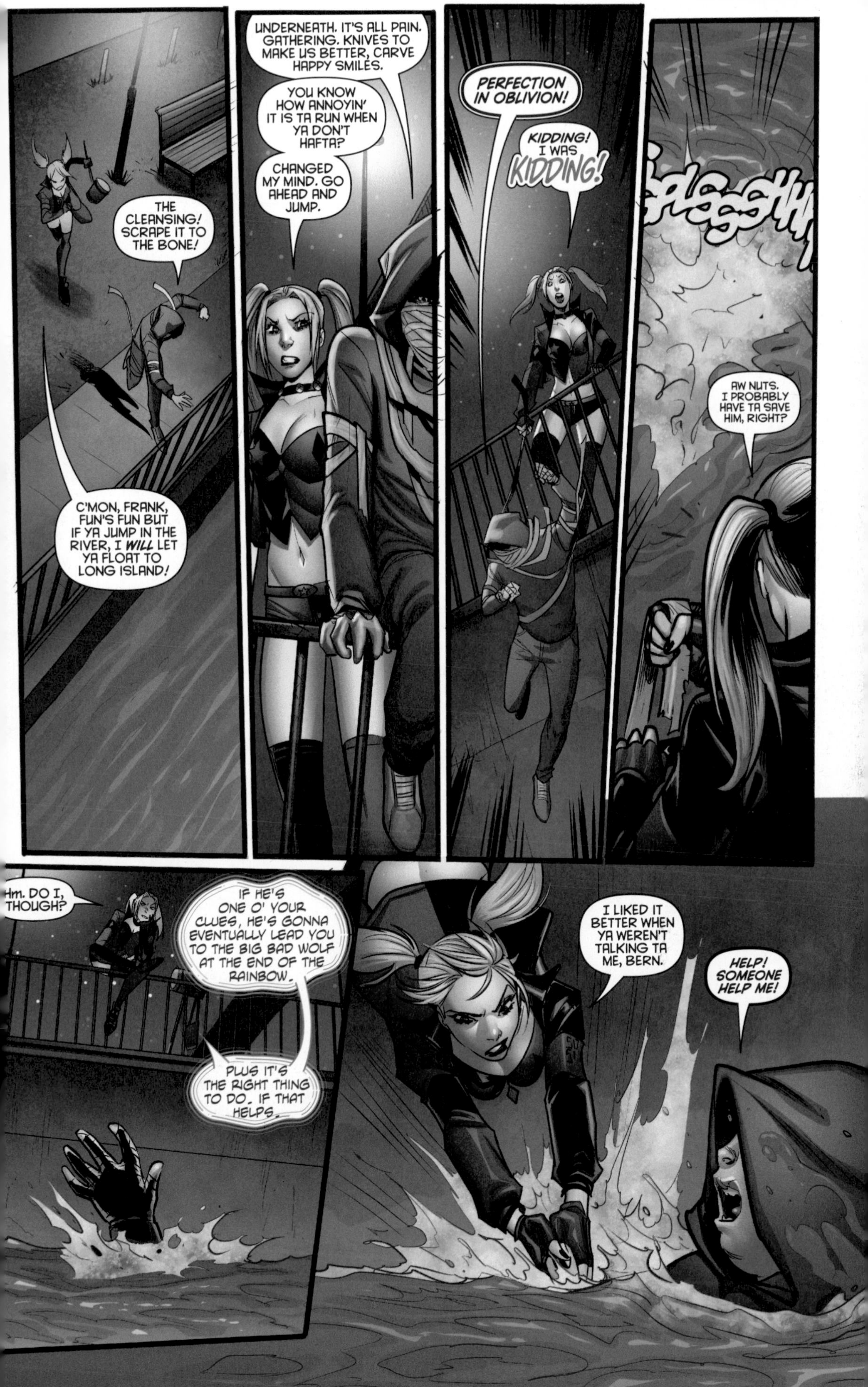
THE CLEANSING! SCRAPE IT TO THE BONE!
C'MON, FRANK, FUN'S FUN BUT IF YA JUMP IN THE RIVER, I WILL LET YA FLOAT TO LONG ISLAND!
UNDERNEATH. IT'S ALL PAIN. GATHERING. KNIVES TO MAKE US BETTER, CARVE HAPPY SMILES.
YOU KNOW HOW ANNOYIN' IT IS TA RUN WHEN YA DON'T HAFTA?
CHANGED MY MIND. GO AHEAD AND JUMP.
PERFECTION IN OBLIVION!
KIDDING! I WAS KIDDING!
AW NUTS. I PROBABLY HAVE TA SAVE HIM, RIGHT?
Hm. DO I, THOUGH?
IF HE'S ONE O' YOUR CLUES, HE'S GONNA EVENTUALLY LEAD YOU TO THE BIG BAD WOLF AT THE END OF THE RAINBOW.
PLUS IT'S THE RIGHT THING TO DO. IF THAT HELPS.
I LIKED IT BETTER WHEN YA WEREN'T TALKING TA ME, BERN.
HELP! SOMEONE HELP ME!

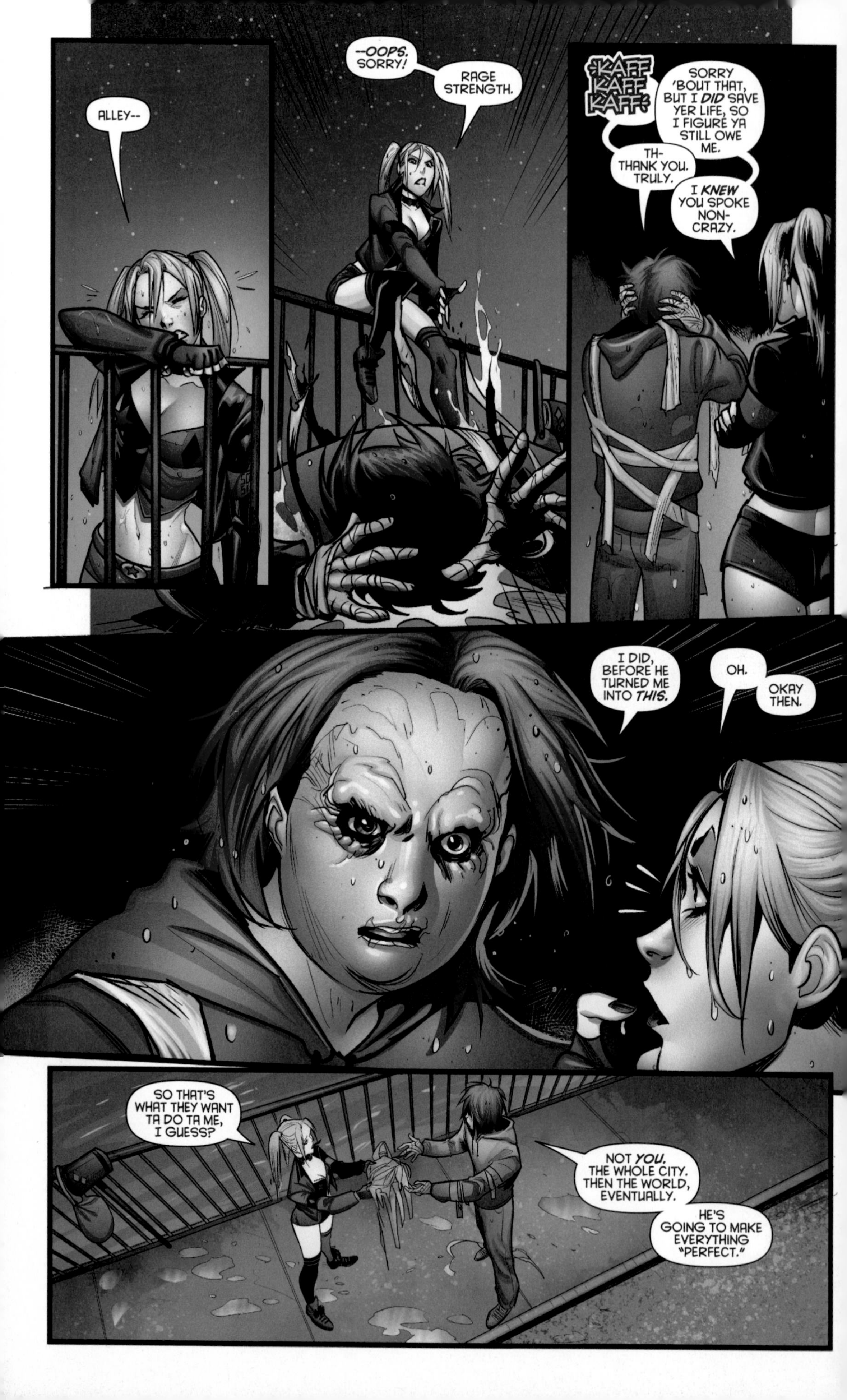
ALLEY--
--OOPS. SORRY!
RAGE STRENGTH.
KAFF KAFF KAFF
SORRY 'BOUT THAT, BUT I DID SAVE YER LIFE, SO I FIGURE YA STILL OWE ME.
TH- THANK YOU. TRULY.
I KNEW YOU SPOKE NON-CRAZY.
I DID, BEFORE HE TURNED ME INTO THIS.
OH.
OKAY THEN.
SO THAT'S WHAT THEY WANT TA DO TA ME, I GUESS?
NOT YOU. THE WHOLE CITY. THEN THE WORLD, EVENTUALLY.
HE'S GOING TO MAKE EVERYTHING "PERFECT."

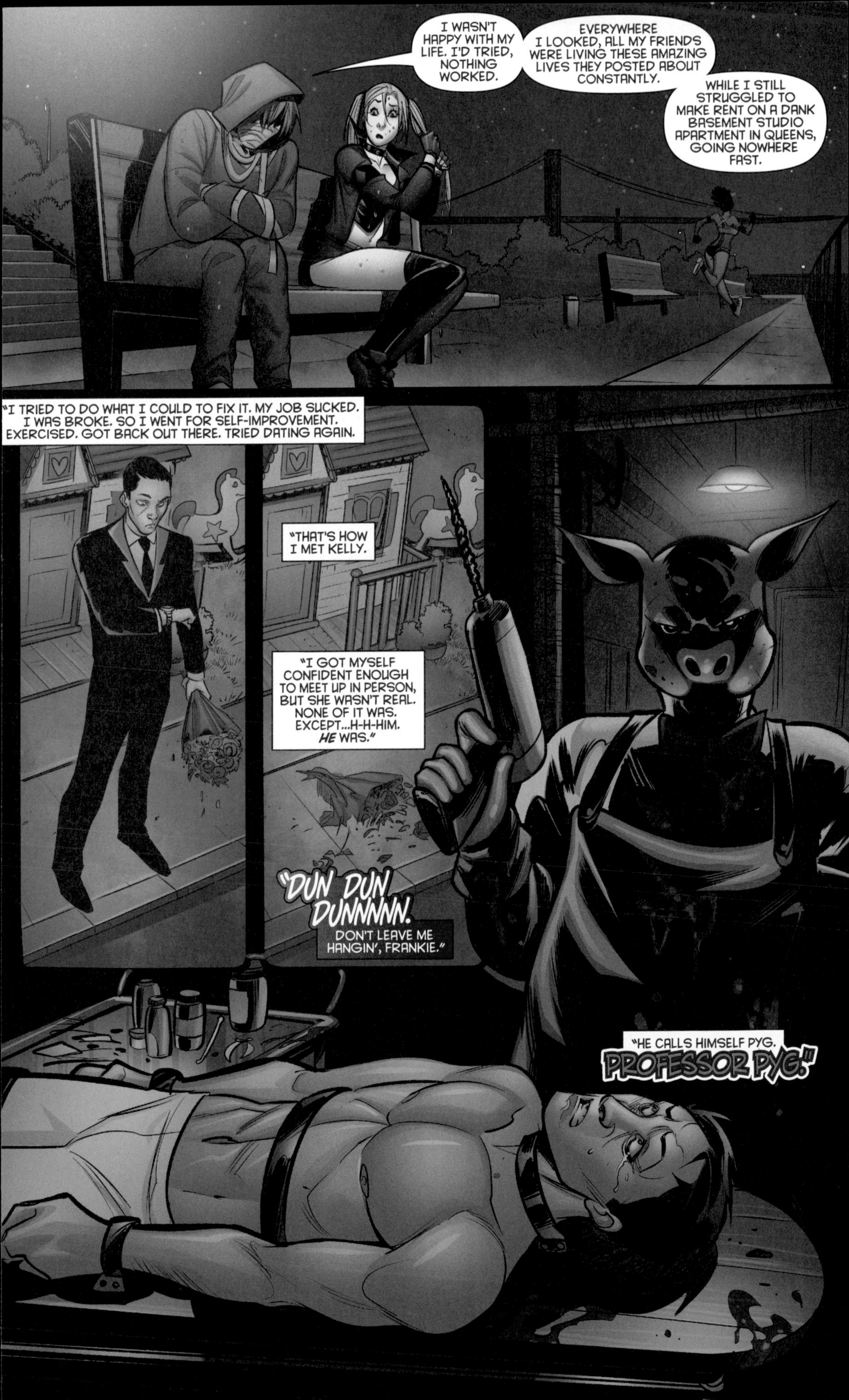
I WASN'T HAPPY WITH MY LIFE. I'D TRIED, NOTHING WORKED.
EVERYWHERE I LOOKED, ALL MY FRIENDS WERE LIVING THESE AMAZING LIVES THEY POSTED ABOUT CONSTANTLY.
WHILE I STILL STRUGGLED TO MAKE RENT ON A DANK BASEMENT STUDIO APARTMENT IN QUEENS, GOING NOWHERE FAST.
"I TRIED TO DO WHAT I COULD TO FIX IT. MY JOB SUCKED. I WAS BROKE. SO I WENT FOR SELF-IMPROVEMENT. EXERCISED. GOT BACK OUT THERE. TRIED DATING AGAIN.
"THAT'S HOW I MET KELLY.
"I GOT MYSELF CONFIDENT ENOUGH TO MEET UP IN PERSON, BUT SHE WASN'T REAL. NONE OF IT WAS. EXCEPT...H-H-HIM. *HE* WAS."
"DUN DUN DUNNNNN.
DON'T LEAVE ME HANGIN', FRANKIE."
"HE CALLS HIMSELF PYG.
PROFESSOR PYG!"

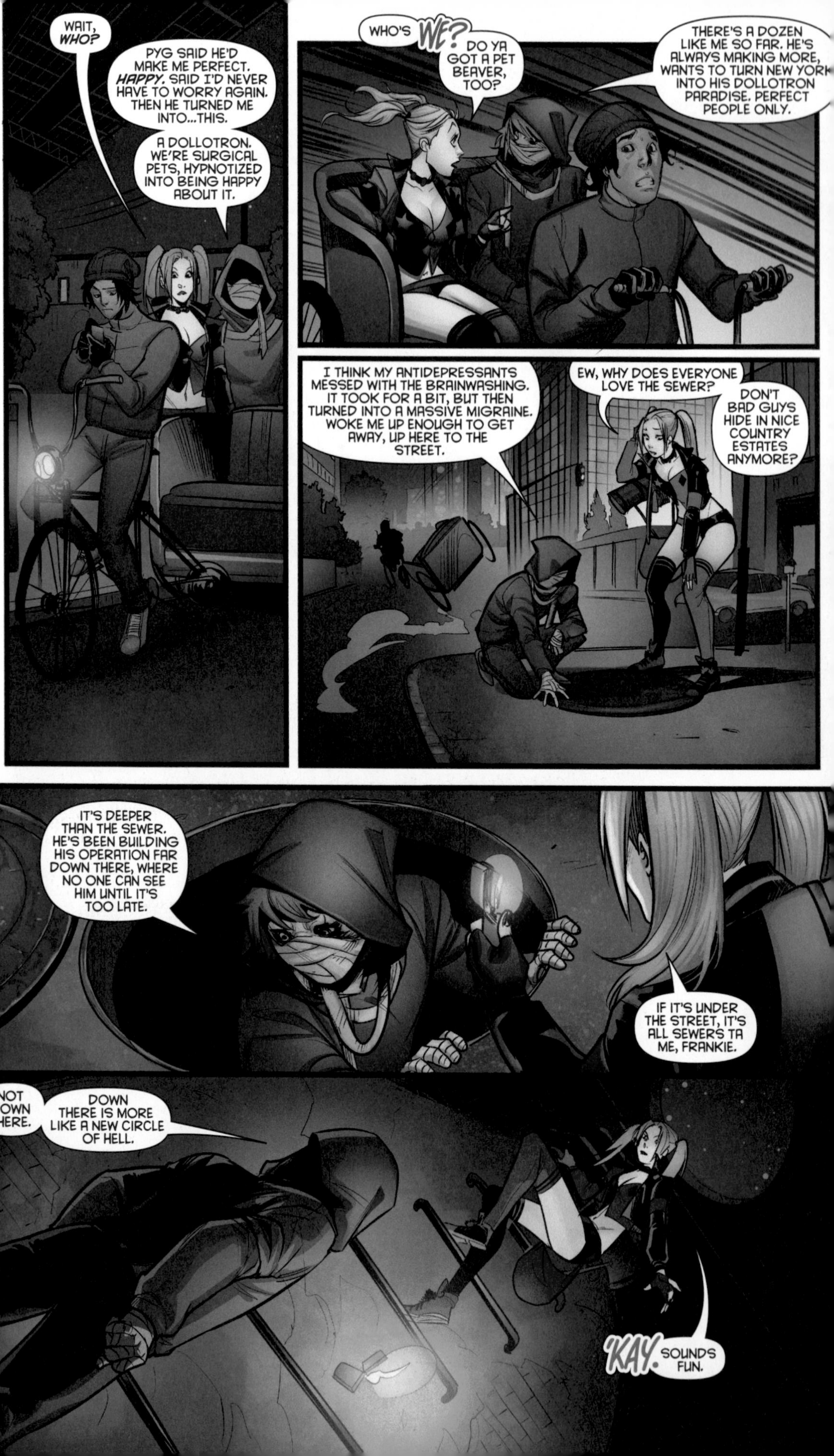
WAIT, WHO?
PYG SAID HE'D MAKE ME PERFECT. HAPPY. SAID I'D NEVER HAVE TO WORRY AGAIN. THEN HE TURNED ME INTO...THIS.
A DOLLOTRON. WE'RE SURGICAL PETS, HYPNOTIZED INTO BEING HAPPY ABOUT IT.
WHO'S WE? DO YA GOT A PET BEAVER, TOO?
THERE'S A DOZEN LIKE ME SO FAR. HE'S ALWAYS MAKING MORE, WANTS TO TURN NEW YORK INTO HIS DOLLOTRON PARADISE. PERFECT PEOPLE ONLY.
I THINK MY ANTIDEPRESSANTS MESSED WITH THE BRAINWASHING. IT TOOK FOR A BIT, BUT THEN TURNED INTO A MASSIVE MIGRAINE. WOKE ME UP ENOUGH TO GET AWAY, UP HERE TO THE STREET.
EW, WHY DOES EVERYONE LOVE THE SEWER?
DON'T BAD GUYS HIDE IN NICE COUNTRY ESTATES ANYMORE?
IT'S DEEPER THAN THE SEWER. HE'S BEEN BUILDING HIS OPERATION FAR DOWN THERE, WHERE NO ONE CAN SEE HIM UNTIL IT'S TOO LATE.
IF IT'S UNDER THE STREET, IT'S ALL SEWERS TA ME, FRANKIE.
NOT DOWN THERE.
DOWN THERE IS MORE LIKE A NEW CIRCLE OF HELL.
'KAY. SOUNDS FUN.

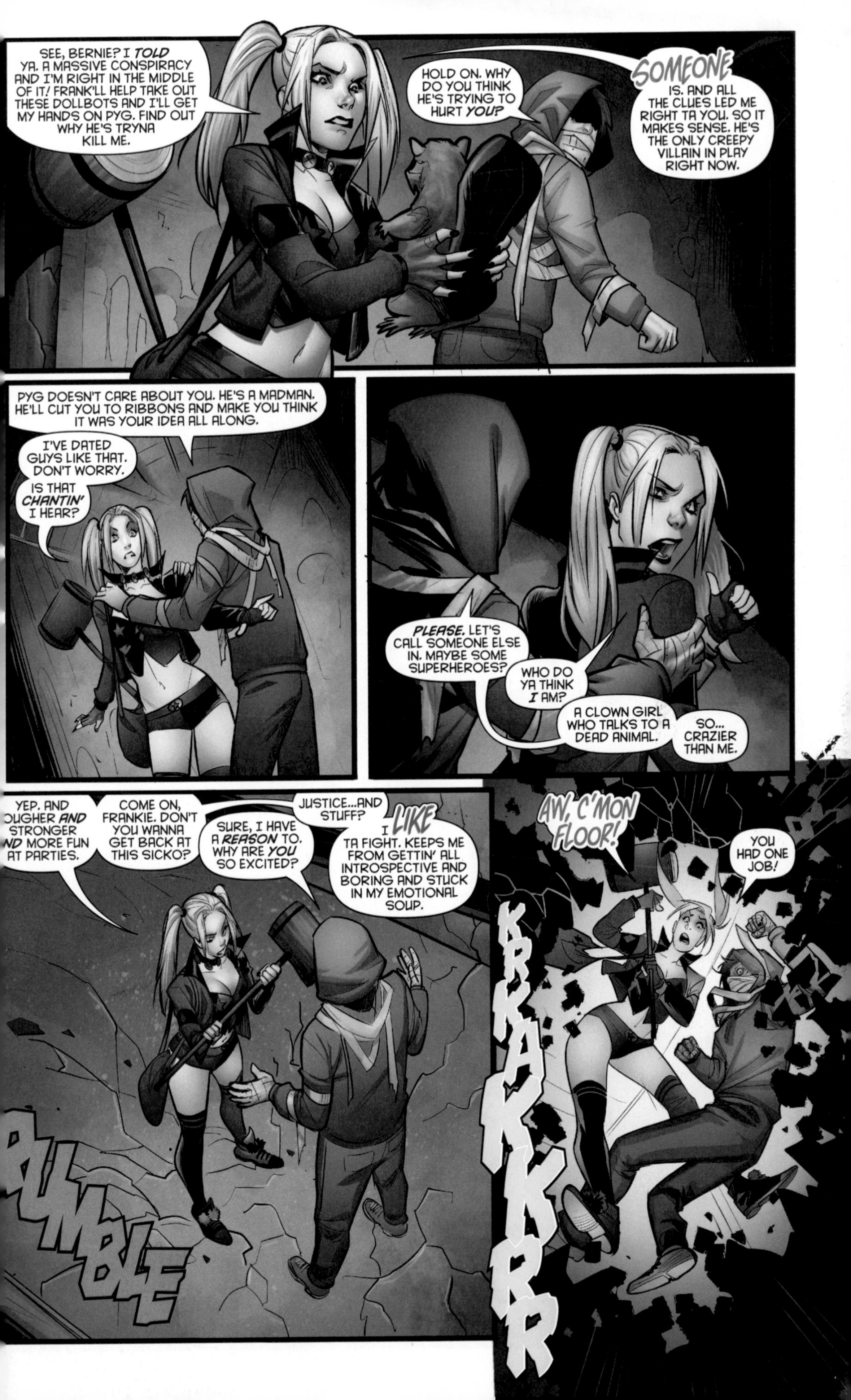
SEE, BERNIE? I TOLD YA. A MASSIVE CONSPIRACY AND I'M RIGHT IN THE MIDDLE OF IT! FRANK'LL HELP TAKE OUT THESE DOLLBOTS AND I'LL GET MY HANDS ON PYG. FIND OUT WHY HE'S TRYNA KILL ME.
HOLD ON. WHY DO YOU THINK HE'S TRYING TO HURT YOU?
SOMEONE IS. AND ALL THE CLUES LED ME RIGHT TA YOU. SO IT MAKES SENSE. HE'S THE ONLY CREEPY VILLAIN IN PLAY RIGHT NOW.
PYG DOESN'T CARE ABOUT YOU. HE'S A MADMAN. HE'LL CUT YOU TO RIBBONS AND MAKE YOU THINK IT WAS YOUR IDEA ALL ALONG.
I'VE DATED GUYS LIKE THAT. DON'T WORRY.
IS THAT CHANTIN' I HEAR?
PLEASE. LET'S CALL SOMEONE ELSE IN. MAYBE SOME SUPERHEROES?
WHO DO YA THINK I AM?
A CLOWN GIRL WHO TALKS TO A DEAD ANIMAL.
SO... CRAZIER THAN ME.
YEP. AND OUGHER AND STRONGER ND MORE FUN AT PARTIES.
COME ON, FRANKIE. DON'T YOU WANNA GET BACK AT THIS SICKO?
SURE, I HAVE A REASON TO. WHY ARE YOU SO EXCITED?
JUSTICE...AND STUFF?
I LIKE TA FIGHT. KEEPS ME FROM GETTIN' ALL INTROSPECTIVE AND BORING AND STUCK IN MY EMOTIONAL SOUP.
RUMBLE
AW, C'MON FLOOR!
YOU HAD ONE JOB!
KRKAKKRR

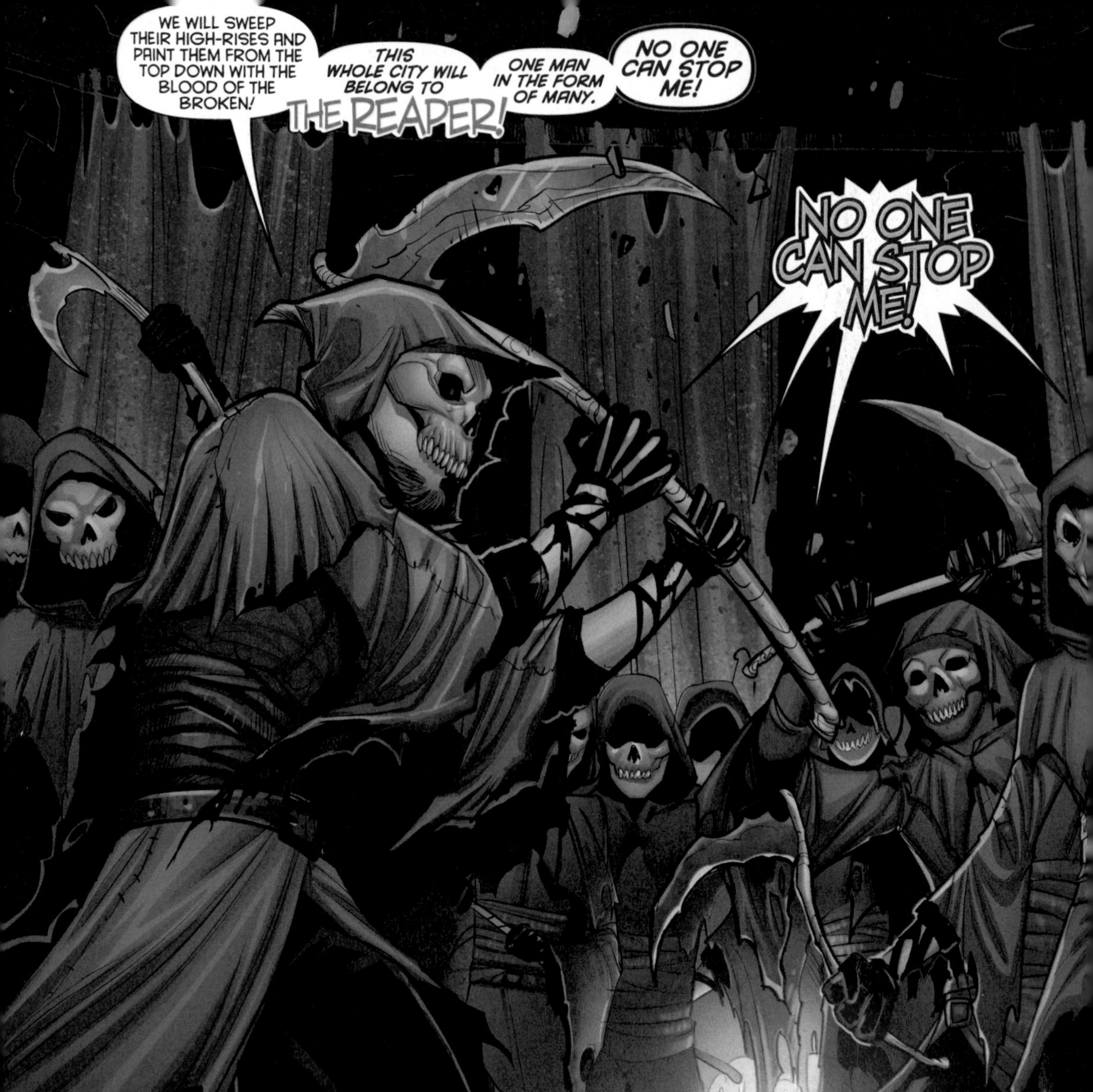
WE WILL SWEEP THEIR HIGH-RISES AND PAINT THEM FROM THE TOP DOWN WITH THE BLOOD OF THE BROKEN!
THIS WHOLE CITY WILL BELONG TO THE REAPER!
ONE MAN IN THE FORM OF MANY.
NO ONE CAN STOP ME!
NO ONE CAN STOP ME!

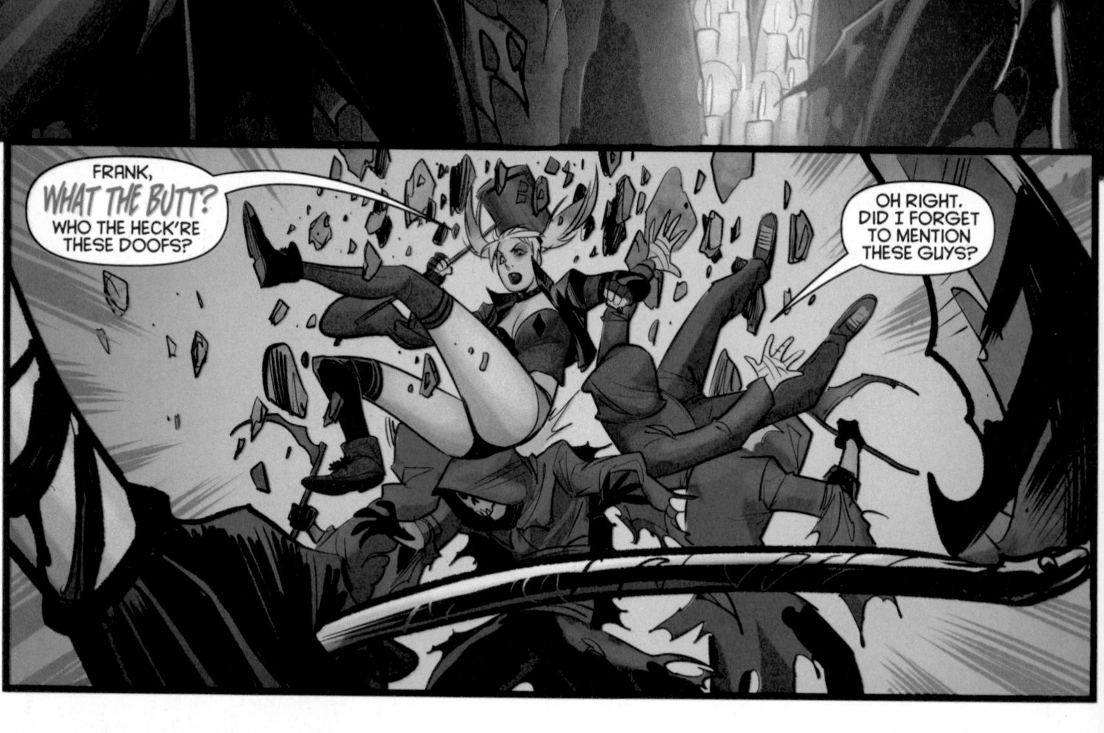
FRANK, WHAT THE BUTT? WHO THE HECK'RE THESE DOOFS?
OH RIGHT. DID I FORGET TO MENTION THESE GUYS?

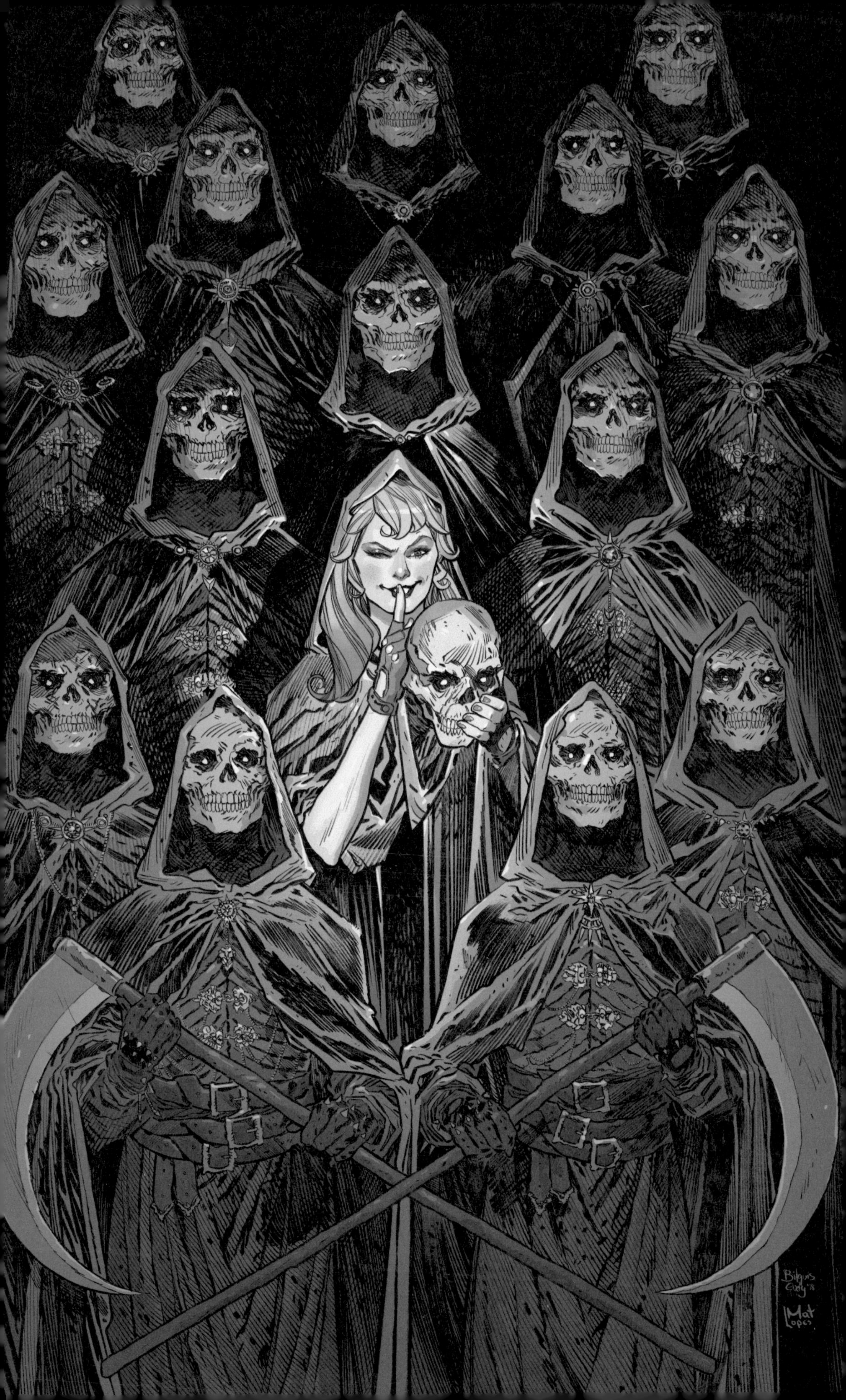
Bilquis Evely '18
Mat Lopes

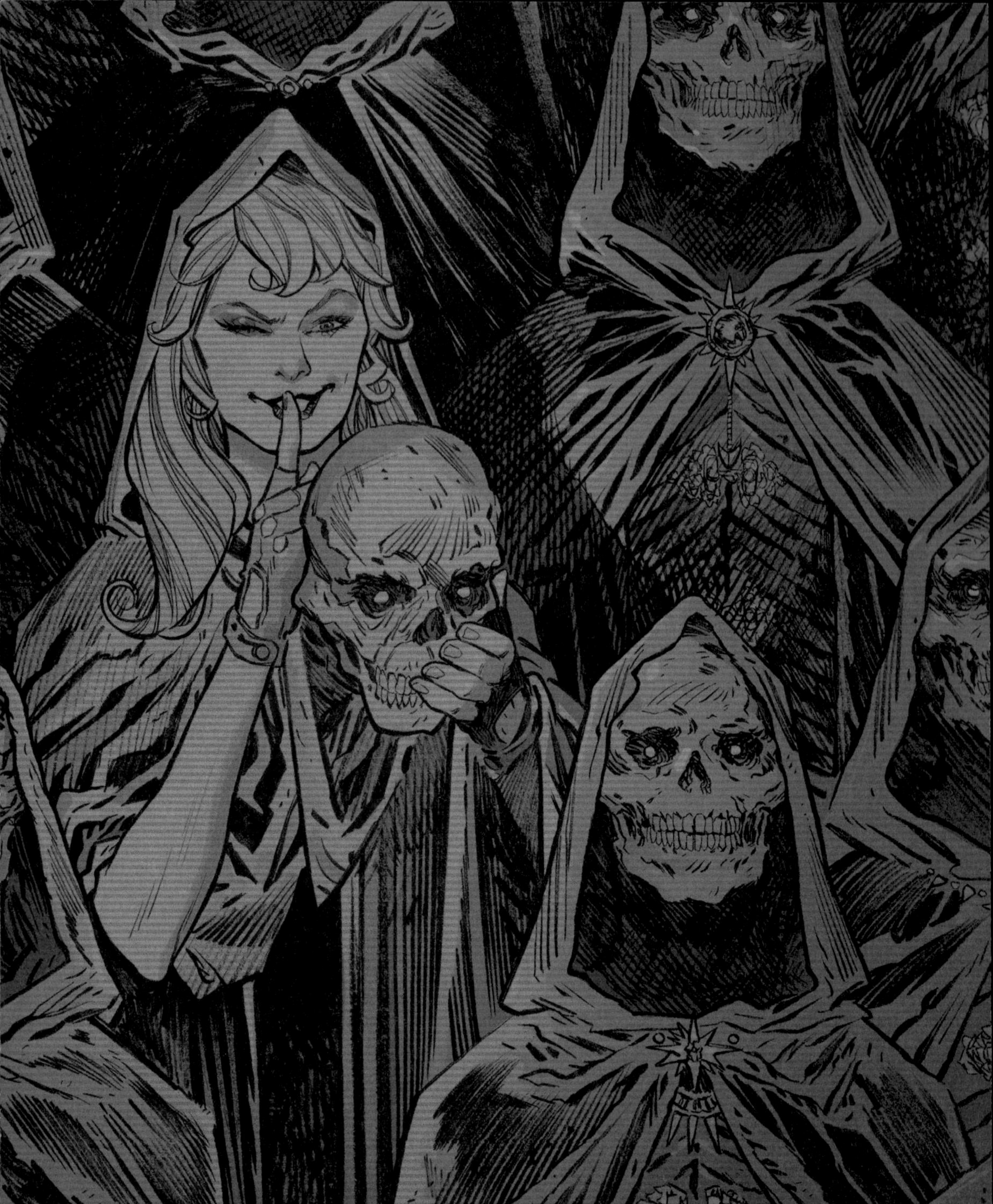

HARLEY QUINN
#44

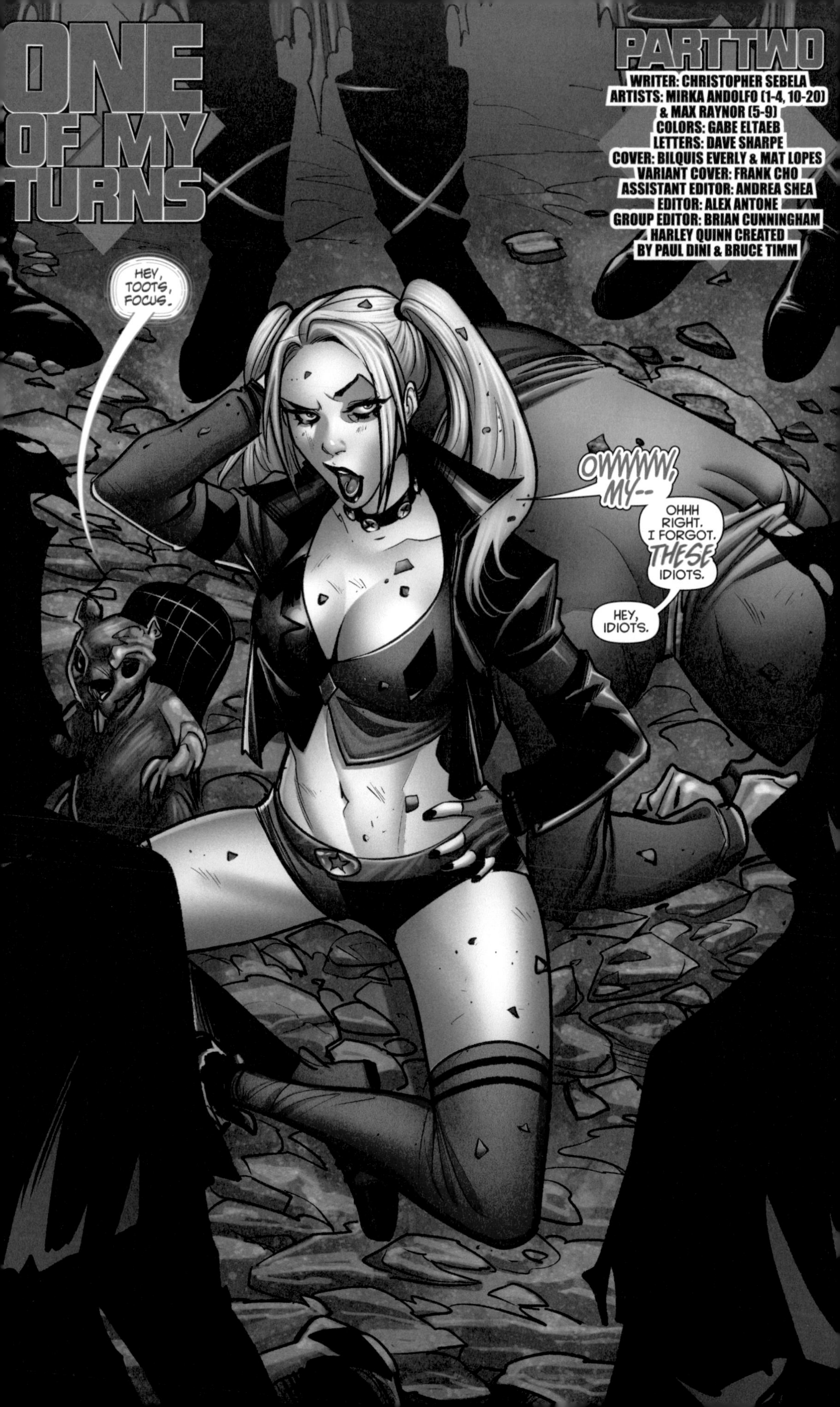
ONE OF MY TURNS
PART TWO
WRITER: CHRISTOPHER SEBELA
ARTISTS: MIRKA ANDOLFO (1-4, 10-20) & MAX RAYNOR (5-9)
COLORS: GABE ELTAEB
LETTERS: DAVE SHARPE
COVER: BILQUIS EVERLY & MAT LOPES
VARIANT COVER: FRANK CHO
ASSISTANT EDITOR: ANDREA SHEA
EDITOR: ALEX ANTONE
GROUP EDITOR: BRIAN CUNNINGHAM
HARLEY QUINN CREATED BY PAUL DINI & BRUCE TIMM
HEY, TOOTS, FOCUS.
OWWWW, MY--
OHHH RIGHT. I FORGOT. THESE IDIOTS.
HEY, IDIOTS.

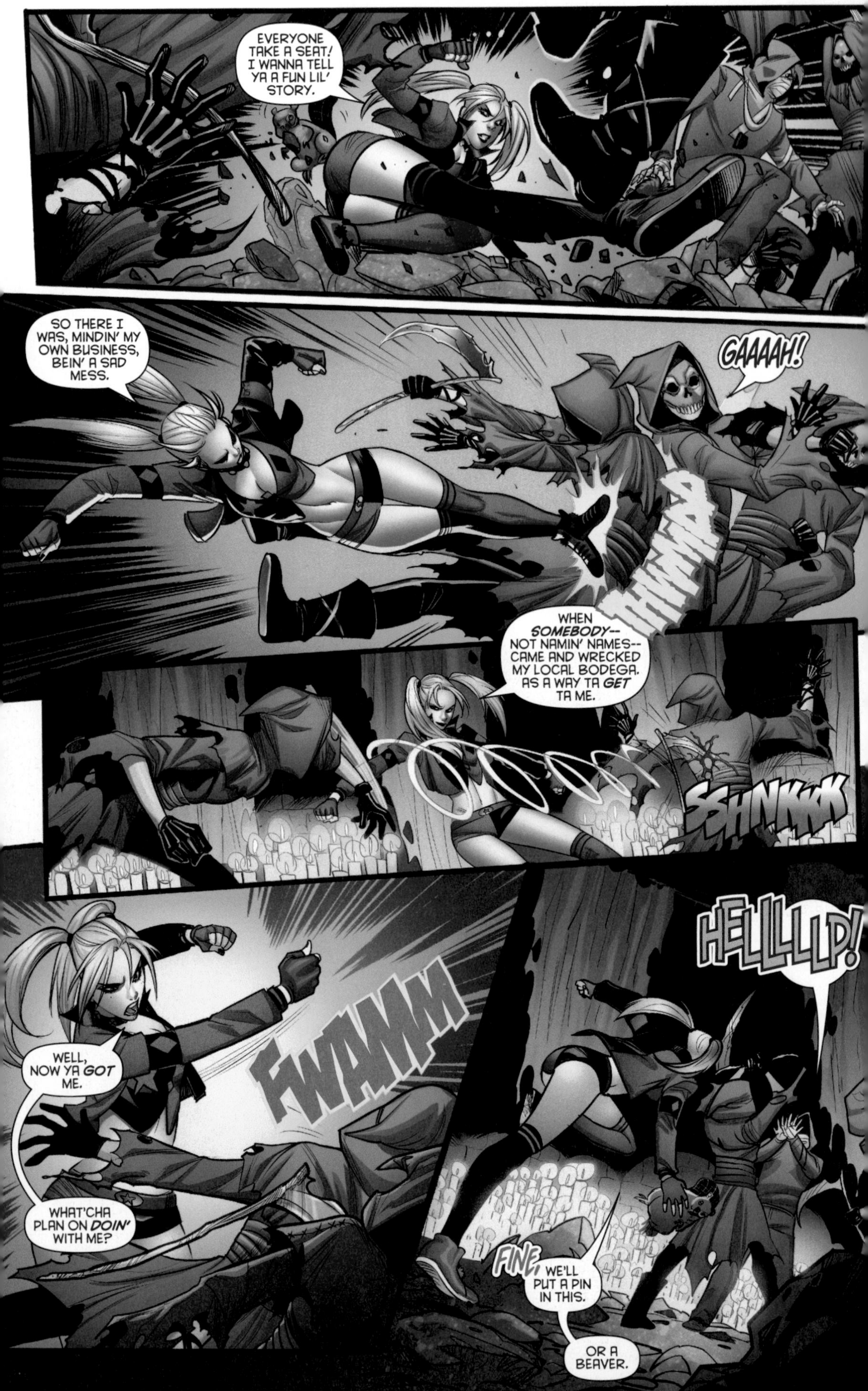
EVERYONE TAKE A SEAT! I WANNA TELL YA A FUN LIL' STORY.
SO THERE I WAS, MINDIN' MY OWN BUSINESS, BEIN' A SAD MESS.
GAAAAH!
THUMP
WHEN SOMEBODY-- NOT NAMIN' NAMES-- CAME AND WRECKED MY LOCAL BODEGA. AS A WAY TA GET TA ME.
SSHNKKK
WELL, NOW YA GOT ME.
FWAMM
WHAT'CHA PLAN ON DOIN' WITH ME?
HELLLLP!
FINE, WE'LL PUT A PIN IN THIS.
OR A BEAVER.

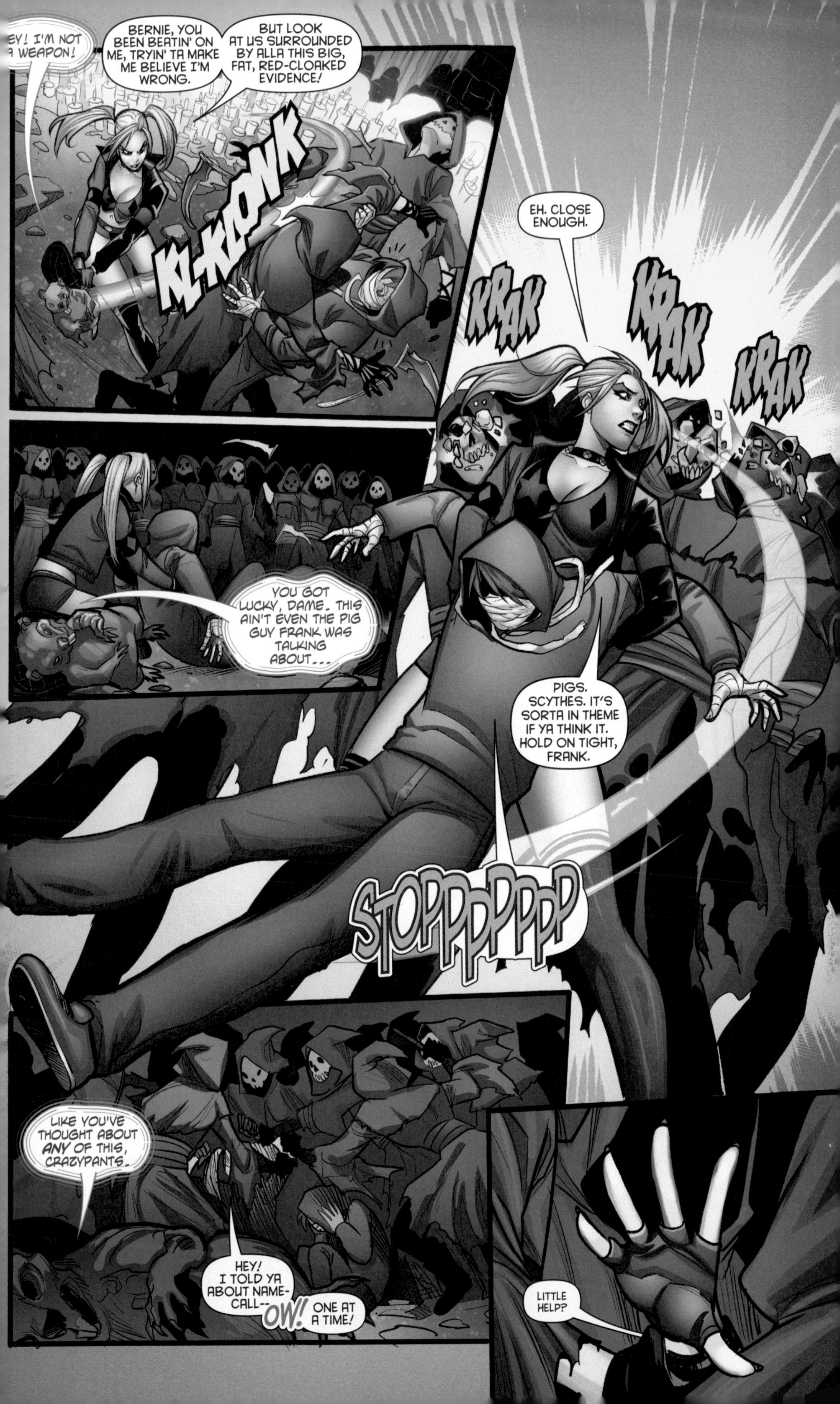

EY! I'M NOT A WEAPON!
BERNIE, YOU BEEN BEATIN' ON ME, TRYIN' TA MAKE ME BELIEVE I'M WRONG.
BUT LOOK AT US SURROUNDED BY ALLA THIS BIG, FAT, RED-CLOAKED EVIDENCE!
KL-KLONK
YOU GOT LUCKY, DAME. THIS AIN'T EVEN THE PIG GUY FRANK WAS TALKING ABOUT...
EH. CLOSE ENOUGH.
KRAK
KRAK
KRAK
PIGS. SCYTHES. IT'S SORTA IN THEME IF YA THINK IT. HOLD ON TIGHT, FRANK.
STOPPPPPPP
LIKE YOU'VE THOUGHT ABOUT ANY OF THIS, CRAZYPANTS.
HEY! I TOLD YA ABOUT NAME-CALL--
OW!
ONE AT A TIME!
LITTLE HELP?

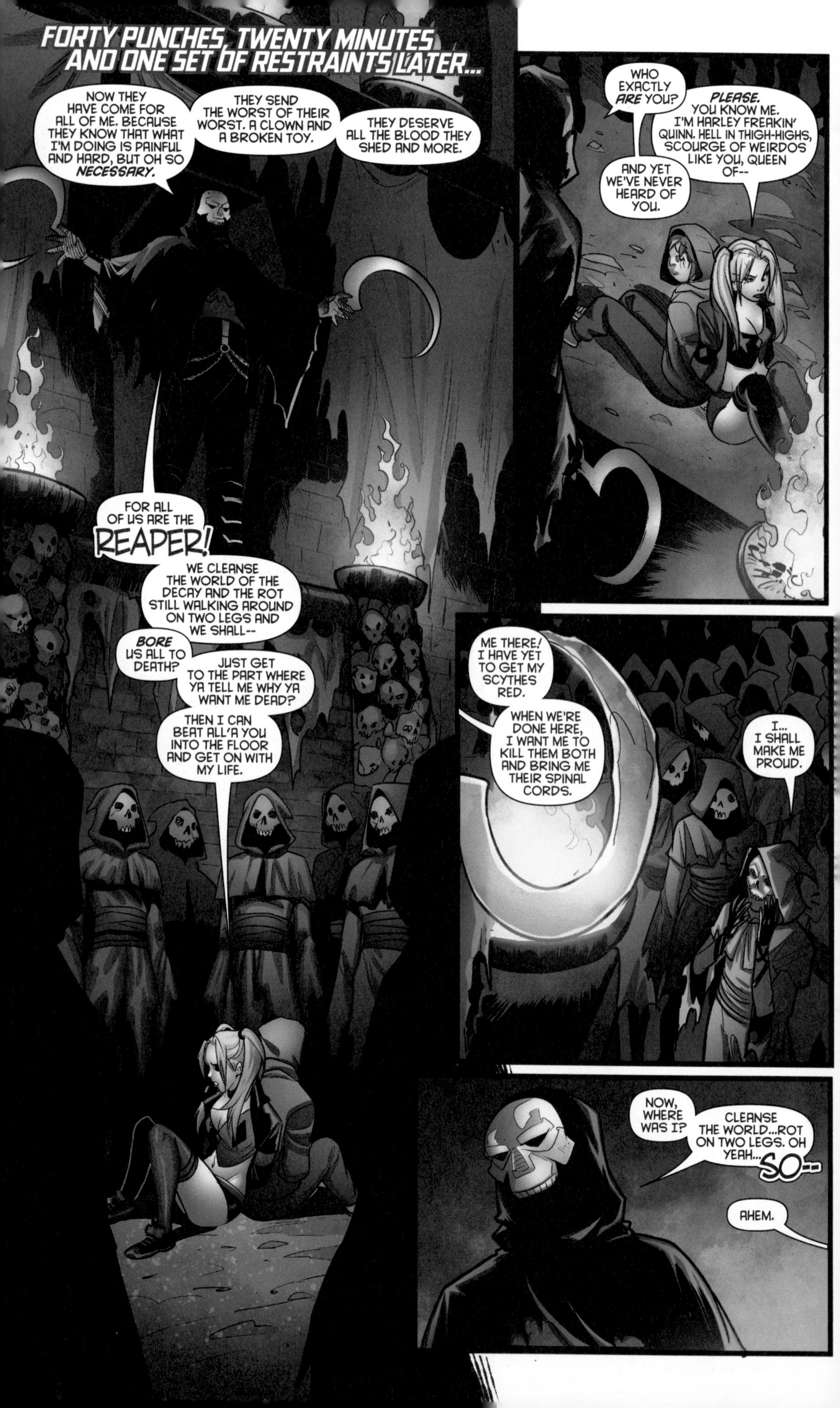

FORTY PUNCHES, TWENTY MINUTES AND ONE SET OF RESTRAINTS LATER...
NOW THEY HAVE COME FOR ALL OF ME. BECAUSE THEY KNOW THAT WHAT I'M DOING IS PAINFUL AND HARD, BUT OH SO NECESSARY.
THEY SEND THE WORST OF THEIR WORST. A CLOWN AND A BROKEN TOY.
THEY DESERVE ALL THE BLOOD THEY SHED AND MORE.
FOR ALL OF US ARE THE REAPER!
WE CLEANSE THE WORLD OF THE DECAY AND THE ROT STILL WALKING AROUND ON TWO LEGS AND WE SHALL--
BORE US ALL TO DEATH?
JUST GET TO THE PART WHERE YA TELL ME WHY YA WANT ME DEAD?
THEN I CAN BEAT ALL'A YOU INTO THE FLOOR AND GET ON WITH MY LIFE.
WHO EXACTLY ARE YOU?
PLEASE. YOU KNOW ME. I'M HARLEY FREAKIN' QUINN. HELL IN THIGH-HIGHS, SCOURGE OF WEIRDOS LIKE YOU, QUEEN OF--
AND YET WE'VE NEVER HEARD OF YOU.
ME THERE! I HAVE YET TO GET MY SCYTHES RED.
WHEN WE'RE DONE HERE, I WANT ME TO KILL THEM BOTH AND BRING ME THEIR SPINAL CORDS.
I... I SHALL MAKE ME PROUD.
NOW, WHERE WAS I?
CLEANSE THE WORLD...ROT ON TWO LEGS. OH YEAH...SO--
AHEM.

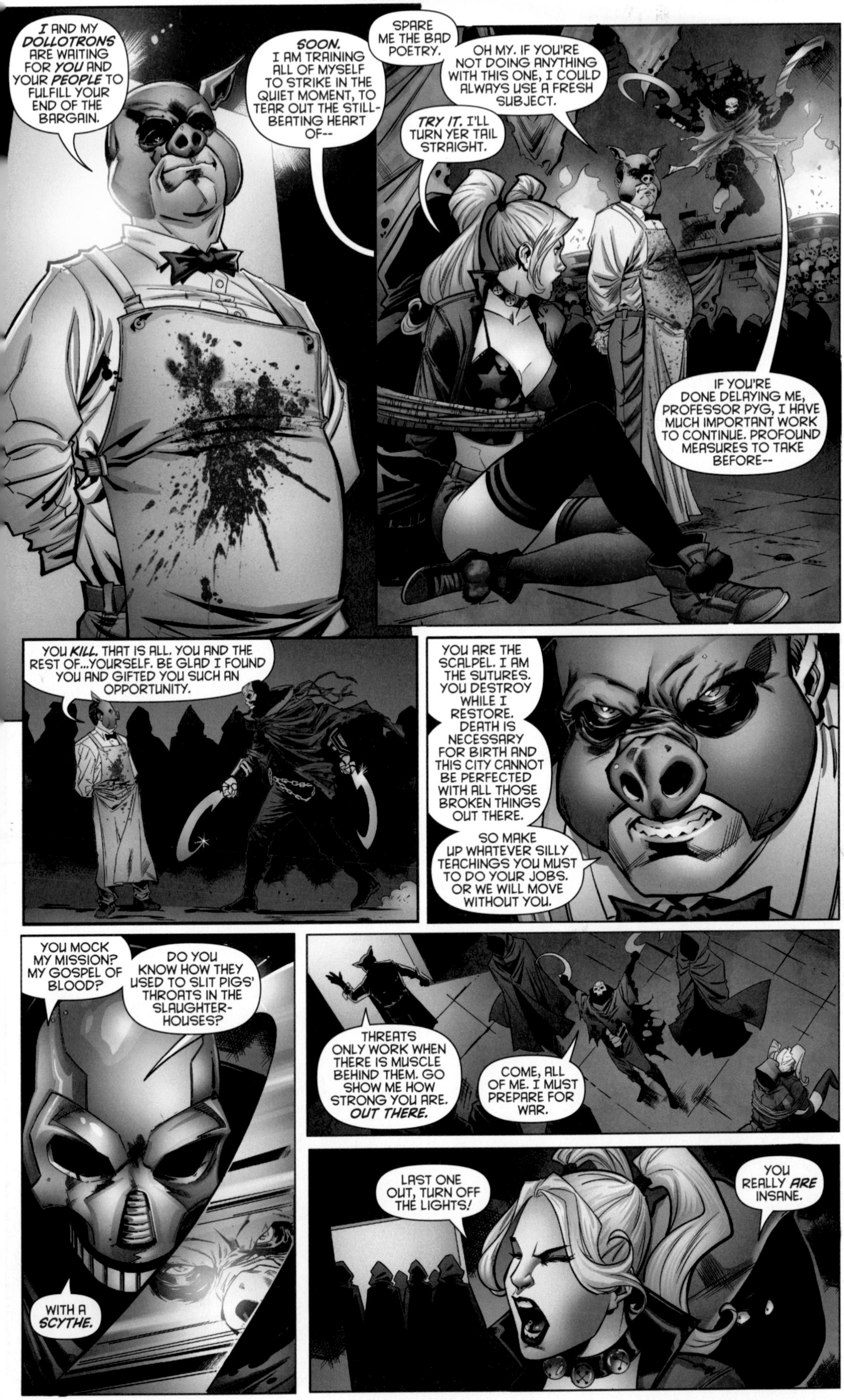
I AND MY DOLLOTRONS ARE WAITING FOR YOU AND YOUR PEOPLE TO FULFILL YOUR END OF THE BARGAIN.
SOON. I AM TRAINING ALL OF MYSELF TO STRIKE IN THE QUIET MOMENT, TO TEAR OUT THE STILL-BEATING HEART OF--
SPARE ME THE BAD POETRY.
OH MY. IF YOU'RE NOT DOING ANYTHING WITH THIS ONE, I COULD ALWAYS USE A FRESH SUBJECT.
TRY IT. I'LL TURN YER TAIL STRAIGHT.
IF YOU'RE DONE DELAYING ME, PROFESSOR PYG, I HAVE MUCH IMPORTANT WORK TO CONTINUE. PROFOUND MEASURES TO TAKE BEFORE--
YOU KILL. THAT IS ALL. YOU AND THE REST OF...YOURSELF. BE GLAD I FOUND YOU AND GIFTED YOU SUCH AN OPPORTUNITY.
YOU ARE THE SCALPEL. I AM THE SUTURES. YOU DESTROY WHILE I RESTORE. DEATH IS NECESSARY FOR BIRTH AND THIS CITY CANNOT BE PERFECTED WITH ALL THOSE BROKEN THINGS OUT THERE.
SO MAKE UP WHATEVER SILLY TEACHINGS YOU MUST TO DO YOUR JOBS. OR WE WILL MOVE WITHOUT YOU.
YOU MOCK MY MISSION? MY GOSPEL OF BLOOD?
DO YOU KNOW HOW THEY USED TO SLIT PIGS' THROATS IN THE SLAUGHTER-HOUSES?
WITH A SCYTHE.
THREATS ONLY WORK WHEN THERE IS MUSCLE BEHIND THEM. GO SHOW ME HOW STRONG YOU ARE. OUT THERE.
COME, ALL OF ME. I MUST PREPARE FOR WAR.
LAST ONE OUT, TURN OFF THE LIGHTS!
YOU REALLY ARE INSANE.

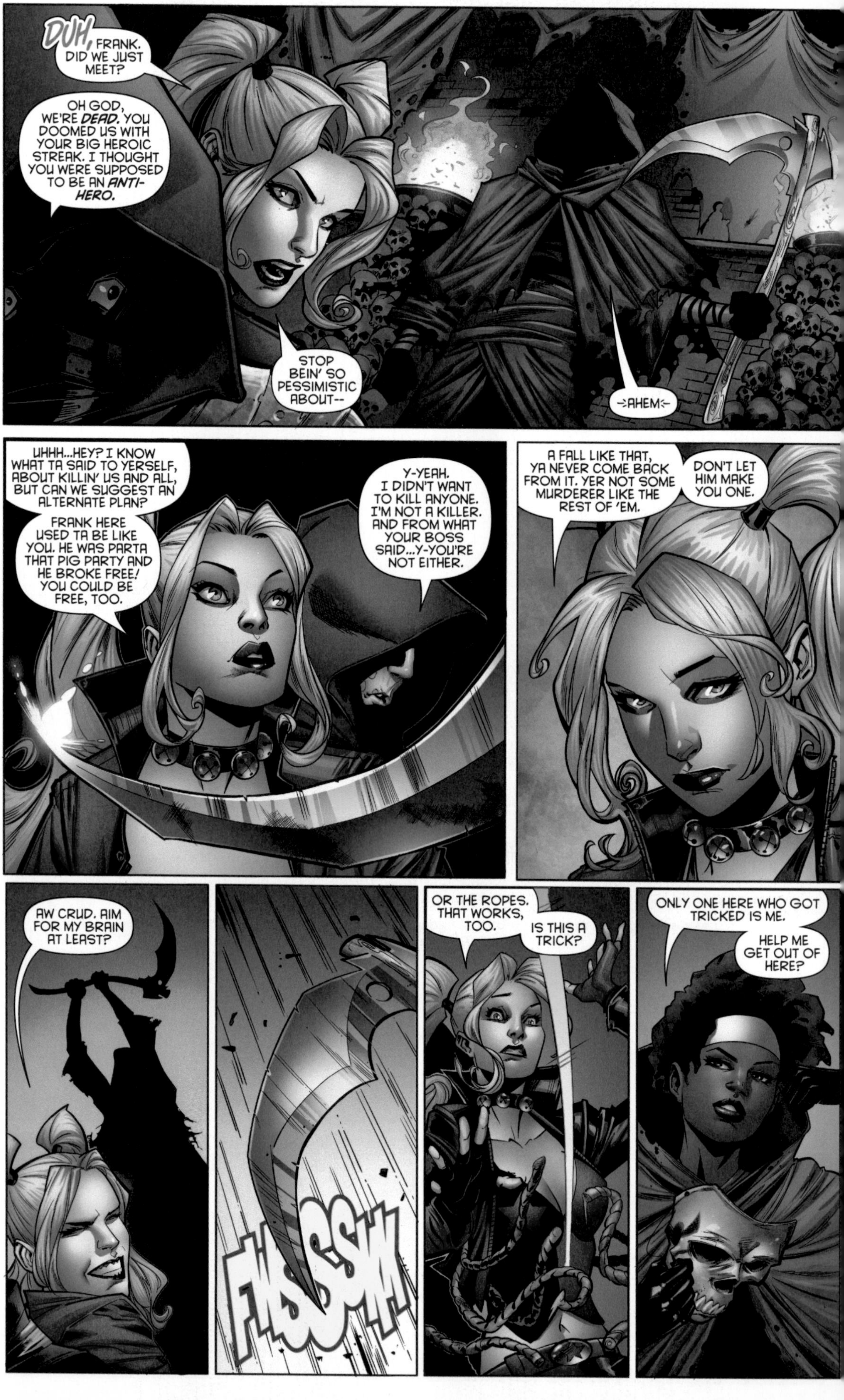
DUH, FRANK. DID WE JUST MEET?
OH GOD, WE'RE DEAD. YOU DOOMED US WITH YOUR BIG HEROIC STREAK. I THOUGHT YOU WERE SUPPOSED TO BE AN ANTI-HERO.
STOP BEIN' SO PESSIMISTIC ABOUT--
AHEM
UHHH...HEY? I KNOW WHAT TA SAID TO YERSELF, ABOUT KILLIN' US AND ALL, BUT CAN WE SUGGEST AN ALTERNATE PLAN?
FRANK HERE USED TA BE LIKE YOU. HE WAS PARTA THAT PIG PARTY AND HE BROKE FREE! YOU COULD BE FREE, TOO.
Y-YEAH. I DIDN'T WANT TO KILL ANYONE. I'M NOT A KILLER. AND FROM WHAT YOUR BOSS SAID...Y-YOU'RE NOT EITHER.
A FALL LIKE THAT, YA NEVER COME BACK FROM IT. YER NOT SOME MURDERER LIKE THE REST OF 'EM.
DON'T LET HIM MAKE YOU ONE.
AW CRUD. AIM FOR MY BRAIN AT LEAST?
FHSSSH
OR THE ROPES. THAT WORKS, TOO.
IS THIS A TRICK?
ONLY ONE HERE WHO GOT TRICKED IS ME.
HELP ME GET OUT OF HERE?

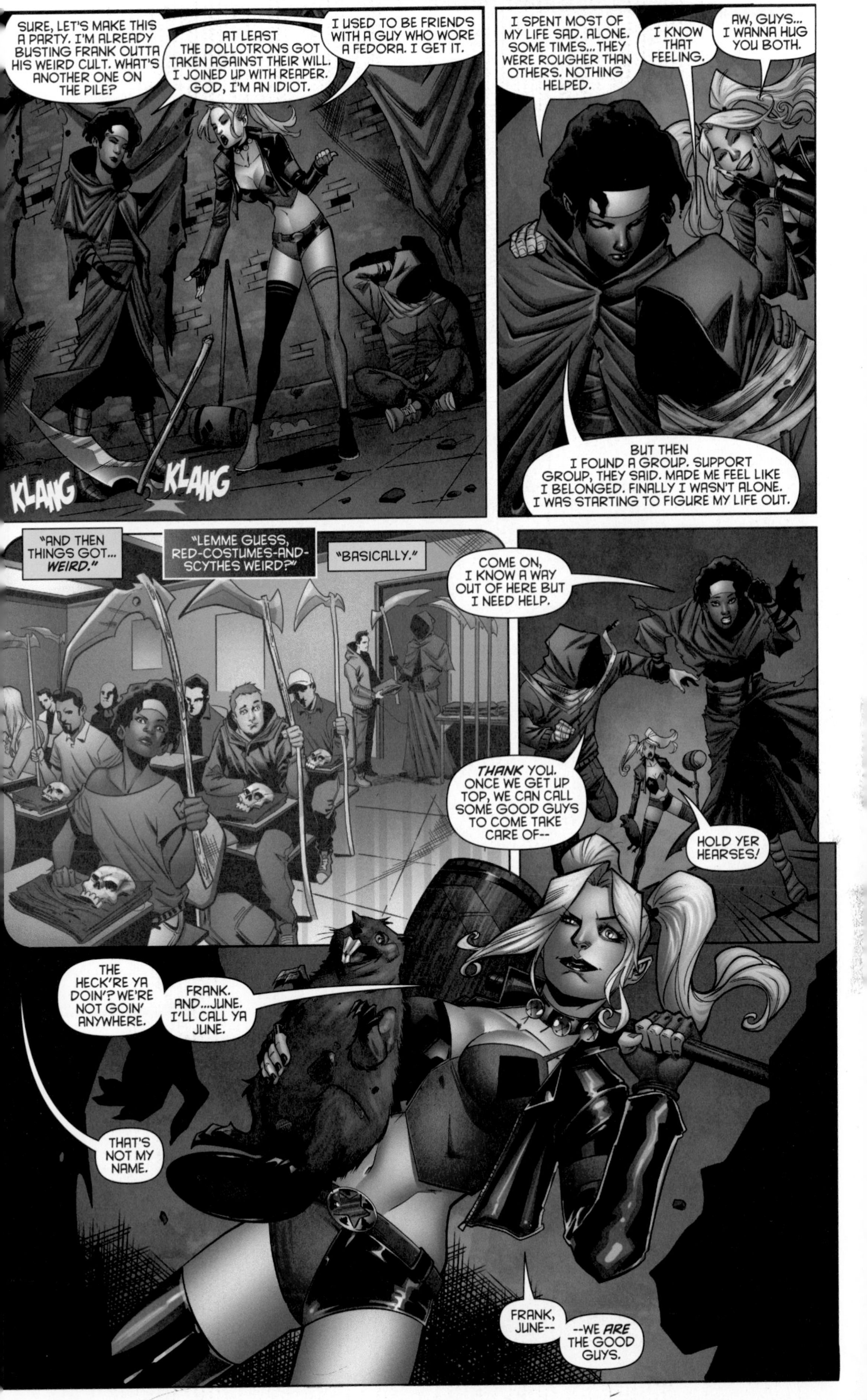
SURE, LET'S MAKE THIS A PARTY. I'M ALREADY BUSTING FRANK OUTTA HIS WEIRD CULT. WHAT'S ANOTHER ONE ON THE PILE?
AT LEAST THE DOLLOTRONS GOT TAKEN AGAINST THEIR WILL. I JOINED UP WITH REAPER. GOD, I'M AN IDIOT.
I USED TO BE FRIENDS WITH A GUY WHO WORE A FEDORA. I GET IT.
KLANG
KLANG
I SPENT MOST OF MY LIFE SAD. ALONE. SOME TIMES...THEY WERE ROUGHER THAN OTHERS. NOTHING HELPED.
I KNOW THAT FEELING.
AW, GUYS... I WANNA HUG YOU BOTH.
BUT THEN I FOUND A GROUP. SUPPORT GROUP, THEY SAID. MADE ME FEEL LIKE I BELONGED. FINALLY I WASN'T ALONE. I WAS STARTING TO FIGURE MY LIFE OUT.
"AND THEN THINGS GOT... WEIRD."
"LEMME GUESS, RED-COSTUMES-AND-SCYTHES WEIRD?"
"BASICALLY."
COME ON, I KNOW A WAY OUT OF HERE BUT I NEED HELP.
THANK YOU. ONCE WE GET UP TOP, WE CAN CALL SOME GOOD GUYS TO COME TAKE CARE OF--
HOLD YER HEARSES!
THE HECK'RE YA DOIN'? WE'RE NOT GOIN' ANYWHERE.
FRANK. AND...JUNE. I'LL CALL YA JUNE.
THAT'S NOT MY NAME.
FRANK, JUNE--
--WE ARE THE GOOD GUYS.

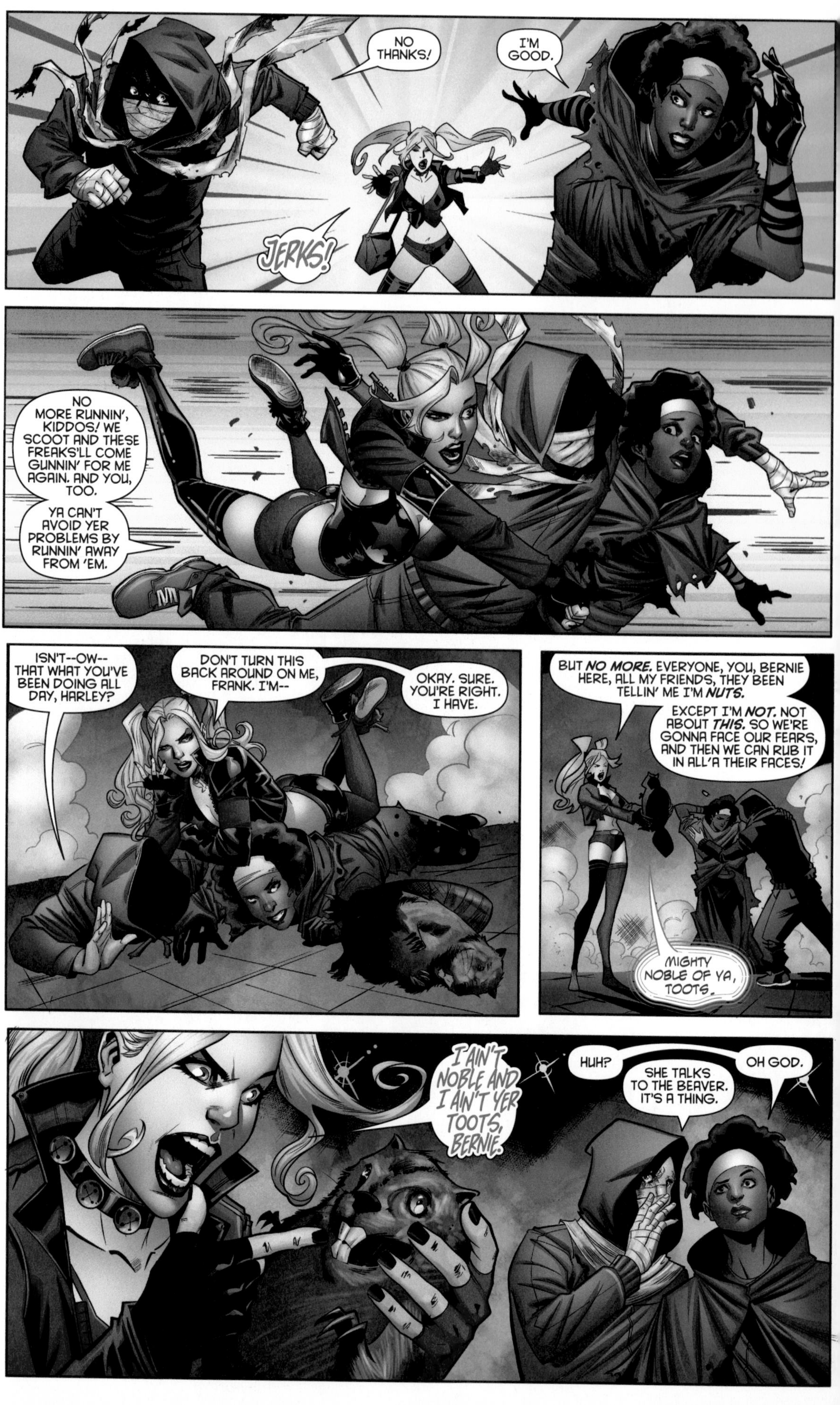
NO THANKS!
I'M GOOD.
JERKS!
NO MORE RUNNIN', KIDDOS! WE SCOOT AND THESE FREAKS'LL COME GUNNIN' FOR ME AGAIN. AND YOU, TOO.
YA CAN'T AVOID YER PROBLEMS BY RUNNIN' AWAY FROM 'EM.
ISN'T--OW--THAT WHAT YOU'VE BEEN DOING ALL DAY, HARLEY?
DON'T TURN THIS BACK AROUND ON ME, FRANK. I'M--
OKAY. SURE. YOU'RE RIGHT. I HAVE.
BUT NO MORE. EVERYONE, YOU, BERNIE HERE, ALL MY FRIENDS, THEY BEEN TELLIN' ME I'M NUTS.
EXCEPT I'M NOT. NOT ABOUT THIS. SO WE'RE GONNA FACE OUR FEARS, AND THEN WE CAN RUB IT IN ALL'A THEIR FACES!
MIGHTY NOBLE OF YA, TOOTS.
I AIN'T NOBLE AND I AIN'T YER TOOTS, BERNIE.
HUH?
SHE TALKS TO THE BEAVER. IT'S A THING.
OH GOD.

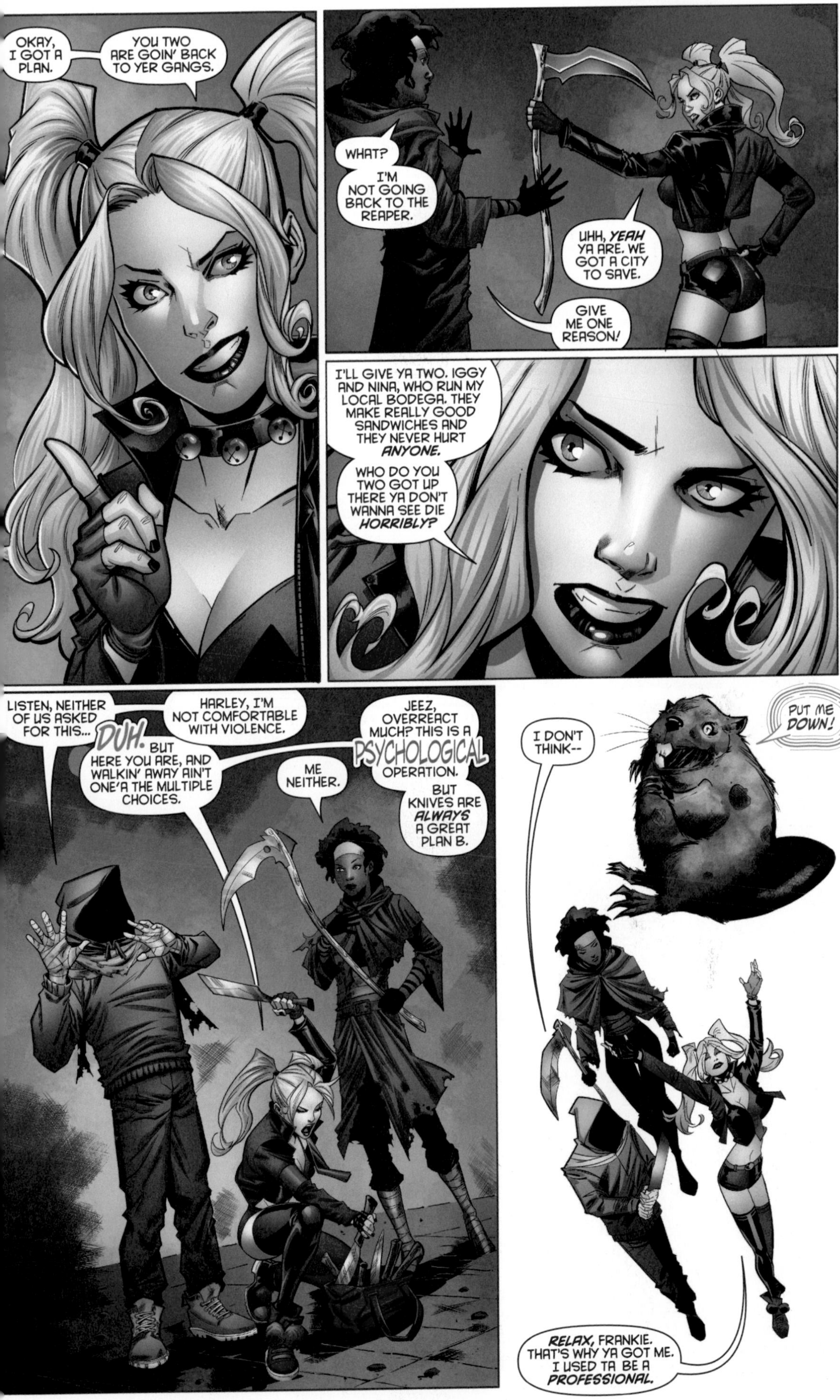

OKAY, I GOT A PLAN.
YOU TWO ARE GOIN' BACK TO YER GANGS.
WHAT?
I'M NOT GOING BACK TO THE REAPER.
UHH, YEAH YA ARE. WE GOT A CITY TO SAVE.
GIVE ME ONE REASON!
I'LL GIVE YA TWO. IGGY AND NINA, WHO RUN MY LOCAL BODEGA. THEY MAKE REALLY GOOD SANDWICHES AND THEY NEVER HURT ANYONE.
WHO DO YOU TWO GOT UP THERE YA DON'T WANNA SEE DIE HORRIBLY?
LISTEN, NEITHER OF US ASKED FOR THIS...
DUH.
BUT HERE YOU ARE, AND WALKIN' AWAY AIN'T ONE'A THE MULTIPLE CHOICES.
HARLEY, I'M NOT COMFORTABLE WITH VIOLENCE.
ME NEITHER.
JEEZ, OVERREACT MUCH? THIS IS A PSYCHOLOGICAL OPERATION.
BUT KNIVES ARE ALWAYS A GREAT PLAN B.
I DON'T THINK--
PUT ME DOWN!
RELAX, FRANKIE. THAT'S WHY YA GOT ME. I USED TA BE A PROFESSIONAL.

"SO WHAT'S YOUR BIG, AMAZING PLAN?"

"EASY-SQUEAZY. YA GO SLIP BACK INTO THE PYG PARTY. BLEND FOR A BIT."

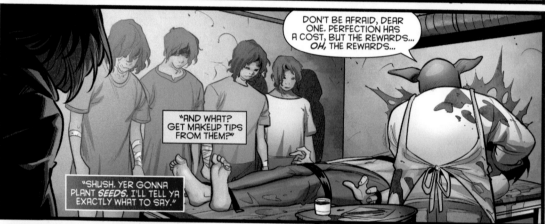

"AND WHAT? GET MAKEUP TIPS FROM THEM?"

DON'T BE AFRAID, DEAR ONE. PERFECTION HAS A COST, BUT THE REWARDS... *OH*, THE REWARDS...

"SHUSH. YER GONNA PLANT *SEEDS*. I'LL TELL YA EXACTLY WHAT TO SAY."

THE CHAFF CAN ONLY BE FELLED WITH A READY BLADE! SHARP ENOUGH TO SPLIT A DROP OF BLOOD!

"JUNE. YA DO WHAT FRANK IS DOING, EXCEPT WITH YER COSTUMED NERDS."

"I CAN'T! THEY'RE GOING TO MAKE ME KILL PEOPLE. LOTS OF PEOPLE. OR THEY'LL KILL ME. HOW CAN I?"

"IF YOU DON'T, THEY *WILL* KILL LOTSA PEOPLE. MYSELF INCLUDED. PROBABLY YOU, TOO, AT SOME POINT."

"AND WHAT EXACTLY WILL *YOU* BE DOING DURING ALL THIS?"

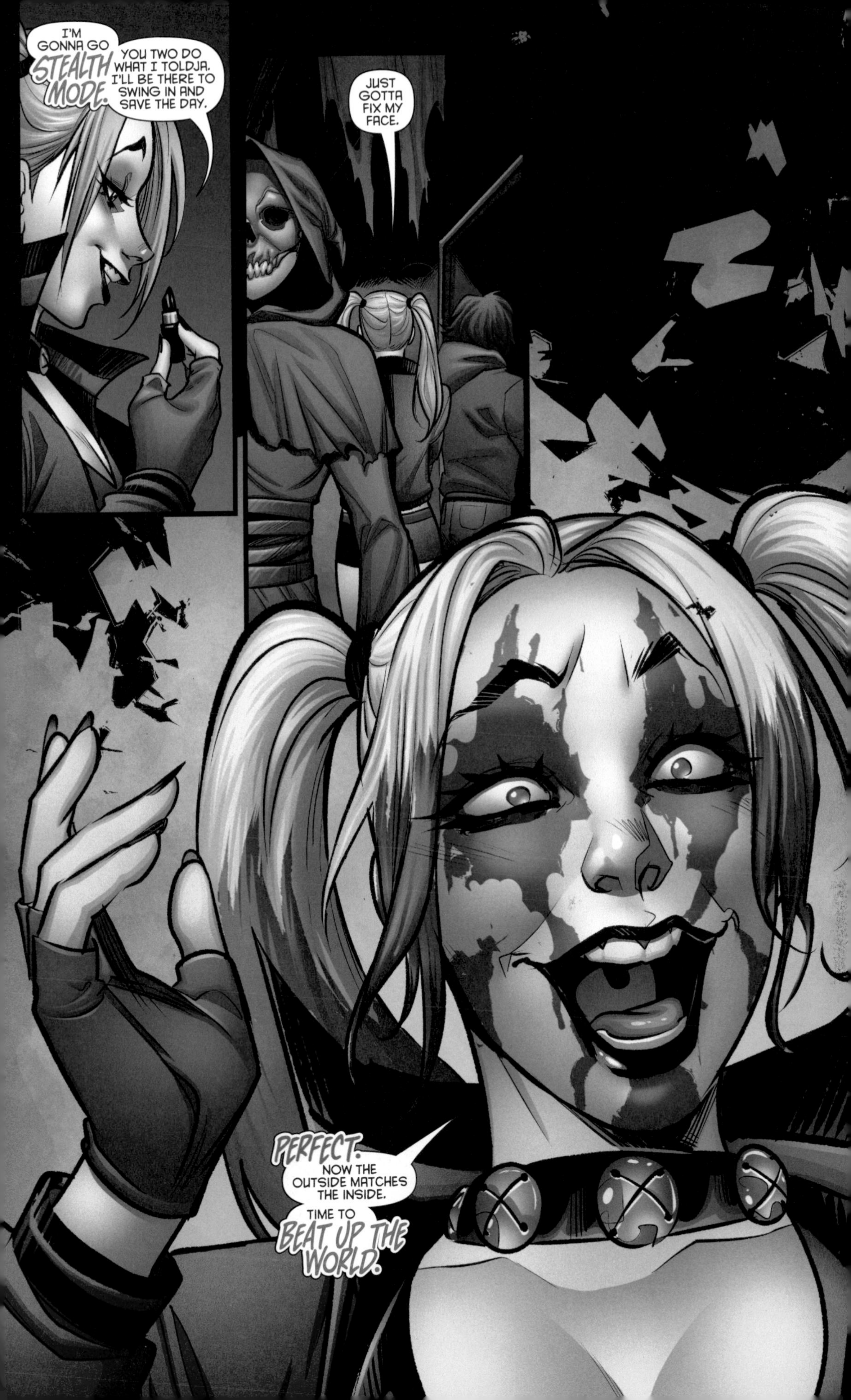
I'M GONNA GO STEALTH MODE.
YOU TWO DO WHAT I TOLDJA. I'LL BE THERE TO SWING IN AND SAVE THE DAY.
JUST GOTTA FIX MY FACE.
PERFECT.
NOW THE OUTSIDE MATCHES THE INSIDE.
TIME TO BEAT UP THE WORLD.

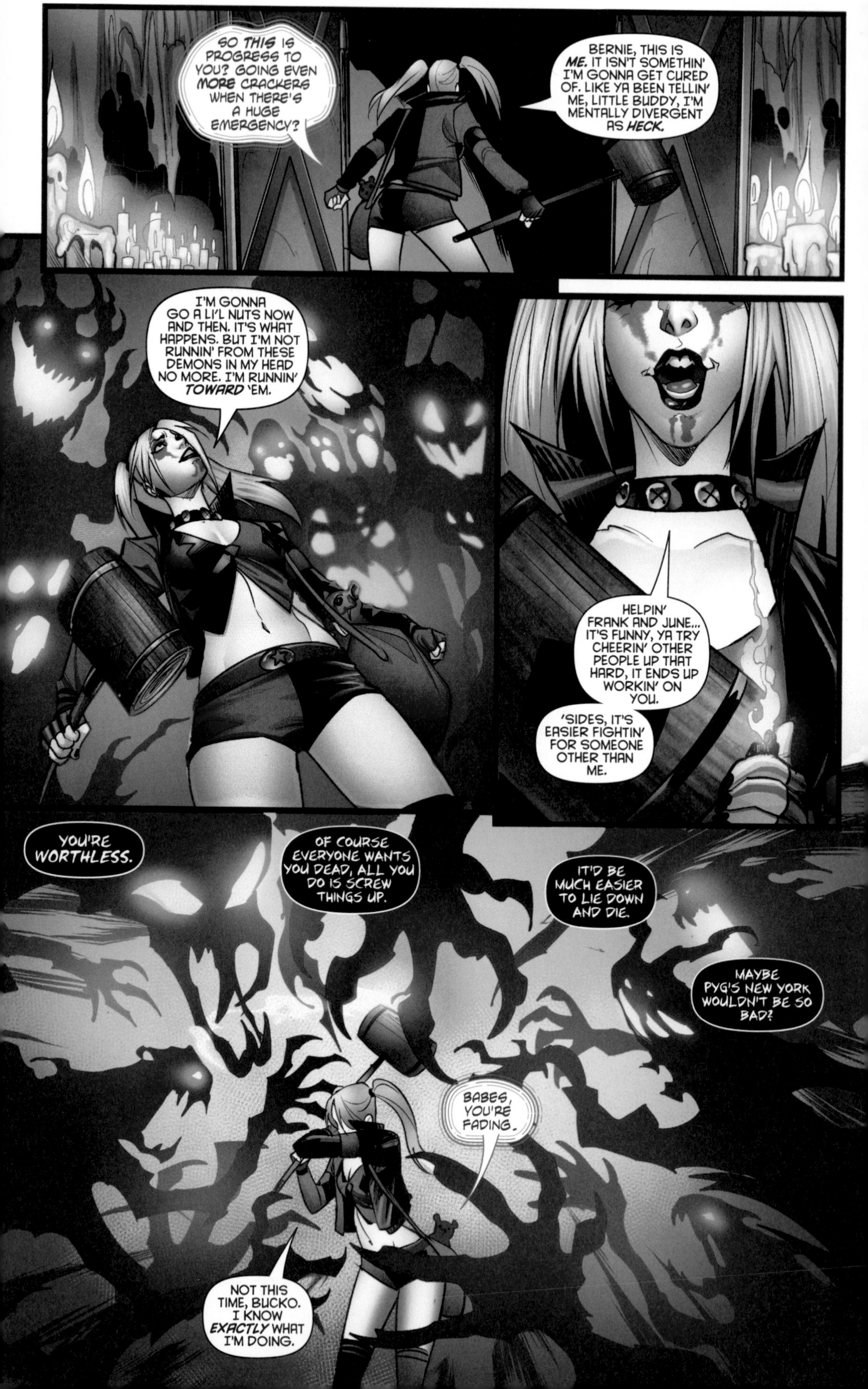
SO THIS IS PROGRESS TO YOU? GOING EVEN MORE CRACKERS WHEN THERE'S A HUGE EMERGENCY?
BERNIE, THIS IS ME. IT ISN'T SOMETHIN' I'M GONNA GET CURED OF. LIKE YA BEEN TELLIN' ME, LITTLE BUDDY, I'M MENTALLY DIVERGENT AS HECK.
I'M GONNA GO A LI'L NUTS NOW AND THEN. IT'S WHAT HAPPENS. BUT I'M NOT RUNNIN' FROM THESE DEMONS IN MY HEAD NO MORE. I'M RUNNIN' TOWARD 'EM.
HELPIN' FRANK AND JUNE... IT'S FUNNY, YA TRY CHEERIN' OTHER PEOPLE UP THAT HARD, IT ENDS UP WORKIN' ON YOU.
'SIDES, IT'S EASIER FIGHTIN' FOR SOMEONE OTHER THAN ME.
YOU'RE WORTHLESS.
OF COURSE EVERYONE WANTS YOU DEAD, ALL YOU DO IS SCREW THINGS UP.
IT'D BE MUCH EASIER TO LIE DOWN AND DIE.
MAYBE PYG'S NEW YORK WOULDN'T BE SO BAD?
BABES, YOU'RE FADING.
NOT THIS TIME, BUCKO. I KNOW EXACTLY WHAT I'M DOING.

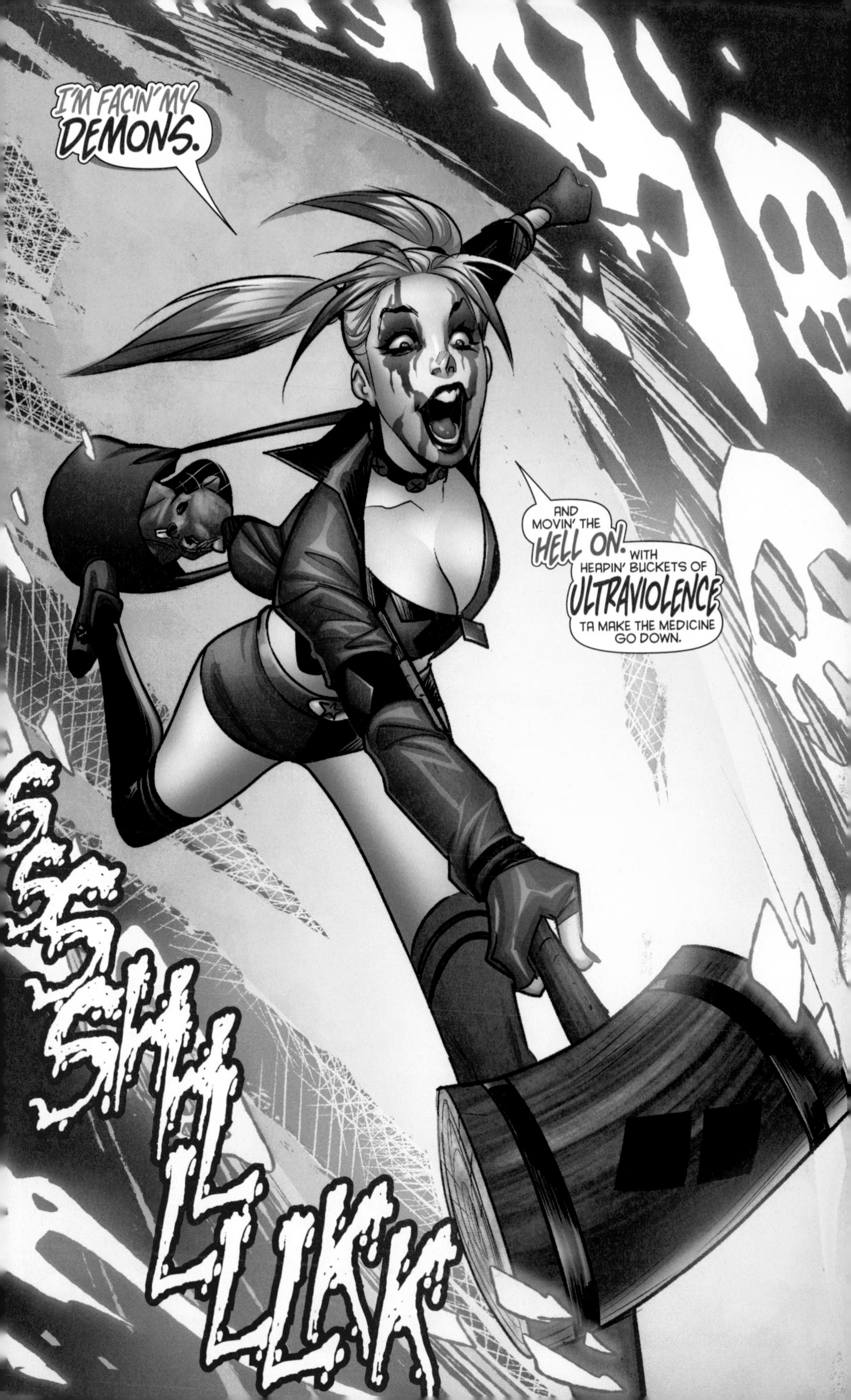
I'M FACIN' MY DEMONS.
AND MOVIN' THE HELL ON. WITH HEAPIN' BUCKETS OF ULTRAVIOLENCE TA MAKE THE MEDICINE GO DOWN.
SSSHHLLLKK

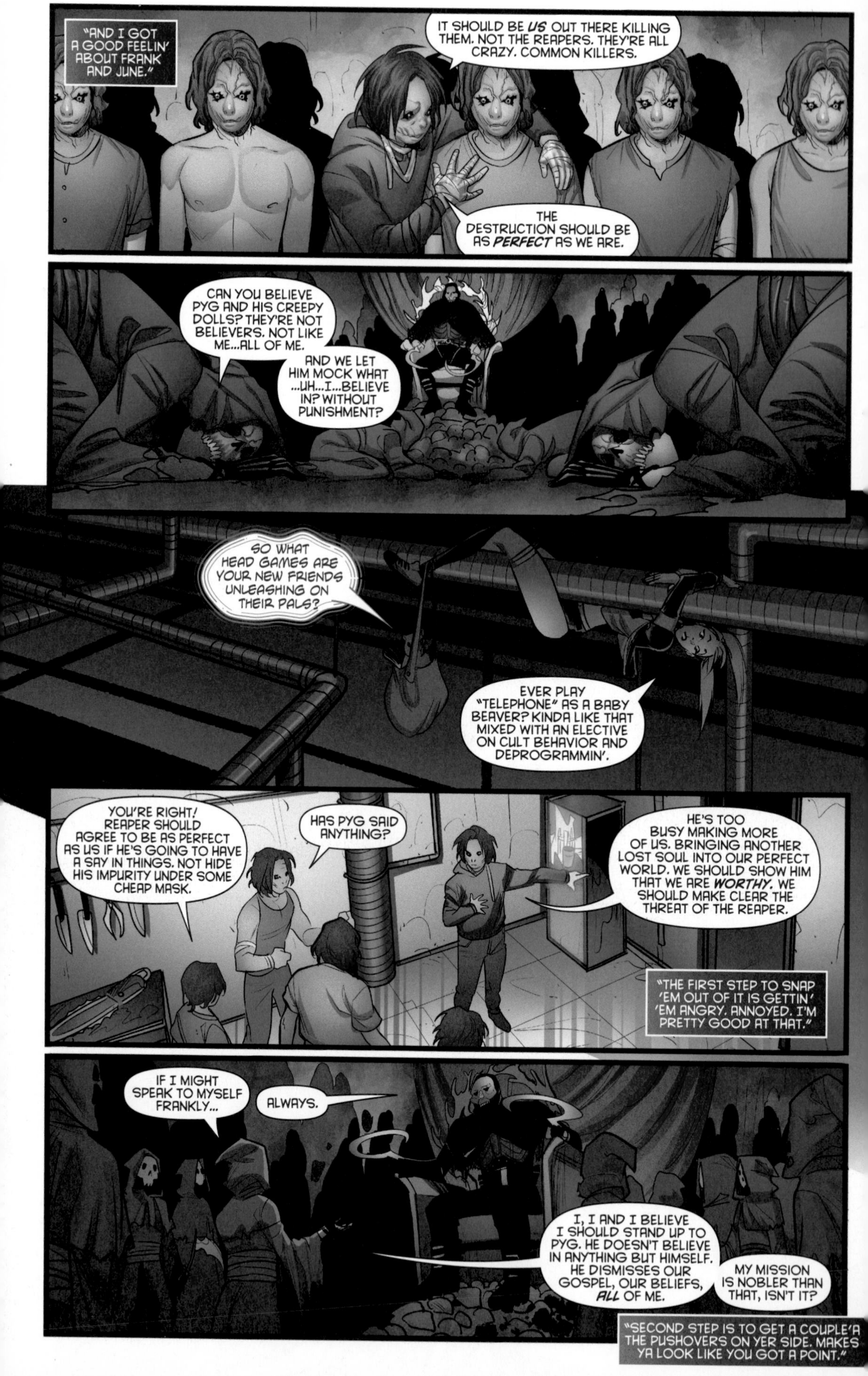

"AND I GOT A GOOD FEELIN' ABOUT FRANK AND JUNE."
IT SHOULD BE US OUT THERE KILLING THEM. NOT THE REAPERS. THEY'RE ALL CRAZY. COMMON KILLERS.
THE DESTRUCTION SHOULD BE AS PERFECT AS WE ARE.
CAN YOU BELIEVE PYG AND HIS CREEPY DOLLS? THEY'RE NOT BELIEVERS. NOT LIKE ME...ALL OF ME.
AND WE LET HIM MOCK WHAT ...UH...I...BELIEVE IN? WITHOUT PUNISHMENT?
SO WHAT HEAD GAMES ARE YOUR NEW FRIENDS UNLEASHING ON THEIR PALS?
EVER PLAY "TELEPHONE" AS A BABY BEAVER? KINDA LIKE THAT MIXED WITH AN ELECTIVE ON CULT BEHAVIOR AND DEPROGRAMMIN'.
YOU'RE RIGHT! REAPER SHOULD AGREE TO BE AS PERFECT AS US IF HE'S GOING TO HAVE A SAY IN THINGS. NOT HIDE HIS IMPURITY UNDER SOME CHEAP MASK.
HAS PYG SAID ANYTHING?
HE'S TOO BUSY MAKING MORE OF US. BRINGING ANOTHER LOST SOUL INTO OUR PERFECT WORLD. WE SHOULD SHOW HIM THAT WE ARE WORTHY. WE SHOULD MAKE CLEAR THE THREAT OF THE REAPER.
"THE FIRST STEP TO SNAP 'EM OUT OF IT IS GETTIN' 'EM ANGRY. ANNOYED. I'M PRETTY GOOD AT THAT."
IF I MIGHT SPEAK TO MYSELF FRANKLY...
ALWAYS.
I, I AND I BELIEVE I SHOULD STAND UP TO PYG. HE DOESN'T BELIEVE IN ANYTHING BUT HIMSELF. HE DISMISSES OUR GOSPEL, OUR BELIEFS, ALL OF ME.
MY MISSION IS NOBLER THAN THAT, ISN'T IT?
"SECOND STEP IS TO GET A COUPLE'A THE PUSHOVERS ON YER SIDE. MAKES YA LOOK LIKE YOU GOT A POINT."

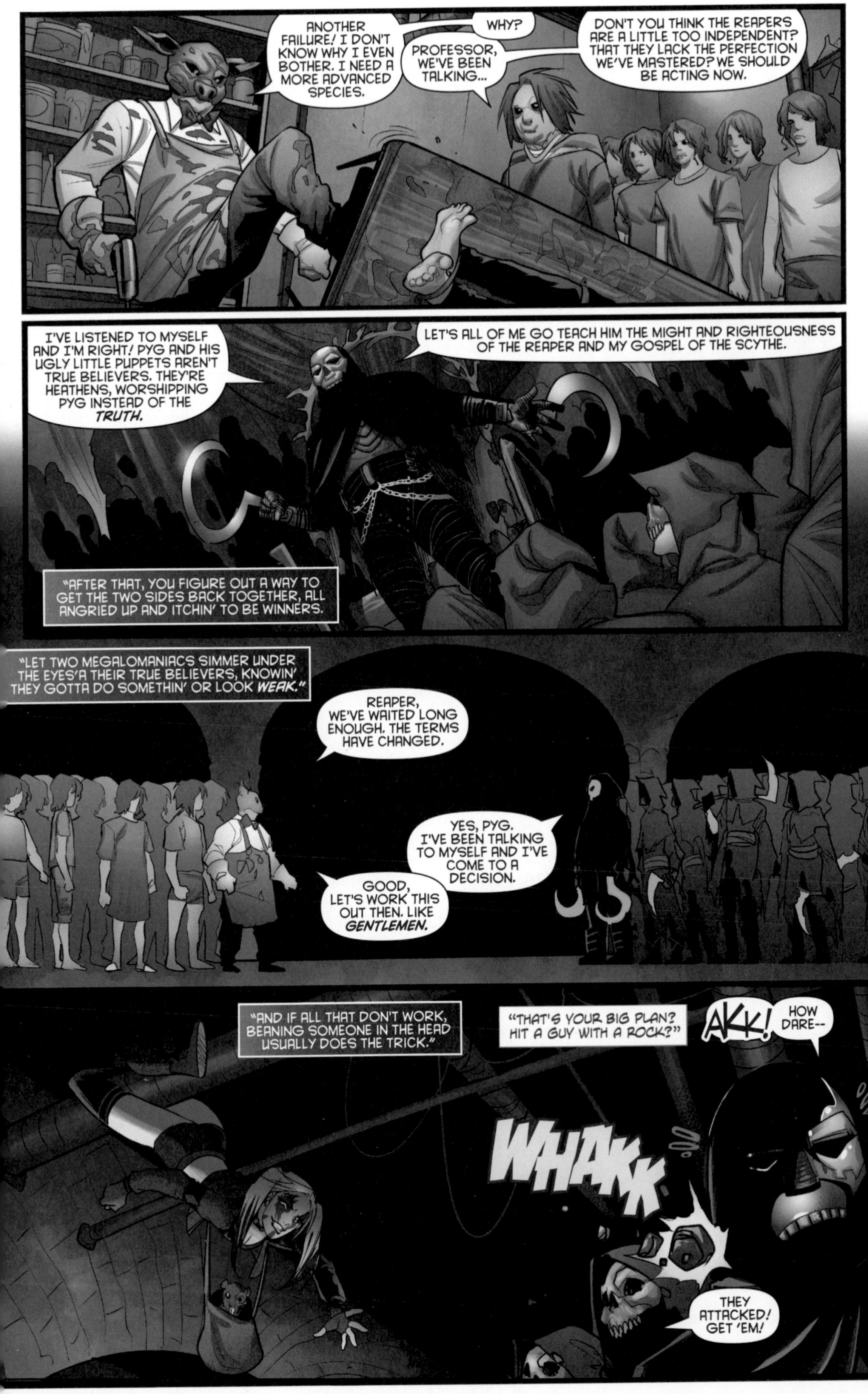
ANOTHER FAILURE! I DON'T KNOW WHY I EVEN BOTHER. I NEED A MORE ADVANCED SPECIES.
WHY?
PROFESSOR, WE'VE BEEN TALKING...
DON'T YOU THINK THE REAPERS ARE A LITTLE TOO INDEPENDENT? THAT THEY LACK THE PERFECTION WE'VE MASTERED? WE SHOULD BE ACTING NOW.
I'VE LISTENED TO MYSELF AND I'M RIGHT! PYG AND HIS UGLY LITTLE PUPPETS AREN'T TRUE BELIEVERS. THEY'RE HEATHENS, WORSHIPPING PYG INSTEAD OF THE *TRUTH*.
LET'S ALL OF ME GO TEACH HIM THE MIGHT AND RIGHTEOUSNESS OF THE REAPER AND MY GOSPEL OF THE SCYTHE.
"AFTER THAT, YOU FIGURE OUT A WAY TO GET THE TWO SIDES BACK TOGETHER, ALL ANGRIED UP AND ITCHIN' TO BE WINNERS.
"LET TWO MEGALOMANIACS SIMMER UNDER THE EYES'A THEIR TRUE BELIEVERS, KNOWIN' THEY GOTTA DO SOMETHIN' OR LOOK *WEAK*."
REAPER, WE'VE WAITED LONG ENOUGH. THE TERMS HAVE CHANGED.
YES, PYG. I'VE BEEN TALKING TO MYSELF AND I'VE COME TO A DECISION.
GOOD, LET'S WORK THIS OUT THEN. LIKE *GENTLEMEN*.
"AND IF ALL THAT DON'T WORK, BEANING SOMEONE IN THE HEAD USUALLY DOES THE TRICK."
"THAT'S YOUR BIG PLAN? HIT A GUY WITH A ROCK?"
AKK!
HOW DARE--
WHAKK
THEY ATTACKED! GET 'EM!

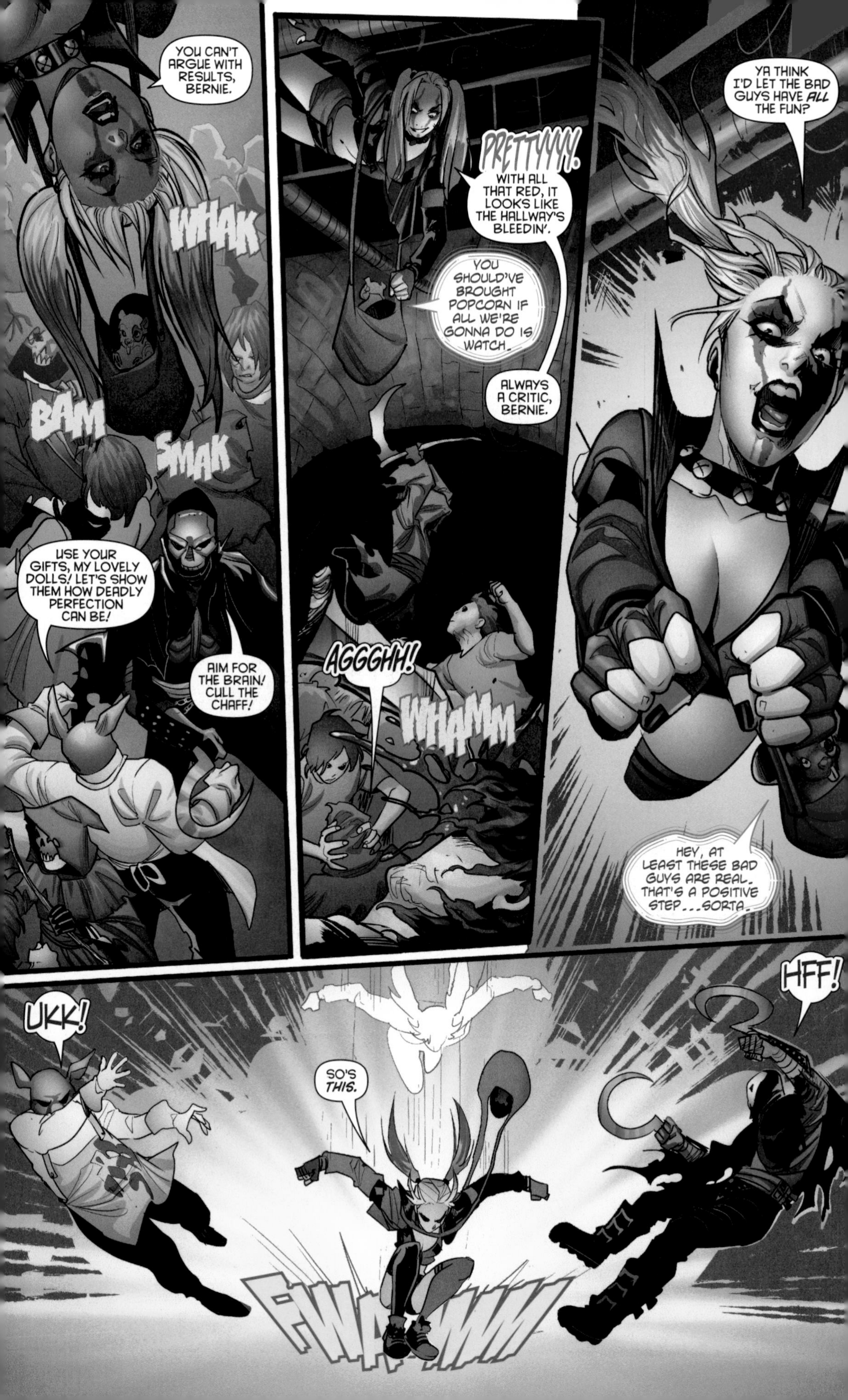
YOU CAN'T ARGUE WITH RESULTS, BERNIE.
WHAK
BAM
SMAK
USE YOUR GIFTS, MY LOVELY DOLLS! LET'S SHOW THEM HOW DEADLY PERFECTION CAN BE!
AIM FOR THE BRAIN! CULL THE CHAFF!
PRETTYYYY.
WITH ALL THAT RED, IT LOOKS LIKE THE HALLWAY'S BLEEDIN'.
YOU SHOULD'VE BROUGHT POPCORN IF ALL WE'RE GONNA DO IS WATCH.
ALWAYS A CRITIC, BERNIE.
AGGGHH!
WHAMM
YA THINK I'D LET THE BAD GUYS HAVE ALL THE FUN?
HEY, AT LEAST THESE BAD GUYS ARE REAL. THAT'S A POSITIVE STEP...SORTA.
UKK!
HFF!
SO'S THIS.
FWAMM

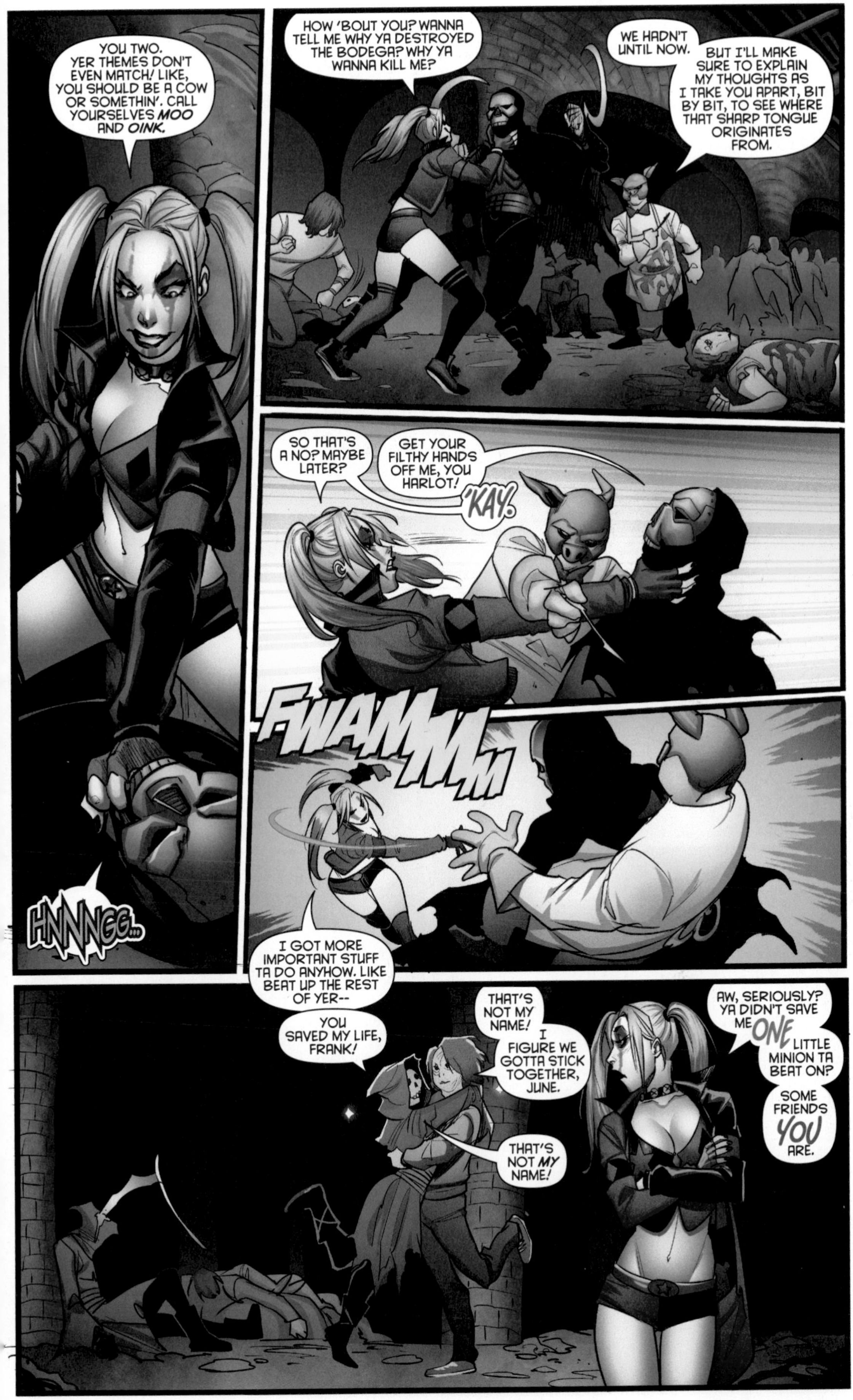
YOU TWO. YER THEMES DON'T EVEN MATCH! LIKE, YOU SHOULD BE A COW OR SOMETHIN'. CALL YOURSELVES MOO AND OINK.
HNNNGG...
HOW 'BOUT YOU? WANNA TELL ME WHY YA DESTROYED THE BODEGA? WHY YA WANNA KILL ME?
WE HADN'T UNTIL NOW.
BUT I'LL MAKE SURE TO EXPLAIN MY THOUGHTS AS I TAKE YOU APART, BIT BY BIT, TO SEE WHERE THAT SHARP TONGUE ORIGINATES FROM.
SO THAT'S A NO? MAYBE LATER?
GET YOUR FILTHY HANDS OFF ME, YOU HARLOT!
'KAY.
FWAMMMM
I GOT MORE IMPORTANT STUFF TA DO ANYHOW. LIKE BEAT UP THE REST OF YER--
YOU SAVED MY LIFE, FRANK!
THAT'S NOT MY NAME!
I FIGURE WE GOTTA STICK TOGETHER, JUNE.
THAT'S NOT MY NAME!
AW, SERIOUSLY? YA DIDN'T SAVE ME ONE LITTLE MINION TA BEAT ON?
SOME FRIENDS YOU ARE.

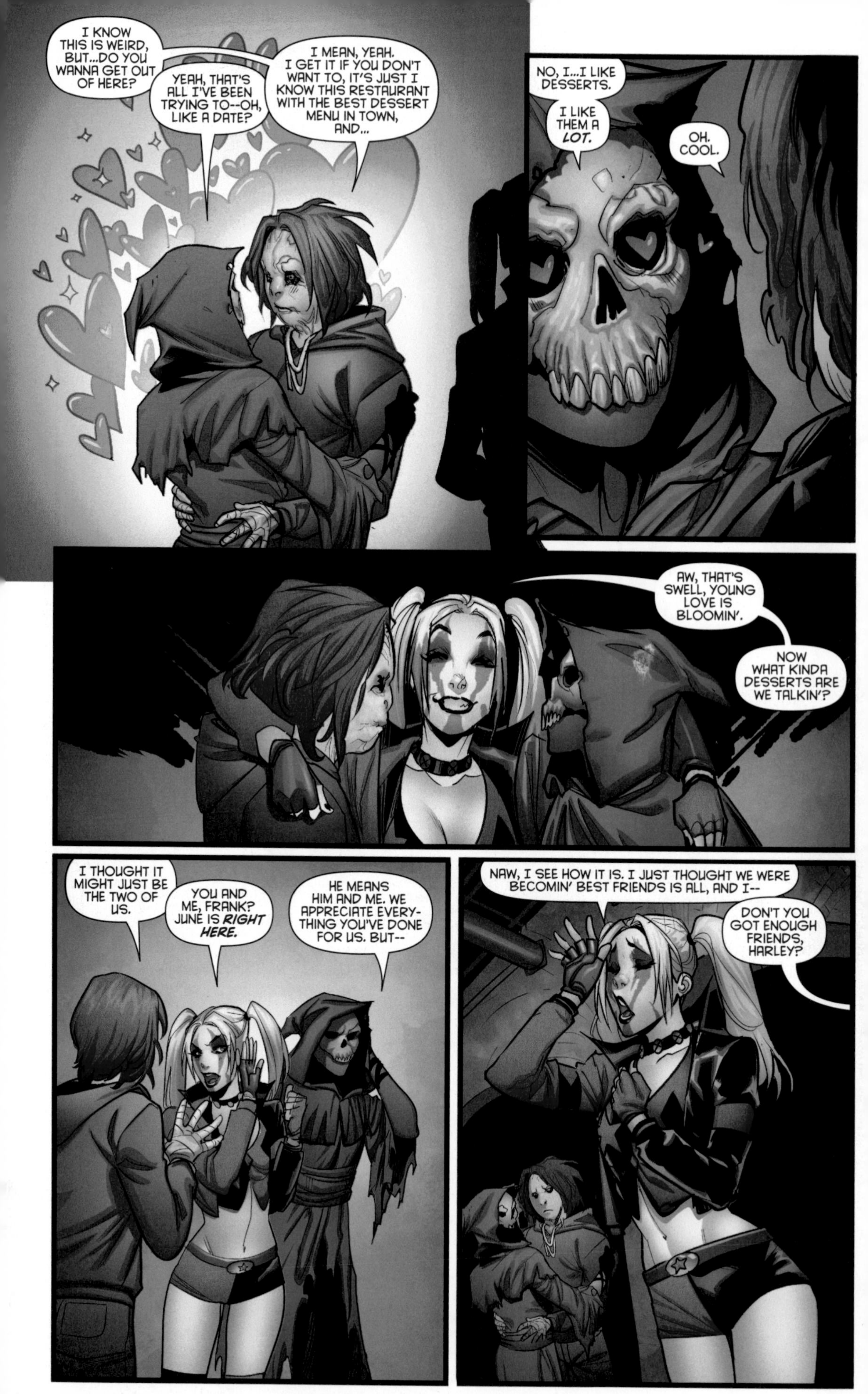
I KNOW THIS IS WEIRD, BUT...DO YOU WANNA GET OUT OF HERE?
YEAH, THAT'S ALL I'VE BEEN TRYING TO--OH, LIKE A DATE?
I MEAN, YEAH. I GET IT IF YOU DON'T WANT TO, IT'S JUST I KNOW THIS RESTAURANT WITH THE BEST DESSERT MENU IN TOWN, AND...
NO, I...I LIKE DESSERTS.
I LIKE THEM A *LOT.*
OH. COOL.
AW, THAT'S SWELL, YOUNG LOVE IS BLOOMIN'.
NOW WHAT KINDA DESSERTS ARE WE TALKIN'?
I THOUGHT IT MIGHT JUST BE THE TWO OF US.
YOU AND ME, FRANK? JUNE IS ***RIGHT HERE.***
HE MEANS HIM AND ME. WE APPRECIATE EVERYTHING YOU'VE DONE FOR US. BUT--
NAW, I SEE HOW IT IS. I JUST THOUGHT WE WERE BECOMIN' BEST FRIENDS IS ALL, AND I--
DON'T YOU GOT ENOUGH FRIENDS, HARLEY?

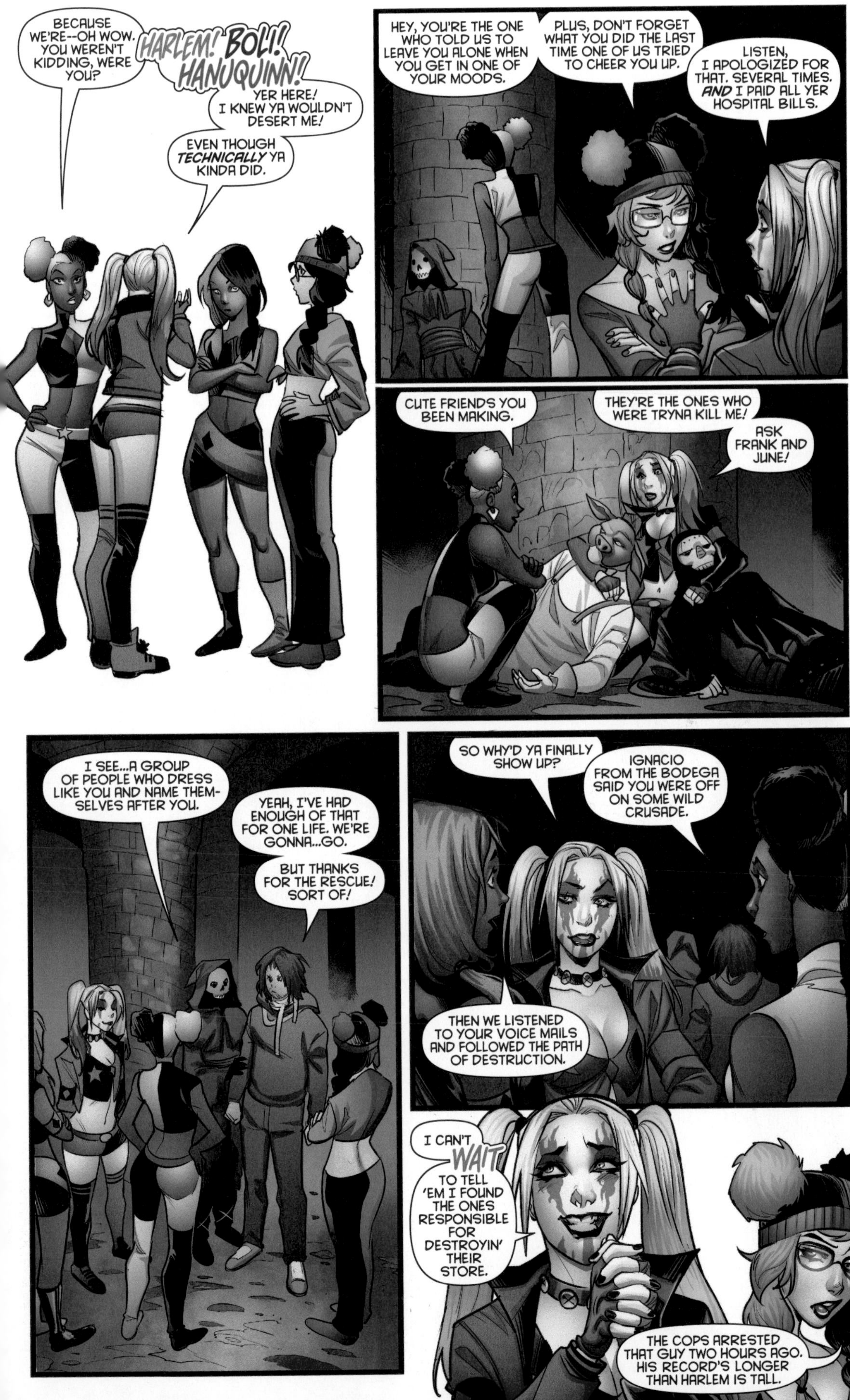
BECAUSE WE'RE--OH WOW. YOU WEREN'T KIDDING, WERE YOU?
HARLEM! BOLI! HANUQUINN!
YER HERE! I KNEW YA WOULDN'T DESERT ME!
EVEN THOUGH TECHNICALLY YA KINDA DID.
HEY, YOU'RE THE ONE WHO TOLD US TO LEAVE YOU ALONE WHEN YOU GET IN ONE OF YOUR MOODS.
PLUS, DON'T FORGET WHAT YOU DID THE LAST TIME ONE OF US TRIED TO CHEER YOU UP.
LISTEN, I APOLOGIZED FOR THAT. SEVERAL TIMES. AND I PAID ALL YER HOSPITAL BILLS.
CUTE FRIENDS YOU BEEN MAKING.
THEY'RE THE ONES WHO WERE TRYNA KILL ME!
ASK FRANK AND JUNE!
I SEE...A GROUP OF PEOPLE WHO DRESS LIKE YOU AND NAME THEMSELVES AFTER YOU.
YEAH, I'VE HAD ENOUGH OF THAT FOR ONE LIFE. WE'RE GONNA...GO.
BUT THANKS FOR THE RESCUE! SORT OF!
SO WHY'D YA FINALLY SHOW UP?
IGNACIO FROM THE BODEGA SAID YOU WERE OFF ON SOME WILD CRUSADE.
THEN WE LISTENED TO YOUR VOICE MAILS AND FOLLOWED THE PATH OF DESTRUCTION.
I CAN'T WAIT TO TELL 'EM I FOUND THE ONES RESPONSIBLE FOR DESTROYIN' THEIR STORE.
THE COPS ARRESTED THAT GUY TWO HOURS AGO. HIS RECORD'S LONGER THAN HARLEM IS TALL.

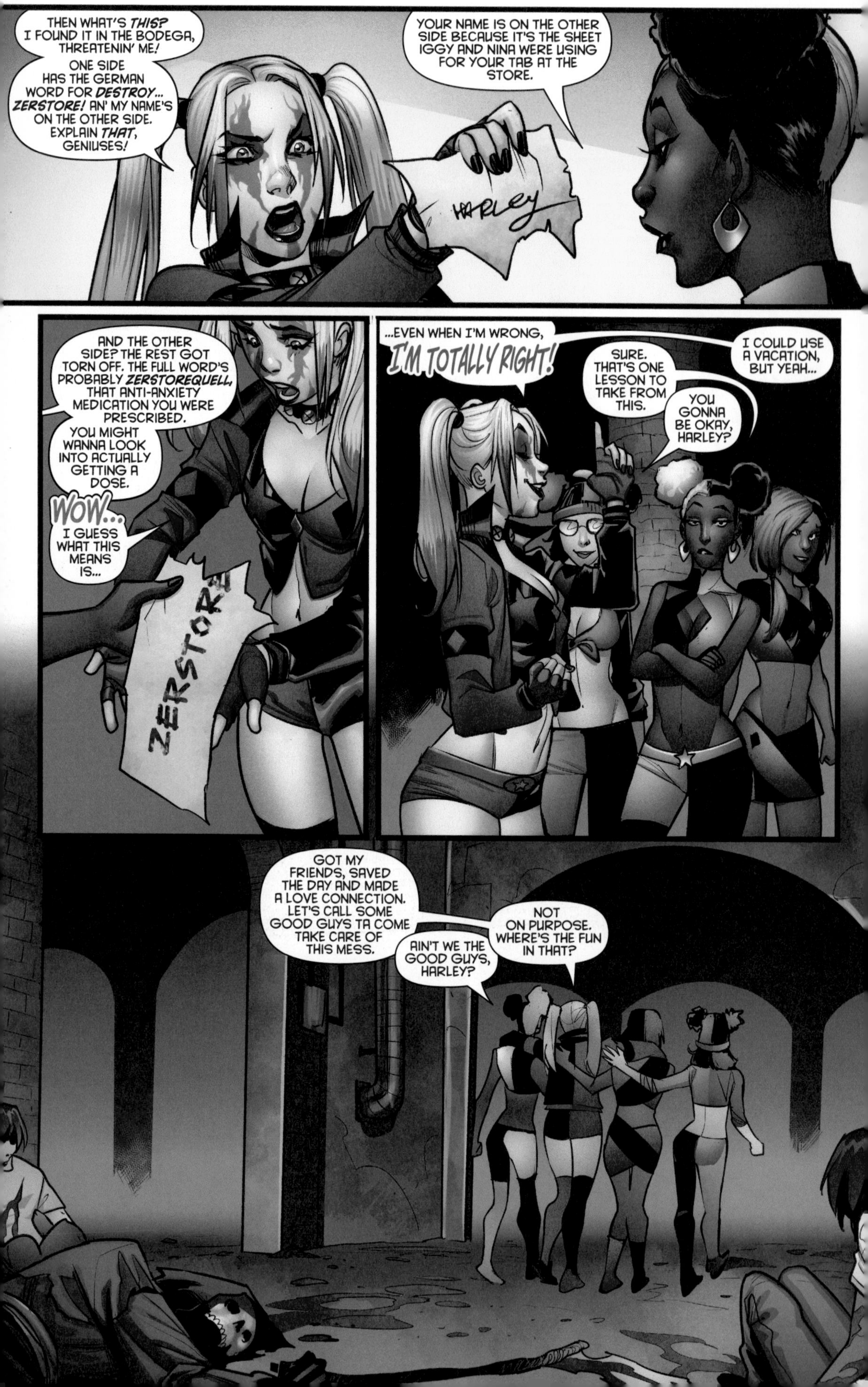
THEN WHAT'S *THIS?* I FOUND IT IN THE BODEGA, THREATENIN' ME!
ONE SIDE HAS THE GERMAN WORD FOR *DESTROY*... *ZERSTORE!* AN' MY NAME'S ON THE OTHER SIDE. EXPLAIN *THAT*, GENIUSES!
YOUR NAME IS ON THE OTHER SIDE BECAUSE IT'S THE SHEET IGGY AND NINA WERE USING FOR YOUR TAB AT THE STORE.
HARLEY
AND THE OTHER SIDE? THE REST GOT TORN OFF. THE FULL WORD'S PROBABLY *ZERSTOREQUELL*, THAT ANTI-ANXIETY MEDICATION YOU WERE PRESCRIBED.
YOU MIGHT WANNA LOOK INTO ACTUALLY GETTING A DOSE.
WOW... I GUESS WHAT THIS MEANS IS...
ZERSTORE
...EVEN WHEN I'M WRONG, I'M TOTALLY RIGHT!
SURE. THAT'S ONE LESSON TO TAKE FROM THIS.
I COULD USE A VACATION, BUT YEAH...
YOU GONNA BE OKAY, HARLEY?
GOT MY FRIENDS, SAVED THE DAY AND MADE A LOVE CONNECTION. LET'S CALL SOME GOOD GUYS TA COME TAKE CARE OF THIS MESS.
AIN'T WE THE GOOD GUYS, HARLEY?
NOT ON PURPOSE. WHERE'S THE FUN IN THAT?

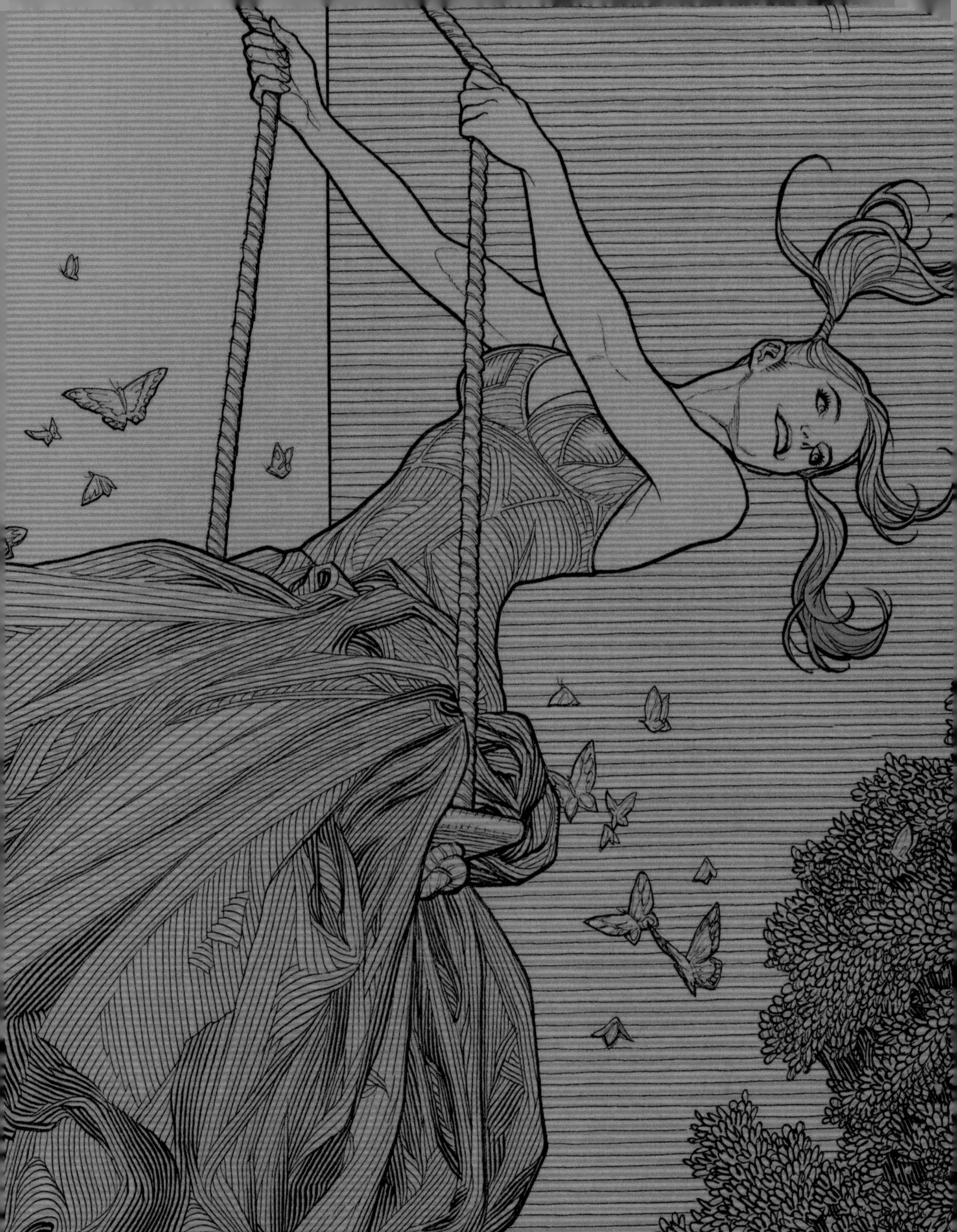

VARIANT COVER GALLERY

HARLEY QUINN #43 variant cover
by FRANK CHO and SABINE RICH

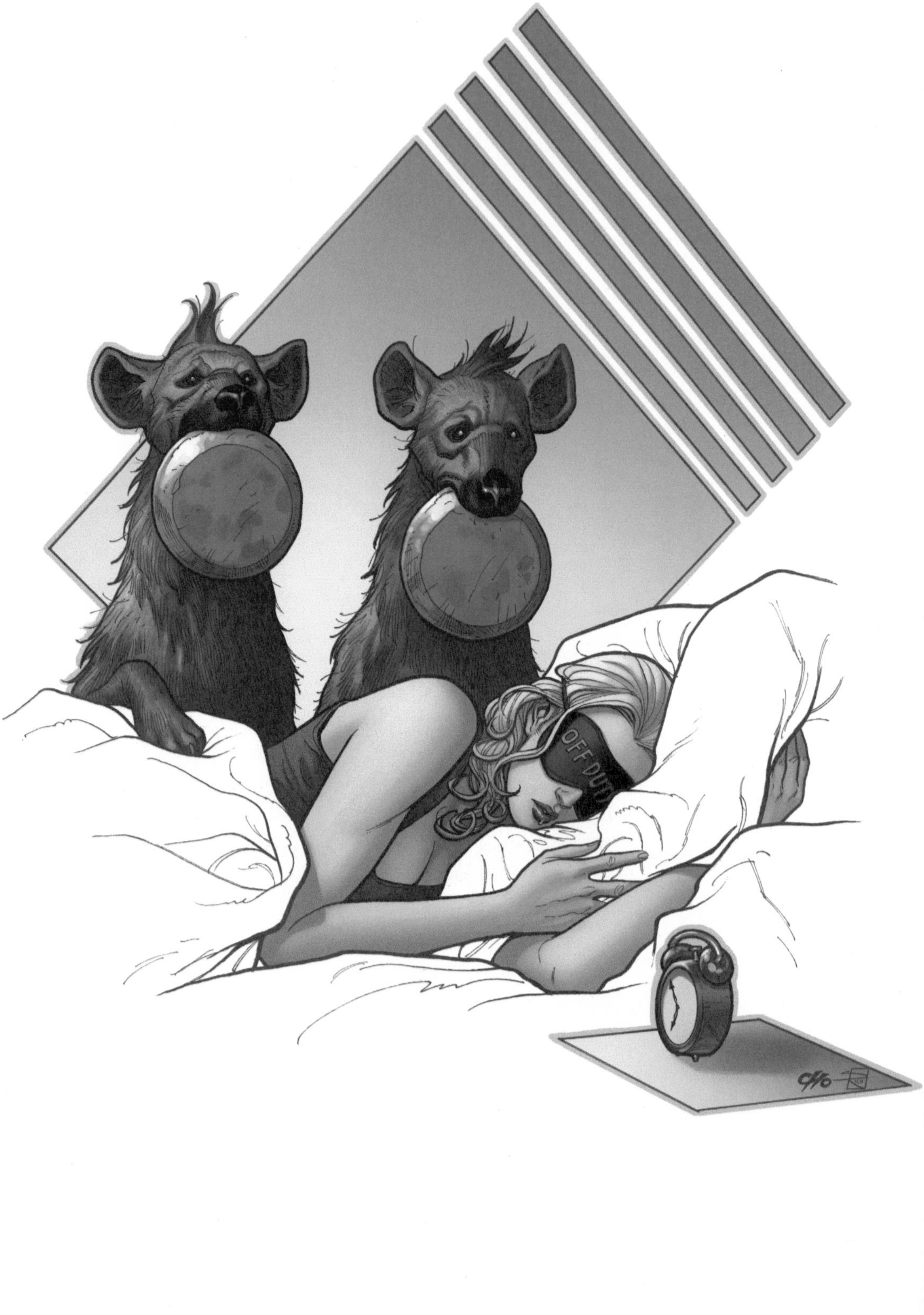

HARLEY QUINN #44 variant cover
by FRANK CHO and SABINE RICH

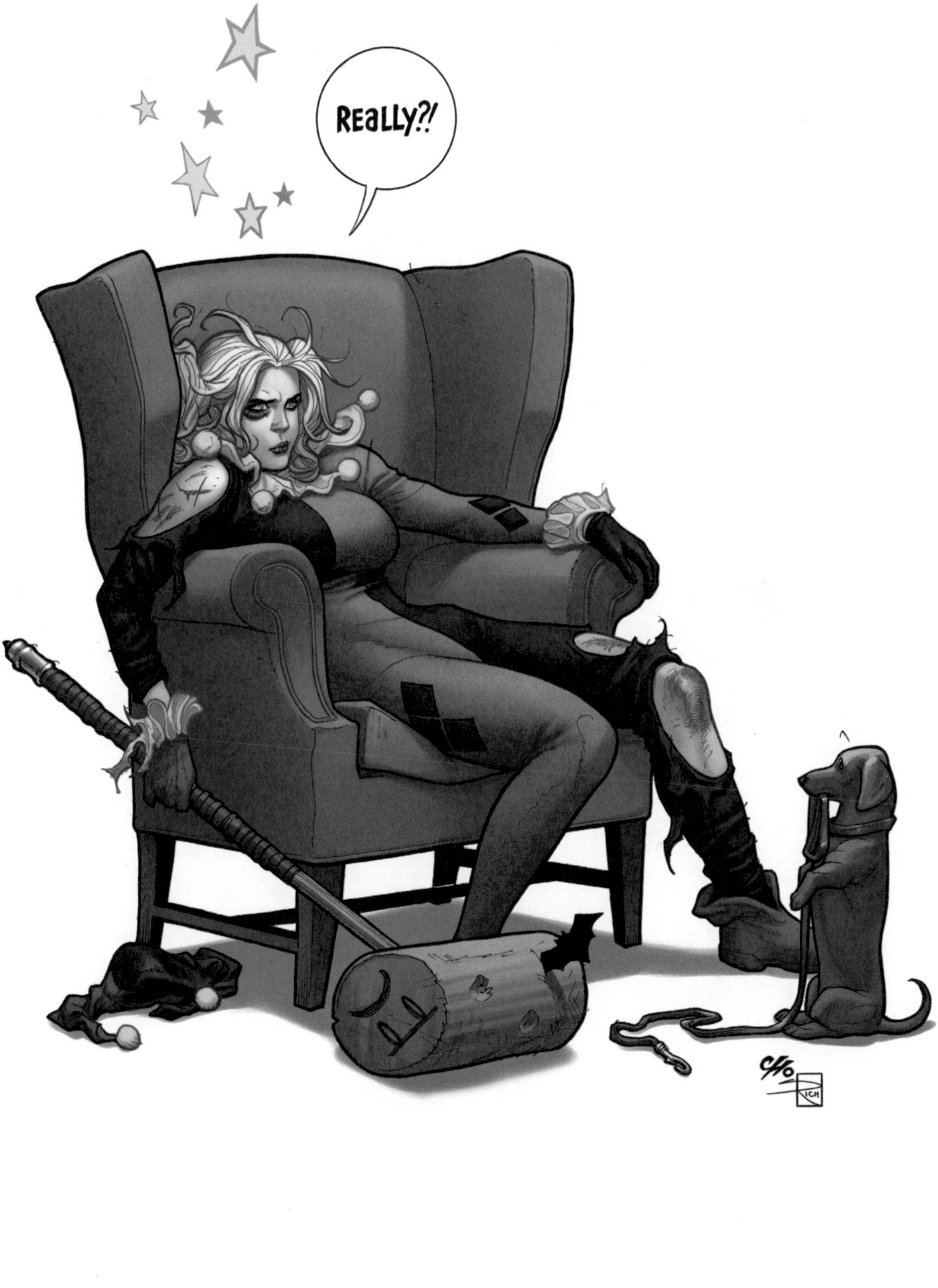
REALLY?!

HARLEY QUINN #45 VARIANT COVER
BY FRANK CHO AND SABINE RICH

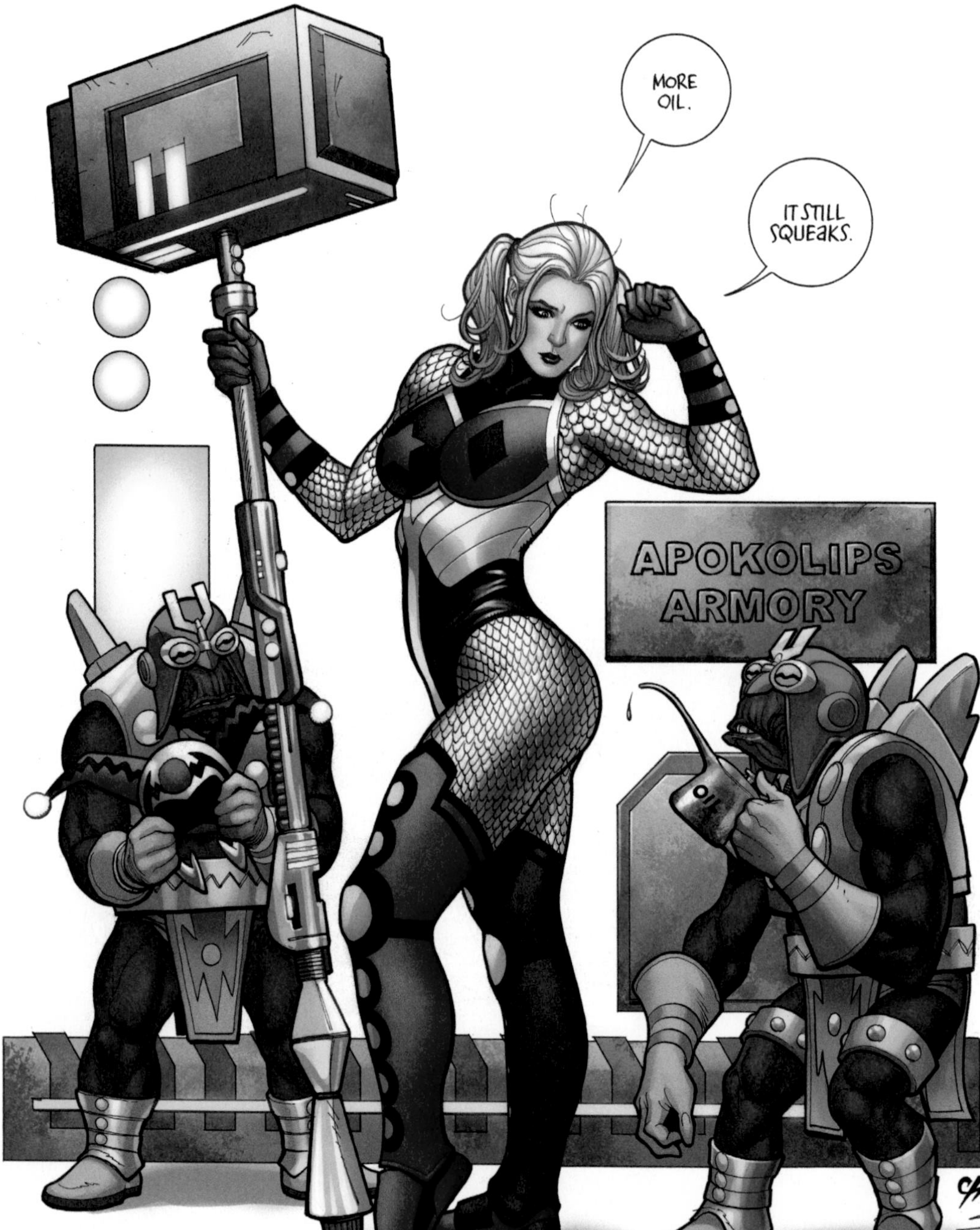
MORE OIL.
IT STILL SQUEAKS.
APOKOLIPS ARMORY
OIL

HARLEY QUINN #46 variant cover
by FRANK CHO and SABINE RICH

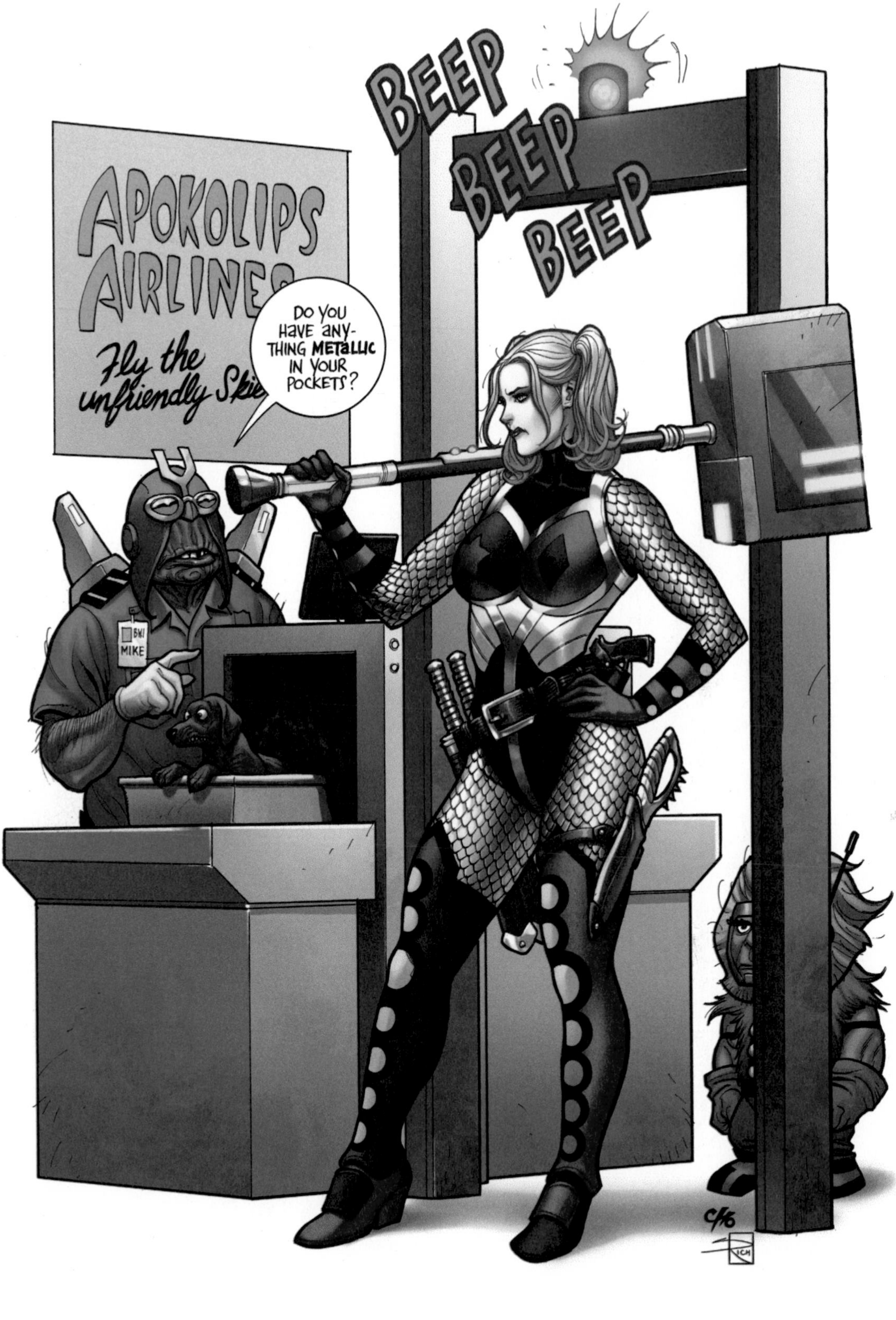
BEEP
BEEP
BEEP
APOKOLIPS AIRLINES
Fly the unfriendly Skies
DO YOU HAVE ANY-THING METALLIC IN YOUR POCKETS?
BWI
MIKE

HARLEY QUINN #47 variant cover
by FRANK CHO

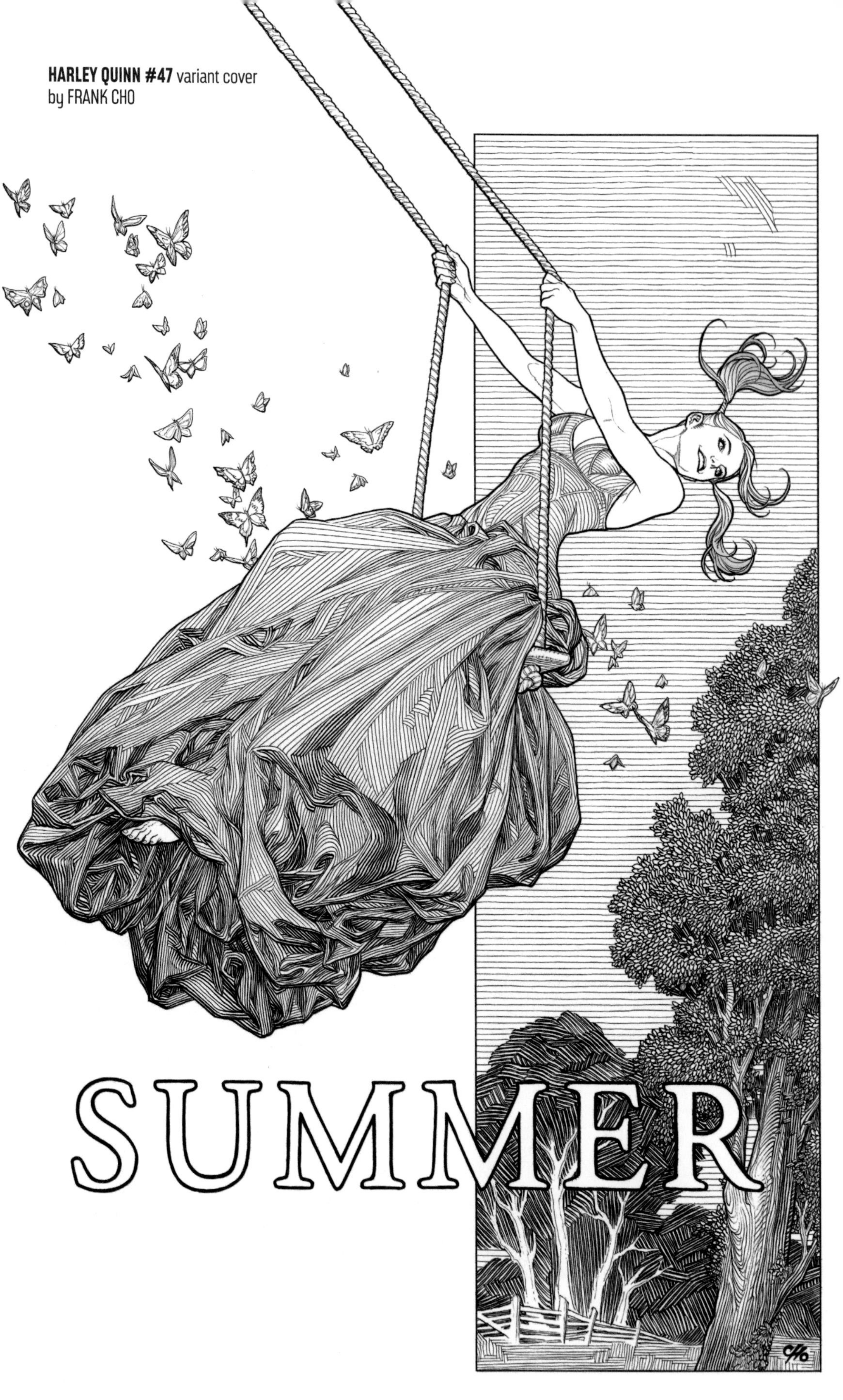
SUMMER
CHO

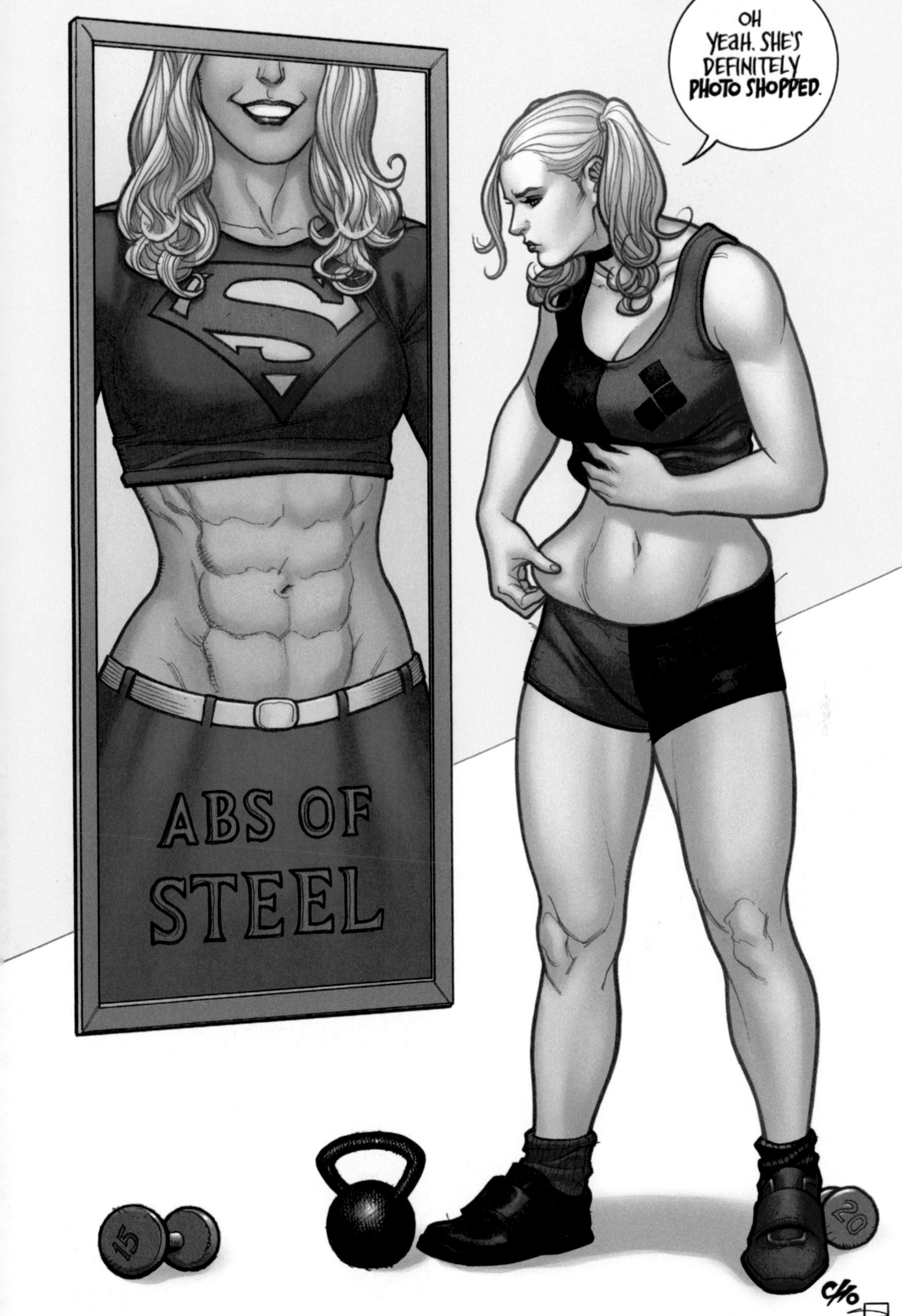

OH YEAH. SHE'S DEFINITELY PHOTO SHOPPED.
ABS OF STEEL
15
20
CHO
RICH

HARLEY QUINN #48 variant cover
by FRANK CHO and SABINE RICH

HARLEY QUINN #49 variant cover
by FRANK CHO

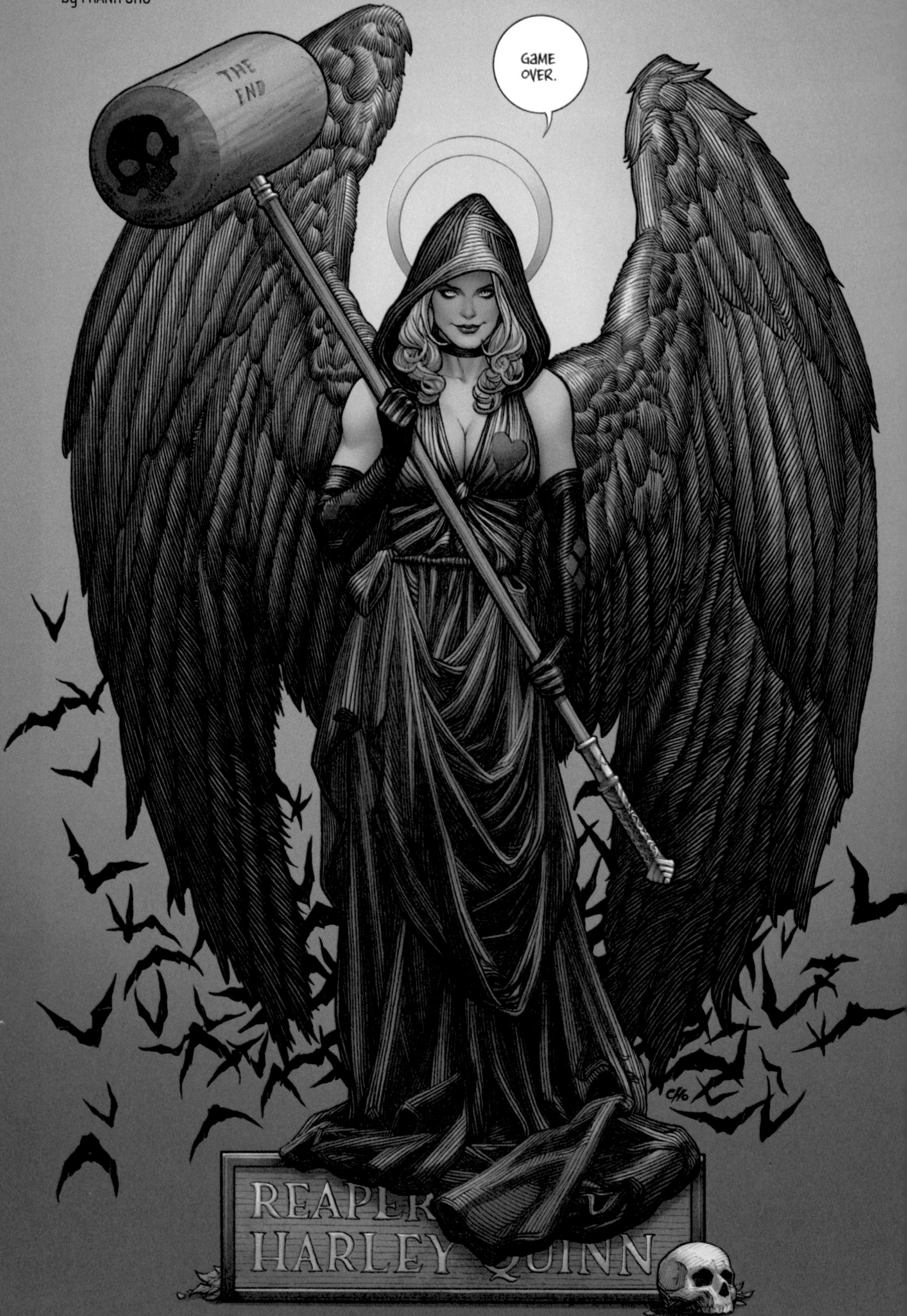
THE END
GAME OVER.
CHO
REAPER HARLEY QUINN

"Chaotic and unabashedly fun."
– IGN

HARLEY QUINN

VOL. 1: HOT IN THE CITY
AMANDA CONNER
with JIMMY PALMIOTTI
& CHAD HARDIN

**HARLEY QUINN
VOL. 2: POWER OUTAGE**

**HARLEY QUINN
VOL. 3: KISS KISS BANG STAB**

READ THE ENTIRE EPIC!

HARLEY QUINN VOL. 4:
A CALL TO ARMS

HARLEY QUINN VOL. 5:
THE JOKER'S LAST LAUGH

"I'm enjoying this a great deal;
it's silly, it's funny, it's irreverent."
– COMIC BOOK RESOURCES

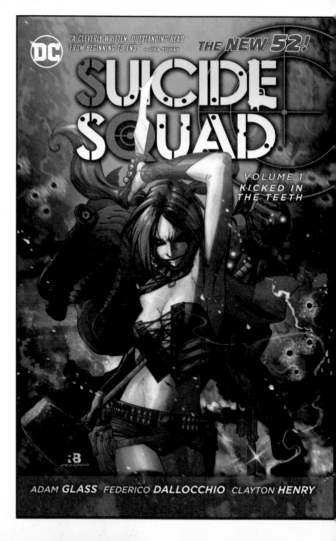

"A pretty irresistible hook..."
– THE ONION A.V. CLUB

SUICIDE SQUAD

VOL. 1: KICKED IN THE TEETH

ADAM GLASS with
FEDERICO DALLOCCHIO

**SUICIDE SQUAD
VOL. 2: BASILISK RISING**

**SUICIDE SQUAD
VOL. 3: DEATH IS FOR SUCKERS**

READ THE ENTIRE EPIC!

SUICIDE SQUAD VOL. 4
DISCIPLINE AND PUNISH

SUICIDE SQUAD VOL. 5
WALLED IN

"A cleverly written, outstanding read from
beginning to end."
– USA TODAY